JONATHAN SWIFT

FOR ROSE

JONATHAN SWIFT
the brave desponder

PATRICK REILLY

SOUTHERN ILLINOIS UNIVERSITY PRESS
CARBONDALE AND EDWARDSVILLE

Published in the United States of America
by the Southern Illinois University Press

ISBN 0-8093-1075-9

Library of Congress Catalog Card Number
81-85639

Printed in Great Britain

CONTENTS

ACKNOWLEDGEMENTS

The debt to Swift scholarship acknowledged in the bibliography is merely the iceberg's tip; students of Swift will easily detect the greater mass submerged within the text.

My chief single obligation is to Mr John A. M. Rillie, head of the Department of English Literature at the University of Glasgow, for advice and encouragement throughout the writing. My colleague Dr Philip Hobsbaum was also generous in suggesting improvements. I am grateful to both while absolving them from all responsibility for the book's defects.

My thanks also go to Professor Ernst Honigmann of the University of Newcastle for his help in the final stage of the work.

I am especially indebted to Miss Irene Elsey, Miss Ingrid Swanson and Mrs Valerie Eden for their patient skill in preparing the manuscript for publication.

Glasgow   September 1981   P.R.

PREFACE

The purpose of this book is to demonstrate the crucial significance of Jonathan Swift for modern man and this aim has determined both its construction and its method. The argument that Swift simultaneously looks towards past and future, back to the crises of the seventeenth century and forward, with uncanny prescience, to the problems of the twentieth, is intended to be the central and unifying theme.

The Introduction announces the various contributory themes which the subsequent chapters examine in detail. This necessitates a return in each chapter to the great prose satires for the illumination they throw upon each part of the argument. The order is organic, with the initial definition of Swift's religious–political position leading naturally to an examination of the satire against corresponding Puritan aberrations in Chapter Three. Similarly, the dislike of Puritan messianism shapes Swift's pessimistic view of history revealed in Chapter Four and makes fully intelligible those crucially contentious creatures, the Houyhnhnms. Chapter Five deals with his abortive attempt (frustrated finally in Ireland) to found a viable social order on the 'realistic' appraisal of man he shared with Hobbes. Chapters Six and Seven, using *Gulliver's Travels* as chief exhibit, concentrate on the major themes of forbidden knowledge and displacement, Swift's sense of alienation in a fearful world. Chapter Eight attempts to synthesize the individual findings of each preceding chapter in examining the central paradoxes of his faith, his attitude to language in general and to satire in particular, and his intolerable divided consciousness.

The method and scope of the work forbid the inclusion of extended passages of analysis of single texts, though it will, it is hoped, be obvious that without such analysis as essential propadeutic the location of Swift's ideas in this wider context would lack all conviction. I have denied myself such detailed examination of the actual texture of the writing for the advantage of standing back and seeing Swift in the context of his age, with continuous reference to the political and religious issues of his time.

I omit extensive treatment of the more 'personal' works, such as the *Journal to Stella* and much of the poetry and correspondence, because, valuable though they are, they only occasionally generate that sense of urgency, of fierce intensity and restless energy, which defines the truly significant Swift and makes him so profound an interpreter of our own contemporary crisis. As much as Yeats, Swift delights in conflict because it is a mode of power and it is the 'public' writer, the satirist–magician, who communicates to us that sense of power, that answering urgency, in a voice from the past whose contemporary genius we cannot afford to ignore. I have not accordingly aimed at an exhaustive treatment of Swift's work and the poetry in particular merits a fuller examination than the present method permits.

Every method imposes its own limitations, every choice is a farewell to other possibilities; one cannot, as Johnson remarks, fill one's cup simultaneously from the source and mouth of the Nile. In inviting the reader to approach Swift from one particular direction, this book seeks to present him as a dauntingly modern writer of the fiercest urgency, not merely relevant but indispensable to an understanding of our present predicament. I should be happy to have it judged by its success or failure in persuading its readers to turn again to the great works for confirmation of this judgement.

ONE

INTRODUCTION

SWIFT OUR CONTEMPORARY

The task of scholarship, approaching a writer of the past, is not to recreate him in a form flattering to modern preoccupations, trendily updating him into a contemporary of ourselves, but rather, through strenuous immersion in the concerns of *his* age, to try as far as possible to make us contemporaries of him. This humility of the scholarly enterprise is all the more mandatory in dealing with a giant like Swift, particularly since Swift himself was an intellectual Orpheus, looking backwards at certain crucially decisive moments, his attitudes hardened in the mould of seventeenth-century history. We shall not understand Swift without realizing that he was, even in his own time, a man of the past, nor without an understanding of that past, that century of revolution which ushered in the relative calm of eighteenth-century England. Yet precisely because he was so intellectually conservative, so thoroughly yesterday's man, conditioned by that age of crisis, of revolution in Church and State, when the last of times seemed to so many daily imminent – 'You are at the edge of the promises and prophecies', in the words of Cromwell's assured millenarianism – Swift speaks to us in our own distraught period with a relevance, a keenness of application, that make him, regardless of our choosing, a living voice, a contemporary writer of the fiercest urgency.

This book derives from a conviction that Swift is a dauntingly modern writer largely because he was so profound an interpreter of seventeenth-century history, that the concerns of that age, with which he grappled so strenuously, have returned, in the most startling of resurrections, as our own contemporary dilemmas. In any age, in periods of serene placidity, Swift will, of course, be esteemed as a great writer, supreme in his chosen mode of satire; but for us he is also a prophetic voice, a wrestler with problems upon whose solution our own salvation depends. His declared purpose was to vex rather than entertain and no one can miss that quality of intimidatory admonition that makes his work as much salvationist as aesthetic. He was forever trying to rescue or redeem someone or other – Sir William Temple, the Tory ministry, the Anglican Church, the Irish people, and, finally, man himself. 'I cannot but warn you once more of the manifest destruction before your eyes, if you do not behave yourselves as you ought.'[1] Who is being addressed? Only a Swift scholar could say for certain, for this is his standard mode of exhortation, for use in all circumstances. But nowhere is he a greater preacher, nowhere more given to the work of salvation, than in his satires – a hellfire preacher, naturally, for he knew that men could not be saved against their will, could not be hauled unwillingly into heaven as the disaffected Gulliver is hauled unwillingly back to England. Swift, like God, will save only those who co-operate with redemption, manifesting by their actions the operation of grace within.

It is this salvationist element that seizes the modern reader, not just because, with the secularization of spirituality, profane literature has increasingly become the prime means of our moral education and hence of our salvation, but also because the problems that bedevilled Swift bear a startling resemblance to those that bewilder us. If today study of the seventeenth century reassumes fresh importance, it is because the styx once separating it from us has narrowed to a step, as recent history conducts us to an ambiguously privileged position for renewed insight. The answering urgency we detect in Swift is connected with the fact that certain key problems of seventeenth-century England, once regarded as safely interred, are resurrected in new guise and walk our world as fearfully intractable as three centuries ago. Dilemmas which by the mid-1700s appeared so far solved as almost to be historical curiosities have, it seems, merely been slumbering, and today, dismayingly, revive and rouse themselves as challenging as ever.

We cannot help hearing in Swift prophetic adumbrations of our own discontents, anticipations of present anxieties – they come unforced, even in situations that on first inspection seem totally distant from the world of the great Dean. Latin American conservatives, surveying with frightened disgust the upsurge of 'liberation' theologies, incensed at those priests who have not simply gone down into the market-place with the people but taken to the hills with the guerrillas, will discover a kinship with Swift confronting revolutionary Puritanism. The fury of those who resent Christ used to legitimize the dictatorship of the proletariat responds sympathetically to Swift's indignation at the rule of the saints justified in the name of King Jesus. Swift's unswerving argument against the dissenters was that they talked religion but meant power, that in their lexicon providence was simply a convenient justification for the violent overthrow of established authority. Religious conservatives in the West today may detect a similar strategy and goal in the curious convergence of certain forms of Marxism and Christianity, united against the great guilty temple of liberal–capitalist civilization. Again, Swift's scepticism as to the peaceful intentions of the dissenters is paralleled in the disbelief of those left cold by the democratic protestations of the Euro-Communists. In both cases, scepticism flows from an inability to believe that a messianic group, convinced that it is God's elect or the instrument of History, will settle for anything less than that total victory, that extermination of its unregenerate opponents, which signal the end of politics.

Prominent, too, among the resurrected dilemmas of the seventeenth century is that of the determinedly recalcitrant minority group, at odds with the law, violently withholding obedience to majority belief and practice. Now starkly political, divested of its old religious garb, the problem confronts us at its harshest and most terrifying in the person of the modern terrorist. Swift, forever discerning in every dissenter a potential Cromwellian trooper, much as Stormont discerned in every Ulster Catholic a potential republican gunman, would immediately have identified the urban guerrilla as spiritual descendant of the Puritan fanatics. To read Conor Cruise O'Brien denouncing the IRA is to acquire fresh insight into the mentality of his great predecessor contemplating the armed saints; we need only change names, be charitable towards minor anachronism, and we have virtually identical arguments.[2] When O'Brien defines the gunmen by the following characteristics – an exalted and unrealistic conception of their objective, a contempt for ordinary people and for what such people are prepared to accept as satisfactory or tolerable, and the conception that willingness to use force constitutes the qualification to be the arbiter of the result – we again hear Swift denouncing his Puritan adversaries. When O'Brien insists that there is no way of dealing *politically* with such people, that their demands are not negotiable, he echoes Swift's scornful opposition to any policy of concession or conciliation towards dissent; what do you concede to those who demand everything? When O'Brien derides the idea of an Ireland capable of including as one of its accepted elements a terrorist faction denying all authority other than its own, he simply repeats Swift's insistence that comprehension of dissenters within the Church of England is absurd since what they really want is not comprehension but conquest.

Advice for handling terrorists is culled straight from the pages of Swift. We must not even talk with the terrorist, 'since though he can argue fluently from his own peculiar premises, he is not accessible to rational argument based on premises other than his own'; hence we must deprive him as far as possible of 'the publicity he so avidly seeks, refusing to be impressed, confused or diverted by the versatility of his propaganda campaigns'. O'Brien's analysis of terrorist psychology – the fanatical devotion to the cause, the pursuit of courses of action which confer not just a sense of righteousness but a feeling of intense gratification – recalls Swift's view of Charles I's executioners. Finally, O'Brien follows the Swiftian insistence on law and order, spurning all hope of a political settlement, a negotiated deal, with men implacably anti-political, who despise negotiation as compromise and deal only in high explosives. He dismisses impatiently the warnings against overreaction by the democratic state, the predictions of disaster if the authorities are stampeded into becoming as repressively intolerant as enemy propaganda alleges, preferring to highlight the, for him, far greater risks of underreaction, citing the Weimar Republic as the classic cautionary example of a state overthrown because it shirked the measures needed to preserve it from sedition. The same hawkish disposition inspires Swift's condemnation of Charles I's deplorably soft policy towards the dissenters which helped to precipitate civil war.[3] For both Irishmen, united in spirit though centuries apart, the deluded search for conciliation is the surest route to disaster, appeasing the flames with petrol; safety lies in the hardline policy of Cromwell facing the menace of the Levellers: 'break them or they will break you'.[4] Once again the seventeenth century speaks to its troubled brother of today, and no disparagement is intended to O'Brien if one remarks that his lecture on the IRA was really delivered nearly three centuries ago by Jonathan Swift.

We, of course, see that here at least, on the issue of dissent, Swift was wrong and Locke right. The policy of extending full civil and religious liberty to the dissenters (denounced by Swift as fatal appeasement) did not entail, as he catastrophically predicted, the violent seizure of power, the overthrow of Church and State. Toleration (the paradox is incontestable) removed rather than intensified dangers, depriving the sectaries of teeth, or, at least, of the motive to use them. But the arguments of Swift, like those of Burke, do not depend entirely upon their particular application, are not rigidly restricted to the special historical case for which they were devised, standing or falling by their accuracy in that single isolated instance. Burke is the critic of revolution rather than of the French Revolution, Swift the perennial hawk forever fulminating against the weakness of concession; we read *Animal Farm* in the light of the one, annotate Chamberlain's conduct at Munich with the aid of the other. The classic formulation of their arguments endows them with a quality of universality, making them constantly available for new situations in which they repossess their initial relevance.

Swift's miscalculation as to eighteenth-century dissent stemmed from a vision conditioned by seventeenth-century history, from his commitment to the past, and it is not so clear, in terms of that past, that he was wrong about the spiritual ancestors of his opponents, the troopers of the New Model Army fired by their fanatical preachers, with a mission from heaven making them as explosively unaccommodating as our contemporary terrorists. Swift's error was to mistake the century he lived in, as he continued to wage a war whose armies were fast disbanding; the age of dynamic, revolutionary puritanism, dedicated to the total renovation of society, was over, but Swift had not seen its passing. Nevertheless, as the whirligig of time brings in its revenges and seventeenth-century history becomes again frighteningly applicable to our own situation, the exploded arguments of Swift, wrong in detail but so recurrently relevant, regain a persuasive cogency for many who contemplate with baffled horror the illimitable claims of the new elects and the atrocities inseparable from their sense of mission. The solution of these dilemmas, the impossible task of distinguishing freedom-fighter from terrorist, racks us as we listen bewildered to the contending voices that solicit our attention: Locke with his calm, optimistic case against overreaction, Hobbes insisting that security is the pearl of great price for which everything else must be abandoned, Cromwell's intransigent contention that it is them or us. The secret is to know which century one lives in and the agony of decision is now ours as it was once Swift's. Our vantage point enables us to mark Swift's error in his overreaction to obsolete threats, but his shade must even now be relishing the irony that we, so adept in solving *his* problems, stand indecisive before those same problems the instant they become our own.

That Swift's arguments, even when wrongheaded or misguided in the particular application, often retain an underlying general validity, a claim to attention which forbids relegation to the dustbin, is also illustrated by his strictures on science and technology. There was undoubtedly an element of hauteur in his attitude towards the Royal Society, the disdain of the gentleman–humanist shaking his head at the curious aberrations of hierarchically-inferior scientists. One initial reaction to the Academy of Lagado is perhaps a surprised embarrassment at the great man's blind spot, his inexplicable myopia concerning the impending glory of the scientific enterprise – the reader may feel impelled to apologise for the shortcoming, much as he might for the sharpness towards Dryden or the bias against Scotland. But there are darker explanations of Swift's hostility towards the Royal Society than simply attributing it to the petulance of a traditionalist who would not or could not appreciate the new disciplines of learning. Swift is made exemplary of the malicious rage of the reactionary, of the dogmatic obscurantism that challenges the whole purpose and strategy of scientific progress. Even Orwell, despite his devotion to Swift and despite his own awareness, so manifest in *Nineteen Eighty Four*, that science could be a destroyer, unaccountably refused to credit the author of the *Travels* with an anticipatory insight into this twentieth-century commonplace. The Houyhnhnm failure to invent the wheel is cited as proof of Swift's culpable ignorance and the hostility to science becomes revelatory of a hatred towards life.[5] Orwell might easily have quoted Joyce to represent what he saw in Swift's rejection of the new scientists: 'A hater of his kind ran from them to the wood of madness, his mane foaming in the moon, his eyeballs stars. Houyhnhnm, horsenostrilled.'[6]

But as the twentieth century moves towards a close and the heady assurances of men like gods modulate into doubt and on to total disenchantment, Swift's views on scientific technology can no longer be so confidently dismissed. Support comes from the unlikeliest of defenders as Bertrand Russell praises Gulliver's third voyage for alerting him to what his education had totally failed to suggest: that science is not necessarily on the side of the angels, but is, at best, neutral, and may easily become an instrument of degradation.[7] What Swift, the King of Brobdingnag and the Houyhnhnm master all sensed in 1725 is today seen by many as the sole guard between man and extinction: the need to regulate the pursuit of scientific technology if certain values, hitherto regarded as axiomatic, are to survive.

With Solzhenitsyn's onslaught on the doctrinaire theoreticians ruining his country, we re-encounter, almost to a duplication of phraseology, the Swift of the third book of the *Travels*. The academic élites, the pharisaical intellectuals, who provoked Swift's scorn in the Royal Society, are again the target as Solzhenitsyn lambasts the Soviet intelligentsia of the Academy of Sciences. It is the same fury at the same folly: the hubris elevating its possessors above ordinary human-ity, the conceit which disdains old, traditional forms, the assumption that wisdom is a new birth, coeval with oneself, and that our fathers all died in the dark. Swift's denunciation of the freethinkers is revived as Solzhenitzyn flays the atheist intelligentsia for dismissing the old religion of Holy Russia as obsolete nonsense, the delusion of peasants who accept God and misunderstand agronomy: 'With peasant agronomy there was grain enough and the soil wasn't exhausted, but now that things are scientifically done we shall soon be without soil altogether'.[8] We are once again with Gulliver in the ravaged country-side of Balnibarbi after the agronomists of Lagado have completed their improvements, until 'except in some very few places, I could not discover one ear of corn or blade of grass'.[9]

In language remarkably Swiftian, Solzhenitsyn contemptuously rejects the anti-peasant arguments of the Moscow intellectuals as motivated by animus against 'the men of the soil' from those whose ideal is 'people of the air, who have lost their roots in everyday existence'. Did Solzhenitsyn, writing this, recollect the inhabitants of the Flying Island, the abstracted theoreticians of Laputa, so enwrapped in cogitation that they need servants to rattle them back to reality and save them from mishaps in the street? Deliberate or not, it would be difficult to better this as a description of the Laputan illuminati, and Swift would surely have identified in the Soviet Academy of Sciences the reincarnated arrogance of the savants of the Royal Society. The memorable image of Lord Munodi's once thriving mill, reduced to rubble by the new technological barbarians in their disastrously voracious pursuit of ever-increased efficiency, is reflected in the tragedy of Matryona's House, symbol of the old traditional Russia, demolished and its owner destroyed (significantly, like Anna Kar-enina, under the wheels of a train) by the new scientific Mongols of Soviet bureaucracy. Solzhenitsyn's contemptuous name for such people, 'smatterers', with its connotations of glib superficiality, of mere outward polish, of an education that despises all ancestral wisdom while gullibly swallowing the newest nonsense of the latest self-styled expert, links up with certain key tenets of *A Tale of a Tub* and *The Battle of the Books* – ridicule of the Moderns, Grub Street and an education which concentrated on learning the index rather than studying the book.

Far from being reprehensibly obscurantist, Swift is really fulfilling the central humanist duty of defending the past against degradation to a mere transit camp on the road to the future. Inevitably, the rôle entails looking to the past as homeland, cherishing its achievements as exemplary, where the scientist, for whom the curve of time is positive, just as naturally dedicates himself to the future. Cultural health depends on a mutually benefical tension between these two root human tendencies, cultural disaster follows when either achieves a sweeping victory over its necessary rival, when Blake is dismissed as a madman or Bruno burned as a heretic. The extremism of Swift's campaign against science is an index of his sense of isolation in what seemed to him a losing struggle. His scepticism, however, surges beyond a mere questioning of the march of science and the inevitability of progress; the audacity of his insight carries him to a point where we are only now catching up with the conjectures of this Augustan writer. If the satire is still so baffling and challenging, still defies definitive summation, it is because it propounds problems that baffle us still.

We see now what Swift suspected long ago, that a totally unregulated science, a technology free of constraint, may produce disaster, that when scientific truth is made into an idol, other values may be sacrificed; we see, too, the intractable problems in man's environment, economy and moral life that the startling advance in scientific technology has brought with it, the enormously high cost of the scientific revolution of the past four centuries. But we still retain a conviction that the price is justified, a Puritan confidence that truth is man's future, lying, like the celestial city, at the end of a long, hard road, and that every single piece of discovered truth, every new acquisition of knowledge, whatever its temporary inconveniences, must lead us closer to that happy destination. Only recently, and in the most tentative way, has a new possibility dared to present itself – the heretical suggestion that perhaps there is a fundamental incompatibility between man's happiness, even his survival, and certain kinds of truth, that man's endurance as a recognizably human creature may depend on censoring certain lines of enquiry, closing certain roads as leading into zones of deadly contamination. The truth, supposed to set us free, may in some areas be too terrible for contemplation, a Medusa face inducing stony inhumanity. The old imperative, that human excellence and happiness can only benefit from the revelation of new truth, that unrestricted enquiry is the guaranteed way to joyful enlightenment, is, for the first time in history, being disputed.

One hesitates to impose a meaning upon satire which sets out to ensnare, which exults in confuting the confident response, and nowhere is this truer than of the 'Digression on Madness', with its deliberate strategy of disorientation, its progressive destruction of the ground beneath us till we are left desperately treading air. The 'Digression' is a high-security prison, designed to make escape impossible; once inside, the reader experiences a sense of moral and intellectual weightlessness, as Swift astoundingly anticipates the techniques of twentieth-century brainwashing. Yet surely it is not over-temerarious to propose as one possible interpretation what strikes us as so shockingly heretical even when advanced today: the idea that man and the truth are not companions along the same road, but that the choice is between the annihilating truth and a delusive happiness that alone guarantees human survival. Even if this is not Swift's final meaning, it is clearly not an idea beyond his power to imagine; if he is only playing, it is a game which almost three centuries later impresses us as intrepidly speculative. To describe Swift as dauntingly modern is not intended as a condescending certification of his fitness for dialogue with us, for it is we who must nerve ourselves to encounter him. His attitude towards science, technology, the extension of knowledge, demands attention, if not approval. Where he doubted the axiomatic value of the compass and gunpowder, we contemplate fearfully fast breeder reactors and genetic engineering; but at root is the same disquiet, the same unease as to the infallible guarantees of science. Today, when the issues are so pregnant with risks of disaster, even those who stay faithful to the promises of science, should, if only for the sake of the cause they serve, learn from Swift that suspecting glance which is our one hope of survival.

This relevance to the largescale problems of society, such as the status of science, our attitude towards the past, the existence of terrorist minorities, is paralleled in the pertinence with which he explores the problem of individual consciousness – this above all has once more made contemporary writers of Swift and Defoe. Despite Swift's contempt for Defoe – 'the fellow who was put in the stocks'[10] – we can retrospectively see both men as closer in certain respects than either would have imagined. Crusoe and Gulliver suffer the same aesthetic myopia, despite splendid opportunities for the appreciation of natural beauty. Crusoe's island is a challenge to puritan know-how, Gulliver's islands are teaching aids in a moral lesson, and we hear much of the history and sociology of these remote nations, little of their landscapes. Swift and Defoe are equally immune to the primitivist temptation so startlingly exhibited by Dryden, when he tells how Columbus in the New World found

> guiltless men, who danc'd away their time,
> Fresh as their groves, and happy as their clime.[11]

The Noble Savage, conscripted to confound ideas of European superiority, the voyage of discovery as a weapon in the anti-Christian arsenal, the contrast between a neurotic Europe, victim of a religion designed to induce misery, and carefree paganism: none of this appears in either Swift or Defoe. The *libertin* writers reinterpreted the fall as *into* Christian civilization, Jesus as the morose Galilean who had disastrously conquered, and their descendant Diderot, in his *Supplement to the Voyage of Admiral Bougainville*, produced an anti-Christian fairy-tale in which Tahiti figures as the new Garden of Eden before the European serpents arrived. Neither Swift nor Defoe shows any inclination to favour *l'homme naturel* against *l'homme artificiel*; the two most famous islands in eighteenth-century literature, Crusoe's and the Houyhnhnm paradise, are free of this kind of primitivism.

Crusoe turns a desert into a thriving agricultural enterprise menaced by primitive intruders. His first response to Friday reveals Defoe's bias – the savage's manly face contains also a European sweetness and softness, especially when he smiled. Far from regarding him as a superior man, Crusoe is patronizingly delighted to find him behaving like a human being, as when Friday rejoices after saving his father from the cannibals. Swift's position is more problematic; although the worst atrocities in the *Travels* are those of allegedly civilized man, it would be a blunder to push Swift into an alliance with Diderot that he would have abhorred. 'Her sinful sons through sinless lands dispersed': Swift would have endorsed only the first half of Swinburne's view of European expansion. There are neither sinless lands nor sinless creatures in Swift, for, if the Yahoos are nauseatingly real, the Houyhnhnms are an impossible dream. Gulliver prefers to risk the murderous savages than return to London, but this merely proves that London savages are worse, not that savages any-where are admirable. What is the Yahoo but Swift's *l'homme naturel*, licentious and undisciplined, checked only by Houyhnhnm superior-ity? We are not to censure the horses for their precautions, even to mass-castration or genocide, against the threat of this savagery. Civilized decadence is still more frightening, but Swift's detestation of the Yahoo is poles apart from Diderot's rhapsody to natural man: here, at least, Swift and Defoe are united.

It is, however, the end of unanimity. Defoe's is a Puritan world, a God-impregnated universe that excludes trifles and chance. God's adversary also fleetingly appears in Defoe's fiction, tempting Moll in the alley, terrifying Crusoe when he discovers the fearful footprint in the sand. Swift insultingly forbids the devil his satire as a shabby attempt by human beings to deny responsibility – the evil exposed is sordidly human, devoid of Satanic glamour, Yahoos and beaux rather than Macbeths and Ahabs. God, too, is a hypothesis the satires can do without. Crusoe forever consoles himself that he lives in God's hand, attested by the shipwreck on the cannibal-less side of the island. He worries over devising a calendar to keep track of the sabbath, while Gulliver indifferently takes each day as it comes. It is the supposedly unregenerate Crusoe who salvages from the wreck a bible and prayer-books; the Lilliputian inventory reveals no such items in Gulliver's possession and he is still managing without them in Houyhnhnmland. In Defoe God is an excellent trading connection and religion a trans-action; in the *Travels* religion enters only as a preposterous source of murderous schism, illustrating Swift's conviction that 'we have just enough religion to make us hate, but not enough to make us love, each other'.[12]

The superiority of European civilization is axiomatic in Defoe, with Crusoe as cultural and religious missionary; Gulliver's last voyage shows how desperately we lack the civilization we pretend to possess. The split is reflected in opposed attitudes to technological progress. Crusoe is Friday's saviour, the instrument of salvation the gun, emblem of Europe's superiority, and already, in the killing of the African leopard, used to overawe a backward people. Crusoe assumes that the gunless man is rightful servant, not just because power grows from its barrel, but because the gun proves intellectual and moral superiority, is both evidence of a higher culture and a heaven-sent means for extending Christian civilization. Friday is a subject who needs a course in Christianity, and Crusoe, believing himself superbly qualified as bearer of light, thanks God for wrecking him in order to save this otherwise abandoned soul. How can he treat as equal a savage who adores the gun and worships gunpowder as 'fire from the gods'? The Giant King, with his different view of gunpowder's provenance, would have set Crusoe a different problem – and had he blundered by arguing from the efficacy of his firearm to that of his bible, his host would have thrown out both together. Defoe believes in Europe's mission, Swift savages the arrogance that thinks we can civilize anyone. The beau's carcase, elegant without, rotten within, is his preferred emblem for European society, but we can be sure that Crusoe's account of England to Friday is completely unironic eulogy.

Swift insults and humiliates, Defoe flatters and encourages. Crusoe is no superman, because Defoe wants, in Coleridge's phrase, a universal representative, a figure for whom every reader can substitute himself. Far from claiming exceptional abilities, Crusoe stresses his mediocrity: a bad carpenter, a worse tailor. The skills he achieves are the product of time and necessity, within any averagely competent man's grasp, and so we identify with him because his survival guarantees ours. What does impress is the will to survive, revealed in the taming of the island. Instead of accepting his invitation to laugh at his clumsy contrivances and home-made clothes, we admire his heroic tackling of obstacles. The modern West has distinguished itself as the Faustian culture, relentlessly reshaping the world, and Crusoe's strivings on the island are part, however tiny, of that titanic programme; trivial in themselves, they celebrate the triumph of Faustian man. But Gulliver comes to denounce, not celebrate. The Giant King, no obscurantist, hails beneficial advance but condemns science without morality and Western man for sacrificing all else to the indiscriminate pursuit of scientific truth. The technologically-backward horses have no Faustian ambitions whatsoever, but theirs is the truly superior culture. Unlike Crusoe, Gulliver exposes himself to ridicule when shipwreck becomes moral and cultural as well as literal, but our laughter, as with Alceste, is a mode of self-defence against this absurd traitor who proposes man as Yahoo, slave rather than tamer of nature. His adulation of the horses is deliberately provocative, intended to needle the reader, as he exasperatingly assumes everyone to be as deferential as himself, bowled over by breathcatching Houyhnhnm graciousness to a lowly human being.

Crusoe, by contrast, confirms what fine fellows we are; the easy assumption of white superiority reflected in Friday's doglike devotion bears no concealed irony. Supporting Defoe is the attitude of a whole civilization at a moment of colonialist expansion convinced of its proselytizing mission. Identifying with Crusoe, we share in the credits as superior partner, whereas the farewell to the Houyhnhnm shockingly reverses this situation, compelling us, to our chagrin, to play Friday to the horse's Crusoe – laughter is the only escape from insult.

Swift courts resentment, forever treats the reader as enemy. Defoe seeks approval for his heroes and, to the extent that it is withheld, it is because the virtues he celebrates, the diligence and ascetic acquisitiveness, are no longer so unreservedly valued: Protestant man takes the dinosaur's trail. In More's *Utopia* gold is used to make chamber pots; in the *Travels* the Yahoos battle for shining stones in a satiric rendition of European bullion markets, with the dealers, in Auden's phrase, howling like beasts on the floor of the bourse: *radix malorum est cupiditas*. Defoe disagrees; sloth is the sin. Trade is the noblest, most important human activity, and if it clashes with religion, Defoe, like Crusoe, is ready to sacrifice the latter. Merchants *are* civilization, and Defoe's heroes rhapsodize over money because it is the ultimate sacrament. Crusoe and Moll's last husband ecstatically thank God for the shower of gold; Swift, with his cynical view of how fortunes are made, would have advised them to thank the other party.

Gulliver's last voyage is, *inter alia*, a polemic against capitalism. Insisting how easily nature is satisfied and how few men's real wants are, he condemns the whole acquisitive ethos and the nascent concept of virtue as material affluence. Five Yahoos, with enough food to satisfy fifty, will battle irrationally for monopoly – the supreme appetite of modern man relegated to a perversion. The wise horse subverts our consumer society in condemning the ingenuity with which men multiply original wants and invent new ones. That the horses do not trade is no surprise when we hear how trade has debauched the English. A wealthy English Yahoo can command the best clothes, houses, women – naturally, everyone wants money. Christianity's disapproval simply proves its sheer irrelevance, yet, appearances notwithstanding, there is no real inconsistency between the weekly routine and its Sunday denunciation, since no one listens to the preacher and sleep is the most innocent of the congregation's pastimes. The name exists, not the thing, and real Christianity can be restored only by overthrowing the civilization that usurps the title.

Houyhnhnmland is a blasphemy against Madison Avenue, an ad-man's nightmare in which Gulliver learns to despise what he once craved, the indispensable rendered odious. *Robinson Crusoe* is a manual of survival, a series of initiative tests, its hero required to find temporary substitutes for all the goods he has sadly forfeited, but to which, God willing, he means to return. We are to commend, despite the apparent irony, Crusoe's decision to keep the gold he finds on the beach. Initially he rejects it as worthless, would readily exchange it for tools – on the island production is wealth. But, far from laughing when he saves it from the sea, we are to approve his prudence, foresight and faith, his determination to return to England, his confidence that God will rescue him some day, when the gold will at once resume its social value. Crusoe is an involuntary castaway, deprived of Europe, not in flight from it, and his retention of the gold affirms his trust in providence.

Crusoe is the apologist, Gulliver the scourge, of western civilization. The Lilliputians mistake Gulliver's watch for his god, since he keeps referring to it for advice; but time *is* given sacrosanct status for Crusoe, as he guards against idleness, never questioning western values, embodiment of puritan virtues, living proof that God sides with the energetic. He is an optimist whose behaviour belies his occasional bouts of despondency; lamenting his damnation, he makes a table and chair. The island is never a choice, for, unlike Gulliver, he has no quarrel with eighteenth-century civilization.

Defoe is retained by the defence, Swift by the prosecution. The search for acquittal is clear in Crusoe's attitude to cannibalism. Revolted but also perplexed, he looks for a formula to cope with the dilemma and settles for what Swift condemned as the pernicious maxim of Tiberius: *deorum offensa diis curae*.[13] Cannibalism is no business of his, and, in his moral isolationism, he decides to leave the cannibals alone if they will reciprocate. His disgust at the 'sin' of another culture contrasts strikingly with Gulliver's revulsion from the sins of men, the natural, unchanging depravity he finds wherever he travels. Similarly, Defoe does not attack colonialism, merely the Spanish variety, its atrocities seen as a consequence of peculiar national malignancy rather than of imperialism itself. Gulliver's refusal to annex dominions stems, by contrast, from detestation of all colonialists, English included, as monsters. Both Crusoe and Gulliver would rather be captured by savages than by the Inquisition, but where Defoe is anti-Catholic, Swift is anti-Europe; Gulliver is no partisan – not Spaniards but man, especially European man, is the enemy. Crusoe, invoking ethical relativity, renounces his right to condemn cannibals; the Giant King, introduced to the novel wickedness of Europe, shows no such tolerance.

Defoe and Swift reach opposite conclusions from identical data. Defoe argues that for cannibals to eat their enemies is analogous to our blowing them up in war – and he is no pacifist. Assuming our innocence, he tolerantly confers acquittal on other cultures. Everyone is innocent, or, in practice the same thing, everyone can be left to God. But in Swift everyone is guilty, as he condemns a wicked society with the implacability of an urban guerrilla. Crusoe moves from European to cannibal innocence, Gulliver from Yahoo corruption to western complicity; Defoe deals in exculpation, Swift in judgement. The different endings supply the final contrast: Gulliver, would-be dropout, dragged back to a detested civilization; Crusoe, reluctant exile, hastening home to the society he pined for, a prodigal son whose wallet is bursting at the seams. His is a success-story, passing from initial misfortune to triumphantly profitable conclusion, Job as eighteenth-century merchant-adventurer, and in nothing is Defoe more faithfully puritan than this final fusion of material and spiritual election. Gulliver, likewise, is never more Swiftian than in his final failure, when, in his alienation, he joins that long line of vanquished figures, Sancroft, Temple, Harley, Bolingbroke, Brutus, Cato, More, Swift himself, suicides, martyrs, losers all, whose integrity is undeniable because it is inseparable from defeat.

Defoe's myths of endurance confront Swift's nightmare of invincible iniquity. The crises of identity and survival, the challenge to the self, which occupy their work, claim kinship with modern anxieties, so that we return to Crusoe and Gulliver, seeking reassurance against our fears or confirmation of our abandonment. Defoe champions the self, the isolated, unsustained self, deprived of any redeeming deputy, against every conceivable threat, internal or external, that might overwhelm it: the devil tempting Moll to strangle the child in the alley, the natural disasters conspiring to destroy Crusoe. Prison, the confinement of the self, is thus a central preoccupation in Defoe – the literal prison of Newgate, the metaphorical prisons of Crusoe's island or plague-encompassed London, the ever-imminent dungeon of bankruptcy and ruin. Camus recognized this in choosing as epigraph for *The Plague* a sentence from the preface to the third volume of *Robinson Crusoe*: 'It is as reasonable to represent one kind of imprisonment by another, as it is to represent anything that really exists by that which exists not!'

Defoe's real theme is, however, not entrapment but escape, the prison broken or, at least, overcome: Moll clawing her way through adversity to a Virginia plantation, Crusoe taming the island, London surviving the plague stronger than ever. Escape, survival, the indomitable self spurning submission and despair – these are Defoe's values, and it is not surprising that Andrey Sinyavsky, fortifying himself in a Soviet prison, should have turned for solace and instruction to *Robinson Crusoe*, 'the most useful, exhilarating and benign novel in the world'.[14] The book's audacity, for him, is that it eschews the easy way out in not beckoning us to a voyage of freedom, but, on the contrary, teaches us to survive without sailing anywhere, without moving from the spot but simply staying in our cage. Sinyavsky's cage was a very real one and it is perhaps extravagantly self-indulgent to link imprisonment so brutally palpable with the metaphorical bondage of modern man, the psychological dungeons of his immuring. Nevertheless, Sinyavsky's tribute to the therapeutic, indeed salvationist, quality of the book reveals the secret of its appeal to contemporary sensibility, with the extremity of his own case highlighting the general relevance of Defoe's parable. In an age when the individual feels puny and insignificant, trapped by vast impersonal forces – class, race, culture, Reason, The Life-Force, Progress, the *Zeitgeist* – whose evolution is identified with human history, man, in an instinctive act of self-preservation, turns to Defoe as celebrant and liberator of the unvanquishable self.

With Swift it is far otherwise. The jailers who, in their attempt to crush man's spirit, would be wise to withhold *Robinson Crusoe* from their captives, might profitably provide them with *Gulliver's Travels*; for the sense of disorientation induced by a close reading might leave them far more uncertain as to that definition of the human upon which resistance must be based. Swift's book is also about entrapment, but a new theme, what Swift called the power of habit, what we identify as brainwashing, appears, and, far from ending in liberation, the book seems almost to deny the possibility of survival. Where Defoe is guardian of the self, Swift's radical scepticism questions if there is a self to guard. The frightening nihilism of the satire, the moral outlawry sensed by so many readers, are inseparable from the unhedged abandon of its root question: is there any central human core beyond the reach of manipulation or conditioning, is there anything essentially *human*, to survive at all? Far more shockingly than *Nineteen Eighty Four*, Swift implies that the few cubic centimetres within the skull which we so confidently proclaim the realm of freedom, an inviolable zone, a no-go area to violence and intimidation, are as casually penetrated as our vulnerable bodies, minds bent as easily as limbs are broken. *Gulliver's Travels* puts on trial the existence of the self as an entity independent of the social system in which it acquires self-awareness. Sinyavsky in prison turns to Defoe to exorcise the terrible doubts unleashed by Lemuel Gulliver.

What makes Gulliver so terrifying is the curiously disturbing way in which he is presented as the human representative, for the book's startling changes of environment reveal him as lacking in any fixed or permanent characteristics: short or tall, clean or unclean only by comparison, a giant among Lilliputians, a Lilliputian among giants, an animal among Houyhnhnms, a horse among men. Every belief, law, custom, attribute, perishes under the laser of this relativity, with disgust alone surviving the experiment. Man, in the sense of some irreducibly human core, some residual quality transcending cultural control, resisting or modifying cultural omnipotence, is shown as fiction and sham, the belief that there is a human *given* exposed as the most pathetic of delusions. 'Fool, do not boast, thou canst not touch the freedom of my mind': this cherished conviction of the Christian–humanist tradition, so rousingly pronounced by Milton's Lady in the power of the enchanter, is scandalously undermined by Swift's great book.

The *Travels* propose instead that man is merely a mechanism, a function of his environment, imprisoned in a system which he evades only to enter another, forever exchanging captivities. Lilliputians, Brobdingnagians, Laputans, Houyhnhnms and Englishmen all live confined in their own social structures, unaware of other modes of life, refusing to credit what they have not been programmed to accept. Gulliver moves from one culture to another, demonstrating that the same belief can be either invincible or ludicrous, depending on its social context; demonstrating, too, just how easily man is conditioned into accepting as natural and inevitable what formerly seemed strange and repulsive. And if man is so infinitely malleable, so much a moral and intellectual weather-vane, what becomes of the boasted freedom of the mind, the inviolable sanctity of the self? What makes the *Travels* so chillingly modern is its anticipation of a major theme of structuralism in suggesting that man is simply the sum of his codes, programmed like a computer to follow instructions, incapable of change until he is reprogrammed.[15] The Brobdingnagian scholars who took Gulliver for an ingenious piece of mechanism which looked, but was not truly, human, are not, it seems, so mistaken after all – or are so only in imagining *themselves* truly human, that is, free, uncondi-tioned, self-directed. Swift's satire is a belated contribution to the Locke–Stillingfleet controversy on the nature of man which had revolved round questions of accident versus essence, shape versus reason, appearance versus reality.[16] Locke had argued that externals are irrelevant, that possession of the shape and appearance of a man is insufficient proof of humanity, since idiots and baboons have both while lacking reason. Swift extrapolates this into a refusal to accept as axiomatic any category distinction between man on the one hand, idiot and baboon on the other.

The *Travels* compel our attention in presenting as fiction what we today fear as fact. Nietzsche in the nineteenth century brought the terrible news of God's death, and today we are warned that Nature may die from man's pollution. Two hundred and fifty years ago Swift made an even more terrifying suggestion – man was dead, had never lived, possessed neither selfhood nor free will, was simply a Cartesian machine, programmed to behave in certain ways, no more able to control the content of his life than the Struldbruggs could the duration of theirs; 'I am not in the least provoked at the sight of a lawyer, a pickpocket, a colonel, a fool, a lord, a gamester, a politician, a whoremonger, a physician, an evidence, a suborner, an attorney, a traitor, or the like: this is all according to the due course of things'.[17] Man is a computerised Yahoo, programmed for lechery, cowardice, theft, drunkenness and the rest.

This concludes *Gulliver's Travels*, summarises the case for the prosecution in a court where the accused is guilty until proved innocent. In addition, Swift will not let man *speak* in his own defence, since speech, 'a kind of jabber', is, like clothes, one of those accidental externals which have no bearing upon essence:[18] a parrot with clothes is not *animal rationale*. Only *action* can overturn the verdict, and here again Swift makes stipulations, for the action must be that of ordinary, everyday humanity – we are not to climb out of the pit clinging to the coat-tails of Cato, Brutus, Thomas More, and similar moral supermen, whose unassailable virtue proves nothing except itself, is irrelevant for the mass of mankind. *Gulliver's Travels* is unique among fictions in its final contemptuous dismissal of the Word as futile and even shameful, its uncompromising insistence that only the Deed is efficacious unto salvation: the Word must be made flesh and dwell among us. Let man, ordinary, everyday man, produce the deeds and at once *nolle prosequi* will be entered, for there will be no case to answer – this is Swift's last offer. Ironically, the bitter opponent of the revolutionary Puritans borrows their activism, their emphasis upon works as the one proof of faith, to frame the unspoken bargain, the implicit challenge, with which his great book ends.

TWO

THE ABSOLUTE ANGLICAN

Swift's literary impulse was primarily political; the parameters of his art are politics, religion and history and any interpretation that neglects these dimensions is likely to go astray. Even his proposal for stabilizing the language is politicized by his association of linguistic and cultural decline: how to make decent English prevail in a land that has been tyrannized by Cromwell and cheated by Walpole? His argument, like Dr Steiner's today on the literature of Hitler's Germany, warns that national and linguistic contamination are facets of a single fall, a pervasive degeneration. Swift, in one sense, never stopped being a political writer; the *Travels* and the *Proposal for Correcting, Improving and Ascertaining the English Tongue* are finally just as partisan as *The Conduct of the Allies* and *The Drapier's Letters*, and he destroys Partridge in belated retaliation for Marston Moor.

But if the political nature of the work is undeniable, dispute rages as to the nature of the politics, and this confusion of the critics reflects division and contradiction in Swift himself. He has been bewilderingly located all along the political spectrum – ally of Hobbes, disciple of Locke, forerunner of Kropotkin. Godwin hailed the Houyhnhnms as model for the coming ideal society, Orwell identified in Swift a distinct English type that he designated Tory–anarchist, and the association is perhaps not so extravagant when we ponder the wild outlawry of the *Tale* or view his life through the lens of Sebastien Faure's definition: 'whoever denies authority and fights against it is an anarchist'.[1] The Irish episcopate might easily have welcomed this as sufficient explanation of their unruly Dean. *Anarchist* is, of course, a term applied to totally different types and temperaments and some readers of the *Travels* might consent to its anarchism while dissenting violently from Godwin's interpretation of both term and text. For him the Houyhnhnms are the heart of the book, Swift's ecstatic vision of a real future when men will live in rational co-operation, responding instinctively to the noble compulsion of reason, without the ugly necessities of police and prison. This is the central tradition that flows from Godwin through Proudhon to Bakunin and Kropotkin. From the 1880s onward, however, there is a counter-tradition relying upon the terrorism of Nechaev, upon propaganda *par le fait*, and those readers of the *Travels* for whom the Yahoo is the central fact may well come away from it convinced that it disseminates terror rather than Kropotkin's mild reasonableness. Asked why he had thrown a bomb into a Paris restaurant packed with innocent people, the anarchist Emile Henry replied with chillingly undebateable certitude, '*Il n'y a pas d'innocents*'.[2] Those who identify the Yahoo as Swiftian man, merely stripped of his disguises of clothes and that jabber called language, may detect a similar remorselessness in the *Travels* and interpret it as a bomb hurled with maximum vindictiveness into the heart of a guilty civilization. This version of anarchism solicits some readers as the true key to Swift's significance.

His libertarian credentials also demand acknowledgement and many prefer to rank him with Locke as the resolute foe of Hobbes; what relation other than stark antagonism can exist between the Drapier and the creator of Leviathan, how reconcile Swift's epitaph with the submission preached by Hobbes? Surely Swift deserves to be counted with those who, in Yeats's words, served human liberty? Quintana refers to the concept of freedom he defended with Roman eloquence and identifies his principles as those of the seventeenth-century parliamentarians who resisted Stuart absolutism, Landa sees him as the heir of Locke and certifies his political theory as that of the Revolution settlement enshrined in the *Second Treatise on Government*.[3] There is certainly much confirmatory evidence: Swift attacked Hobbes outright for confusing legislative power with executive authority and extolled the merits of mixed or 'Gothic' government, thereby upholding the Lockean separation of powers against the Hobbesian monolith; he dismissed Bodin as a *coquin* for his adulation of Louis XIV and it was Bodin's theory of indivisible sovereignty that Hobbes developed in *Leviathan*.[4] It seems sensible to take Swift at his own valuation as a moderate man who disliked extremism, who claimed with justice to be 'no bigot in religion, and I am sure . . . none in government'.[5] Apart from a general agreement on what orthodox

Christianity would have called man's depravity, there seems small
justification for linking Swift to Hobbes in any relationship outside
flat hostility.

But there is still less for matching them as foes, even when there
is no quarrel between them. So anxious are some critics to fumigate
Swift from all taint of absolutism that they manufacture disagreement
where none exists. Gulliver's flight from Lilliput is sometimes cited
as an allegorical rebuff to Hobbes, Swift showing that the social
contract is only as good as Leviathan's enforcing power and that no
government can expect to be preferred before self-preservation.[6]
Hobbes is perhaps vulnerable to a charge that his totally selfish
creature would never initially accept the prostration required by
Leviathan or enter a society where he is naked before the sovereign.
Locke argues that Hobbe's citizens are better off in the state of nature;
instead of a multitude of individual threats, each now hangs on the
whim of an omnipotent tyrant and Locke prefers to risk the jungle
than antagonize Big Brother.[7]

But, possible inconsistency apart, Hobbes would have been amazed
to hear that Gulliver's flight disproved his system. Selfishness creates
Leviathan, and man's salvation, in this secularized version of the Fall,
comes from fulfilling, not transcending, his nature as passionate
egotist. If he voluntarily transfers his rights, it is naturally to promote
his own good, and some rights are accordingly not alienable. Just as
for Mill a free man cannot give away his freedom, so for Hobbes
selfish man cannot renounce the right to life or fail to resist his would-
be killer – on trial he can even refuse to incriminate himself unless
previously guaranteed immunity. The runaway Gulliver is a good
Hobbesian, since 'no law can oblige a man to abandon his own
preservation', and he could have silenced Lilliputian accusations that
flight proved treason by reminding them that 'he that wants protec-
tion may seek it anywhere'.[8] Hobbes would instantly have endorsed
Gulliver's plea that 'his majesty's present severities acquitted me of all
past obligations'.[9]

Self-preservation is not, in any case, a monopoly of the innocent;
even traitors may defend their lives, rebels unite in self-protection –
the initial act is certainly unjust, but from then on only an amnesty
makes further resistance unlawful. If Gulliver stands for self-preservation above obedience, he reinforces rather than refutes Hobbes.
Hobbesian absolutism is far removed from the utter submission of
Job, the self-abnegating trust in the Lord who slays; Hobbesian man

is not Desdemona, loving despite murder, defending her killer while dying. Selfish man makes the contract for selfish reasons, not from an urge towards self-immolation. Hobbes would have been startled to learn that his system did not give due place to human selfishness and the last place to seek a rift between Swift and Hobbes is in their view of human nature. The same selfishness that creates Leviathan is baptised by Swift as Christianity's cornerstone, constituting its superiority to all other religious systems, alone in satisfying man's craving for eternal felicity – Swift has no patience with utopian moralists who decry selfishness, since Christianity is fuelled, for him, by the enlightened self-interest that seeks its reward in heaven.

This similarity of view is a convenient starting-point for investigating Swift's relationship to Hobbes. We may, after all, reasonably suspect affinity between a man's psychology and his politics on the ground that theories of government are almost always bespoke, tailored to suit the concept of human nature already held. They originate below the level of conscious, articulate expression, reflect their creator's personality, with differing expectations of man necessarily issuing in very different systems. Rousseau, dedicated to natural goodness, must attribute evil to tainted institutions and a corrupt society; Locke, convinced that the writ of natural law runs even in the wilderness, will try to curtail State power and oppose arbitrary decree; Hobbes, interpreting nature as a jungle struggle, inevitably equates law with force and seeks the strongest possible government. Behind every absolutist theory, as *Leviathan* shows, lurks a disparaging view of man. Swift exhibits a kinship with certain basic Hobbesian attitudes and on the crucial question of religious conformity is undeniably closer to Hobbes than to the *Letter Concerning Toleration*.

Kinship emerges in a shared realism towards human nature: an axiom of ubiquitous selfishness, vindication of terror and bribery as the only feasible disciplines, rejection of altruistic virtue as a dream of starstruck idealists, as badly in need of flappers as Laputan theoreticians. Swift and Hobbes are, by contrast, wideawake and lynx-eyed. In prelapsarian Lilliput the State rewards good conduct and the little people cannot credit that Europeans rely simply on penalties. Lilliput, with its special fund to encourage the law-abiding, follows Swift's *Project* in making reward and punishment the hinges on which all government turns; Hobbes's equivalent metaphor is to describe them as the nerves of the artificial man, Leviathan, by which every joint and member is moved to perform its duty.[10] If the view is not un-common, Swift's consistency in preaching it is striking. Every single human act, however seemingly altruistic, those of martyrs and saints included, is traceable to self-love. 'Human nature is so constituted that we can never pursue anything heartily but upon hopes of a reward'; neglecting this, the great pagan philosophers ruined their fine moral programmes, catering for it, Christianity vindicates its superiority to all other systems.[11] The only real social problem is how to make selfish man behave decently.

In *The Republic* Plato presents Gyges as the unjust man. Acquiring a ring that confers invisibility, Gyges, immunity guaranteed, kills the king, seduces the queen and makes himself tyrant. Unlike Raskolni-kov's, his is a story of crime and impunity, because Plato, upholding the supreme value of virtue, sunders it from all consideration of reward or retribution to impress that its value is finally indistinguish-able from its uselessness. It is its own reward and even the possession of Gyges's ring will not seduce the truly virtuous man from virtue's service. But for Swift and Hobbes a virtuous Gyges is a self-contradic-tion, as absurd as 'incorporeal substance' or 'round quadrangle'; to possess the power of Gyges is to act like him, for where power is sufficient, a man acts, power being simply a synonym for cause, act for effect. As well ask water not to run downhill as expect Gyges to behave otherwise. Human behaviour is simply a subdivision of the study of dynamics, a problem in vector analysis. The Yahoo, the beau, the marauding kite, John Churchill, Walpole and the Duchess of Kendal all do as they must, and, instead of foolishly dreaming of a willed reformation, we must devise a new force-field compelling changes of direction.

Hence hell's importance for Swift as the final countervailing power, the fulcrum of moral pressure. True, people often behave well because they fear public opinion and know that a reputation for dishonesty is a social hindrance. But since, as Glaucon argues, the most accomp-lished form of injustice is to seem just when one is not, what must we expect from a man clever enough to combine the greatest crimes with a spotless reputation? Swift is unhesitant: 'But let it consist with such a man's interest and safety to wrong you, and then it will be im-possible you can have any hold upon him; because there is nothing left to give him a check, or to put in the balance against his profit. For, if he hath nothing to govern himself by, but the opinion of the World, as long as he can conceal his injustice from the World, he thinks he is safe.'[12] The atheist Wharton, contemptuously indifferent to public opinion, is a monster whom Swift would dearly love to exterminate, Gyges is a Yahoo licensed to bestiality without risk of retribution. Only if both can be induced to believe in hell will society be safe. 'To expect that strength will not manifest itself as strength, as the desire to overcome . . . is every bit as absurd as to expect that weakness will manifest itself as strength. A quantum of strength is equivalent to a quantum of will, urge, activity.'[13] No wonder Nietzsche raged against Christ, who claimed to be irresistible power sacrificing itself, omnipotence embracing crucifixion, for, if true, Nietzsche's central axiom is shattered. Swift unquestionably sees the dissenters as power-seekers rather than candidates for self-sacrifice, and, since they can manifest their strength only by overthrowing the Church, the Church in turn must try to keep them as weak as possible.

The Giant King's un-Gygean response to the gunpowder offer should stagger us as much as Gulliver. He interprets such self-neglect as folly, pernicious consequence of a provincial education, a defect from which all European rulers (and men) are fortunately free. Despite brave efforts from his position of cultural superiority to extenuate the King's offence, it finally defies both understanding and charity. For, as Glaucon says in defence of Gyges, 'if anyone who had the liberty of which we have been speaking neither wronged nor robbed his neighbour, men would think him a most miserable idiot'.[14] Finding a virtuous Gyges in Brobdingnag stuns Gulliver and Glaucon's is for him the only satisfactory explanation of the monstrosity; but, though his evaluation would have been very different, Swift would have been just as amazed to meet such a paragon of disinterestedness in real life as to find a phoenix among pigeons.

The problem is to balance the evidence that ties Swift to Locke, found, understandably enough, in the explicitly political writings such as the *Letter to Pope* and *The Sentiments of a Church of England Man*, with other evidence, less specific but powerfully pervasive through his work as a whole, that suggests affinities with Hobbes, particularly parallel solutions to the problems of a similarly conceived human nature. The debt to Locke is plain in Swift's attack on tyranny as the worst of evils and the advocacy of balanced government, King, Lords and People, as the necessary safeguard. He praises the wisdom of annual parliaments and demands their restoration as precondition of liberty. He echoes Locke in his claim that 'the possessors of the soil are the best judges of what is for the advantage of the kingdom'[15] —

though 'soil' is the emphasis, since this prefaces an attack upon the
new moneyed men of the Whig Bank of England. He rejects 'the
necessity of suspending any law upon which the liberty of the most
innocent persons depended', not just because this encourages arbitrary power and a system of wholesale delation, but because it is
'opposite to that maxim, which declareth it better that ten guilty men
should escape, than one innocent suffer', in sharp rebuttal of Leviathan's assumption that no price is too steep for that *summum bonum*,
a stable society.[16] Orwell, for whom Swift was a progress-hating
reactionary, found nevertheless in the *Travels* the first instinctive
awareness of the modern police-state with its rigmarole of spurious
plots and rigged trials.[17] The case seems solid for assigning Swift once
and for all to the anti-Hobbesian liberal camp.

Yet it is unsafe to take Swift at his liberal word without investigating
what he really means. Beneath the Lockean surface seethe unresolved
tensions, the old authoritarian Adam poised behind the champion of
freedom, and when his passions are up, as with the subject of religion,
this latent authoritarianism ignites. Swift exemplifies, not hypocrisy
or dissimulation, rather a species of unawareness, which, pushed to an
extreme, becomes doublethink. A casual reader, ignorant of Swift's
life and new to his attack on the party political system, might forgiv-
ably conclude that the writer detested and strenuously avoided all
contact with the whole filthy business. Learning that Swift was the
ablest political propagandist of his day, playing a major role in keeping
one party in and the other out, the newcomer's reaction will probably
be one of amused indignation, perhaps a wry admiration for the nerve
of so adroit a confidence-man. The irony is that, like the great mad
proselytysers of the 'Digression on Madness', Swift is first his own
dupe, taking himself in rather than deliberately deceiving others.
Party and Whig are for him synonyms, party rule means Whig
government, whereas the Tories are *not* a political party but the
nation's representatives. The word 'faction' is similarly employed in
his lexicon; the Whigs, even in power, are a faction, the Tories, even
in the doldrums, embody the national will – Swift knew all about silent
majorities, even if he never heard the expression. When he lashes
party politics, he means Whig plots to gain office, and he would have
been furious to hear this described as dishonest.[18]

The unwary reader can so easily mistake as the conclusions of a
coherent political theory what is really a scatter of isolated judgements,
occasioned by the exigencies of specific situations. Swift, as political

journalist, aimed less at philosophical consistency than at scoring over his enemies – he is contending in the hot strife of the chamber, not theorizing in the secluded calm of the study. He began his career by defending the House of Lords as bulwark against popular tyranny, citing classical parallels to condemn the attempted impeachment by the Commons of his friends, the Whig lords, stigmatizing the Tory lower house as irresponsible demagogues. Years later, with the Lords blocking the Treaty of Utrecht, he elatedly welcomed the new peerage creations proposed by the Tory ministry to thwart the intransigence of the erstwhile bulwark against popular tyranny.[19] But, if not a consistent political philosopher, neither was he an unscrupulous opportunist or time-server. He always fought bravely for what he believed in and it was substantially always the same cause – his apparent swervings are really fidelity to values tenaciously maintained while the world changed, for the world rather than Swift was turn-coat. He is opportunist towards means, never towards ends, and will use Locke, Hobbes or anyone else to defend these ultimate values. We must forever guard against judging him by some isolated state-ment, whose meaning is restricted to a particular context without perhaps representing his basic convictions. These ultimate values and convictions found finally no abiding home within the structures of Lockean liberalism.

His attitude towards censorship is especially revealing. His liber-tarian admirers argue that he willingly extended toleration to all writings not against the English constitution; but this isn't very helpful, given his tendency to identify the constitution with his own beliefs, so that when the latter were outraged, the former was threat-ened. He demands the banning of Tindal's covert attack on the Erastian framework of the established Church, badgers Bolingbroke to silence the anti-peace pamphleteers who oppose the Treaty of Utrecht.[20] He assumes a universal consensus as to what differentiates poisons from cordials so that we can easily outlaw the public sale of the one while permitting the other – any awkward hint that one man's poison is another's cordial is stringently suppressed. He applauds the arrest of a number of booksellers and printers in 1711, conveniently forgetting how he had formerly made political capital in the *Examiner* of the freedom granted the fallen Whigs by their triumphant rivals, boastfully contrasting Tory toleration with Whig restriction.[21] The sting here was that the Whigs prided themselves as the party of liberty and used the word as warcry.

But it is difficult not to interpret his celebration of Tory magnanimity as a piece of political infighting, the exploitation of a temporary
advantage, rather than the fruit of profound conviction, for deep
down he believes that error has no rights. The Whigs can justifiably
be silenced at any time, and, temporary expedient apart, Swift is
convinced that the only sensible, long-term policy is repression:
'Why not restrain the press to those who would confound religion, as
in civil matters?'[22] – an ominous demand in so sectarian a thinker.
He wants banned what he dislikes, protests angrily when his own
principle is invoked against him, exhibits in general the characteristics
of an authoritarian rather than a liberal temper. When Walpole rules,
Swift preaches 'the old Whiggish principle . . . of standing up for the
liberty of the press' and lashes his enemy for the very policy that he
urged upon Bolingbroke.[23] The Christian maxim of doing to others
as you would be done to is clearly not extended by Swift to matters of
press publication, the tangle of self-contradiction explicable only in
the light of Dr Johnson's remark that 'the liberty of the press is a
blessing when we are inclined to write against others, and a calamity
when we find ourselves overborne'.[24]

Swift is consistent only in his inconsistency, partisanly utilising
or discarding any argument to secure his overall aim. Anglican
hegemony is unashamedly defended with the most outrageously
provocative coattrailing – 'we are the majority and we are in possession'; but that this stems not from a reverence for majorities as such
is clear when, at the Union of Parliaments in 1707, he derides the
notion of *vox populi vox dei*.[25] He was not the last Irishman to extol
majorities that agreed with him and excoriate those that didn't. His
call for chastisement of the enemies of the Utrecht peace is forgotten
as he ends a sermon encouraging resistance to Wood with the naive
remark, 'and this, I am sure, cannot be called meddling in affairs of
state'.[26] In its *ingénu* quality of wide-eyed simplicity as vehicle of
political dynamite, this is worthy of Gulliver himself. Swift would
naturally have denied inconsistency: a peace-loving citizen is not
inconsistent when forcibly arresting a burglar and for Swift the
Whigs are simply burglars who have somehow captured the police
station. The Tories as rightful occupants may use any means to overcome the intruders and restore legitimate order. Lockean terminology
in Swift's mouth may have strayed far from its original intention, and,
without imputing deliberate deception to Swift, it is difficult not to
conclude that, praising liberty, he means that of himself and his

friends, inclining otherwise towards Filmer's view of the desire of
liberty as first cause of Adam's fall. 'Freedom only for members of
one party – that is no freedom at all. Freedom is always and exclusively
freedom for the one who thinks differently.'[27] Rosa Luxemburg
might perhaps have accepted Locke as a man who at least strove to
bring nearer her exalted ideal; it is very doubtful that she would have
similarly saluted Swift.

Locke himself might well have declined the alliance with Swift so
confidently proposed by the critics, and, had he foreseen Swift's
views on those vital topics, the state of nature and the doctrine of
sovereignty, would probably have been indignant at the attempt to
foist upon him so dangerous a Hobbesian. Any social contract theory
leans heavily upon these two concepts, which depend in turn on the
view of human nature held. Irretrievably selfish men must create an
intolerable state of nature, a nightmare existence, to be evaded at any
cost. But if men are not wholly selfish, then their natural condition is
not so hellish nor the pressure to escape it so desperate. Its members
are consequently in a much stronger bargaining position as to the
kind of government they will accept in return for quitting their
natural state, and this must influence the theory of sovereignty
proposed. Hobbes's theory of sovereignty is a lifeline thrown to a
drowning man who would have to be lunatic to question the condition
of the lifeboat before consenting to leave the water. Locke's view of
the contract as an invitation to a number of reasonably prosperous,
sensible individuals to consider the benefits of mutual co-operation
is radically different and his theory of sovereignty differs accordingly.
In this radical separation, Swift, despite talking sometimes like Locke,
is in fact closer to Hobbes.

Both hold the same theory of psychological egoism, with not just
the lions and foxes of the political élite but all men avidly pursuing
power, seeking safety in domination since every fellow man is a
potential competitor. Anglican security requires suppression of the
sectaries on the Hobbesian assumption that they want power, not
toleration. To know oneself is to distrust others: 'whosoever looketh
into himself . . . shall thereby read and know, what are the thoughts
and passions of all other men, upon the like occasion'.[28] *Quantum
sumus scimus.* Looking inward we recognize Hobbesian man, outward
the Hobbesian state of nature, which requires for its amendment a
sovereign capable of preventing the anarchy that erupts when subsidiary associations compete for the subjects' allegiance. Hobbes calls

such groups 'factions', 'lesser commonwealths in the bowels of a greater, like worms in the entrails of a natural man', existing only by leave of the sovereign, abolishable at will.[29]

This contradicts Aristotle's pluralistic thesis that competing associations are the best defence against despotic centralism. Aristotle first recognized the State as harmoniser of those differences of opinion inevitable among men, whereas the distinguishing feature of totalitarianism is a hatred of diversifying groups and institutions. Rousseau insists that for the general will to be truly expressed, the State must excise subsidiary groups and pays tribute to the magnificent achievement of Lycurgus in establishing the only State of that kind ever known. Swift, significantly, hailed Lycurgus as a model of how the wise ruler should handle nonconformists.[30] Locke, by contrast, supports the Aristotelian notion of competition and pluralism, later developed by Mill and de Tocqueville. The State is but one of several institutions in society, existing alongside religious, educational and economic institutions with their own totally autonomous purposes. As a political, not social, agent, the State must confine itself to strictly political matters. Locke's distinction between government and society enables him to argue that society can survive the fall of government,[31] whereas for Hobbes both are conterminous – to overthrow government is to abolish society and return to nature. Locke dodges the Hobbesian dilemma, chaos or tyranny, by reprimanding those who confuse the state of nature with a state of war, making the clinching *reductio ad absurdum* that, if true, 'all society is abolished, and all faith, which is the bond of society'.[32] But fear rather than faith cements Leviathan.

Naturally each man has a very different view of what is permissible in the state of nature. For Hobbes the sovereign is like Dostoevsky's God – without him everything is permitted; the state of nature is a state of war without Genevan conventions, where nothing is unjust because justice does not yet exist and right and power are synonymous. Locke denies that the liberty of the state of nature is licence – the law of reason, which is the law of nature, binds all men to mutual respect and toleration. Locke will not be panicked into staking everything on absolutism: 'Men living together according to reason without a common superior on earth, with authority to judge between them, is properly the state of nature.'[33] This describes not the life of savages but a community of virtuous anarchists who need neither police nor law courts because they obey reason. It is the state of nature enjoyed by the Houyhnhnms – liberty without licence, persuasion without force, a life of peace and benevolence, all those elements that inspired Godwin's dream of a brave new world. But in twisting the book into an anarchist prophecy of the coming utopia, Godwin is guilty of intellectual hijacking, diverting the *Travels* from Swift's intended destination towards his own imaginative Algeria. What he ignores is that Swift embodied reason in the horses in provocative dismissal of the claim that it exists in men, and that, maiming to our self-esteem, the state of nature in the book towards which we are herded as our proper habitat is that of the Hobbesian Yahoos, nasty, brutish and short, rather than the rational Eden of the Lockean Houyhnhnms.

The sovereign who establishes peace is for Hobbes above reproach, whereas Locke tolerates government as an improvement upon nature only in so far as it enlarges preexistent rights – his state of nature is already a political society, its members already political animals. Social stability is the assumption, not the problem, of his theory. Hobbes, our one great political writer to live through a period of chaos in which society seemed close to dissolution, reveres the State as redemptive institution, secular equivalent of Calvary, not just an instrument, however, useful, for improving man's life – salvation, not improvement, is his theme and he finds in government the answer to the age-old question, who shall deliver me from the body of this death? Hobbes and Locke reenact on a new arena the ancient quarrel of Augustine and Pelagius. For Locke 'truth and keeping of faith belong to men as men, and not as members of society',[34] while Hobbes distinguishes between laws which bind *in foro interno* and laws which bind *in foro externo* in order to prove that society is anterior to morality.[35] Both agree that 'in the beginning all was America',[36] but differ violently as to what 'America' means – a brutish struggle from which Leviathan rescues us, or a mode of life far from desperate but regrettably deficient in guaranteeing property rights. Government, for Locke, secures property, whereas Hobbes, rejecting the claim to absolute private property, sees wealth, like religion, as held at the sovereign's pleasure. Swift's admission that Church property, including tithes, could be revoked at will by the sovereign, stations him once more with Hobbes. Locke, finally, insists that peace can come too dear and prefers nature to tyranny; absolute monarchy is as if men protected themselves against pole-cats and foxes, 'but are content, nay think it safety, to be devoured by lions'.[37]

Swift likewise condemns 'arbitrary power . . . notwithstanding all that Hobbes, Filmer, and others have said to its advantage', describing it as 'a greater evil than anarchy itself; as much as a savage is in a happier state of life than a slave at the oar'.[38] Tyranny or savagery is, however, the Hobbesian choice that a thoroughgoing Lockean would at once have denied; even in rejecting Hobbes, Swift seems dominated by his categories, not surprisingly, given that the state of nature is a construct premised on one's analysis of man. Their divergent views on original sin alone reveal the gulf between Swift and Locke. For Swift, human depravity is not a dogma demanding faith but a fact of experience; for Locke, death, not depravity, is the general penalty of Adam's transgression. Men are mortal, not wicked, and Locke points out that the New Testament nowhere mentions this alleged universal corruption. A spiritual catastrophe is transformed to a biological characteristic, with the Augustinianism that informs the Hobbes–Swift state of nature utterly rejected. Hobbes follows Augustine in regarding society as arising from a defect in man's nature, government as the badge of our lost innocence, while Locke, reacting against Augustinian pessimism, agrees with Aristotle and Aquinas that society is natural to man, the State the highest expression of human fellowship. Swift has no sympathy with the growing meliorism exemplified by Locke, the more optimistic view of man's destiny as the pursuit of earthly happiness – that the rational horses regard European Yahoos as even more noxious than those of Houyhnhnm-land shows where his sympathies finally lie.

Hobbesian affinities are revealed in his description of humanity as a republic of dogs, where peace and full bellies are identical.[39] The dog who seizes a bone for himself is a tyrant, when a few friends share there is oligarchy. Aggressiveness is the dominant characteristic – Hobbes dismisses as irrelevant to so intensely competitive an animal as man the Aristotelian argument that many creatures, such as bees and ants, live in amicable co-operation – and Swift's presentation of the canine kingdom where 'the most ancient and natural grounds of quarrel are lust and avarice' is identical to the pre-Leviathan situation. In this condition, there is no mine or thine, only the right of the strong to take what he can, as the commotion caused by a bitch in heat clearly reveals, for, there being no individual right of possession, 'the whole commonwealth of the street is reduced to a manifest state of war, of every citizen against every citizen; till some one of more courage, conduct, or fortune than the rest seizes and enjoys the prize'.[40] The frivolity masks a deadly serious view of man as ruthlessly competitive.

Locke may stress man's co-operative tendencies, Swift believes that even his games betray man as aggressor: 'most kinds of diversion in men, children, and other animals are an imitation of fighting.'[41]

The state of nature is so evidently a state of war that he ignores the contrary view: 'Quadrille, in particular, bears some resemblance to a state of nature, which we are told, is a state of war, wherein every woman is against every woman'.[42] Even a joke can be revealing; we at once recognize the teller as Hobbes, and Locke would surely have been piqued at so cavalier a disregard of his own very different information. Swift's commitment to Hobbesian categories is such that he even seems unaware that they have been refuted. When Tindal remarks that some crimes may justly be punished in the state of nature, Swift raps him for the schoolboy howler in totally misunderstanding the concept he borrows from Hobbes.[43] But Tindal was Locke's disciple and, far from blundering, was simply restating what the master, pledged to natural law, repeatedly maintained against Hobbes – that even the state of nature is subject to ethics, that all is *not* permitted in the sovereign's absence. Swift's apparent ignorance of rival interpretations is a measure of his immersion in Hobbesian ideology.

This emerges again in a shared theory of sovereignty. Hobbes was often attacked by people, Swift included, who misunderstood him. The basic political question is the sovereign's power rather than identity, as Mill and de Tocqueville discovered. Hobbes's advocacy of monarchy is purely adventitious, a consequence of historical factors which can and do alter without affecting the basic doctrine. A world without kings doesn't turn *Leviathan* to scrap. The sovereign's powers – the end for which the form of the state is simply, for Hobbes, a means – depend on an assumed constant human nature. Any form, monarchy, aristocracy, democracy, suits Hobbes, provided sovereignty is absolute and peace assured. He loves peace, not kings – he simply thought that kings were more likely to achieve it.

The historical period through which Hobbes lived and which obsessed Swift converted both to absolutist solutions. In 1628 when the Petition of Right was presented, Hobbes translated Thucydides to attack democratic anarchy and the war confirmed his distrust of liberty as a tumultuous force. Swift similarly traces all the troubles of his times to a restless Puritan 'faction' and interprets the war as a second Fall. Since revolution is forever imminent, they never relax – their politics are those of a state of emergency, a threatened city

fearfully awaiting assault. Locke, by contrast, inhabits a mental
world free of war hysteria. The cost of peace may be exorbitant, its
tranquility that of Polyphemus's den, where men, passively obedient,
await patiently their turn to be devoured. Disliking both Strafford's
despotism and Anabaptist excess, Locke devises a system of checks
and balances, with power deliberately divided and the right to protest
jealously preserved. We need dig very little to expose, beneath
surface similarities, the basic disagreement between Swift and Locke.

Swift's assertion that 'law, in a free country, is, or ought to be, the
determination of the majority of those who have property in land',[44]
might have come from the *Second Treatise on Government*, but, significantly, he does not follow Locke in proclaiming the right to resist
an abuse of legislative power. He is, of course, against divine right,
absolute monarchy and passive obedience – how could he be otherwise after 1688 and not be a Jacobite? – but this makes him Filmer's
adversary, not Hobbes's. Divine right and Hobbesian absolutism are
very different. Far from welcoming *Leviathan* as useful adjunct,
royal absolutists were horrified by it, and Hobbes's boast in 1656
that his teaching had persuaded many potential rebels to accept the
Protectorate did not endear him to the cavalier *émigrés*.[45] *Leviathan*
supported winners – Locke argued that, far from securing peace, it
incited the disorder it claimed to prevent by a naked invitation to
strike for power. But this encouragement to caps in the ring, disliked
by Locke, was just as detestable to pre-1688 Tories, aghast at Hobbesian brutality. There is no argument that Swift opposed Filmer, but
Filmer is not Hobbes. Swift avoids the stigma of divine right (abandoned by all save fanatical Jacobites) but confers the old power on a
'divine' legislature, supremely irresistible and enforcing unqualified
obedience; the old high doctrines return in a terminology appropriate
to the post-revolutionary period. Knowing what 1688 means, Swift
rejects the old obsolete absolutism for a new Hobbesian model.

The contract theory, used throughout the Reformation period as a
weapon of religious minorities against persecution and by Locke to
justify the overthrow of tyrants, became in Hobbes a device for enforcing total obedience. Divine right is given a secular facelift, stripped
of its outmoded religious trappings and reintroduced, with scepticism
rather than faith the new rationale, force rather than legitimacy its
justification. After the Revolution it was futile to pine for the old
authority and Hobbes supplied the only realistic alternative for those
reluctant to embrace the new open society implied in Locke. Swift's

legislature, like Leviathan, demands absolute obedience, especially in religion, whereas Locke endorses a pluralistic society where diverse loyalties are encouraged rather than reprehended. Writing at a time when it seemed to him inconceivable that an assembly could be as efficient as a king, Hobbes preferred monarchy as best adapted to Leviathan's requirements, but his arguments apply equally to all forms of government where one supreme authority towers illimitably over all other institutions. If we accept this as the definition of despotic government, attend to the power a government commands rather than the name it calls itself, we shall identify Swift's system as authoritarian, Locke's as liberal.

Confusion results from a basically authoritarian man like Swift using the vocabulary of liberalism. Taking such sentiments at modern valuation is like concluding that the critic of Walpole's censorship upholds the principles of *Areopagitica*. Occasional sniping at tyranny notwithstanding, Swift's real concern is the danger of anarchy and to quell it he creates his omnipotent legislature. No area of life, private property and religious worship included, is a sanctuary from government. Against Locke's claim that the supreme power cannot deprive any man of his goods without his consent, Hobbes regards property rights as valid against other subjects but not against the sovereign. Government, like God, can do as it pleases with its own creation. Swift likewise maintains that within all actions capable of execution by force, government is supreme.[46] Both men view with suspicion the ancient distinction between the things of God and of Caesar and reinterpret it so as to let Caesar rest quietly without worrying over rebellions provoked by uneasy consciences. Only a Caesar aspiring to Big Brotherhood would think of disputing the things of God as defined by Swift and Hobbes. The one exception to their absolutist embrace is the sphere of private belief, the inward domain of consciousness, the few cubic centimetres within the skull, but, far from being generous, they are simply making a virtue of necessity; even the most devout totalitarians have yet to discover a foolproof method of making an inventory of a man's head and to claim credit for permitting what cannot be prevented is a piece of insulting legerdemain – as well make a merit out of the free movement of bowels as the free movement of thought, thus defined.

Their libertarian credentials are the more dubious when we suspect uneasily that they would manipulate opinion if only they could, that the mind is safe from them simply because they lack the key to unlock it. Despite his insistence that the sovereign requires external obedience only and doesn't meddle with inward convictions, Hobbes pronounces ominously that subversive thoughts produce subversive actions: 'the actions of men proceed from their opinions, and in the well-governing of opinions consists the well-governing of men's actions'.[47] The rulers of Oceania, nodding agreement, take the appropriate steps. Bunyan, banned by the government from public preaching, protests the logic of the decision: where is the sense in preventing him from addressing a crowd on the ground that he is seducing them, yet simultaneously allowing him to persuade individuals?[48] If the one action is wrong, then so is the other. Hobbes, Swift and the Giant King accept the challenge: both actions are wrong, he must stop converting individuals as well as crowds and be content to hold his beliefs in the privacy of his own mind. Orwell's O'Brien carries this to its logical terminus by totally prohibiting heretical opinions and purifying the mind that harbours them. Are Hobbes and Swift a pair of would-be O'Briens who simply lack the scientific expertise to perform such an operation? Given the absolutist tendency of Hobbes's State, his remark about subversive thoughts makes sense only within a context of 're-education', and it masks the brutal reality of a sovereign exterminating all those incorrigibles who become neither indoctrinated nor successful hypocrites.

Swift is equally sensitive to the interdependence of thought and action: 'when we consider our thoughts, as they are the seeds of words and actions, we cannot but agree, that they ought to be kept under the strictest regulation'.[49] For him, as for Pascal, thinking well is the first principle of morality, and thinking well is the opposite of free-thinking – avoiding being one's own carver, sticking to the *consensus gentium*. Yet here too we find contradiction in Swift. Bolgolam's argument for executing Gulliver – that, since he is already a traitor at heart, it is a mere matter of time before he is so in deed[50] – is the logic of Brutus; one doesn't wait for the serpent to leave the shell before crushing it:

> so Caesar may;
> Then, lest he may, prevent –

Swift is clearly attacking in Bolgolam those who condemn thoughts, regardless of action, yet his own rebukes to Tindal and Burnet show how dangerously close to Bolgolam he could be, and when peaceful dissenters plead their conduct as surety for their claim to civic rights,

Swift invokes Brutus's argument — rather than any past act of aggression, he fears what they *might*, and indeed *must* logically, do, for all sects inevitably seek domination just as all kites eat chickens.[51]

Justifying his exhortations to fellow-Anglicans is the conviction that dissent must be crushed before it grows strong enough to do the crushing; fearing under- rather than over-reaction, he favours the pre-emptive strike and this fighter-pilot mentality makes one suspect his wholehearted commitment to the Giant King's indifferentism towards inward dispositions. Because correct belief is crucial, free-thinking is dangerous, since 'if you do happen to think there is no hell, there certainly is none, and consequently you cannot be damned'.[52] It is fear of damnation that keeps men virtuous. Brecht's Herr Keuner advises that we ask ourselves if ceasing to believe in God will influence our behaviour for the worse; if the answer is affirmative, we must strive to go on believing. But the question is superfluous for Swift, since nobody can honestly respond in the negative; rejecting hellfire means automatic membership of the Kit-Kat Club, for those who think wrongly, act wrongly. Dr Johnson's Rochester, who, 'finding it not convenient to admit the authority of laws which he was resolved not to obey, sheltered his wickedness behind infidelity',[53] is the patron saint of freethinking as conceived by Swift, for why else do men turn against religion if not, in Pirandello's phrase, *a fare il porco*? If Swift 'permits' liberty of belief, it is surely not through discounting the importance of thought in determining action, and at least some readers may suspect it is really because he knew no way of curtailing such liberty — men may think as they please for how can they be prevented?

However unfair, one cannot help speculating, provoked by Swift himself, how he might have reacted had some means of detecting silent dissent been discovered. Given the essential link between thought and action accepted by him, he might have been hard pressed, subjected to the same 'logical' techniques, the *ad hominem* arguments he used against his enemies, atheists, freethinkers, dissenters, Milton, Burnet, Tindal, Whigs and Ulster Presbyterians, to justify a refusal to go for total conformity, were such a programme technically feasible. 'You may force men, by interest or punishment, to say or swear they believed, and to act as if they believed: You can go no further'.[54]

One can easily imagine this uttered with elated defiance by Mill or the still unbroken Winston Smith, but did Swift deliver it with the slightest twinge of regret? May we wonder as to his reaction had he been assured that one *could* go much further? Swift, for one, could not complain, for his own favourite strategy in debate, the discrediting of the opponent by what Plekhanov describes as first sticking the convict's badge on him and then examining his case, entails a continual recourse to hypothetical argument. Locke would unquestionably have denounced indoctrination or 're-education' as a violation of liberty. Swift, without alluding to its morality, merely points to its impracticality, but there is, disquietingly, no denial that in the right hands it might be both permissible and even laudable – the objections are technical, not moral. Isn't a Gulliver redeemed by Houyhnhnm re-education an improvement upon the corrupt jingoist who enters Houyhnhnmland? Perhaps the wrong temptation was offered the Giant King. Would the good man who recoiled disgusted from gunpowder have done likewise to a promise of painless conformity, the bloodless triumph of virtue, the rehabilitation of the recalcitrant and the assured docility of the citizen, all easily achieved by those latest marvels of western technology, aversion therapy and behaviourist conditioning? Even if the Giant King had remained steadfast as Guyon in the Cave of Mammon, is it unfair to feel doubtful about his creator? – certainly, no freethinker or dissenter would have slept absolutely secure in a rehabilitation centre run by Swift. Yet, as Locke shows, one can share Swift's unease about possible abuses of liberty of thought without necessarily adopting the theory of sovereignty proposed by him as the one barrier to anarchy. To take the single instance of religious freedom, Locke provides against abuses of this right, such as offering human sacrifices, without removing the right itself, as Swift is disposed to do.

Completely opposed interpretations of law mark another radical separation between them. Locke's concept of natural law and his strict separation of spiritual and temporal powers link him, via medieval scholasticism, with Cicero.[55] For Cicero law cannot be determined by simply consulting a digest of praetors' edicts, government decrees or existing statutes, all of which often have about as much right to be called law as the rules of the Mafia. Bad laws exist and to accept as justice what peoples, princes and judges have often approved may mean justifying abominations like the Final Solution. Cicero insists that votes and decrees cannot change the laws of nature or turn bad into good. Law is not just a command issued by powerful authority – the orders of a Caligula have a status very different from those of an Alfred the Great – for to deserve the name it must avoid moral, as much as political, anarchy. Cicero anticipates Thoreau's rejection of the idea that the citizen must resign his conscience to the legislator, even when the 'justice' being administered is clearly unjust; he can appeal instead to a law of nature, superior to actual laws and to which they ought to conform. Laws which fail to do so are bad laws, against reason, and, as the Nuremburg judges insisted, they must not be obeyed. From Cicero the idea descends through Aquinas to Hooker and Locke. Aquinas, discussing the Roman legal text, *quod principi placet legis habet vigorem*, declares that only commands regulated by reason have legal authority, otherwise the ruler's will is lawlessness rather than law; whatever contravenes the law of nature is a perversion of law, no matter how many votes or bayonets support it – Gyges is powerful but wicked, the violence of legislators is still violence. Locke, inheriting this tradition, is Antigone's champion, invoking natural law and immutable justice against the brute force of authority.

In the sixteenth and seventeenth centuries the whole concept of natural law was menaced by a revivified scepticism. Men like Montaigne advanced doctrines of ethical relativism, often buttressed by data from the new geographical discoveries, to discredit the belief in an unchanging moral law common to all men. Morality was, on this view, mere custom, with a change of meridian producing a complete revolution in moral attitudes, and Montaigne, having revealed the rat-hole in the temple, warns, somewhat illogically, against the dangerous practice of investigating the source of sacred laws lest we uncover the irrational basis on which they stand. Beneath all these diverse attacks on the traditional doctrine, from Hobbesian positivism to Pascal's Jansenism, was a profound scepticism concerning human reason, a conviction that man is not *animal rationale* but a creature driven by passion. Yet demoting morality to custom and exploding the law of nature leaves only power, for the choice, as Montaigne and Pascal, Hobbes and Swift, each in his own way, recognize is finally *Recht* or *Macht*.

For Hobbes positive law is not limited by a prior, superior law against which it is to be judged for its moral validity. No law, by definition, can be unjust, since injustice is what law forbids. A law is authoritative, not through some deluded conformity to the conclusions of reason, but through its origin in the sovereign's will. Before the sovereign exists, there is neither justice or injustice, right or wrong – law and religion both are artificial constructs, established by arbitrary institutions, the sovereign's achievements, not his credentials. All that Hobbes confusingly retains of the traditional doctrine of natural law is the name; Cicero notwithstanding, law *is* simply the command of a superior to an inferior – law defines justice, not vice versa. Hobbes uses the same terminology as Locke and Grotius, just as today people use a word like democracy to describe both the United States and China, but, though the words are the same, the things are very different. When Hobbes refers to natural right he means that man outside society may employ his strength and cunning like any other beast of prey, while by natural law he means prudential calculation, the sense not to get caught. Cicero uses these concepts to raise man above the animals, Hobbes to reinstate him with the rest of the pack, obsessed with survival, both the fiercest of predators and the most ferociously successful of intra-specific killers, as Gulliver's description of European warfare so clearly attests.

The doctrine that dominion stems from power alone was not startingly new, as Goneril's response to her husband's accusation of adultery and murder exemplifies:

> Say if I do, the laws are mine, not thine;
> Who can arraign me for it?[56]

The Emperor Valentinian, forcing himself upon the chaste Lucina in Fletcher's *Valentinian* provides an even clearer example:

> *Lucina*: As long as there is motion in my body
>   And life to give words, I'll cry for justice.
> *Valentinian*: Justice shall never hear ye. I am justice.[57]

What is both new and significant is that this doctrine, hitherto the infallible stigma of the villainous, becomes in Hobbes a straight scientific description of political reality, to be accepted without any moral fulminations against its wickedness. *Leviathan* secularizes the Scotist idea of God. The medieval dispute between Aquinas and Scotus on the nature of God turned upon the question of whether law was *jus quia justum* or *jus quia jussum*, and Hobbes and Locke reenact this confrontation between voluntarism and intellectualism. Hobbes follows Scotus; the rights which God possesses over men come not from the fact that he is their creator and benefactor, 'but from his irresistible power', and 'that mortal God', Leviathan, is adored to the degree that it wields power.[58] The God of Scotus and Leviathan determines by an act of will, by pure fiat, what is and is not law, right and justice. So sacrosanct is this authority that Hobbes is driven to exalt it above even egoism. The subject, in making out a blank cheque to the sovereign, surrenders all right to complain at injustice, no matter the sovereign's conduct. Even David, seducing Bathsheba and arranging Uriah's death, did no injury to Uriah, since the King's 'right' to do all this – 'right' and 'power' are clearly interchangeable – was given him by Uriah himself.[59]

Swift, like Hobbes, makes the sovereign absolute and legally impeccable. Difference as to the sovereign's person is trivial when set against their agreement on his power. 'Force is a physical power; I do not see how its effects could produce morality. To yield to force is an act of necessity, not of will; it is at best an act of prudence. In what sense can it be a moral duty? . . . Surely it must be admitted, then, that might does not make right, and that the duty of obedience is only to legitimate powers.'[60] Rousseau's words are supremely valuable as a reminder that power, even raised to omnipotence, is not *ipso facto* alchemized into justice. Hobbes and Swift are, by contrast, so anxious to prevent the anarchy implicit in the claim that only legitimate power need be obeyed that they treat power as its own legitimization. Authorities must be obeyed, for the alternative is unthinkable. The liberal historian Acton declared that whereas the issue of ancient politics was an absolute state planted on slavery, that of the Middle Ages was a system in which authority was restricted by the representation of powerful classes, by privileged associations, and by the acknowledgement of duties superior to those imposed by men. The link between this ideal and the liberal democracy promulgated by Locke and developed by Mill and de Tocqueville is obvious, just as are Hobbes's envious yearnings towards ancient authoritarianism. What should be equally plain today when concepts of majoritarian tyranny and totalitarian democracy clash with Lockean ideals of liberal democracy, is that Acton's sombre warning applies just as forcibly to Swift's as to any other theory of absolute sovereignty: '. . . that government by the whole people, being the government of the most numerous and most powerful class, is an evil of the same nature as unmixed monarchy and requires, for nearly the same reasons, institutions that shall protect it against itself and shall uphold the permanent reign of law against arbitrary revolutions of opinion'.[61]

Nowhere is the affinity between Swift and Hobbes better revealed or their vulnerability to authoritarian temptation better demonstrated than in their attitude to the relationship of Church and State and the tensions provoked in the individual by the problems of dual loyalty.

These are Swift's paramount concerns: his politics were a function of the Church's needs and he judged Whig and Tory from the pulpit's viewpoint.[62] He left the Whigs, not as opportunist or renegade, but from a conviction that the Tories were the Church party and it is no exaggeration to find here the key to his personality. The Church–State relationship was the great political question of the seventeenth century, and Swift always remained mentally a man of that period. Between 1558 and the English Revolution the pressing task was to find a solution to the breakdown of the medieval religious polity. One answer, deism via Cartesian rationalism, involved toleration and the secularisation of politics, with religion, in Tawney's words, ceasing to be the master-interest of mankind and dwindling instead into a department of life with boundaries which it is extravagant to overstep.[63] Another option was the establishment of a national religion based on authority rather than reason or faith, aiming at social stability rather than individual salvation. Erastianism, a State Church, a ministry of religion, seemed to many the only way to save orthodoxy from its heretical and rationalist enemies. Ever since Luther's revolt religion had become a potentially disruptive force, but the Church as government department could promote social harmony. The first alternative found its rationale in Locke's *Letter Concerning Toleration*, the second in *Leviathan*, and it is significant that in this, his major concern, Swift leans towards Hobbes rather than Locke.

It makes every other possible disagreement between them seem of marginal importance. The sovereign power alone prevents ruinous religious anarchy. It is an essentially reactionary outlook because for men of Locke's persuasion the new and very different priority is to safeguard individual rights against a too-powerful sovereign. The spectre of 1642 continues to haunt Swift when many already see religious toleration as the necessary guarantee of social stability – where the State's survival had once seemed to depend on repression, it now was increasingly seen as inseparable from toleration. The advocates of toleration as good in itself could also plead its practical benefits, as the militant sects, burgeoning under persecution, declined when tolerated. Yet Swift clung to the Hobbesian dictum that religion, as inevitable instigator of civil strife, must be subject to State control, with its corollary that dissent threatened national security.

The remedy, already noted, was to confer an absolute law-making power on government. Whatever the legislators decree, ecclesiastical or civil, at once becomes law: 'their decrees may be against equity, truth, reason, and religion, but they are not against law', since law *is* what they decide – 'in short, they may do anything within the compass of human power'.[64] Hobbes also insists that the sovereign is as powerful as is humanly possible, that even if he can commit iniquity, he cannot commit injustice. Whatever shades of difference may still lurk behind their respective definitions are of minor significance in the light of their alliance against Cicero as a tout for anarchy – men, misgivings notwithstanding, must obey the law, even when they dislike it. What is the point of Swift saying that Parliament cannot create a bishop, since the laying on of hands comes from God, when he adds that it can give anyone it chooses the revenue and powers of a bishop and compel all men to treat him as such? What ruler outside *Nineteen Eighty Four* wants more? For Swift is, of course, *not* inciting rebellion or even passive resistance to improper appointment; within all action capable of execution by force – what does this leave out? – government is supreme. As Hobbes puts it, 'by a good law I mean not a just law: for no law can be unjust'.[65]

Swift enlists the Bible in support of a State-enforced religion, arguing that Old Testament kings were judged good or bad according as they punished or permitted idolatry.[66] Locke, by contrast, denies any parallel between the divinely-instituted theocracy of Israel, where God himself was legislator, and modern States. Israel is unique and in any case foreigners were not coerced to renounce their own creeds and observe the Mosaical law.[67] Swift disagrees: 'we are sure Christianity is the only true religion . . . and therefore it should be the magistrate's chief care to propagate it; and that God should be worshipped in that form, that those who are the teachers think most proper'.[68] There could be no more outright rebuttal of Locke's claim that neither sin nor religion is the province of the magistrate. Locke campaigns to separate Church and State, dismissing them to different directions so that, never meeting, they will never quarrel, one to tend the material good of society, the other to devote itself to the cure of souls. Swift stigmatises this as a modern exemplification of the pernicious maxim of Tiberius, *deorum offensa diis curae*; guilt by association could scarcely be more damaging, for, given the infamous source, there is no need to discuss the wickedness of Locke's argument.[69]

Swift, for his part, is eager to help God chastise his enemies. Foolish rulers fail to see that heresy and rebellion, sin and crime, are mutually reinforcing, reciprocal in fertilization; sedition may be more dramatically dangerous but heresy leads just as surely to civil tumult, 'as natural and probable . . . though more remote',[70] just as the liver may be damaged suddenly or by gradual alcoholic assault. Blasphemy must be punished, since the rebel against God is merely rehearsing his onslaught on society – sin *is* the province of the wise magistrate. Locke is effectually rejecting any established Church, let alone one that requires the police to provide a congregation, and Swift's disgust is attested in his vitriolic review of a book by Locke's disciple, Tindal, which was a barely-disguised attack upon the idea of a national, State-supported Church. Swift naturally resented this as undermining his chief, perhaps only, argument in favour of Anglicanism: 'I beg you Sir, not to overlook these last words, religion as by law established'.[71] Where religion is concerned, possession is for Swift the whole of the law.

Hobbes and Swift break with Locke in the alacrity with which they surrender to the sovereign 'the right of judging what doctrines are fit for peace, and to be taught the subjects',[72] even to the point of deciding if the State is to have any religion at all – as Leslie Stephen remarks, on Hobbesian premises, Charles II was to decide whether the world had a beginning.[73] Hobbes pillories the Church–State separation proposed later by Locke: 'Temporal and spiritual government are but two words brought into the world to make men see double and mistake their lawful sovereign', when the truth is that 'both State and Church are the same men', subject to the one authority.[74] Swift naturally accepts the principle of religious toleration as an essential element of the Revolution settlement to which he repeatedly and sincerely declared his allegiance, where Hobbes would have denounced this as a door open to anarchy.

But perhaps all this betokens is the difference between living before and after the Revolution. Swift's is certainly a most grudging concession, toleration reluctantly accepted as *fait accompli*, past blunders having permitted heresy to flourish to a point where it cannot be extirpated without grave risk of civil war – Charles I, like the Weimar Government after 1919, is Swift's cautionary model against the folly of under-reaction. He is adamant that toleration as such is both displeasing to God and noxious to the State. Sects, he assures us, 'seem only tolerated with any reason, because they are already spread. . . . But the greatest advocates for general liberty of conscience will allow that they ought to be checked in their beginnings, if they will allow them to be an evil at all; or, which is the same thing, if they will only grant it were better for the peace of the state that there should be none'.[75] This splendidly exemplifies a strategy in disputation much favoured by Swift and his admirer Orwell – assuming as self-evidently incontrovertible a belief which the antagonist, far from sharing, as is pretended, violently rejects. Locke declines to accept 'evil' and 'disturbance of the peace' as synonomous; the peace of a Nero is far better disturbed than sheltered by passive obedience. But, dissenting even more radically from Swift's provocative assumption, Locke flatly denies that mankind's division into different sects is 'obstructive of the salvation of souls', insisting that God is offended only by evil living, whether by orthodox or heterodox.[76]

Welcoming, as he does, religious diversity, Locke might well be the target of Swift's attack on those 'who would make [schism] no crime at all; and argue at a wild rate, that God Almighty is delighted with the variety of faith and worship, as he is with the varieties of nature . . . to such absurdities are men carried by the affectations of free-thinking'.[77] One must always be prepared for inconsistency, even self-contradiction, in Swift, finding the same belief sometimes ridiculed, sometimes upheld:

> You who in different Sects have shamm'd,
> And come to see each Other damn'd,
> So some Folks told you, but they knew
> No more of Jove's Designs than you.[78]

This is, of course, not a 'Lockean' poem – Locke is just as vulnerable to a charge of claiming to be God's confidant – but, in the present context, it seems much easier to give it a Lockean interpretation, to reconcile it with the *Letter Concerning Toleration* rather than with the no-surrender intransigence of bellicose Anglicanism, Swift's modern rendition of *extra ecclesia nulla salus*.

The notion that God favours one particular religion above all others could be pressed to justify a holy war to convert the whole world to the true faith, but Swift, like Hobbes, sees religion in strictly national terms, protected within political boundaries. Far from being a Jesuit-type crusader, he simply wants to enforce the Hobbesian lesson that Church and State are the same men, to correct the deplorable double vision of Locke and show that since a commonwealth is finally one person, it ought to exhibit one worship. As sensitive as

Bossuet to the fissiparity of Protestantism, he looks to the civil power
to resist the tendency to fragmentation and disunity inherent in the
very soul of Reformation: the revolt of the individual conscience
against intrusive authority in matters of faith. Schism entails religious
civil war: 'most religious wars have been caused by schisms. . . . The
national religion always desireth peace, even in her notions, for its
interests'.[79] This holds good for any national religion, Protestant,
Catholic or Mahometan, and Swift's approval is indiscriminately
extended to all such preservers of peace, just as, conversely, his
anger is trained upon all contumelious schismatics as spoilers of
harmony.

The seditious character of dissent makes any concession, short of
total capitulation, futile, for dissenters, like all men, will stop asking
only when they possess everything. In Swift's parable the Church
is a much-desired woman, while the dissenters are an importunate
lover who will betray the instant they enjoy. The lady, if wise, will
go on being 'cruel', since surrender will leave her helpless in a world
where if you can't bargain, you won't survive.[80] It is only 'natural'
that dissenters should unite with Whigs, just as formerly 'at the
Restoration the Presbyterians, Anabaptists, Independents, and other
sects did all with every good reason unite and solder up their schemes
against the Church'.[81] Swift is not blaming the dissenters for seeking,
as they must, domination, but neither should they complain if
Anglicans decline to dig their own graves. The use of expressions
like 'natural', 'good reason', 'natural temper of mankind', and so on,
reveals the extent of Swift's thirlage to the idea of self-interest as the
all-sufficient key to human behaviour. He expects and is accordingly
unshocked by the scheming of sectaries; his perplexed indignation is
reserved, not for dissenters naturally bent on dislodging Anglicans,
but for his own criminally besotted co-religionists who would suicidally
allow their enemies full civic rights.

That selfishness is natural, all according to the due course of things,
enforces the need to take precautions – the marauding kite is not
to be spared for behaving naturally. Its nature is to kill chickens but
the farmer's is to kill kites; retribution is natural too.[82] The
Hobbesian war is waged in a poultry yard where the laws of life
exclude both blame and indignation. The Houyhnhnms know the
Yahoos are incurable, but to understand is not to pardon; knowing
one's enemy is a precondition for thwarting him.

Toleration is, in any case, futile, for nobody really wants it.

Dissent is egoism hunting an excuse, cussedness posing as principle. La Rochefoucauld suggests cynically that nonconformity is pride in a pet; when all the best places are taken, some people prefer to be awkward sooner than settle for a back seat.[83] Comprehension within the Church is doomed, 'for what imports it, how large a gate you open, if there will be always left a number, who place a pride and a merit in refusing to enter?'[84] The problem is not religious but psychological, the province of the alienist rather than the churchman. The heretic wants to be different – like Jack in the *Tale* or Brecht's poet in 'The Burning of the Books', he solicits persecution as proof of significance; toleration, in denying his importance, will simply inflame him to seek some new, more outrageous heresy, since his true craving is confrontation. Ibsen once warned would-be progressives against trying to keep up with him, since they would reach his present position only to find he had moved on.[85] Swift attributes a similar mentality to his religious adversaries in order to decry a policy of concession – why foolishly be a dove when the enemy is so resolutely hawk?

He will not treat dissent as a straight religious problem: the demand for toleration is either psychological or political in motivation, the perversity of people mad for the limelight or a ruse of unscrupulous power-seekers. How, asks Swift, will the dissenting preachers react when toleration makes them redundant? Will they, the principle secured, willingly withdraw into obscurity, or will they, as is far more probable, their appetite for power titillated, cast around for fresh pretexts to withhold their flocks and attract new proselytes by further innovation?[86] Finally, can't all this be deduced, with no need for empirical verification, simply by considering 'the natural temper of mankind in general'? Militants with a vested interest in strife will respond to concessions by escalating demands, and no individual plea for toleration need be examined on its merits once we accept Swift's prior assumption that all dissenters are militants at heart if not yet in deed. Rival sects scheme each other's overthrow in a Hobbesian state of nature, so that dissenters protesting their innocence of all aggressive intent are not to be believed. Bunyan denies any similarity between himself and Fifth Monarchy fanatics – 'that practice of theirs, I abhor, said I; yet it does not follow that because they did so, therefore all others will do so'.[87] For Swift, however, a docile dissenter is as illogical as a virtuous atheist or a just Gyges, since domination 'is natural for all sects to desire' and 'they cannot justify by any consistent principles, if they do not endeavour' to obtain it.[88] The unreliable whims of those who are peaceful against logic may alter overnight, transforming them into the dangerous foes they ought to be. As much as with Henry and his roomful of Paris bourgeois, abstract logic prevails over everyday experience, syllogism over fact, and people who seem innocent are at heart irreclaimably guilty.

Swift derides the policy of low profile and counters Tindal's claim that the wise lawgiver makes allowance for religious diversity by citing Lycurgus, greatest of ancient legislators, who gave his people not what they wanted but what was good for them; and, in any case, 'the Scripture is full against schism'.[89] Swift and Locke proceed from identical data towards opposite conclusions, the one insisting that dangerous men must be put down, the other that oppressed men become dangerous. Locke's analysis leads logically to an open society where Church and State are separated, Swift's to a uniformity imposed through their identification. It is, however, one thing to ask the State to defend orthodoxy, another to identify it, especially when, as Locke caustically observes, 'every church is orthodox to itself; to others, erroneous or heretical'.[90] The problem is particularly awkward for Swift, with his conviction that all sects seek power, 'which they cannot succeed in, without the utmost danger to the public peace'.[91] His response to Locke's challenge is to invite the sovereign to define orthodoxy, thus subordinating church to state: *cuius regio eius religio*. The government can, at pleasure, take away the tithes. It had already expelled the non-jurors from their livings over the oath to William III. It could, if it saw fit, disestablish the Church or even abolish Christianity altogether and set up another religion, Jewish, Mahometan or heathen.[92] The sovereign, in Hobbes's words, has 'the right of judging what doctrines are fit for peace, and to be taught the subjects'.[93] A seventeenth-century Cicero might have objected that some doctrines fit for peace may be totally unfit for salvation, but both Hobbes and Swift sheer away from this slope to anarchy. They flatly contradict Locke's dictum that the civil power has no jurisdiction over religious beliefs. The resultant paradox is that Locke, frontrunner in the movement from dogma towards rationalism, upholds Anglican autonomy (with, admittedly, that of every other Christian sect) against State interference, while Swift, champion of Anglicanism, delivers his Church to the State and is reconciled even to its possible abolition, rather than concede equality to dissent.

For Locke, faith being a matter of inward commitment, compulsory worship is absurd; Aquinas, whom Acton called the first Whig, likewise insists that infidels should not be dragooned into the Church, 'for belief depends upon the will', and an unwilling believer is a self-contradiction.[94] The problem vanishes when inward belief coincides with outward conformity, but, lacking a highly developed propaganda machine and advanced brain-washing techniques, such coincidence over large numbers is most improbable. Swift doesn't burke the problem. Should Church and State, conscience and law, clash, the good citizen will obey the latter; even if parliament decides to abolish episcopacy in favour of the detestable Presbyterians, 'without question all peaceful subjects ought passively to submit'.[95] Plato's maxim that men should worship the gods established by law is cited in support – a shrewd thrust, since Plato was often claimed by deists and freethinkers as spiritual ancestor.[96] Swift prefers a State Church to the risk of civil war and his definition of schism is pure Erastianism: ''tis certain that, in the sense of the law, the schism lies on that side which opposes itself to the national religion'.[97] God is on the side of the legal battalions. To identify schism by theological criteria is, as Locke points out, difficult if not impossible; Swift, avoiding theological squabbles, settles for the less disputable, if less spiritually satisfying, weapon of legal enforcement, policemen being easier to recognize than prophets. Forget inspiration and acknowledge power: Swift, anticipating the who–whom argument of Lenin, refuses with breathtaking brutality to grant civil equality to dissenters: 'we are the majority and we are in possession'.

Swift is in consequence, whatever his inmost beliefs, committed to a Hobbesian view in which the maintenance of national unity and peace trumps all else. The use, not truth, of religion becomes paramount. Hobbes, to be sure, distinguishes between religion and superstition, but only on grounds of legal status: 'Fear of power invisible, feigned by the mind, or imagined from tales publicly allowed, religion; not allowed, superstition. And when the power imagined is truly such as we imagine, true religion.'[98] Catholicism is religion under Henry VIII, superstition under Edward VI, recovers under Mary, and relapses for good under Elizabeth; or, geographically expressed, Catholicism is superstition in England, Protestantism superstition in Spain, and both are superstition at Constantinople. As for *true* religion, Hobbes is surely speaking tongue in cheek, for how can we verify what we imagine? True religion, a purely theoretical construct like the *Ding-an-sich*, is bafflingly unknowable, otherwise why the need to call in the sovereign in the first place? Pascal, admitting that

we cannot make justice strong, settles for making strength justice;[99]
the Hobbesian variant is that since we cannot make 'true' religion
prevail, we must make the prevailing religion 'true'. Both Hobbes
and Swift define heresy and schism as refusal to obey the sovereign
on religious matters; conversely, what the sovereign commands cannot
by definition be heretical. Being orthodox means obeying the law.

Swift refuses to debate with dissenters, stands Shylock-like for
law and insists that every country needs a national religion, whether
bishops or bonzes. The practice is 'universal and founded upon the
strongest reasons', for otherwise, fearful prospect, 'a nation may have
an hundred sects with their leaders; every one of which hath an equal
right to plead that they must obey God rather than man'. Compulsory
uniformity is the sole stay to anarchy. Only when the established
religion grows exorbitantly corrupt or when a massive majority of
landed people on the government side turns against it, may it be
superseded, 'provided the work might be done without blood or
confusion'.[100] The dilemma of seventeenth-century Protestant conservatives was to justify their revolt against Rome without sanctioning
further rebellions to the left, and Swift strenuously devises a set of
preconditions so improbable in conjunction as to make further change
virtually impossible. The time for change is when it can't be avoided
and Swift resented James II above all for forcing revolution on
England.

Resolved on Anglican supremacy, he is none the less compelled by
his argument's logic to applaud uniformity as good in itself, whatever
the religion. He recommends the abolition of their native language as a
means of civilizing the Irish, so preparing them for the national
religion, 'whatever kind may then happen to be established'.[101]
Ideally, everyone should be Anglican, but the next best thing is a
nation where Church and State are the same men. He tartly informs his
Catholic friend Pope that he has no more to do with the constitution of
Church and State than a Christian at Constantinople, in rebuttal of
Locke's contention that full citizenship must never depend on religious
belief: 'Neither pagan nor Mahometan nor Jew ought to be excluded
from the civil rights of the commonwealth because of his religion'.[102]
For Swift, however, stability and conformity are so close as to justify
the Erastian price. 'All true believers shall break their eggs at the
convenient end'; in this Lilliputian solution, what other meaning,
given Swift's definition of schism, can 'convenient' have than 'what
conduces to public peace'?[103]

Locke argues that since we cannot identify orthodoxy, we must accept toleration – unable to agree, we must agree to differ. Hobbes and Swift accept the premise but not the conclusion; since we undeniably cannot agree, the magistrate must decide – the policeman's truncheon is the determinative argument. Yet if true religion means inward assent, how can men be justifiably forced to do what they abhor? Coercive religion is nonsensical and the impossibility of harmonizing inward belief and outward conformity proves the tolerationist case.

Swift readily agrees that only outward behaviour can be controlled – his remark that one can go no further than enforce verbal assent or external compliance is pure Locke, and he similarly asserts that 'to say a man is bound to believe, is neither truth nor sense', since each man must 'believe according to [his] own impartial reason'.[104] But, far from deducing the absurdity of a coercive creed, he denies any essential identity between belief and action or that men must act as they believe, maintaining instead the paradoxical converse: 'Every man, as a member of the commonwealth, ought to be content with the possession of his own opinions in private, without perplexing his neighbours or disturbing the public'.[105]

The plea for liberty of conscience is specious, since all men already possess it, without fear of deprivation: 'Liberty of conscience, properly speaking, is no more than liberty of possessing our own thoughts and opinions, which every man enjoys without fear of the magistrate. But how far he shall publicly act in pursuance of those opinions, is to be regulated by the laws of the country'.[106] Believe in cannibalism if you please but don't eat your neighbour. Intolerance, as the exemplary Giant King demonstrates, is violation of another's mind, not the essential regulation of his conduct. Swift can praise even the arch-enemy Cromwell for sensibly discriminating between action and belief, when, defending his veto of the Mass in Ireland, he denies that this injured anyone's conscience. Dr Johnson gives classic formulation to this much-favoured distinction of conservative thinkers: 'people confound liberty of thinking with liberty of talking, nay, with liberty of preaching. Every man has a physical right to think as he pleases; for it cannot be discovered how he thinks . . . But, Sir, no member of a society has a right to *teach* any doctrine contrary to what the society holds to be true'.[107] Hobbes resolves the awkward problem of a sovereign who forbids belief in Christ by pointing out that such commands are futile since belief cannot be dictated. Caesa may force you to sprinkle incense, but Christ abides undetected in the heart. Why, then, this fuss over a liberty which everyone unpreventably enjoys?[108] Once again a merely verbal agreement masks an irretrievable antagonism as both men use the same expression to mean totally different things: within liberty of conscience Locke includes the rights to argue, discuss, express, publish and campaign, whereas Swift grants only what cannot be withheld.

Swift also frames an intellectual definition of conscience, intended to put it so far above the mass of men that they could never invoke it against authority. It is 'that knowledge which a man has within himself of his own thoughts and actions . . . the knowledge we have of what we are thinking and doing'.[109] Innocent though this sounds, conscience's stalwarts may sense a threat in the deduction that therefore 'a man's conscience can go no higher than his knowledge'. Experts alone may entertain doubts, the rest of us, too ignorant to afford scruples, must humbly submit to external authority or be classed as conceited dunces. Hobbes likewise insists that conscience depends upon a highly fallible judgement, that men 'pretend to know [their ideas] are true, when they know at most but that they think so'.[110] What makes men, so prone to error everywhere else, assume that their conscience is never wrong? The strategy is so to disparage and discredit conscience that men will be reluctant to trust it against established authority.

The animus against the inner voice stems from a conviction that wherever it is encouraged, the law will be flouted, especially by those deluded enough to promote their dreams to divine instructions: 'in all things not contrary to the moral law [that is to say to the law of nature] all subjects are bound to obey that for divine law, which is declared to be so by the laws of the commonwealth'.[111] Since by law of nature Hobbes means merely a set of prudential recommendations that sensible men follow, this effectively ensures obedience by all save a few inspired dupes who can safely be left to the police. Whether emanating from crazy fanatics or ambitious schemers, liberty of conscience, in Locke's sense, is the instigator of disorder, and Hobbes arraigns the worst of seditious doctrines – that every individual is judge of good and evil ('every man his own carver') and that to oppose one's conscience is sin. Religion cannot be a matter of 'supernatural inspiration or infusion', for this would make every Christian a prophet, preferring his inner light to the law of the land. Men who leave nature for society abdicate the right to be their own judges. Swift, too,

denounces the abuse of the word conscience by people 'who apply
meanings to it which God Almighty never intended', the most outrageous being its misuse as 'our director and guide' when opposed to
established law and religion.[112] Dr Johnson condemns the doctrine
of inward light as incompatible with political and religious security.[113]
The issue of the individual conscience did not of course die when the
problem of religious toleration was solved – it transcends particular
animosities, is inseparable from man's social existence, has merely
moved house from religion to other quarters. Wherever individuals
confront unjust laws, the problem that beset Hobbes, Locke and
Swift is revived, though the form be different. It would be anachronistic to saddle men centuries dead with views on modern problems
they never envisaged, yet it is difficult not to hear sounding through
their pages anticipations of quarrels that continue to plague us, and
we read them today as much to find the clue to our own perplexities
as to enlighten ourselves on theirs.

Swift willingly concedes that his policy must produce hypocrisy –
there are, as the *Project* says, far worse things than hypocrisy: better
a Tartuffe than a boastfully wicked Sawbridge or Charteris. Hobbes,
too, easily befriends hypocrisy, arguing that God is not offended by a
profession simply of the tongue. The Bible supplies a precedent in
Naaman who was completely exonerated by Elisha after obeying a
command to kneel before idols. Even infidel princes must be obeyed;
Hobbes's sole concession to Christians ruled by heathens is a right to
die for their beliefs, never to fight for them. A certain testiness creeps
in as he chides the excessive zeal of resolved martyrs. Their faith is,
after all, 'internal and invisible', and there is no need, as Naaman
shows, to court self-destruction. But if they must be pigheaded, 'they
ought to expect their reward in heaven, and not complain of their
lawful sovereign, much less make war upon him'.[114]

Despite the large measure of agreement that it would be wrong to
ignore, Swift is clearly no disciple of Hobbes. He preferred the
English system of his day to continental absolutism, and, his own
words notwithstanding, one scarcely imagines him functioning
placidly within the puppet Church of Hobbes. There are, besides,
crucial differences between them. Hobbes makes his dark assessment
of human nature with a scientist's dispassionate equanimity, applying
his beloved geometry to the solution of human problems, untroubled
by the least aspiration towards nobler remedies. Swift, by contrast,
confronting depravity, continues to revere the exalted virtue of a

Thomas More or Giant King and cherish ideals, however difficult to attain; strive as he may, he is never at ease with Hobbesian mechanism, lacks the detachment that would permit him to examine the odious little vermin without losing his temper.

That he often agrees with Hobbes is indisputable, but sometimes it seems to us no more than verbal. For it is equally undeniable that in word and deed he often defies Hobbesian doctrines he elsewhere approves. Whigs and bishops would have snorted in angry derision at hearing Swift labelled a law-and-order man – only, they would have said, when it was *his* law and order. As Drapier he was outlawed for spurning the obedience enjoined by Leviathan, and his hero Thomas More died rather than imitate Naaman. Swift is not to be docketed and pigeonholed, neatly and conveniently slotted into any one political niche, Hobbesian, Lockean, Godwinian or anything else. His authoritarian paternalism is balanced by the wild outlawry that so many from Queen Anne to Yeats have sensed in him, and his greatness is that of contradiction, as defined by Pascal, rather than consistency: 'I do not admire a virtue like valour when it is pushed to excess, if I do not see at the same time the excess of the opposite virtue, as one does in Epaminondas, who displayed extreme valour and extreme benevolence. For otherwise it is not an ascent, but a fall. We do not display our greatness by placing ourselves at one extremity, but rather by being at both at the same time, and filling up the whole of the space between them'.[115] That Swift can legitimately be claimed but not owned by so many contending parties proves how completely he fulfils the Pascalian prescription for greatness.

Must we, however, conclude that his Hobbesian role is pure impersonation, mere double-talk, advice delivered to others that he would have contemned addressed to himself? Is Hobbes simply a convenience, arguments Swift really dislikes being employed because they are expedient? It is easy to insist on majority rule when we are the majority, claim the established religion must be obeyed when it is ours, swear that, were we the minority, we would peacefully accede to majority wishes – what member of the winning team isn't a good loser? Many who say such things are doubtless sincere, but was Swift? The major theme of his satire, startling in a great writer, is the futility, indeed the offensiveness, of words divorced from action: men say they are rational but act like Yahoos. If we judge Swift, as he so devastatingly judged men, by the language of conduct, we must surely conclude that Swift in opposition is very different from Swift in power, that the mentor of authoritarianism is astoundingly transformed into wild rebel.

Locke's liberal arguments, denounced when they seek to unseat Anglican orthodoxy, are appropriated by Swift when he feels his own cause threatened. Though not a political absolutist, he had one absolute devotion: loyalty to Anglicanism. This is always his overriding priority, his highest value, and he will sacrifice anything, his own career included, to defend it. To this end all else is subordinate and he will unashamedly use arguments from any source, Hobbes, Locke or anyone else, to sustain it. He is always an Anglican churchman rather than a doctrinaire politician. The Anglican controversialist who uses Hobbes to prove that dissent causes civil war, will just as readily exploit Locke's argument supporting parliamentary sovereignty to point out that *his* religion is established by law. He will travel the road with either for as long as it suits the Church, part company the instant it doesn't. There is no hypocrisy, for there is no attempt to deceive – when he left the Whigs and his hopes of preferment to join the Tories, Swift openly declared to the world where his deepest loyalties lay. These affections could not finally settle comfortably within the house that Locke built – Swift is ultimately no more at home in Locke than in Hobbes. He is his own man and it is because he is so absolutely Anglican that we suspect the total conviction of his Hobbesian stance – it is too pat, altogether too convenient, to be believable.

Swift is perfectly willing to speculate about the citizen's duty in the highly unlikely event of a government ban on Christianity just as long as the current reality of Anglican hegemony is vigilantly guarded – that great fish is well worth any number of hypothetical sprats; but had the speculation become shocking fact and the Christian Church been chased back to the catacombs by a new Nero, does anyone doubt that another series of letters, from the Dean rather than the Drapier, would soon have been circulating, summoning the persecuted to resist and endure? He calmly discusses the proscription of Christianity because he knows it will not happen. He is, certainly, no disciple of Locke, but this does not automatically dismiss him to the despots. It is true that if we accept political liberty in the modern world as resulting from the struggle of religious organisms to live, with modern ideas of freedom and human rights directly traceable to the fight for religious toleration in the seventeenth century, then Swift's solution to the Church–State, authority–conscience dilemma, resembling *Leviathan* rather than the *Letter Concerning Toleration*, should make us pause before confidently assigning him to the libertarian tradition of Locke.[116] Liberty is, however, a complex product that comes to us historically from many diverse, sometimes highly surprising, sources. Only those who demand a monopoly for Lockean liberalism will feel uneasy at Yeat's great claim on behalf of Swift; the others who know Swift's life and works will never doubt that he too served human liberty.

THREE

FANATICISM AND FREEDOM

The seventeenth century posed in an agonizingly urgent form the problem of freedom and discipline, the poisons that a man might legitimately keep at home locked up in the cabinet and those that he might without reprisal vend abroad as cordials. The Reformation, especially in its more radical manifestations, had intensified the dilemma by causing to sprout all over western Europe a host of determinedly recalcitrant minority groups, at odds with established law, often violently withholding obedience to majority beliefs, sometimes prepared to attempt armed rebellion, always impelled by a conviction that men, meaning themselves, should be free to live and worship as they pleased. Such a conviction led to the founding of New England and the reshaping of Old Europe, but emigration and revolution were practical answers to a problem that bristled with theoretical enigmas. There was a corresponding inner emigration, an internal speculative revolution, that drove many to reappraise the meaning of freedom, and from Hobbes to Locke, from Milton to Winstanley and beyond to the wild men of the antinomian left, there appeared a new set of answers to the incorrigibly stubborn old question.

That Swift felt its pull we need not doubt – scratch the surface of his writings and the concern with freedom and order soon reveals itself, not surprising in an art so bounded by the parameters of politics, religion and history. What is the behaviour consonant with the claim to be *animal rationale* that justifies conjectures of superiority? In *Gulliver's Travels* he is still trying to disentangle, as his hero moves from one mode of imprisonment to another, the meaning and possibility of freedom, whether conditioning can ever be eluded or habituation broken, and the recurring theme of chains and liberty alerts us to the ubiquitous presence of the problem. What is freedom? Hobbes's brisk, no-nonsense definition, incisively cutting the metaphysical cackle, attracts by its tone of wholesome simplicity: 'By liberty, is understood, according to the proper signification of the word, the absence of external impediments'.[1] The instinctive reaction is to clutch at this in relief, especially in our own century, as embodying the fundamental sense of freedom as freedom from chains, from imprisonment, from enslavement by others – the rest is extension of this sense or else metaphor. A man who is not chained but is doing what he wants to do is free. What could be more straightforward, more gratifyingly purged of all those awkward reservations, those exasperating qualifications, metaphysical, moral, psychological, that open the door to doubletalk and smart-alec logic – Rousseau forcing us to be free or Hegel, in Russell's interpretation, granting us the liberty to obey the police?[2]

Hobbes's definition makes it easy to tell when Gulliver is not a free man. Lying bound on the beach at Lilliput, vainly imploring his liberty and being told that, temporarily at least, he must remain a prisoner, he is manifestly not free and the chains are the confirmation of Hobbes's good sense. The same is substantially true of his sojourn in Brobdingnag even if the chains have been dispensed with – that the giants don't even need to bind him simply reinforces a sense of captivity. Compelled to 'the continual drudgery of entertaining the rabble every hour of the day'[3] – the show must go on, all the more so when the star is a slave – he comforts himself by reflecting that the disgrace is not personal, since even the King of Great Britain, similarly circumstanced, would also have had to submit. Why bother to lock up someone so unreservedly vulnerable that he dare not rebel or even flee? Revolution is absurd, emigration ruled out; at the mercy of every trivial event of everyday life, immersed in the terror of the ordinary and banal, petrified by the flashing of cutlery at dinner, brained by falling apples or pounded senseless by hailstones, suffocating in cream or drowning in soup, prey of the first hungry pup or kitten – where can Gulliver escape *to*? Yet he goes on dreaming of deliverance and is finally airlifted back to freedom, to the society of his equals and the absence of external restraints.

The beautiful simplicity of the first two voyages in determining what freedom means vanishes with the perplexing final voyage and the dilemma is dramatised beyond any possibility of evasion in that it both opens and ends with the hero in chains – in, that is, from

Hobbes's standpoint, situations of identical servitude. It is, however, far from clear that Swift views each imprisonment as substantially the same. The opening imprisonment is straightforward, presents no problem. The villains he is forced to recruit at Barbadoes corrupt the crew and lead a mutiny in which Captain Gulliver is overpowered and chained to his bed, with a sentry ordered to shoot 'if I attempted my liberty'.[4] It is this loss of freedom that causes him to be marooned in the land of the Houyhnhnms. But the second chaining forces us to look again at Hobbes's definition as perhaps inadequate and over-simplistic and challenges the reader as to how confidently he can interpret this particular captivity. Exiled by the horses, Gulliver sails first to an island where he narrowly escapes an attack by naked savages – he will carry the arrow-mark to the grave – and from there to a second island where he is picked up by the Portuguese landing party. 'Picked up' is the appropriate expression, for Gulliver, who would have been overjoyed to have met them on the shores of Lilliput or Brobdingnag, has now completely altered – and so too has his notion of the meaning of freedom. He no longer wants the society of his equals, tries to dodge rescue, would rather go back to poisoned arrows than accompany these sophisticated Yahoos to 'civilized' Europe. Despite being treated 'with great humanity' (an evidence of linguistic bondage, since the word no longer possesses its ancient associations for the newborn Gulliver) he begs to be set free – 'I fell on my knees to preserve my liberty' – but is dragged aboard Don Pedro's ship. The captain's great kindness leaves Gulliver 'silent and sullen', and, left alone, he tries to jump over-board; Don Pedro, confronted by such crazy behaviour, has no choice, as he sees it, but to chain Gulliver in his cabin. In my end is my beginning.

But the book's full circle forces us to differentiate between Gulliver as prisoner of Lilliputians or mutineers and Gulliver as compulsory guest of Don Pedro; *then*, his own good totally disregarded, he is chained to suit his captors' convenience, *now*, rightly or wrongly, Don Pedro is acting against Gulliver's wishes but in what he genuinely believes to be Gulliver's best interests – perhaps he might even have used Rousseau's formula, had it been available, to argue that he was really forcing Gulliver to be free. In any case, the reluctant rescuee has to give his word of honour not to go over the side before his chains are removed and he is again set at liberty. His pleas to be allowed to perish either in the ocean or at the hands of savages are denied, for Don Pedro is not John Stuart Mill; he knows what is best for

Gulliver and, gentle and generous though he is, is willing to back up his judgement with force. The reader is challenged to decide if he endorses or condemns this interference with freedom or to judge if it is so. Can we unhesitatingly affirm that Don Pedro is wrong, however well-intentioned, that we would cheerfully have allowed Gulliver to destroy himself if that's what he wanted? From being obligingly pellucid, the word freedom suddenly becomes opaquely problematic, as the Hobbesian interpretation falters before life's complexity.

Hobbes's failure suggests that there may be another, more complex explication which does not surrender its total content to a definition that takes account only of chains and similar external constraints upon voluntary action. Regardless of the particular instance illustrated and what we think of Gulliver's repudiation of his species, the generous Don Pedro included, as incurable Yahoos (the rationale for his decision to go overboard) another concept of freedom proposes itself for consideration: liberty, in Montesquieu's phrase, as the power of doing what we ought to will, freedom as the recognition of necessity, or some equivalent variant — Plato's justice, Augustine's emancipating truth, Milton's self-disciplined quest for disenthralment, some formula that associates true freedom with absence of delusion as much as chains. For if freedom means, *tout court*, doing what you will, then Gulliver is equally unfree chained up by the good captain as by the rascally mutineers and we must resolutely reject Burke's contention that the individual has a 'right' to be restrained in his own interest. But if we agree with Locke that where there is no law there is no freedom, or with T. H. Green that the ideal of true freedom is the maximum of power for all the members of human society alike to make the best of themselves, then Don Pedro's immovable paternalism will seem less a deplorable infringement of another's freedom than the commendable rescue of a demented man from self-destruction.

Back in Lisbon, Don Pedro fires another gun in his capaign to redeem Gulliver for decent, civilized conduct, urging that 'as a point of honour and conscience . . . I ought to return to my native country, and live at home with my wife and children'.[5] The introduction of the idea of obligation violates the simplicity of the Hobbesian position, for Hobbes regards every voluntary act as constituting its own justification: 'of the voluntary acts of every man, the object is some good to himself'[6] — and Hobbes resolutely sticks to this even when the 'good' chosen is bad, like arsenic or heroin. What a man shuns or flees from is bad, what he embraces or strives after is good — for him: that is what bad and good mean in Hobbes's tautological definition and there is no other meaning we can assign to them.

Gulliver, leaping overboard, refusing to go home, is acting voluntarily and therefore aiming at his own good, and who is a better judge of this than Gulliver himself? Don Pedro is, however, not a Hobbesian who believes that the will is simply the last appetite in deliberating, like the last gladiator on his feet in the arena and champion for that reason, that the final choice can only mean the best choice; for him the will is not a contestant similar to all the other appetites, even if *primus inter pares*, not just a superior desire, but rather the presiding umpire who decides which contestant is to be champion and who should do so not by simply caving in to the strongest – if so, why is the will needed at all? – but by awarding the prize to the 'best'. Don Pedro believes in a right course of action that Gulliver, regardless of desire, ought to follow, even if this involves self-discipline, for no one, as Fichte says, has rights against reason, and, as Don Pedro judges, Gulliver is behaving in a thoroughly irrational manner.

We have, of course, arrived at one of the most contentious moments in a highly contentious book. Someone is undoubtedly brainwashed, is the unwitting resident of a mental prison where he is as inescapably trapped as he would be in the dungeons of the Inquisition, and that he doesn't even see his metaphorical chains makes the imprisonment all the more fearfully adamantine. Is it the deluded worshipper of Houyhnhnm virtue or is it the gentle captain and behind him, even more shockingly, the gentle reader, each so conditioned to Yahoo filth that, unawares, he lives, moves and has his being within it? Or is it, as Swift's nihilistic insight pierces to new bathymetric levels, all of us, Gulliver, Don Pedro and reader combined, co-partners in a process of ubiquitous, unavoidable conditioning in which there are only victims but no privileged observers? We think we are free when we are merely programmed; if, by some *bouleversement*, we succeed in changing our habits, it is, like Orwell's animals, only to saddle ourselves with new masters; we dig ourselves out of our mental prisons and end up as hopelessly immured in other cells, like Edmond Dantès in the Chateau d'If. It is frighteningly possible that Swift's world is one vast, high-security prison in which there is no escape.

Sensibly, Don Pedro advises his errant companion to return to the old home and the old life, but what if Gulliver, anticipating Laing, Cooper and other 'anti-psychiatrist' enemies of the family today, is right and it is the old home and life which are so hideously wrong?

Dare we, with a writer so hostile to the reader as Swift – and hostile for no other reason than that the reader *is* a reader – and in a book so treacherous to our critical foothold, dismiss this hypothesis as wildly untenable? And if Europe is only Yahooland tarted up, clothes, language and a *soupçon* of depraved culture added, is it sensible, on anything other than a Hobbesian perspective, to call a life lived in squalid subjection to such norms a life of freedom? If man is, as Gulliver with vitriolic casualness remarks, merely a programmed Yahoo, incapable of amendment by precept or example, isn't it nonsense to dignify his addiction to evil by calling it freedom? The alcoholic, the drug addict and the erotomaniac are unchained but unfree, and chains or straitjackets might even in extreme cases be, paradoxically, the indispensable propadeutic for freedom.

There is, notoriously, no unanimity as to Swift's intention at the end of the book. His admiration for Don Pedro does not necessarily mean that he derides the association of man and Yahoo – for Arbuthnot no less than Don Pedro would serve equally well, were the procedure valid, in disproving the identification, and there is no need to wait till the end of the *Travels* to learn that Swift believed there were a few good men in the world. Yet Jehovah did not spare the cities of the plain because Lot was in the vicinity. Even if we insist, as seems likely, that Swift was a paternalist libertarian, an exponent of that positive idea of liberty as the right to do what is right, with its corollary that no man is free in doing evil and that to prevent him is to set him free, even if Swift's life-work was an unremitting denial of a man's right to go to hell untroubled in his own way, doing his own thing – however true in general, this wouldn't help us in the particular application, unless we beg the question by assuming that Gulliver must be doing evil when he tries to avoid going back home. Did Bunyan want *his* runaway to go back home? *Gulliver's Travels* is a challenging, difficult book because beneath its deceptively pellucid surface it entraps us in unceasing self-questioning concerning what it means to be human, free and responsible. We shall never have done with it, never 'solve' it, because the necessary evidence is in life rather than in literature and every new day brings fresh supplies in a perpetual process of revision and reconsideration.

Nothing could be more futile or contrary to its creator's intention than to try solving the book internally, arguing from the text as to whether man is *animal rationale* or Yahoo, able to listen and save himself or incapable of amendment by precept or example, crown of the evolutionary process (whether in Darwin's or de Chardin's sense) or a doomed, idiotic *lusus naturae*. We have no business judging a book designed to judge us and Swift's literary strategy aims at keeping the reader nervously aware of his inferior status. Not till history itself ends will we be able to put Swift's masterpiece away as obsolete, something outgrown. It is his greatest sermon, perhaps *the* greatest sermon, and its artistic triumph is, paradoxically, its refusal to be turned into art as a covert means of taming it, to be accommodated under a soothing and recognized aesthetic rubric that would make its readers feel easier.

A Tale of a Tub and *The Mechanical Operation of the Spirit* are works of a radically different status. No longer does our unease come from a realization that we too are the jest of the book's meaning, tantalizing in its ambiguity yet somehow sensed by us as serenely controlled by an author manipulating Gulliver as well as ourselves; it comes now from a disconcerting suspicion that a breakdown of control is continually imminent, as the author in the text, lacking any back-up elsewhere and himself affected by the hysteria he describes, struggles desperately to master his material. Hence the manic energy of the form that matches the madness of the content – the book's frenzied structure, its erratic leaps and wild digressions, do not, as the *Travels* do, indicate a mind securely in possession of its experience. We pass through it as we would through Bedlam, shocked and frightened, praying that in the end there will be an unlocked door and beyond it the cool air of the quiet world. The book *is* Bedlam.

But, however bafflingly difficult these early satires are, there is surely one point (and, for an understanding of Swift, not a secondary one) upon which every reader will agree: that in the conduct and claims of the Saints, Swift exposes for our unqualified condemnation a bogus liberation of the spirit which is really a sordid enslavement to matter in its most odious form. The sectaries who purport to bring a new, exciting freedom from old barren forms and outmoded beliefs – behold, I make all things new – leave men even more inescapably confined to a world that is urinal, brothel, Bedlam cell, and junkie den in one stiflingly narrow chamber: infinite squalor in a little room. Promising a new heaven, they lead us to a new hell, devoid of whatever makes Dante's a place of tragically impressive retribution, retaining and emphasizing only the elements that shame and nauseate, a hell custom-built for Yahoo man. Within this barred room, men belch, urinate, fart, excrete, ejaculate, get stoned, employing their bodies in a degrading series of mechanical operations involving wind and semen, which they have the foolish effrontery to pass off as an exaltation above matter.

There is a large and important argument as to how deeply implicated Swift himself is in the madness he exhibits, whether he is the warder securely showing us round Bedlam or merely a privileged resident with a limited franchise as tourist guide – an argument that has raged unresolved from William Wotton to our own day – but there is surely a consensus as to what Swift attacks and why: a presumptuous attempt to scale heaven must end in the foul ditch, since matter can at best be decently, resignedly administered, but never left behind. Here in these satires, in the least equivocal, most readily intelligible form, we find Swift's critique of freedom in the negative sense as the ability to do as one pleases, to go wherever one's inclinations lead. Deluded men are not free, can at best merely experience the euphorically false conviction of freedom that delusion brings, like a drunk wildly overestimating his own talents. The young Swift, his reading still fresh in his head, had, in confirmation of this truth, turned his satiric gaze upon that great experiment in radical freedom occurring between 1640 and 1660 when the world was turned upside down by the armed Saints. The *Tale* and *The Mechanical Operation* are frighteningly comic demonstrations of the disasters that follow when liberty is confused with licence and the gratification of base instinct is hailed as an extension of freedom.

His mind saturated in seventeenth-century history and intensely interested in madness, individual and collective, Swift looked back to the period of upheaval as a nightmarish upsurge of lawless energy, usually and thankfully repressed. What for some was a time of glorious innovation, of ancient fetters broken, is mocked by him as the manic interval when 'this island of ours was under the dominion of grace'[7] – and the full devastating force of this judgement can be gauged only after considering how 'grace' is manufactured by the spiritual handymen of *The Mechanical Operation*. What Christopher Hill enthuses over as 'this period of unique liberty'[8] is depicted in Swift's satire as a lapse into madness, when blasphemy and sexual mania became deliberate artifacts under the guise of inspiration and the self-induced trance was cultivated as a way to bestial indulgence.

Today we are schooled to distinguish between two revolutions, one successful, one abortive, that took place in mid-seventeenth-century England: the triumph of the Protestant ethic, the attack upon king, aristocracy and Church and the destruction of old hierarchies in favour of a new propertied class, whose great representative figure is Cromwell; and, intermittently threatening but never happening, a much more radically utopian project, involving communism, democracy and a new sexual ethic, whose heroes are Ranters, Levellers and other dissenting extremists. While the makers of the first revolution sought the help of the second group against the Royalist enemy, they feared and abhorred them almost as much as traditional conservatives did and moved against them when it was safe to do so. Swift as polemicist conflates the two revolutions, selecting as paradigmatic enemy the fanatics of the left who blasphemously tried to legitimize the killing of the king and their antinomian excesses by offering them as the will of heaven. They are, unhappily, not hypocrites, Tartuffe's brothers, cynically exploiting religion to pursue power, but immeasurably more dangerous – honest men who mean what they say, sincere madmen who attract converts by first imposing upon themselves.

This explains why Jack is so much more grotesquely important than Peter as the *Tale* progresses: Jack is a madman, Peter only a clever rogue. There are, of course, other shaping elements of the religious satire, notably the Ulster matrix of the *Tale*. Swift lived at Kilroot as Anglican divine surrounded by Presbyterian descendants of Scottish settlers at a time when Catholicism, however doctrinally repugnant, had ceased to be a political threat. The Williamite settlement after Limerick ended for centuries the possibility of a Catholic property-owning class dominating Ireland and throughout the island the Catholics were reduced to helpless, impoverished servitude. The united Protestant front that had beaten the Popish, Gaelic threat could now break into its component parts, and in Ulster dissenters complained they had overthrown papal absolutism only to make a minority of Anglicans their new masters. Their grievances aroused Swift's angry contempt – he retorted sarcastically that he thought they had fought for the religious freedom which they now enjoyed; but freedom was apparently only the pretext to pursue power and the overthrow of the established Church.[9]

Their alarmist nonsense about a continuing Catholic menace was either a foolish misreading of the situation, or, more probably, a trick to con the gullible into giving them power as the only defence against rampant Popery. This pose as the indefatigable, suffering champions of Irish Protestantism is ridiculed in the comic spectacle of Jack

returning home 'full of terrible accounts of what he had undergone
for the public good' to exhibit his wounds: 'Neighbours mine, this
broken head deserves a plaster; had poor Jack been tender of his
noddle, you would have seen the Pope and the French King, long
before this time of day, among your wives and your warehouses'.[10]
The alliteration recalls Shylock's conjunction of daughter and ducats
and is meant to be equally derisory. Swift's contempt at so glaring an
imposture is intensified by a conviction that the real threat to the
Church comes from these very dissenters who impudently offer
themselves as the shock anti-papist troops. The papist-under-the-bed
argument was being advanced by rowdy dissenters who were stamping
all over it. So Jack is more important than Peter not because Swift is
soft on Catholicism, simply that as alert Anglican he knows the quarter
from which danger now blows.

But even more important than his awareness of the contemporary
political situation is Swift's fascination with madness, especially
successful madness, lunatics who end up not chained in cells but
sitting on thrones, presiding over philosophical societies or leading
religious revolutions. Peter is just a clever mountebank and the papal
impostures are simple, straightforward swindles to augment the
power and wealth of Rome. Jack, by contrast – it is the measure both
of his menace and his fascination – is not amenable to any such easy
formula; he is a sincere man who believes in himself and who can
communicate this belief to others as if by contagion. If he is far more
laughable than Peter, this is not because Swift finds madness funny
but because he finds it dangerous – derision is the countervailing
power to resist the madness of militant Puritanism. Swift, who in
certain moods was tolerant towards hypocrisy as a force that could
be taught to aid virtue, always regarded madness with fascinated
horror, saw in madmen the new lepers as the decline of leprosy in
modern Europe and the closing of the lazar houses was followed by the
opening of places of confinement for the mad. The success of revolutionary Puritanism for him was as if the lazar houses had been thrown
open and their inmates set free to infect the nation.

Even their present-day admirers do not dispute the madness of
some of these men, but, in the accredited modern strategy, turn it into
a plus quality by arguing that madness may be a form of protest
against social norms or that it is really a form of knowledge which the
dominant culture can not understand. The madman is metamorphosed
into saviour bravely rejecting the intolerable conditions to which the

sane and well-adjusted tamely submit. The perennial arrogance of the drilled majority spurning as lunatics those whom the future will justify as prophetically wise – this, on such a view, is the formula of Swift's satirically brilliant onslaught on Puritanism and the comedy should not conceal the impulse towards retrospective vaticide that is its true motivation. It was one of these prophets who appealed to his countrymen to join him in redemptive madness and make the island not Great Britain but Great Bedlam.[11]

Swift, who disliked the expression Great Britain,[12] had even less sympathy with the notion of cleansing or renovative madness and no wish whatsoever to become a citizen of Great Bedlam. He would not have denied vaticidal intent if we reinterpret it to mean his campaign to expose those deluded enough to claim to be God's agents and persuasive enough to get it believed. Self-constituted élites, claiming privileged insight and special power, were for him the rabble, even when they were Fellows of the Royal Society or eminent classical scholars, men made more barbarous by their learning and more in-humane by their study of humanity – he was not likely, condemning these, to look more favourably upon an élite of fanatics. When the persona opens the *Tale* by touting his forthcoming treatise entitled 'A modest Defence of the Proceedings of the Rabble in all Ages', we are not to mark this down to Swift's aristocratic prejudices or understand by this term that reprobate group, anathema to progressivists every-where and stigmatized by Marx as *lumpenproletariat,* who, brutally bigoted, are forever to hand when the ruling class needs a weapon to use against heretically enlightened élites or advanced minorities; by rabble Swift means precisely those élitist minorities who hubristi-cally seek to turn the world upside down. Swift's comic genius selects for its satiric prey things that are, for him, finally no joking matter – his work is a constant struggle to disarm the psychopath by putting him into a clown's costume. At our historical distance it is easy to be deceived, often with his connivance, into mistaking serious criticism for pure bagatelle, as when he buries within a list of absurd titles of non-existent books some of his most profoundly held convic-tions about human affairs.

Consider, for example, the passage in *The Mechanical Operation* where he mockingly examines the objection that the Holy Spirit is barred from descending upon the modern Saints as He did upon the Apostles at Pentecost because these contemporary candidates for grace, unlike their predecessors in the upstairs room, insist on keeping their hats on: 'The modern artists do utterly exclude all approaches of the spirit and bar up its ancient way of entering, by covering themselves so close, and so industriously a top. For, they will needs have it as a point clearly gained, that the cloven tongues never sat upon the Apostles' heads, while their hats were on'.[13] We shall not appreciate the humour less by realizing the skill with which he attacks his adversaries in one of their symbolic strongholds.

He begins by pointing out the objection's irrelevance – hats impede only a genuine supernatural assistance coming from without, but neither godsent inspiration nor its diabolic counterpart is the topic of discussion. Neither is he talking about the frenzy that springs from purely natural causes, the grief of Empedocles plunging into the gulf or the chagrin of Jack, furious at his own bedraggled coat and maddened at Martin's politely sensible refusal to join him in tatters. 'Artist' is the clue, for Swift is examining a method for madness, a technique easily learned, and the modern Saints are inspirational handymen, do-it-yourself experts in raising the soul above matter, technicians of artifical trance. The mechanical operation so beloved of our British workmen is self-induced inspiration, a trade like any other with its masters and apprentices, where practice makes perfection. To those who doubt if artifice can ever merge so indistinguishably into nature, he offers two clinching instances, ancient and modern – how our ancestors the Scythians deliberately bred within a few generations a race of longheaded people and how our fathers emulated this in producing another curious mutation known as Roundheads, conclusively demonstrating that nature can be taught to follow art.[14]

The allusion to Roundheads, a word used especially as a term of opprobrium against political radicals, is the second clue to Swift's target. What seems to us a trivial, inconsequential, perhaps absurd matter – keeping one's hat on at church – had become during the years of revolutionary turmoil a dramatically provocative symbol of a wild upsurge against all authority.[15] Hats and freedom were intimately connected in the minds of radicals and conservatives alike; the man who kept his hat on in the presence of social superiors, far from being a harmless eccentric, was either a brave Promethean rebel or a seditious malcontent, depending upon one's position in the political spectrum. A long tradition of egalitarian protest fuelled the refusal to bare the head and as late as 1789 Barrière is affirming it as a revolutionary symbol – 'le chapeau est le signe de l'affranchisement' –

and insisting that the militantly democratic Third Estate remain covered in the royal presence. Trivial in itself, it was potent as a symbol of insubordination, like the defiant flaunting of the black berets of paramilitary groups in Ulster streets today. Outraged traditionalists detected in it a rehearsal for full scale attack on every form of superiority, wealth included.

The debate extended to the religious sphere when some extremists received direct commands from God that hats should be worn during prayers – logically enough, since if every man was his own Christ, as the Ranters insisted, why should he doff his hat to his father in heaven any more than he did to his various fathers, literal, kingly or magisterial, on earth? Conversely, if God the Father was, as this implied, a democratic egalitarian, then the present earthly system of hierarchical privilege, so dear to traditionalists, must come from His adversary, Satan. Swift was no democrat but cherished, despite his slashing indictment of existing aristocracies, a Platonic ideal of aristocratic excellence, and it is no surprise to learn that among the ideal Houyhnhnms there is an established natural hierarchy tranquilly serving society because there are no rancorous, levelling, upstart horses to disrupt it. What he thinks of the Ranters' claim to individual autonomy is sufficiently indicated by the persona's recommendation, among other modern books, of one entitled 'Every man his own carver', and the same arrogant individualism that led to the denial of hat-honour had also, for Swift, spawned the revolution that killed the King. His genius for combining gravity and humour, for wisecracking about what he detests, is exemplified in the comically irrefutable contention that in cases of self-generated inspiration, a tight-fitting hat, far from being a deterrent, keeps the inner ecstasy at perspiration point. The comic climax is also a devastating exposé of the disreputable origin of Puritan grace and freedom.

Another mechanic aid to ecstasy was tobacco, and Swift, with his comic sketch of the primitive Irish smoking and humming themselves into a state of stupefaction, is also deriding those extreme sectaries who found meditation easier with the assistance of ale and 'the creature called tobacco'.[16] Pipe-smoking was a feature of Baptist services, while some radicals extolled drunkenness as 'a help to see Christ the better by'. Tobacco was the marijuana of the age and was used along with alcohol by certain groups engaged in communal love-feasts to heighten and intensify spiritual vision. The parallel with modern group drug-taking is strong and the Saints would have nodded approvingly at the psychedelic challenge: how can you come to your senses until you go out of your mind? We must always be alert for symbolism in the extravagant gestures of seventeenth-century radicals, seeing in their drunkenness, blasphemy and tobacco-trances symbolic expressions of freedom from moral restraints, a release of the repressions that gave the Puritan middle class their moral energy.

Swift, as *The Mechanical Operation* shows, agrees with this as a description but despises the 'freedom' achieved. Marcuse tells us that 'in the great historical revolutions, the imagination was, for a short period, relaxed and free to enter into the projects of a new social morality and of new institutions of freedom'.[17] Swift, who disliked projects and projectors, enlightens us as to the kind of liberation sought by the Saints in their strategies of self-stupefaction. They have perfected a technique for overcoming the requirements of reason, putting it to sleep and encouraging 'a thousand deliriums over the brain', discarding judgement in favour of 'mere spontaneous impulse'. What Marcuse celebrates as an exhilarating breakthrough is condemned by Swift as a lapse into animalism, a return to the zoo; his stance anticipates Freud rather than Marcuse's utopianism, Eros *or* civilization rather than some impossible fusion of the two.

His description of the spirit-manufacturing process is dual: how it is produced by the preacher and how it is distributed to the group. Prominent among the anti-rational strategies, styptics to the rational faculty, is music, the narcotic humming of the pipe-smoking Irish, the senseless droning of the contemptible little preacher, the nasal, singsong twang of dissenters in general. The 'musicalization' of modern culture has its unarguably irrational aspects: as immediate common ground of shared inner experience and participatory emotion, incommunicable in words; as group narcotic or stimulant; as reflecting a longing for magical, transrational forms, no longer assuaged by institutional religion; as the one true reconciling force in human life, the primal universal language, says Lévi-Strauss, comprehensible to all, untranslatable into any other idiom. Language separates us, music heals the breach; politicians declare war on each other in their respective tongues while the young from Los Angeles to Moscow dance to the same disco records. God's curse on those who tried to take heaven by force – the division of mankind at Babel into its many languages – is frustrated by the discovery of music and man storms heaven, God notwithstanding, by the power of this irrational energy. Had Satan been musician rather than armaments manufacturer, perhaps the war in heaven would have taken a different turn.

It is music as the mindblowing medium detected by Nietzsche, the mode of pre-eminent energy, that arouses the fearful suspicion of the rationalist sensitive to reason's vulnerability – Settembrini's melo-dramatic warning to the young Hans Castorp in *The Magic Mountain* against music as an anti-rational force is later justified when we see his pupil dropping out of the world of civilized discourse in his addiction to the newly acquired gramophone. In *Doctor Faustus* music is the paramount mode of diabolic possession, belonging to a demonic realm, a gift from hell rather than heaven, interfused throughout the book with sexuality, disease, decay and death. What Mann, following upon Freud, presents as tragedy – man's wish to be sick, in Leverkühn's case the liberating effect of syphilis on creative power – had already been given comic formulation by Swift in the dissenters' strategy for getting 'stoned' as a prelude towards spiritual 'liberation'. But behind the comedy is the portentous insight, as crucial for Swift as for Marlowe, that such a liberation is really enslavement, that the real question is not whether a man *can* do what he wants with his own soul but rather what *ought* he to do with it, that piety means forgoing the freedom to sin given to men by God.

The link between inspiration and sexuality, dramatized so fearfully in Adrian Leverkühn, appears in appropriate derisory form in Swift. 'The favourite arena of the demons, the given point of attack for God's adversary', as Mann's decently bourgeois narrator points out, is the sexual area; 'for God had conceded him [Satan] greater magic power over the venereal act than over any other human activity'.[18] Swift, equally fascinated with the irrationalism of sexual desire, has made it clear from the outset that demonology as a source of Puritan inspira-tion has been ruled out in his mechanical operation of the spirit – common good sense forbids us to believe that either heaven or hell is at all interested in such nasty nonsense. Swift denies man the romantic satisfaction of thinking himself a great sinner when he is merely vermin; nobody ever secretly hankered to be a Yahoo or his equally disgusting brother the beau as some do dream of being Ahab or Milton's Satan, the chief of sinners. The demonic is noticeably absent from Swift's work, is invoked at all only to be derided as a shabby trick by nasty man to shift blame on to someone else's shoulders. From the beginning man has been an alibi-hunting animal – the woman tempted me and I did eat – and Swift is scornfully aware of this universal tendency for wriggling away from responsibility. Surveying the whole gamut of human folly from a little boy playing truant to a lost maidenhead and a highwayman dying on the gallows, Swift derides the ubiquitous search for a scapegoat:

> Their loads they all on Satan lay:
> The D——l did the deed, not they![19]

The peculiar intensity of Swiftian satire comes from a fusion of contradictory viewpoints – man is conditioned yet responsible – and, anticipating a central tenet of modern existentialism, he insists that the deeds are ours and not the devil's, that we are, as Middleton's De Flores says, the deed's creature. But, although refusing man the tragic significance accorded to Marlowe's Faustus and Mann's Leverkühn as the battleground for a contest between God and Satan, Swift anticipates Mann's association of sex and inspiration. The nasal, singsong mode of address of dissenters leads Swift by an easy catena from snuffling to noses to venereal disease. The links between conquerors, philosophers and fanatics established throughout the *Tale,* the connection between the three empires of power, learning and religious dissent, are exploited to show how similar in their mode of acquisition are the kingdoms of Darius and the Saints.[20] Yahoo lust motivates Henry IV's preparations for continental war, Europe convulsed and history made because of a royal erection; Yahoo cunning, as Herodotus relates, inspires Darius's plan for making himself ruler of Persia, when a randy horse smelling a mare is successfully passed off as a sign from heaven.

Darius is the first mechanical operator of the spirit, who mounts a throne because his horse first mounted a mare and who deceives his rivals into accepting as God-inspired what is really a piece of slick engineering, a conditioned reflex. He manipulates not his own but his horse's spirit, is a cunning rogue like Peter rather than a deluded fanatic like Jack, a Puritan in Ben Jonson's sense rather than Swift's, a hypocrite who deceives others but is undeceived himself. But the Saints, those modern descendants of Darius in one sense, are sincere, and they combine his cunning with Henry's lasciviousness, conditioning themselves, so that they do both the mounting and the empire-building simultaneously and personally. Danton, protesting to Robespierre that 'you can't conspire and f—— at the same time',[21] advances this as incontrovertibly true, but Swift attacks the Puritans for doing both.

The Ranters were denounced as knowing no law but their own lusts and for dismissing sin as purely subjective and Jack's self-exculpatory credo provides a variant of this antinomian attitude in his assertion that the filthy must go on being so without blame or recrimination.[22] The Puritan revolution had its sexual as well as political extremists and moved steadily leftwards during the upheaval. It began by inciting young people to marry for love, using sexual passion to overthrow property marriage and parental domination. Certain extremists attacked church marriage as a facet of ecclesiastical tyranny and the next easy step was to denounce marriage itself in proclaiming a theory of complete sexual freedom. The monogamous family was attacked by the Ranter Abiezer Coppe – 'Give over thy stinking family duties'. This is not, however, Gulliverian asceticism, a loathing for the body, but a passport to promiscuity – 'I can . . . kiss and hug ladies, and love my neighbour's wife as myself, without sin'.[23] To the pure all things, adultery included, were pure; indeed, at a paradoxical extreme, only the avid adulterer had risen above sin. Like Swift's Jack, Ranters proclaimed the right of natural man to behave naturally, 'all according to the due course of things', as Gulliver says at the end of the *Travels*. Certainly, there was also an ascetic element in certain Puritan quarters; George Fox 'never thought of such things' as the procreation of children because 'I judged such things as below me'.[24] However relevant this *might* be to the misanthropic Gulliver, it has no connection whatsoever with Puritanism as reflected in *The Mechanical Operation* – there it is the extravagantly libertine side of the revolution that Swift exploits.

To all this Swift's attitude is unmistakably clear. He was not an enthusiast for any kind of marriage, but profoundly despised romantic marriage which made passion its own justification. Milton might endow angels with sex, write a paean to wedded love, and make of Adam an almost tragic figure, nobly admirable, as he wavers agonizedly between romantic love and duty towards God. Swift, with grim satisfaction, assures us that in heaven they neither marry nor give in marriage and his categorical clarity concerning man's priorities would have exorcised any real dilemma from Book IX of *Paradise Lost*: his castigation of the Tory lady in waiting who at a critical juncture left her political post to nurse her dying child tells us how he would have judged Adam's decision to forsake God for love of woman.[25]

Passion governs, says Franklin, and she never governs wisely; Swift, forever striving to dethrone passion, would have denounced

Adam's conduct as a shameful capitulation to animal desire. Perhaps there is no final ambiguity in Milton's poem, but had Swift written it the very suggestion of a tragic collision between love and duty would never have arisen. 'Romantic' is always for him a term of contempt and even an interpretation of Adam's decision as an act of self-sacrifice, evoking from love's champions a sense of wondering admiration, would have left him coldly derisive – it was precisely England's 'romantic disposition' in unnaturally sacrificing her own interests to those of her Dutch allies that incurred Swift's exasperated censure.[26] Ireland as Injured Lady is also culpably romantic when in a fit of foolish, loving generosity she fails to wring concessions from an England in difficulties.[27] The disastrous consequences of defying parents and marrying for love, advocated by Puritans, are cruelly exemplified in 'The Progress of Love' when the young 'heroine' of romance ends up a syphilitic whore whose husband is her pimp.[28]

Swift's chillingly unromantic advice to the young lady about to marry, coupled with the exemplary Houyhnhnm attitude to marriage, so methodical, sensible and practical, are designed to destroy romance and dismay romantics, and if Swift views married love so tepidly, it is easy to conceive his disgust at the extra-marital excesses recommended by Ranters and similar extremists. Because sex is anti-rational, it must be all the more circumspectly regulated by sensible men. 'Although reason were intended by Providence to govern our passions, yet it seems that, in two points of the greatest moment to the being and continuation of the world, God hath intended our passions to prevail over reason. The first is, the propagation of our species, since no wise man ever married from the dictates of reason. The other is, the love of life, which, from the dictates of reason, every man would despise, and wish it at an end, or that it never had a beginning'.[29]

But if God has decided that passion must win, Swift intends the victory to be as marginal as possible. The Houyhnhnms have perfected the ideal strategy for taming this dangerous force to a tolerable level. They have no notion of courtship or love: 'the young couple meet and are joined, merely because it is the determination of their parents and friends: it is what they see done every day, and they look upon it as one of the necessary actions of a reasonable being'.[30] With so humdrum, even resigned, an outlook, it is no surprise to hear that adultery and all other sexual misconduct are unknown among the rational horses. Providence has made us sexual creatures and we must accept our sexual destiny, but clear-eyed resignation is very different from Ranter excess and we must not dive headlong into the pit because we can't avoid getting our shoes muddy. This is why Ranters and Romantics alike are so criminally wrong, in trumpeting an unavoidable chore as the noblest of all activities: 'to be called a libertine is the most glorious title under heaven'.[31] Calvinism's occupational hazard, its vulnerability to an antinomian rejection of all bonds and restraints on the assumption that the elect, since Christ's sacrifice, are free of the law, led some extremists to identify freedom and libertinism, so that the more one fornicated, the freer one became. Certain apparently justificatory texts in Calvin and Luther – 'the consciences of believers . . . may forget the whole righteousness of the Law'; 'pecca fortiter' – were available for those who, in Swift's brutal formulation, simply wanted an excuse to whore on and defy the parson.[32]

Yet this, as *The Mechanical Operation* demonstrates, is the real goal towards which all self-induced inspiration aspires. Tobacco, alcohol, music, and all other anti-rational devices are merely means to an end: the *agape,* the communal love-in, following upon the anaesthetization of the usual moral and rational inhibitors. When the police fall asleep, the city plunges into licence. The excitement of being liberated from reason, the deliberate cultivation of drugs, trance, music and the derangement of personality, has at its root the exaltation of Dionysius over Apollo, the non-ethical, sexual energies triumphing over the moral reason. This is not the liberty advocated by Milton, the stress upon self-discipline as axle, or as card and compass, so vital if man is to discover the paradise within – such sentiments are unthinkable in Ranter mouths, and Swift, overlooking Milton, polemically selects the Ranters as truly representative of what the Saints in general want.

The idea that religious enthusiasm is inextricably mingled with sexual excitement is an old one, as a glance at Ronald Knox's *Enthusiasm* shows. Swift, in his derisive account of the ancient game of leap-frog played between flesh and spirit, gives a new turn to the old accusation.[33] His spoof history of fanaticism from ancient times to his own day, ranging through Greek mystery cults to early Christian heresies and on to Luther's rebellion and the consequent proliferation of extremist sects, is too near the knuckle to be just good-humoured, if rather irreverent, fun. From the mythological Orpheus to the revolutionary Family of Love and Sweet Singers of Israel, he claims to have identified one common factor in all these different upheavals, and this 'one fundamental point' is 'the community of women'.[34] Just as Henry IV put all Europe in uproar because a female Yahoo had passed into a rival kingdom, so the New Model marched and conquered that the Saints might communally couple whenever the lust took them. Cleopatra's nose, Henry's genitals, Louis XIV's back-passage – these are the unprepossessing regions where history is made and the armed Saints, refuting Danton, making love and war simultaneously, are the latest representatives of a tradition at least as old as the cult of Orpheus.

'It is a curious fact that with every great revolutionary movement the question of free love comes into the foreground. With one set of people as a revolutionary progress, as a shaking off of old traditional fetters, no longer necessary; with others as a welcome doctrine, comfortably covering all sorts of free and easy practices between man and woman.'[35] Swift finds it not at all curious and declines to make Engels's distinction between the two sets of revolutionaries. He does not, of course, accuse the Saints of hypocrisy – the true measure of the menace is that they believe their own pernicious nonsense: 'But when a man's fancy gets astride on his reason; when imagination is at cuffs with the senses, and common understanding as well as common sense is kicked out of doors, the first proselyte he makes is himself, and when that is once compassed, the difficulty is not so great in bringing over others, a strong delusion always operating from without as vigorously as from within'.[36] What Nietzsche identifies as the underlying cause of this release of primal energies, this Dionysian upsurge against Apollonian order, is also recognised by Swift, but with acid contempt rather than exaltation. Ecstasy is simply the way towards orgy – 'an entire mixture and confusion of sexes' – and the wine of Bacchus like the ale and tobacco of the Ranters facilitates the descent into sexual frenzy. The vocabulary associated with the Greek mysteries is combed, in mock scholarly fashion, for its sexual connotations – thus ivy and wine are emblems of cleaving and clinging, the fir tree secretes the semen-like turpentine, the rods carried are phallic symbols, and the satyrs, goats and asses upon which the bacchanals ride are fit companions for those engaged in 'affairs of gallantry'. Orpheus dies as victim of frustrated female sexual frenzy, a salutary caution to his modern descendants not to raise expectations they cannot assuage – though this is unlikely, since, from John of Leyden on, modern dissenters are so vigorously obliging that their visions and revelations always climax in their 'leading about half a dozen sisters, apiece' and 'making that practice a fundamental part of their system'.[37]

Swift exploits the vocabulary of Dissent, as he has that of Orphic ritual, for purposes of degrading deflation. Seizing upon the term *vessel*, used in dissenting discourse to mean the receptacle into which grace is poured by the favouring deity, he gives it a nautical meaning as the vehicle in which we journey through life, our pilgrim's progress over the ocean rather than along the highway. He next praises the randy Saints for their perspicacity; for, just as prudent sailors lay in enough meat for a long sea voyage, so the Saints embark with a sufficient quantity of female flesh to keep their vessels adequately provisioned. He ends 'this brief survey' of erotic enthusiasm – he has, after all, left out Mahometans and others who could have supplied confirmatory evidence – by discussing the links between romantic excess and religious fanaticism, the ogling of lovers and the canting of Saints, practices equally irrational and spurned by sensible men.[38] But beneath the surface of playful humour, we realize that Swift is not debating anything so innocuously straightforward as simple hypocrisy; the material he exploits is nearer to Krafft-Ebing than to Tartuffe, to perverts rather than playboys, clinical delusion rather than duplicity. It is a satiric rendition of the fevered jumbling of love and devotion depicted by Pope in the intense emotionalism of Eloisa, trapped between God and man. Swift's victims are, of course, unlike Eloisa, viewed with satiric animus as he recounts an eminent medical friend's observations on female sexual mania and finds in the nymphomania of female Quaker patients a contemporary version of the Bacchic women. Those who identify the counter-culture of underground Puritanism as an exhilarating Dionysian revolt against repressive Apollonianism and lament its eventual failure would secure Swift's agreement as to the description but not to the attached valuation; he feared and despised the Dionysian spirit, welcomed its defeat, and demanded that precautions be taken to prevent its recrudescence.

Swift's tendency to see aberrations as situated in circular rather than linear form, so that errors which seem at opposite extremes are in reality closely related, if not identical – one recalls how Jack's desperate endeavours to be different from Peter only make them look more similar (Swift's strategy for upholding sensible Anglicanism against its enemies to left and right) – is equally operative in his attack upon Yahoos and romantic enthusiasts. They only seem different but identity is disclosed when they end as companions in the same pit. The first error is a brutal capitulation to the material world, Yahoo immersion in sordid matter, Jack's avid surrender to the inescapable filth, the natural right of natural man to be his disgusting self; the blatantly rampant sexuality of the Yahoo is this error in its most extreme form.

The second error is even more dangerous in that it prides itself upon a deludedly impossible emancipation from the material world, 'a lifting up of the soul or its faculties above matter'.[39] This is why, however initially dissimilar, romantic lovers and Puritan fanatics are finally united. Inspiration and orgasm are intimately related, whether the ecstasy is poetic or prophetic. Subtending every romantic dream, every vatic vision, is a bedrock of physiology. This explains the otherwise baffling mystery as to how even the ugliest of enthusiastic preachers has his following of besotted females, like modern groupies pursuing their guitar heroes. Preacher and pop star, inconspicuous in themselves, incarnate a sexual promise which spreads like rut through their hearers, and where the bewildered rationalist, seeing only the external man, warts and all, can only ponder the folly of female fans, pop and devotional, the women sense and respond to the sexual urgency latent in the sermon's peroration or the instrument's crescendo. But, however sublimated or disguised, it ends up as inescapably enmeshed in matter as Yahoo brutality and the final consummation is identical.

The Mechanical Operation ends with a scoffing indictment of those who presumptuously try to rise above matter, with the unfortunate Thales selected as archetypal image of such blunderers. Swift passes over Icarus and Phaethon, not just because they have been used *ad nauseam* – we recall how coldly unimpressed Gulliver was when the rescuing captain compared the fall of Gulliver's house from the giant bird's beak to the fall of Phaethon: 'the comparison of Phaethon was so obvious, that he could not forbear applying it, although I did not much admire the conceit';[40] and Gulliver's contempt for the trite and banal is inherited from his creator. The *Polite Conversation* is enough in itself to indicate Swift's Flaubertian disgust for cliché and threadbare commonplace, and his own writing is always successfully organised to resist the obvious.

But, even more important, he overlooks Phaethon because he doesn't want a fiery consummation, dramatically disastrous, and soliciting, despite its element of the culpably headstrong, a kind of admiration, just as he doesn't use Icarus because he doesn't want a

fall into the sea. Each is a suitable candidate as far as pride goes, but
lacks, for Swift's requirements, the marvellously appropriate nemesis
of Thales' fall, particularly the place where his heavenly aspirations
end. Swift wants a fall into filthy matter, a pit, a slimy hole in the earth,
because this terminus, in keeping with the whole preceding thrust of
his satire, can be given an explicitly sexual interpretation. However
highfalutin the spiritual intriguer, romantic or religious, he is rooted
in earth because 'too intense a contemplation is not the business of
flesh and blood';[41] he may delude himself that the spirit has left him
and is soaring high in the empyrean, but in an obscenely ironical
sense missed by the Puritans who frequently used the expression,
the root of the matter is forever in him. What goes up must come down
in spiritual as in other affairs, and ecstasies, romantic or devotional,
are finally of the earth, earthly. Lovers are just another sort of Pla-
tonics pretending to be engrossed with the stars in their ladies'
eyes when the real business is with regions much lower – 'but the same
pit is provided for both' – and Thales, the starstruck philosopher
so rapt in celestial contemplation that he tumbles 'seduced by his
lower parts into a ditch', is the perfect cautionary example of what
invariably happens.[42] The fall of enthusiastic man is essentially
sexual and the foul ditch in which he lies besmirched is the same place
of excrement where Yeats tormentedly located love's mansion. The
exalted rigmarole of poetic or spiritual declamation is in the end the
justificatory prelude to sordid tussles no different from Yahoos
coupling in bushes. The hubristic claim to a freedom greater than man
can enjoy ends in an enslavement more vile than he need endure.

For even if the ditch cannot be completely avoided, there is no need
to roll about in its pollution. That is the criminal error of Yahoo and
Platonist, those deluded brothers of *The Mechanical Operation* as
Peter and Jack are of the *Tale*. But where the latter pair have within
their satire an example of sensible, decent conduct in brother Martin,
from whom they can learn if only they will, the other deluded two-
some are left brotherless and without correction at the bottom of
their pit. They have, it is true, as fellow-creatures of Swift's imagination, a sister, if only they knew of her existence, but she lives, not in a
satire, but in the completely straightforward 'Letter to a Young Lady
on her Marriage'.[43] She, suitably tutored by Swift, will tell them how
to live properly, accepting life and its imperatives, including its sexual
imperatives, in a commendably sober, disillusioned way, without
dressing them up as more than they are.

The first lesson is the Houyhnhnm one that marriage and procreation are the expected duties of ordinary human beings, the second that marriage will quickly become a tedious wrangle unless the young lady enters immediately upon a course of unremitting self-improvement: 'the grand affair of your life will be to gain and preserve the friendship and esteem of your husband'.[44] If Emma Bovary protests at such chillingly unromantic limitations, that simply proves what a Yahoo she is. Marriage is a race between the speedy decay of beauty and the painful acquisition of culture: 'you have but a very few years to be young and handsome in the eyes of the world; and as few months to be so in the eyes of a husband, who is not a fool'. The young lady must get in a stock of education as quickly as possible to forestall the danger of becoming in time 'a thing indifferent and perhaps contemptible'. Meanwhile, it is worse than foolish, it is criminally disastrous to dream of charms and raptures which marriage brutally liquidates; the young lady is lucky in that hers is a match of prudence and good-liking, totally disinfected of 'that ridiculous passion which hath no being, but in play-books and romances'. Those who find this about as enticing as a cold bath must remember how deeply Swift disliked Ciceronian eloquence and all rhetoric designed to inflame the passions and preferred Demosthenes' appeal towards reason and understanding. Swift will be the young lady's 'director' – the role for which he was born and forever aspired to – and he warns her to 'beware of despising or neglecting my instructions'; it is her happiness, not Swift's, that's at hazard.[45]

The only drawback in all this is that the young lady is too much of a Houyhnhnm heroine – prudent, sensible, unadventurous and dull, rather like Martin in the *Tale*, whereas Jack, the beau and the Yahoo are always corrupt and always interesting. Perhaps this is a damaging sign of our own itch for Bedlam, our inner kinship with corruption, but if so it is a complicity that the satirist surely shares. Swift's imagination takes fire only when he is lashing human folly, not providing recipes for sensible wedlock or sensible religion. When he writes directly about order and decency, we nod approvingly, but when he exposes the fanatics of freedom as licentious madmen, we applaud his genius.

FOUR

THE RUINED MILL

In an age when literature tended to be the hostage of politics, it is heartening to find Swift and Johnson uniting to praise John Bunyan. Johnson found in *The Pilgrim's Progress* 'great merit, both for invention, imagination, and the conduct of the story', and awarded it his own supreme accolade, 'the general and continued approbation of mankind'.[1] Swift, despite living closer than Johnson in time and much closer in imagination to that hateful upsurge of revolutionary Puritanism in which Bunyan had served, nevertheless admired the enemy's masterpiece. Arbuthnot's letter complimenting Swift upon the success of the *Travels* and predicting 'as great a run as John Bunyan', surely proves this, for he would not have been so inept as to convey his sense of his friend's achievement by linking it with a writer Swift disliked.[2]

But we know from Swift himself how highly he rated Bunyan, since it is to him he turns, in his advice to the young gentleman about to enter the Anglican ministry, to enforce his point that 'a divine hath nothing to say to the wisest congregation of any parish in this kingdom, which he may not express in a manner to be understood by the meanest among them'.[3] Tillotson and his like are bad models for someone who wants to write 'a plain sermon intended for the middle or lower size of people'. Against the high, ornate style that inevitably leads to obscurity, Swift upholds 'that simplicity, without which no human performance can arrive to any great perfection', and praises Lord Falkland for consulting a servant whenever he was tempted to use a word of doubtful intelligibility: the vulgar are the final judges, especially in sermons 'where the meanest heart is supposed to be concerned'. After banning Latin and Greek from the pulpit as pedantic affectation, Swift denounces the foolish practice of larding a sermon with metaphysico-philosophical jargon and cites Bunyan as the healthy antidote: 'I have been better entertained and more informed by a chapter in the *Pilgrim's Progress* than by a long discourse upon the will and the intellect'. Entertainment is mandatory, for we cannot learn unless we stay awake. Scorners may be converted but sleepers are beyond reclamation, and the modern preacher, who can easily surpass St Paul at putting people to sleep, will not be able to restore them to life if they follow Eutychus over the balcony and kill themselves. Bunyan's readers run no such risk – even in a task so daunting as describing his soul's experience of salvation, he has mastered the art of holding the reader's attention. This anti-soporific secret is clearly a matter of art rather than theology, and Swift praises the child of Stourbridge Fair rather than the convert of Geneva, the creator of Giant Despair rather than the conventicler mulling over Calvinist texts. What he admired in Bunyan is what we admire in Swift, and identifying it will take us to the heart of his own artistic strategy.

The greatness of *The Pilgrim's Progress* comes from Bunyan's incarnating his high theme on the level of an unsophisticated adventure story – uniting his mature concern with the spiritual life to his youthful delight in old wives' tales and chapbook romances, each fitting the other like a glove: the whole man became thus profoundly engaged. The old stories are used as a kind of imaginative shorthand for his inner experience, in which moral significance is inseparable from sensuous form. His long training in addressing unlettered audiences lies behind that remarkable fusion of ancient romance and homely immediacy which makes it impossible to snooze through the story of his soul's adventures, and the constant movement from concept to image strikingly enriches the concept, giving dramatic life to what would otherwise be chill abstraction. A brilliant visual imagination, a gift for making the word flesh, breathing life into theological formulae and rendering the abstract in vividly dramatic tableaux, pictures rather than diagrams – this is what Swift both admired in Bunyan and sought in his own work.

The motive was equally didactic – the *Travels* would wonderfully mend the world – and Swift, who told Delany of his ambition to be a great preacher,[4] follows his own advice to the young clergyman and presents in his own greatest sermons, the major satires, not the discursive philosophizing that would send all but the insatiably intellectual to sleep, but the sharp dramatisation, the vivid depiction, the apologue, parable or fable, the image rather than the concept. He shares with Bunyan an imagistic genius for making the abstract concrete, for finding the sign, figure, symbol, vignette, emblem that is so much more irrefutably cogent than libraries of syllogisms. He will not waste time analysing the philosophical fallacies of stoicism but briefly alludes to the folly of cutting off our feet because we lack shoes, and the image of bloody stumps makes further argument redundant.[5] He declines the tedious catalogue of claims and counterclaims by ancients and moderns, inventing instead a bee and spider to enact the whole dispute before our eyes, so comprehensively that Aesop sums up for all of us – 'that in all his life, he had never known two cases so parallel and adapt to each other, as that in the window and this upon the shelves'.[6] He does not write a long refutation of Cicero's account of the compensations of old age, simply projects his nightmare vision of the Struldbruggs, 'the most mortifying sight I ever beheld, and the women more horrible than the men'.[7]

There is no arguing with images and these images are particularly potent. The wars of religion are egg-shaped, the history of primitive Christianity and its subsequent perversion is dramatized in the parable of the coats, and the rarefied dispute over transubstantiation becomes a wrangle at dinner as a trickster browbeats a slice of bread into a shoulder of mutton: 'Pray Sir, says Peter, eat your vittles and leave off your impertinence'.[8] Wherever we look in Swift, we find this visual power, this dramatic gift for the image that serves as objective correlative of an attitude towards experience or statement about life: the flayed woman, the beau's carcass, the little odious vermin of the Giant King, Gulliver fighting off the amorous she-Yahoo in the stream or fainting away in the embrace of that odious animal, his wife. Swift trades in icons rather than arguments, emblems rather than propositions, as part of his anti-intellectual stance: he will *show* us the truth but will not stop to contest the matter; he that has eyes to see will see, the rest are in darkness beyond the artist–preacher's reach. Swift and Bunyan are great moralists because they are great artists and their deepest convictions about life are always presented in emblematic form.

Swift, who was as fearful as Johnson of 'the fury of innovation', supplies in 'A Voyage to Laputa' the justificatory emblem for all conservatives sceptical of utopian change. The fruits of innovative zeal are everywhere evident as Gulliver is conducted by Lord Munodi through devastated Balnibarbi, a land ruined by the barbarous technocrats who are the heirs of Huns and Vandals: 'I never knew a soil so unhappily cultivated, houses so ill contrived and so ruinous, or a people whose countenances and habit expressed so much misery and want'.9 Munodi's estate, by contrast, is 'magnificent, regular and polite', reward for fidelity to ancient method and a reluctance to entertain the newfangled. The Academy of Lagado, founded forty years before Gulliver's visit to Balnibarbi, is the centre of utopian expectations and revolutionary promises: palaces to be built in a week that will stand for ever, new tools that will make work obsolete, crops compelled from the earth regardless of season, production multiplied a hundred fold. The sole inconvenience is that these triumphs are still confined to the drawing-board, and the country, while attending the miraculous abundance, is reduced to beggary; only a handful of obscurantists, traitors to the progressive commonwealth, continue to live in decency and comfort 'in the old forms . . . without innovation'.

In one single instance Munodi's stand against novelty has faltered, with disastrous consequences. He shows Gulliver a ruined building upon a hillside, once 'a very convenient mill', turned by a current from a large river, which had sufficed for many of his tenants as well as his own family.10 The mill worked well because man, in exemplary Burkean fashion, submitted to and co-operated with nature. The 'improvers', rash professors of novelty who despise history and tradition, seek to coerce nature rather than patiently accept a subsidiary partnership. They hustle Munodi into destroying the old, 'natural' mill and replacing it with a new, artificial one on the wrong side of the mountain, requiring a whole new assembly of machines; they defend this foolish flouting of nature with scientific doubletalk and the promise of a far greater future productive capacity. Two years and a hundred workmen later the scheme collapses, the projectors blame Munodi before departing to wreak similar havoc elsewhere, and a pile of crumbling stones is all that remains of a once flourishing mill.

From Halifax through Burke to modern conservative apologists we find this attack on utopian speculation tyrannizing over nature and ancient usage, but seldom delivered with the devastatingly ironic artistry of Swift's parable. Halifax, rejecting the chimera of perfectionism — 'those who look for perfection in this world may look as long as the Jews have done for their Messiah' — advises us to settle for the good we possess rather than hare after the impossibly perfect; if a system 'hath more excellencies and fewer faults than any other we know, it is enough to recommend it to our esteem'.[11] Burke denounces schemes upon paper – 'their abstract perfection is their practical defect' – and exhorts his hearers to choose 'our nature rather than our speculations'. He has clearly just come from meditating Munodi's distressing experience as he formulates the lessons of the ruined mill in generalised philosophic terms: 'very plausible schemes, with very pleasing commencements, have often shameful and lamentable conclusions', and therefore 'it is with infinite caution that any man ought to venture upon pulling down an edifice which has answered in any tolerable degree for ages the common purposes of society, or of building it up again without having models and patterns of approved utility before his eyes'.[12]

Swift eschews general laws in favour of the discrete image, but the whole conservative philosophy is implicit in this teaching by parable: approved utility, tradition, experience, respect for ancient rights and deference to prescriptive authority, a strong sense of the untried as risky, opposition to revolutionary change based on abstract doctrine and a contempt for paper schemes for the millenium, above all an insistence upon society as organism rather than the mechanical model of the planners – all of this is rendered with consummate artistic economy in the emblem of the ruined mill. Burke's organic metaphor, the most important of all 'Tory' concepts, is linked to his deep anti-intellectualism, that wariness towards intelligence and suspicion of thought which are integral to his philosophy – it is because he distrusts speculation that he banks on habit as the mainstay of human action.

Munodi, 'old and wilful, and weak', i.e., sensibly resistant to change, shunning 'modern usage' and so building 'a noble structure' according to the best rules of ancient architecture, 'content to go on in the old forms, to live in the houses his ancestors had built, and act as they did in every part of life without innovation', is the exemplary Burkean hero, the paridigmatic conservative man of the *Travels*, as his spiritual brother Martin is of the *Tale*.[13] In his anti-Catholic frenzy, Jack tears his coat to tatters, hatred of Rome prevailing over sensible reform, so obsessed with getting rid of Peter's excrescences that he damages the fabric itself and dignifies this mania for destruction with the newly coined expression, zeal. Martin, by contrast, prudently halts as soon as he sees the danger of excessive reform. Of course, it would be splendid to restore the garment to its pristine purity, but the coat now belongs to history and the accretions are now to some degree inextricably interwoven with the original material; the choice facing the brothers as universal representatives of mankind is between a ruinous perfectionism or a sensible toleration of minor blemishes for the sake of the overall good: utopia or history.

In Hawthorne's short story *The Birthmark* the idealistic hero is so tormented by the tiny defect in his wife's beauty that he is driven to remove it, but her life is the price. Martin is the unidealistic hero of the *Tale* because he sees that the coat as part of history has become the stuff of life itself, and the stuff of life, whether the emblem chosen be coat or mill, is disciplined by its own internal necessities rather than by the fiat of some demented idealist who foolishly thinks he can legislate for nature or dictate to reality. When such a man is powerless, he is simply a poor, pitiable lunatic, but when able to coerce other men he becomes as dangerously destructive as the Saints of Great Bedlam or the projectors of Lagado, for it is the conjunction of dreaming and ruling that generates tyranny. Munodi and Martin are the wise antagonists of these dreaming tyrants, creatures of prudent habit who possess that maturity which makes concessions to the real world, tolerating unavoidable imperfection and preferring nature to speculation. Munodi knows that nature cannot be frogmarched to human whims; we can certainly destroy the mills she allows but we cannot replace them where she withholds permission. Martin's cautious reformism exposes the revolutionary excess of his frenzied brother; Jack may have been driven mad by injustice in the first place, but explaining his dementia leaves him as dangerously deranged as ever, and, in his reckless quest for pristine purity, he prefigures Gulliver in the land of the Houyhnhnms – each believes wrongly that history can be discounted and perfection recovered. Martin, in approved conservative fashion, sees that the delicate task of picking out the offensive threads without damaging the allied fabric must be 'a work of time', and the final proof of his moderationist temper is the judicious decision to let abuses alone when the risks of removal are excessive.

It is the threat of total breakdown which induces the conservative to tolerate inefficiences, and even injustices, rather than put social stability at risk. Swift exhibits a like mentality when he advances, in a totally unironical context, the argument that it is wiser to let even a false belief remain in a body of religious dogma than by plucking it out to cause doubts among some of the faithful: 'To remove opinions fundamental in religion is impossible, and the attempt wicked whether those opinions be true or false; unless your avowed design be to abolish that religion altogether. So, for instance, in the famous doctrine of Christ's divinity, which hath been universally received by all bodies of Christians, since the condemnation of Arianism under Constantine and his successors: Wherefore the proceedings of the Socinians are both vain and unwarrantable; because they will never be able to advance their own opinion, or meet any other success than breeding doubts and disturbances in the world. *Qui ratione sua disturbant moenia mundi.*'[14]

These twin parables of Martin's coat and Munodi's mill reveal Swift as intellectual Orpheus, looking backwards at certain crucially decisive moments. We cannot sufficiently emphasize the extent to which the author of the *Tale* had his intellectual roots in the seventeenth century; the key to Swift is his Rip van Winkle attachment to the past, his resolve to view eighteenth-century events through seventeenth-century eyes. At a time when it is being increasingly realized that religious toleration need not entail social anarchy, Swift still sides with Bodin and Hobbes rather than Locke and Montesquieu. His politics, dominated by the spectre of 1642, are those of a state of emergency; when he thinks of dissenters, they are all wearing New Model Army uniforms. To Locke's argument that persecution produces conspiracy, toleration peace, he replies that dangerous men must be put down and that toleration both displeases God and harms the State – a more vigilantly thorough Charles I would not have lost his head. Grudgingly he allows a minimum toleration to sects unhappily permitted to spread by past neglect, but, too late to destroy them, insists that national security depends upon treating their adherents as second-class citizens. Like Hobbes, he regards religion as a source of potential strife which must be subject to State control. We today see that the sects which multiplied under persecution withered with toleration, but such a prediction would have seemed as absurd in the seventeenth century as legitimizing terrorist groups in the twentieth, and Swift is, as we have seen, very much a seventeenth-century man, his outlook conditioned by his reading of that period. So when the abolition of the Test Act is proposed, he resists what the events of the previous century have schooled him to see as another attempt to destroy the Church.

A similar conditioning informs his response to the debate on the decay of nature between Godfrey Goodman and George Hakewill in the first half of the seventeenth century.[15] Goodman believed in inevitable decay, a steady decline of man and nature from pristine perfection to moral and physical corruption. Hakewill, rejecting deteriorationism, insisted upon the virility of nature as a condition of faith in a beneficent Providence, an argument used later to attack those who upheld the ancients as exemplars of a bygone, unattainable excellence. Since no single factor was so responsible for the feeling of inferiority as the belief that the world was sinking into Struldbrugg senility, it was vital for the moderns to show that nature, if not improving, was at least constant. So well did they succeed that to many, as the century progressed, the world seemed less and less the derelict ruin lamented by Goodman. But Swift, unimpressed by the accumulated instances of virility cited to justify the new optimistic view, held fast to deteriorationism, and his work is an updated restatement of Goodman's thesis on irreversible human corruption. Yet that Swift's deteriorationism, like his insistence upon religious uniformity, links him with the past, is still insufficiently recognized. We are told to interpret his calls for return to real or imagined earlier practices nearer to perfection as merely the platitudes of an age habituated to belief in the world's decline.[16] In fact, Swift's age was rapidly abandoning this belief and its more optimistic spirits were already feeling their way towards a doctrine of progress. If Swift contemptuously spurns any hint of betterment, this simply underlines his commitment to an earlier, more pessimistic *Weltanschauung*.

Failure to grasp this prevents us from properly evaluating his excruciatingly acute sense of decay and can also lead to a misinterpretation of his intervention in the ancients–moderns quarrel in purely personal terms: his patron had been attacked, his Oxford friends had all been opposed to the new philosophy, his own unpleasant experience in getting his degree *gratia speciali* and his dislike of mathematics set him against 'pedantic' learning. All true, of course, but it leaves the most interesting questions unanswered. Why did he dislike mathematics? Was it pure coincidence that his Oxford friends opposed the new philosophy or was a shared antipathy the basis for friendship in the first place? And doesn't it unduly trivialize an important issue to regard Swift merely as a literary hatchet-man, obliging a friend by cutting up a couple of pedantic boors but otherwise indifferent to the dispute and its background? Certainly, Swift regarded Bentley as an intellectual mugger and was happy to assume the role of vigilante chastising bully-boys, but the affair surely transcends the purely personal.

In the light of its vital significance for the rise of the idea of progress, it is inexcusable to endorse Macaulay's dismissal of the ancients–moderns dispute as a childishly contemptible controversy.[17] A quarrel that has been described as a skirmish in the onslaught of science upon religion and as a local engagement in the clash between the perenially opposed forces of tradition and progress, is not so casually demoted.[18] The conservatives blamed the new ideas for the religious factions disrupting England, and there was unquestionably a close relationship between Puritanism and the new science. The quest for personal religious experience, reflected in Puritan diaries and autobiographies, is closely akin to the experimental spirit in science, and many who were seekers in the one field extended their enquiries into the other.[19] The motto of the Royal Society, *nullius in verba*, insisting upon a personal investigation of traditional ortho-doxies, was a threat to national peace and unity when applied to religious matters. The radicals' abandonment of the dogma of human sinfulness coalesced with Baconian optimism to produce a Joachimite vision of a perfect world – hubristic folly to those who would not be deflected from man's depravity by the tale of his new material achievements. Swift surely disliked modern pretentions even before Temple was roughed up, identified them as another gang of enthusiasts with no more claim to respect than their religious allies. His scornful attitude to projectors and his insistence that all men are selfish were partly provoked by what he saw as the cant of Puritan scientists posing as martyrs for mankind. Swift cared little for the authenticity of Aesop and Phalaris, and to that extent his intervention may simply be an attempt to defend Temple, but his pessimistic view of history would have set him against the moderns in any case. Judged solely by his beliefs and writings, he is on the side we would expect; his wounded friends were simply an additional motive for attacking what he already detested.

Swift's deteriorationism needs emphasizing because by his day cyclical theory had undergone a sea-change in assuming optimistic rather than pessimistic implications. Polybius, whose theory grew out of national defeat, had stressed the downward turn of fortune's wheel, but the cycle could be optimistic with emphasis upon renewal rather than decay – an unfamiliar idea for twentieth-century western-ers accustomed to regard cyclical theory as the characteristic ideology of a society in decline. But in the seventeenth century cyclical theory was used to attack the concept of regression, of an absolute, irreversible fall from ancient excellence, and thus pave the way for a doctrine of progress. It was argued that the ancients had had their turn and that after the fallow medieval period the wheel was again turning upwards towards a new age of achievement. Not content with trumpeting their superiority to the Middle Ages, men began to claim that in certain fields they were outstripping the ancients themselves. The doctrine of the accumulation of knowledge meant that modern superiority was historically guaranteed – the moderns, coming later in time, must know more than the ancients, just as a boy sitting on his father's shoulders must see farther. No need for nature to be more prolific in genius, since, given Hakewill's idea of nature's constancy, sheer accumulation of examples is itself an advantage. To pay excessive veneration to the ancients as such is foolish, since, as Bacon argues, it is we who are really the ancients: *antiquitas seculi iuventus mundi*. Cyclical theory, with this optimistic face-lift, could be used to vindicate Hakewill against Goodman in rejecting the hitherto dominant tenet of degeneration. But Swift's brand of cyclical theory remains bleakly Polybian and it is abuses, not knowledge, that he finds accumulating – the more trash is put in the dustbin, the filthier it becomes.

The distinction between material progress and human corruption was still commonplace in Swift's day; total progress in all realms of being is a late-eighteenth-century French concept, with Saint-Simon the first to claim that moral progress kept pace with scientific, technological advance. Swift as moralist judges every alleged achievement in terms of how it promotes or retards moral progress: what does it profit a man if he gains the world and loses his soul? Men drunk with their achievements need to be reminded of this truth and all men need reminders more than new information. Material advance may disguise moral regress; reason itself is not an unqualified good if it becomes the yes-man to Yahoo passion. It is a challenge rather than a gift; properly used, not in the merely Hobbesian sense of a faculty for making correct deductions, but as the candle of the Lord, the handmaid of virtue, it is a blessing – otherwise it is what Faustus made of it, the instrument of damnation. The prelapsarian Lilliputians prefer honest mediocrity to unprincipled ability and fear the clever villain as the greatest social menace, believing with Swift that 'great abilities without the fear of God are more dangerous instruments when they are trusted with power'.[20] This is what determines Swift's attitude towards science and his evaluation of modern inventions and discoveries.

His refusal to be overawed by modern triumphs is seen in his casual, almost contemptuous remark that 'the greatest inventions were produced in times of ignorance; as the use of the compass, gunpowder and printing; and by the dullest nations, as the Germans'.[21] These were the three inventions cited *ad nauseam* to prove modern superiority.[22] Some qualms might arise over gunpowder but even here the normal attitude, clergy included, is to score it up on the credit side; on the frontispiece to Sprat's *History of the Royal Society* a gun is prominent among the emblems of experimental success. Optimistic Anglican ministers, anxious to discredit Goodman, hailed the gun as proof of progress; old-fashioned thinkers like Temple, Swift and the King of Brobdingnag admit the genius but condemn it as evil, to the genuinely bewildered indignation of that moral defective, the perfect modern, Lemuel Gulliver. The Giant King is not some anti-scientific know-nothing flat-earther – he honours the man whose expertise can produce two blades of grass where there was formerly only one; outrage, not timid obscurantism, motivates his horrified refusal of Gulliver's offer, and the moral bankruptcy of the age is manifested in the myopia that can hail gunpowder as proof of greatness. Only those who identify scientific advance with progress will accuse Swift of being a reactionary obscurantist. Bertrand Russell credits Swift with the revelation that science is ethically neutral and can be used for evil as well as good : 'It is to feeling, not to knowledge, that we must appeal if science is to be beneficent. Laputa showed me the possibility of scientific horrors and made me realise that, however scientific, they remain horrors'.[23] Swift might have jibbed at Russell's terminology, but 'feeling' is not very far removed from the moral intuitionism that Giant King and Houyhnhnm rely on to identify the morally detestable, especially when it is also scientifically admirable. The whirligig of time may have given pre-Hiroshima scientists their revenge on Swift, but today he is surely rehabilitated, his moral scrutiny of science a precondition of human survival; only highly developed technological societies could carry through those miracles of social engineering, the extermination of the Jews and the pollution of the environment.

Swift also follows Temple in regarding printing as a dubious blessing.[24] For Temple books may help, but are not essential to, learning: Mexico and Peru are bookless but cultured, Ireland, once lavish with libraries, is now savage, and Temple cites the wise, virtuous Indian Brahmans to prove that tradition is often a better preserver of learning than writing. Swift agrees with the Giant King that too many books indicate decadence: 'If books and laws continue to increase as they have done for fifty years past, I am in some concern for future ages, how any man will be learned, or any man a lawyer'.[25] The Houyhn-hnms trust completely to tradition. The conservative sceptic has always distrusted the press as a seed-bed of heresy, and Swift is no exception. His attitude to censorship shows that he views the press as he does reason: properly used, i.e., to uphold traditional values, it is good, otherwise it is an evil, disruptive force, contumeliously heretic. Books might be all Milton claimed, but Swift insists they behave themselves like other citizens and is ready to suppress them when they turn seditious and threaten public order.

The invention of the compass leading to geographical expansion was the strongest card in the moderns' hand, for here the ancients had been indisputably surpassed. Even Dryden deserts his habitual scepticism to hail Columbus for rescuing our 'free-born reason' from the age-long tyranny of Aristotle.[26] Those moderns who were uneasy about gunpowder could take comfort in assuming that geographical expansion has been wholly beneficial, with compass and gunpowder the God-given means of extending the unqualified blessing of western Christian civilization to benighted heathens. For Temple the compass is admittedly a great invention but it has promoted luxury, not know-ledge. Our moral superiors, the ancients, would have used it for good; modern men have prostituted it to Yahoo bestiality. Far from bringing light to savage peoples, 'we have treated them as if we hardly esteemed them to be a part of mankind'.[27] Temple's un-impassioned argument becomes in Swift acid condemnation. Modern commerce panders to male intemperance and female vanity, the earth gone round three times to provide breakfast for a rich she-Yahoo, essential commodities exchanged for 'the materials of diseases, folly and vice'.[28] Criminal ostentation by a few, a brutal, degraded popu-lace, vice everywhere, are the fruits of our vaunted commercial civilization and its geographical exploits. As for the cant of bringing Christian civilization to backward peoples, Gulliver tells us exactly how and why dominions are acquired: Pizarro and Cortez are the shameful truth behind the humbug of a cultural mission. No wonder Gulliver dreams instead of the horses massacring an invading army before undertaking the mammoth task of civilizing Europe. To Swift it was the nadir of moral blindness and brazen effrontery for men living in the stink of English corruption to advocate piously the extension of our civilization to other lands.

The moderns also claimed superiority by virtue of their possession of the truths of Christianity. Nothing angers Swift more than to see religion, the whole purpose of which is to convict man of sin, perverted into buttressing human egoism. It is the foolish modern of the *Tale* who identifies the reader's repose, both of body and mind, as 'the true ultimate end of ethics'[29] – its proper aim, for Swift, is to make men uneasy and intimidate pride. Unable to deny the moderns' claim, he derides it instead. The egregious modern in the *Tale* clinches his indictment of Homer by exposing his gross ignorance of the doctrine and discipline of the Anglican Church – a *reductio ad absurdum* of the idiocy of blaming the ancients for being born before, and praising ourselves for being born after, the Incarnation.[30] The young clergyman is warned against the insufferable cant of disparaging the ancient philosophers whose fault is 'that they were ignorant of certain facts which happened long after their death'.[31] Swift rejects natural religion and rational Christianity, denies that the unaided reason can lead one to religious truth. If we are Christians, we owe it solely to a gratuitous revelation; if the ancient philosophers never achieved a satisfactory idea of God, what more can be expected of reason without revelation?

Swift even praises those who, in the absence of revelation, abandoned such inquiry as futile: 'the wisest among them laid aside all notion after a Diety, as a disquisition vain and fruitless, which indeed it was, upon unrevealed principles'.[32] The likeliest hypothesis, on strictly rational grounds, is Manichean division rather than the mystery of an all-powerful, all-loving deity.[33] Since God, then, is a *deus absconditus* who has mercifully revealed himself to us, how dare we blasphemously turn this to personal credit, especially when, lacking this revelation, we should be sunk in far greater ignorance than ever the ancients were? Even without Christianity, the ancients are our moral superiors, coming as near to Christian truth as was possible before the Incarnation. Their writings form the best commentary on the moral part of the Gospel; Plato even anticipates the supreme Christian injunction to love one's enemies. Certainly Swift will not allow the ancient philosophers to be used by deists as a stick to beat Christianity with, or to imply that Christian doctrine is superfluous; but neither will he allow modern Christians to flaunt their religion as proof of superiority to those who lived before Christ's birth.[34]

The historical nature of Christianity posed a problem increasingly debated in the early eighteenth century.[35] The idea of progress, of a progressive revelation, was fast becoming almost mandatory if Christianity were to withstand deist attacks. The main criticism derived from the premise that any religion claiming to be universally valid for *all* men must be, and always have been, available to all men. To Pascal's rhetorical question, is it not enough that miracles are performed in one place and that Providence appears in one people? – the deists returned a resounding negative.[36] How can belief in Christian doctrine be essential for salvation if temporal and geographical factors ensure that most men have never heard of Christ? The deist standards for a true universal religion are designed to disqualify any historical religion, and Christianity is rooted in history. Where is the universal application of a system deriving from the religious customs of the Jews, a primitive, nomadic people inhabiting an obscure desert, remote, secret, unapproachable? Why, if Christianity is vital for salvation, was it not revealed to all men at the beginning of history instead of to a handful of ignorant peasants and fishermen scratching a living around the Sea of Galilee?

To counter such attacks many Christian apologists came to rely increasingly on the idea of a progressive revelation. Christianity had been given to the world at the precise moment it could be understood, God dispensing His truth in small doses until the time was ripe for the full message to be grasped when Christ was born. This was the view, justified by certain texts in Augustine and Aquinas, that was adopted to refute the deists. But it is altogether characteristic of Swift's distrust of rational argumentation and doctrinal polemic, as well as his aversion to the idea of progress in any form whatsoever, that he ridicules rather than answers deist arguments. The freethinker who takes upon himself the task of putting Anthony Collins's book on freethinking into plain English for the use of the poor, repeats the central deist arguments in so absurd a fashion that we are clearly intended to be amused rather than disconcerted: 'The Bible says, the Jews were a nation favoured by God; but I who am a Free-thinker say, that cannot be, because the Jews lived in a corner of the earth, and free-thinking makes it clear, that those who live in corners cannot be favourites of God. The New Testament all along asserts the truth of Christianity, but Free-thinking denies it; because Christianity was communicated but to a few; and whatever is communicated but to a few, cannot be true; for that is like whispering, and the proverb says, that there is no whispering without lying'.[37] The deist device of discrediting Christianity by pointing to its Judaic origins appears in the wish that the great freethinker Josephus 'had chosen a better subject to write on, than those ignorant, barbarous, ridiculous scoundrels the Jews, whom God (if we may believe the priests) thought fit to chuse for his own people'.[38] Ridicule always came easier to Swift than reasoned refutation.

An alternative way, different from that of the Anglican progressivists, of solving the problem of Christianity's historical nature was to assimilate whatever in Christianity was amenable to the new religion of reason, i.e., reconcile it with deism, and jettison the rest. True Christianity is really as old as the creation. Swift's freethinker insists that Socrates, who rejected superstitious stories about the Gods, was a true Christian, despite living long before Christ, because 'Christ is nothing else but Reason, and I hope you do not think Socrates lived before reason'.[39] And since Socrates knew nothing about mysteries, the less truck we have with them the better. Swift ridicules deism, ignores progressivism, and demands unquestioning obedience to Christian doctrine. If the theory of progress in religion or progressive revelation makes no appeal to him, this is because the very idea of progress smacks, for him, of that self-approbation that is man's besetting folly.

Pride is the unforgivable, the unnatural sin: 'I never wonder to see men wicked, but I often wonder to see them not ashamed'.[40] Gulliver is baffled how such an animal and such a vice can tally together. The moderns are the pinnacle of human presumption, intellectual Pharisees, scorners of other men and other ages. A contemporary admirer describes the members of the Royal Society as 'placed in a rank specially different from the rest of grovelling humanity', men who have laid 'a new foundation of a more magnificent philosophy, never to be overthrown . . . a true and permanent philosophy'.[41] But the Giant King, in denouncing grovelling humanity, does not exempt the virtuosi of Gresham College and the shade of Aristotle summoned to the island of sorcerers reveals what Swift thought of that chimera, a true and permanent philosophy.[42] The doctrine upon which the moderns' case rested, the progressive accumulation of knowledge, is for Swift just a joke, and Bacon's paradox is exposed as outrageous nonsense when Swift's foolish moderns present themselves as the true ancients.[43] The notion that learning is accumulative is exploded when the author of the *Tale*, in a manner testifying to his manifest folly, claims as the freshest modern a despotic power over all previous writers.[44] The raving of a crackpot, conceited enthusiast merits contemptuous dismissal, not reasoned refutation.

Modern pride is the more inexcusable when set against the age's corruption – 'this polite and learned age', in the savagely ironical encomium of the *Tale*. Man is an outrageous creature, the one animal daily degenerating through auto-intoxication.[45] In his *Project*, where we learn that even Queen Anne's splendid example has failed to discourage wickedness, Swift is anxious to prevent his fulminations being discounted as standard laments or homiletic commonplaces, the clichés of the preacher. That fraud is rampant among the English to a degree unknown in any other Christian land is no surprise considering our unparalleled neglect of religion – one minister and two curates to every twenty thousand souls in London.[46] The moderns, peddling their pernicious rubbish about progress, stand between man and his true image, quacks assuring men mortally ill that they are in prime condition. Kant tells us that man has three possibilities: constant progression, constant regression, or an eternal moral marking-time.[47] There is surely no doubt where we shall find Swift.

Deterioration is present in the *Travels* both as theme and structure. Shipwrecked by a storm, abandoned by companions who save themselves, captured by pirates and set adrift in an open boat through the malice of a Dutch Christian, betrayed from within by a mutiny of his own crew, Gulliver's adventures record a transition from purely natural disaster through human frailty to the blackest of human deeds, spite and treachery. The movement is one of deepening evil and the process of internalizing evil and giving it human features culminates when Gulliver, embraced by the she-Yahoo, acknowledges his kinship in a corruption not monopolized by pirates and mutineers. Deterioration is also a major theme. We hear of the admirable, prelapsarian institutions of Lilliput before they succumb to 'the degenerate nature of man'. The Giant King concludes that European society has deteriorated from a once tolerable original. On Glubdubbdrib, where Gulliver is initiated into the sordid reality of history, degeneration is made explicit by contrasting a Roman senate with a modern English parliament and some English yeomen of the old stamp with their contemptible present-day descendants. When

Gulliver's Struldbrugg dream fails and with it the last hope of foiling the deteriorationism that rules history, he is forced to admit inevitable decay.[48] One suggestion of Yahoo origins is that they are the degenerate descendants of castaway Europeans – the descent of man, indeed.[49]

Decay is a major theme in all of Swift's work and the fact that he can also occasionally burlesque it (as in the Brobdingnagian treatise lamenting the shrunken present) should not mislead us into minimizing its significance.[50] Swift is, of course, sufficiently Augustan to concern himself with man rather than nature – Goodman's argument that trees and animals share in the decline, growing punier with each generation, is irrelevant for Swift's moral purpose, and the physical aspects of human corruption are significant for him chiefly as symbols of moral decay. If depraved aristocrats can produce only diseased offspring, this vindicates the moral law that God is not mocked; the sins of the fathers are literally visited upon the children, and Swift, with grim relish, notes that here at least moral and physical decay are appropriately matched.[51] The clinching proof of unavoidable corruption is seen in Gulliver's horror at return to England, for what most unnerves him is the inevitable recrudescence of his own depravity. If Gulliver, granted a vision of Houyhnhnm perfection, must relapse, who can claim to be exempt from corruption? Hostile critics surely have enough evidence against Gulliver without fabricating more, and those who deplore his pride must concede that, unlike that of the Royal Society, it never extends to regarding himself as superior to the doom imposed on all men; he may be deluded in seeing man as diseased but he never asserts his own immunity from contagion.

Historical deteriorationism is reinforced in Swift by a pessimistic view of life. Far from seeing life as a blessing, he describes it as a tragedy where we look on for a while before playing our own parts, and argues that God sends misfortunes, sickness, the death of friends, to cure us of our inexplicable reluctance to let go of life. Since life is the prize and stamping-ground of the evil man, death is really a benefit, Hobbes's *summum malum* transformed to a liberation. The premature death of the virtuous while thousands of wretches go on littering the earth is enough for Swift to dispel any foolish notion that God meant life as a blessing. The Houyhnhnm attitude to death is clearly intended as exemplary. Far from raging against the dying of the light, they return, calm and unafraid, to their first mother, a model, however difficult, for human imitation, since 'it is impossible that

anything so natural, so necessary and so universal as death should
ever have been designed by providence as an evil to mankind'.[52]
Freud would have been on safer ground had he looked to Swift
rather than *King Lear* for the spirit that teaches us to make friends
with the necessity of dying.

The crucial disagreement over Swift's pessimism is between those
who would tame it to Christian purposes and those who argue that, if
only occasionally, it overflows the Christian mould generally accom-
modating it to threaten fundamental Christiam assumptions, that
intermittently one senses here a pessimism rooted less in the offically-
sanctioned Christian depreciation of this life in favour of the next
than in revulsion from the horror of life itself. The onslaught in 'The
Day of Judgement' is not restricted to erring individuals or sects but
implicates the whole offending race of human kind, especially those
who deceive themselves and others into thinking they are God's
confidants. If God's designs are as deliberately inscrutable as the
poem implies, then we are all, Anglicans included, in the same
deluded hazard as the drivelling little imbecile in *The Mechanical
Operation of the Spirit*.[53] It is hard to reconcile this with any form of
Christianity or see how the adherents of any revealed religion can
take comfort from Jove's parting pronouncement. Perhaps this is
merely a trope or an exaggeration in the sense of a truth that has lost
its temper, an instance of Swift's tendency to say more than he means;
when the persona of the *Tale* confesses to being a person whose
imaginations are hard-mouthed and exceedingly disposed to run
away with his reason, is he simultaneously revealing his creator's
secret?[54] Or perhaps the poem marks a point where scepticism becomes so intense and pessimism so bitter that they diverge from
Christianity, opposing rather than reinforcing it, challenging not just
Pelagian presumption but basic Christian tenets.

The Struldbruggs have, predictably, become a battleground for
those conflicting views. That they *can* be used to drive home a
Christian moral proves nothing as to Swift's intention in creating
them. They certainly embody a recurrent problem in the Swift who
declared that 'no wise man ever wished to be younger', and, 'every
man desires to live long; but no man would be old'.[55] Those who
assume that the satire of a clergyman must be Christian satire insist
on interpreting the Struldbrugg episode within a context of Christian
apologetics. In ridiculing Gulliver's dream of immortality Swift
attacks the freethinkers' blasphemous desire to evade God's judge-

ment that death for all Adam's posterity is the penalty for original sin.[56] Such a view clearly puts the Christian rabbits into the hat before triumphantly producing them – it assumes what it seeks to prove. For how do we know that Swift wrote the *Travels* as a Christian propagandist, unless we assume that every denunciation of life by a Christian divine, even when he is Jonathan Swift, must be motivated by Christian requirements? Silenus, too, did not regard life as a blessing: *optimum non nasci, aut cito mori*; Socrates described it as a disease and instructed Crito to sacrifice a cock as a thanks-offering for his deliverance; Marcus Aurelius praises death as a release from the twitchings of appetite and the service of the flesh. Must we include them too as Christian moralists? Schopenhauer claimed he was Christianity's truest interpreter, expressing (he said) its innermost thought: deliverance from the self, from the tyranny of the will-to-live. If the Struldbruggs really embody Christian teaching and desire for death is the distinguishing mark of the Christian thinker, it will be difficult to refute his claim.

But there is no need to confine ourselves to Christian orthodoxy in interpreting the Struldbruggs. Swift uses the myth to assault long-cherished but illusory sources of human satisfaction – it exhibits the folly of believing life is good rather than the blasphemy of seeking immortality. Those who insist that he is attacking not life itself but its perversion, that he is simply saying that to prolong life beyond its normal span is against both God and nature, that above all we must not confuse ordinary life with Struldbrugg existence, do so because they feel that anything more radical would be discreditable in an Anglican clergyman. Yet who told us that clergyman and satirist are totally identical or that Swift wrote the *Travels* to defend Christianity? Swift himself tells us, in a context free of irony, that it is only because God has rigged the game against us to begin with by implanting within us sexual desire and the instinct of self-preservation that we are hoodwinked into going on living at all; emancipated from passion, we would see and shun the horror of existence.[57] This is closer to Camus's remark that suicide is the most important philosophical problem of our time than to the reiterated emphasis of Genesis that God saw His creation as good.[58]

Is Swift simply attacking the heretical longing for immortality or questioning the value of life itself? Lilliput may provide the answer. The Lilliputians, holding that life is simply a by-product of animal concupiscence, deny that children are obligated to their parents for begetting them.[59] This is not just because the parents were solely concerned with their own selfish pleasure when conception occurred, not just that gratitude for the gift is cancelled by the donors' egoism, but because it is not a gift at all, 'neither a benefit in itself nor intended so by his parents'. Why should anyone, contemplating 'the miseries of human life', feel grateful for so calamitous a legacy? It needs only one more step to arrive at Hamm's question to his father: 'Scoundrel! Why did you engender me?'[60] Beckett sees all fathers, from God downward, as guilty; in Swift guilt is inseparable from the sexual instinct that men cannot escape and seldom wish to. Nothing could be plainer as a denial of the value of life and there seems no reason for saying that Swift is satirising the Lilliputian view or that they speak only for themselves. The pessimism is Swift's own and it is the critic's duty to determine its nature and provenance, even if this means removing it from the clerical incubator which is its usual domicile. We may regret this pessimism but we must face it.

The dread of destructive innovation dramatised in the ruined mill, the longing to conserve revealed in Martin's sensible treatment of his coat, the preference for simplicity over refinement, the aversion from life itself as a servitude to shameful appetites – all of this supplies the key to unlock the meaning of Swift's most contentious creation, the Houyhnhnms. Most readers find the Houyhnhnms unattractive, but too many assume that what displeases them must also displease Swift. We use great writers like echo-chambers; it comforts us to share beliefs with a genius and to treat his superiority as no more than a verbal gift, a power of expression. Hence the temptation to promote our own personal preferences as though they were his. We pick and choose among Houyhnhnm attitudes according to our own pre-dilections, perhaps praising their wise population programme (increasingly favoured today), or their enlightened policy of female education, endorsed by Swift but even more relevantly by us. But when we learn that they know nothing of iron and next to nothing of astronomy, we probably interpret this disparagingly – though Swift may be applauding their priorities, their equine equivalent of the humanist tradition that the truly valuable knowledge is of man rather than nature. Their restriction of sex to marriage and procreation will not win many votes today, yet Swift may have found this just as commendable as the education of women. Even a genius is entitled to his own opinions, however jarring, and if unconvinced we should at least refrain from moulding him into some king-size version of ourselves. Perhaps Swift admired the Houyhnhnms even though we find them intolerable.

But how, it will be said, could anyone – the brainwashed Gulliver and William Godwin apart – ever see anything to admire in such repulsive creatures?[61] Surely the book's purpose is to expose Gulliver as a gull and where is this more evident than in his absurd adulation of the horses? The victim of the Houyhnhnm propaganda machine may deserve sympathy, but his sycophancy is to be deplored, not endorsed. As for Godwin, Orwell has shown that the substitution of exhortation for force among the horses is simply the replacement of a physical by a moral tyranny, no recommendation to those schooled by Mill to see this as the most fearful kind, not over the body but over the mind.[62] Mill's indictment of social democracy as potentially more oppressive than overt authoritarianism is available for use against Houyhnhnm society. All this makes it easier to see the horses as part of a satiric target rather than an image of Utopia, and if Gulliver is heartbroken when they refuse him political asylum, this only proves what an oddball he is. They are dislikeable so Swift must have disliked them, and if Gulliver and Godwin like them, so much the worse for them.

Yet it should not surprise us if Swift did fail to create an attractive Utopia, since in this he is no different from all the others who have tried. As travel-agents they would go broke, despite the fact that these travel-agents of the imagination are enviably secure from the awkward reality that threatens their real counterparts – the glowing brochures exposed as lies, the sense of let-down, the fury of outraged expectations. Like Adam what they dream is fact; they only have to sell the brochure, convince us that what they desire is desirable. Yet we leave their paradises not with regret that they are not practical, however desirable, but with a conviction that they are not desirable, however practical. Perhaps by being too precise in defining paradise, they provoke controversy rather than consensus – unlike St Paul who, when caught up into heaven, heard secret words that man may not repeat. How can anyone quarrel with his 'description' of paradise, that the eye has not seen nor the ear heard nor the heart conceived what things God has prepared for them that love Him? Perhaps people just cannot recognize a good thing when they see it – Rousseau talks of forcing them to be free, Marcuse sees them as slaves who love their chains – still, Utopias have never been chart-toppers. It may be true that of all the emigration-agents Swift is the biggest failure, in box-office terms Houyhnhnmland the biggest flop, since apparently rational horses cannot persuade nor wild horses drag people to live there; in a world of realised Utopias Houyhnhnmland would probably become a penal settlement, a Devil's Island for incorrigible recidivists. Yet even if the horses are non-starters in the Utopia stakes, they were entered to win: Houyhnhnmland is for Swift, with one significant qualification, an image of Utopia.

Although the central critical dispute is the relation of Swift to Gulliver, thus preventing us from assuming that Gulliver speaks for Swift, there are surely at least moments when we sense a second voice reinforcing Gulliver's. When Gulliver communicates his disgust with modern history, after having been taken backstage and shown how history is made, will anyone deny that this is Swift expressing his own views?[63] That history is not just what Voltaire calls it, a pack of lies we play on the dead, but is also propaganda, a pack of lies played on the living, with truth as difficult to get at as in *Nineteen Eighty-Four* – Gulliver succeeds only because his witnesses are dead men for whom lying is redundant – this all sounds remarkably like the Swift who, in *The Battle of the Books*, ranked historians as mercenaries. Similarly, the long passage where Gulliver describes his happy life among the horses – enjoying health of mind and body, fearing no treachery or oppression, not having to flatter, pimp or bribe – sounds very much like Swift trouncing English corruption.[64] There seems no reason here at least to suspect irony at Gulliver's expense or to think him a fool for preferring this life to the risk of being burned by the Inquisition.

Houyhnhnmland here is what Moor Park was for Sir William Temple: a decent refuge from the cesspool of English politics. Temple believed that politics was a simple, straightforward business, and ascribed his own success as a diplomat to candour and plain-dealing. Like the Giant King denouncing whole libraries devoted to the art of government as proof of decadence, Temple detested the whole *arcana imperi* tradition and relied instead on simple honesty; only rascals refine politics into intrigue. So when he discovered that under Charles II the rope-dancers of Lilliput invariably won, he became a political drop-out and retreated to Moor Park, refusing to re-enter politics and writing his memoirs as a record of public spirit thwarted by chicanery. Macaulay blamed him for a selfishness that took him gardening while politics deteriorated but Swift admired him as a political analogue of Bunyan's hero withdrawing from a City of

Destruction. Gulliver's attempt at a similar withdrawal fails when he is expelled from Houyhnhnmland, and, not unnaturally, he views his return to English corruption much as Temple would have regarded being forcibly detained to serve a court whose perfidy disgusted him.

We can see what Swift admired in the Houyhnhnms if we emphasize this simplicity–corruption antithesis in the light of his pessimistic view of history as the chronicle of an inevitable transition from pristine simplicity to refined corruption, what happens to the father's decently plain coat when the extravagant sons get hold of it. This process of 'refinement' (Swift's synonym for corruption) is both ubiquitous and irreversible; the most we can hope for is to keep vice temporarily at a stand. It is the view of a defeated man but Swift held it long before his actual defeat. In his earliest, most optimistic political pamphlet, the *Contests and Dissensions*, he cites Polybius as proof that decay is unavoidable, that the greatest states share man's mortality.[65] So the usual explanation of his pessimism – that it simply results from the chagrin of being a loser and missing a bishopric – will not do. Swift was not a loser when he found in Polybius an attraction far deeper than the mere ups and downs of party politics under Queen Anne. When he read in Polybius that 'wherever it is possible to find out the cause of what is happening, one should not have recourse to the gods',[66] he welcomed this as confirmation of his own contempt for the Puritan tendency to see the hand of God at work everywhere: 'I think it is in life as in tragedy, where it is held a conviction of great defect, both in order and intention, to interpose the assistance of preternatural power without an absolute and last necessity.'[67]

His dislike of the Puritan habit of using God as a kind of joker for claiming otherwise untakcable tricks emerges in his concern that Captain Creichton should supply a purely naturalistic interpretation of the dreams that help him hunt down the outlawed Covenanting preachers.[68] Since only quacks and fanatics claim a hot line direct to heaven (see 'The Day of Judgement'), it was all the more vital that Creichton should avoid being classed as charlatan or lunatic along with the Saints. Swift flatly denies the Puritan belief in ubiquitous divine intervention that led them to see earthly prosperity as sacramental, an outward sign of inward grace: 'Power, wealth and the like outward advantages are so far from being the marks of God's approving or preferring those on whom they are bestowed, that, on the contrary, he is pleased to suffer them to be almost engrossed by those who have the least title to his favour'. For, 'if Heaven had looked upon riches to be a valuable thing, it would not have given them to such a scoundrel'.[69] Why drag in God to account for a man's being a millionaire when it is all perfectly explicable in terms of rapacity and corruption? The notion that John Churchill and the Duchess of Kendal owe their prosperity to heavenly favour provokes Swift to angry derision. It is the devil who looks after his own and men may boast less of their wealth when reminded of this. And since human affairs are such a disgusting mess, how can anyone believe that God is in the driver's seat? Much easier to conclude that we live in a God-abandoned world where only the vicious can flourish; Swift's God is the *deus absconditus* of Pascal and success is anti-sacramental.

But if God does not rule history, what does? Swift found a congenial explanation in Polybius' emphasis on chance as a determinant of history. Polybius was the first historian to occupy himself with chance in a systematic way because, as a Greek under Roman domination, he wanted some other explanation for his country's plight than plain inferiority. He decided that everything depends upon fortune, not merit. Again it must be emphasised that it was not the Tory debacle that drew Swift to this view. It is a novice's blunder to imagine that Swift turned pessimist overnight when Queen Anne died too soon and he was shipped off to an Irish exile. These disasters merely intensified a temperamental pessimism in one who was always something of a desponder, confirming his prophetic forebodings, telling him what he already knew, that he was, like his hero Harley, one 'more formed for adversity than prosperity'.[70] That great fish, which he had so narrowly missed catching as a boy, loomed over his whole life as an image of impending disappointment.[71] To a born loser like Swift the idea that chance, not God, is the real lord of history presented itself with persuasive force.

How can history be amenable to law when a gust of passion or a sudden whim in some strategically-situated individual can send it careering off in some totally unpredictable direction? This aleatory interpretation consoles the loser, as when Trotsky ascribes his defeat by Stalin to a headcold caught while duck-shooting in the country, which prevented his attending Lenin's funeral in Moscow – only this ridiculous accident allowed his rival to pose successfully as Lenin's heir. But the Cleopatra's-nose view also comes instinctively to all who reject the *animal rationale* hypothesis and instead see the passions as the fuel of history. To reveal the trivial, corrupt origins of historical causation is to put man in his place and scotch at birth foolish pretensions to glory. Behind Henry IV's projected attack on the Empire is Yahoo lust, all Europe on the march because of a royal erection – but for the numbers he commands, he is any frustrated bully throwing stones at a whore's window; the sordid reality behind the *grand siècle* is a fistula in the royal anus; Marlborough will not make peace because his Yahoo lust for shining stones is served by the war's continuance. From being a flattering mirror of human achievement, history is reduced to a record of depravity, its glittering surface a mere cover for the filthiest impulses.

Predictably, history so conceived presents the uninterrupted triumph of evil: virtue is a handicap, honesty a clog, and Swift has barred supernatural aid in rejecting the *deus ex machina*. History, like the Mass, is a daily reenactment of goodness crucified: 'This world is made for Caesar – as Cato said, for ambitious, false or flattering people to domineer in'.[72] The wages of sin is success. Gulliver is driven to sea when his business fails because he refuses to cheat like everyone else – a moral Gresham's Law. The world is rigged against genius and virtue: 'When a true genius appears in the world, you may know him by this infallible sign; that the dunces are all in confederacy against him'.[73] Swift's heroes are all defeated men, failures, suicides, martyrs: Robert of Gloucester, Socrates, Cato, Brutus, Thomas More, Harley; his villains are the winners: Octavius, Henry VIII, John Churchill, Walpole.[74] His odes, save that to King William, are about good men undone by rogues; even in that to the Athenian Society he introduces a Polybian vision of future defeat by barbarian hordes. He ascribes his own failure to a refusal to prostitute his pen, whereas to succeed you must

> Write worse then if you can – be wise –
> Believe me 'tis the way to rise.[75]

This pessimism is a natural companion of the historical view he found in Polybius.

Polybius provided him not only with an interpretation of history but also with a programme for handling contemporary social problems. States, like men, having only a limited life-span, the aim of political health is to preserve the state till its appointed time. For States too can commit suicide, and just as there are libertines destroying their bodies, so there are men lusting for change, political debauchees who just as surely ruin the body politic.[76] Swift's prescription as political physician is simple: resist change. His jocular recommendation of Charondas' scheme for restricting innovation – hanging those whose proposals are rejected – should not blind us to its serious implications.[77] Mill thought that 'people who defend this mode of treating benefactors cannot be supposed to set much value on the benefit', but Swift does not regard reformers as benefactors and clearly favours the drastic stop to innovation that must follow. His benefactors are the primitive lawgivers like Solon and Lycurgus and he reserves his praise for those who stick to the original command, preserving as best they can the father's coat. He extols the early Christians for meeting heresy with violence, thus preventing the corruption of true religion.[79] His respectful references to Lycurgus become significant when we recall that Sparta was admired by the Greeks for reputedly maintaining intact over an unusually long period a system established by this inspired lawgiver; Swift admires him as the man who came closest to achieving a human equivalent of the static civilization of Houyhnhnmland.[80] Fear of change emerges in linguistic terms in his proposal for fixing our language for ever where he argues, as if exhausting the available options, that stable imperfection is preferable to continual, disastrous change – Martin's rebuke to his crazy brother.[81] Similarly, in politics and religion he insists that dissenters and freethinkers must be resisted all along the line, with no outpost too negligible to be surrendered; every ditch is a last ditch, nothing is negotiable since any concession, human nature being what it is, simply provokes more exorbitant demands, as Ireland in her role of Injured Lady so ruefully discovers.[82]

The ruined mill is history in microcosm, a parabolic demonstration of what must happen when corrupt, hare-brained meddlers tinker with the social structure; the statesman's task should be conservation, patching up defects, 'else time alone will bring all to ruin; how much more the common accidents of storm and rain?'[83] For, meddlers apart, the mill is fighting a losing battle with time itself. Unlike Bacon, for whom time is man's ally in the struggle to subdue nature – *veritas temporis filia* – Swift, like Shakespeare in the *Sonnets*, sees it as a force inimical to man: *damnosa quid non imminuit dies*. Time itself is the culprit, history the enemy. So the essential problem for Swift comes down to this: how can man evade the deterioration implicit in time, how escape from history? We have seen his contemptuous rejection of the doctrine of historical progress, his championship of the ancients because he views history as a losing struggle to preserve the values achieved by antiquity, his longing for stability because he fears a new, engulfing barbarism – the invasions of the Goths were not just historical facts but moral symbols and future warnings.[84] If it is true that there are two chief modes of historical perception, two opposed archetypal shapes of history, the circle and the straight line, man lashed like Ixion to the perpetually revolving wheel or dreaming with Jacob of the ladder that leads to heaven, and that almost everyone betrays a preference for one of these opposing conceptions, then we must interpret Swift's outlook in terms of the pessimistic wheel rather than the optimistic ladder.[85] The Houyhnhnms are intelligible only in the light of Swift's desire to escape from history into a realm of stability and permanence, to stop the clock of history and with it the inevitable slide from simplicity to corruption.

Simplicity prevails throughout Houyhnhnm society, in diet, manners, education, ethics, language, and what Gulliver discovers among them is how easily nature is satisfied. If a decadent palate at first finds milk and oats very insipid, the benefit is never an hour's sickness while on the island; the contrast is with the self-inflicted diseases of refined society caused by gluttony and intemperance. Swift's primitivism extends beyond mere culinary matters to all aspects of human behaviour: the simple, health-giving diet belongs to the state of nature, the rich, unnatural food to artificial society. The implication is that in other matters, as well as diet, a perverted search for novelty, excitement, 'experience', will just as surely end in disease and disorder. The condemnation of European diet is moral as well as medical – disease, the result of repletion, and gluttony, the sin so prominent in the Fall, go together.

In manners the Houyhnhnms are polite but not foppish, preserving 'decency and civility in the highest degree but . . . altogether ignorant of ceremony' – ceremony being for Swift the point where manners turn rotten, like the elegant beau's disgusting body under the fashionable clothes.[86] They have no books or literature, and no disputes since their reason is uncontaminated by prejudice – as Hobbes puts it, men do not massacre each other for the truths of mathematics as they do for those of religion; their language is simple, with nothing in their conversation but what is useful, expressed in the fewest, most significant words; they have no words for lying or for anything evil save what they borrow from Yahoo defects – and we are to see this linguistic purity as the index of a moral one. Their bewilderment at human depravity is for Swift not culpable ignorance but laudable innocence; when, horror-stricken, they close their ears to the doings of men lest the mere telling contaminate, we are not meant to censure their ostrich attitude but admire their strategy of moral survival based on withdrawal. That this strategy is no longer admired today is beside the point; the horses are no more peccant for wishing to stay undefiled than is the Giant King when he commands Gulliver on pain of death never to mention gunpowder again. We may no longer approve of this idea of forbidden knowledge but Swift is not obliged to agree with us.

Their economics is as simple as their ethics: they neither manufacture nor trade but practise an agrarian subsistence economy. They have no money and none of the glaring social inequalities of England where 'the bulk of our people' toil miserably to maintain a few rich men in criminal ostentation. When we contrast what it costs to clothe Gulliver and his wife as they 'ought' to be – the ambiguity is deliberately disconcerting – with how 'the bulk of our people' live, we recognize an eighteenth-century adumbration of the private opulence, public squalor thesis.[87] In the Yahoo lust for the shining stones we are invited to denounce as a perversion what Tawney calls the supreme appetite of modern western man.[88] When Gulliver insists how easily nature is satisfied and how few men's real wants are, he condemns the whole acquisitive ethos of capitalism. When his master observes that men have been very successful in multiplying their original wants and in inventing new ones, he attacks our consumer-society as unnatural.[89] Predictably, in view of Swift's criticism of the compass as abetting Yahoo wickedness, the Houyhnhnms are not a trading nation. Houyhnhnmland, where Gulliver learns to do without, to despise things once craved as indispensable, is an ad-man's nightmare; it will never boast a Madison Avenue.

Everywhere Houyhnhnm simplicity confronts European corruption. Orwell saw in them proof that Swift's aim is a static, incurious civilization, but it is fairer to see them as representing for Swift a holiday from history, an escape from the brutal wheel to which man is inexorably lashed. In contracting out of history they evade deterioration. Without letters and relying solely upon tradition for their knowledge, they nevertheless manage perfectly, for, 'there happening few events of any moment among a people so well united, naturally disposed to every virtue, wholly governed by reason, and cut off from commerce with other nations, the historical part is easily preserved without burthening their memories'.[90] This is entirely credible since nothing really happens in Houyhnhnmland besides the biological business of living until the time comes to retire to one's first mother, and by shielding them from the contagion of commerce Swift clearly means to keep it that way. If we attack this life as boring, Swift implies that this is because we prefer corruption to simplicity, novelty to stability, excitement to serenity, sensation to thought, evil to good, exotic dishes to wholesome food: *'plutôt la barbarie que l'ennui'* is precisely the rationalization a contemptuous Swift expects from sophisticated Yahoos.

But our revulsion from Houyhnhnm society is perhaps less indicative of our innate depravity than of our commitment to a conception of history radically different from Swift's.[91] Ever since Augustine attacked the pagan despair of Polybian circularity, the West has made a huge emotional investment in a mode of historical perception at once linear and progressive: history as moving towards an appointed consummation – the City of God, the Rule of the Saints, the heavenly city of the eighteenth-century philosophers, the classless society. What all these mutations of the pursuit of the millenium have in common is a view of history as significant, novelty-creating and always variant. Against this stands the second great mode of historical perception, history as a cycle, eternal recurrence, sheer recapitulation. Augustine denounced this view, advanced by Polybius as a Stoic bulwark against a meaningless existence, as proof of the Psalm, *'in circuitu impii ambulant'*; the Incarnation, climax of God's covenant with his pilgrim people, has broken the circle and converted history into a straight line. But shortly after God died in the nineteenth century, the belief in progress took to its bed – not altogether surprising when one recalls their close historical connection, how easy it was to pass from the Augustinian *procursus* via Bishop Otto's *progressus* to the nineteenth-century idea of progress.

The revival of cyclic theory at this historical moment is the index of a growing pessimism, a sign that history as meaningful progression was in retreat before the 'tale told by an idiot' view. Yet linear orthodoxy must deny this heresy of meaningless repetition. The agonized demand at the end of Owen's 'Futility' is not just for an explanation of this single death but of the whole human experiment. The greatest blasphemy against linear orthodoxy is to declare with Chekhov's Tuzenbach, when asked the purpose of life, that it has no more meaning than a fall of snow. Against this Masha insists that life must have a significance beyond the triviality of daily existence, that it can only be redeemed by the goal towards which history is moving, otherwise 'nothing matters . . . everything's just wild grass.'⁹² Not pain but meaninglessness is what is finally unbearable, and Faulkner's heroine destroys herself rather than endure the purposelessness of a life where we 'eat and evacuate and sleep warm so that we can get up and eat and evacuate in order to sleep warm again'.⁹³ What we dread above all is the horror of mere repetition, imbecile circularity, and the failure of 'collectivist' solutions to the problem (Christianity, Marxism) has led to the rise of 'private' solutions – mysticism, drugs, all the various ways of cultivating the Inner Life – but in every case the impetus is the anguished refusal to let Tuesday be the same as Monday. Western society is today polarised between two groups: the 'Old Believers' who still affirm some form of progress and the sensation-mongers, trying to stave off boredom by a frenzied hunt after experience. Naturally neither group finds much to admire in Houyhnhnm society where the *status quo*, with its creator's obvious approval, is guaranteed for ever.

Orwell's dislike of the Houyhnhnms is really a rejection of uneventful repetition. To his criticism that the horses have no notion that life here and now could be worth living, it is enough to answer that for Gulliver and the horses everyday life in Houyhnhnmland is the *only* life worth living – simple, decent, uneventful, distractionless, 'boring', just as the mass of men since history began have, viewed from the outside, led boring, uneventful lives. Orwell is entitled to attack this as boring but not to assume that the horses are bored. Boredom may after all be as much a judgement on the person bored as on the cause of boredom – Mary Crawford is bored where Fanny Price isn't, Emma Bovary is driven crazy by what most wives accept as normal, Nathanael West's 'cheated' are so tired of affluence that they hang about airports praying for disasters to break the monotony, Count Pococurante finds everything a drag – and within the *Travels* boredom is so uncomfortably akin to Yahoo spleen that one might on that account alone be deterred from confessing it. But when Orwell attacks the horses for having no notion that life could be made worth living by sacrificing the present for some future good, he gives the game away. The chief offence of Houyhnhnm society is its contented immersion in the present; Houyhnhnmland is a dreary place because it has no doctrine of progress: 'The Houyhnhnms, creatures without a history, continue for generation after generation to live prudently, maintaining their population at exactly the same level, avoiding all passion, suffering from no diseases, meeting death indifferently, training up their young in the same principles – and all for what? In order that the same process may continue indefinitely'.[94] It is Faulkner's Charlotte Rittenmeyer all over again; Orwell clearly regards Houyhnhnm life as a total waste of time. The charge against the horses is that levelled by Goncharov against the slothful, complacent Oblomovkans: 'they did not think life existed so that man should constantly strive for some barely apprehended aims'.[95] The Socialist Orwell, like the Christian Eliot, sees a life of mere repetition as an arid wasteland of birth, copulation and death; they simply disagree about the nature of the goal which redeems routine existence from otherwise unavoidable banality. The loss of progress, as of God, leads to the same blank sterility.

But the Houyhnhnms lack that strain of apocalyptic millenarianism that hungers after some great upheaval, new birth or second coming, that will transform everyday life, and that loathing for the present that motivates the revolutionary, whether he looks back to Eden or forward to Utopia. They have never left Eden, have achieved Utopia. They are guilty of the heinous sin of being happy in the present, are ignorant of that discontent which, says Wilde, is the first step in the progress of a man or a nation.[96] All that is needed for a decent, happy life they already possess; what we think they lack is what Swift thinks any truly rational creature would gladly reject. They have no ambition but in heaven ambition is satanic. If we dislike their lack of curiosity, they would be appalled at our mania for sensation, our modern delinquents murdering 'just for a giggle', killing time by killing others. If 'nothing' happens in Houyhnhnmland – no wars, crimes, disasters, 'everything there promises a calm, long life, till the hair turns white with age and death comes unawares like sleep'[97] – this is because no news is good news; newsmen, with a vested interest in disaster, will naturally prefer Vietnam.

Goncharov regards the Oblomovkan prayer thanking God that nothing happened today and asking Him to let nothing happen tomorrow as a sign of sloth, shamefully quietist; Swift, in a world sinking daily into corruption, where the most we can hope is to keep vice at a stand, may think otherwise. If the Houyhnhnms have no history, it is not so clear that Ulster is better off; presumably there are many in the Six Counties for whom the dullness of Houyhnhnm 'history' is no drawback, who might enviously echo Montesquieu's remark, 'happy the people whose annals are tiresome'. The Lilliputians, with their long catalogue of massacre, have plenty of history as defined by Voltaire – *un ramas de crimes, de folies, et de malheurs* – yet even a modern European might prefer Houyhnhnmland to Lilliput, and for Swift we all live in Lilliput.

One of the most malicious Chinese curses is 'may you live in interesting times'. The horses do not live in interesting times; they have no words for power, government, war, law, punishment – and history stripped of these concepts is a pretty blank page. They never dispute and have only one debate, whether or not to exterminate the Yahoos; that they will decide this without civil bloodshed is not necessarily to their discredit. If they do not believe in sacrificing the present generation to future progress, are they so clearly inferior to the pioneers of Five Year Plans, gas chambers and Ukraine famines? And if we damn them for eschewing social revolution in favour of everyday domesticity, do we not implicitly condemn the mass of ordinary men since time immemorial? Even those who insist that all progress comes via the heretic and revolutionary will admit that the average man is neither, that he worries less about social renovation than about his own personal concerns, often to the furious despair of the militant reformer outraged by such blind irresponsibility. There is, paradoxically, a tinge of this antidemocratic contempt in Orwell himself (despite his sympathy at other times with the minutiae of everyday life) when he rages at the common man for caring more about Manchester United than the fall of Spain, or at the common woman for rioting over a shortage of saucepans while indifferent to the political abominations of Big Brother.[98] The frustration of the militant moralist at the apathetic mass can so easily topple over into an élitist, embittered disdain, as the 'Modest Proposal' demonstrates. But the simple life of the Houyhnhnms, for Orwell a dereliction of social responsibility, is Swift's equivalent of the reign of the Saints or the classless society – their quiescence is analogous to that praised by St James in the Father, 'with whom there is no change, nor shadow of alteration', and to attack them for lacking an idea of progress is about as reasonable as faulting the beatific vision or the Marxist paradise for the same deficiency.

Apart from any specific values they embody, the horses really signify a triumph over history, values preserved because, in contrast to real society, time is divorced from deterioration. As individuals the horses grow old and die, but decay is restricted to a biological minimum; socially they exist in a timeless continuum outside history. It is appropriate that they have not invented the wheel, for they are going nowhere. Those who locate the highest value in continual adaptation to change will regard such an ideal as pusillanimous or perverted; Milton's refusal to praise 'a fugitive and cloister'd virtue' because it is really cowardice might be used against Houyhnhnm civilization. But underlying this is the optimistic belief that growth is, as Dewey says, a moral end in itself, or that change, though evil, can be overcome. Swift would have rejected the first as meaningless and the second as false.

Houyhnhnmland is an image of Utopia created by a man too tough-minded to believe that Utopia is feasible. Swift admires Houyhnhnm virtues but knows how unattainable they are; the wish is never allowed to become the fact, the error of Jack and all others who think to restore by fiat the irrecoverable purity of ancient Christianity. Despite Swift's praise of Temple, he finally sides with the Puritans in rejecting the strategy of dropping out. 'The way to the Celestial City lies just through this town, where this lusty Fair is kept; and he that will go to the City, and yet not go through this town must needs go out of the world.'99 The way to heaven is hard; it is the primrose path that leads to the everlasting bonfire. Bunyan, so unforgiving to the folly of looking for short cuts, would have scorned Houyhnhnmland as an attempt to bypass the Fair. Milton would have been equally scathing: 'to sequester out of this world into Atlantic and Utopian politics which never can be drawn into use, will not mend our condition'.100 The drop-out, monastic or otherwise, is guilty of moral evasion, and Houyhnhnmland another deplorable attempt to obtain the garland 'without dust and heat'.

But Swift, with his relentless realism, is equally aware of the impossibility of Utopia. It is Gulliver, not Swift, who hails the Struldbruggs as the great hope of foiling historical deterioration, and it is because the Struldbruggs, human like ourselves, could so easily become a flattering consolation to us that Swift ruthlessly blows Gulliver's dream skyhigh. There is to be no consolation, far less flattery, in the *Travels*. Precisely because we cannot identify with the horses, and, far from achieving a vicarious elation in their success, are offended by it, Swift delights in making these alien creatures the perfection of nature. He flaunts their triumph before us like a tricolour in the Shankill Road; they are an insulting impossibility, meant to provoke in us envy and chagrin, not emulation.101 Swift knows that the lusty Fair cannot be circumvented; the difference between him and the Puritans is that they optimistically welcome

struggle: 'that which purifies us is trial, and trial is by what is contrary'. They despise those who want the prize without the contest not
only because they believe in the psychological necessity of struggle –
Eden is wasted on the prelapsarian – but also because they believe
they cannot lose with God in their corner.

Swift's vision of struggle and its end is very different – 'dying like
a poisoned rat in a hole'[102] – and his pessimism makes dropping-out
more attractive, if only as a temporary dream, though he never
abandons himself to it. Despite his frequent adoption of the language
of the drop-out – his refusal to go on prescribing a dose for the dead,
his assertion that he had long since given up all hopes of Church or
Christianity, his unwillingness to put his shoulder to a falling wall or
stay in a storm-tossed ship when he could no longer do service in it,
his claim to have long ago forsworn politics or to have been cured of
Irish politics by despair[103] – Swift is always a fighter even when there
is no hope of victory; he always despairs, never surrenders. He may
approve the strategy of withdrawal in others, may even pretend to
be Temple, but the pose conflicts with his partisan, combative nature:
'no cloyster is retired enough to keep politicks out, and I will own
they raise my passions whenever they come in my way'.[104] Temple's
imperturbable nature allowed him to garden in peace while corruption
flourished, but for Swift human evils 'require more of the Stoick than
I am master of to support it';[105] he could never stop fretting over the
misdeeds of the ungodly.

He lacked the philosophic calm of Pope, the happy ability of
Bolingbroke to grieve less at what he could not mend[106] – when we
read Pope's description of Bolingbroke as 'a man driven by a violent
wind, from the sea into a calm harbour',[107] the contrast with Swift
strikes us forcibly; Dublin was no calm harbour for Swift. The only
calm harbour he ever found was an imaginary one, the island where
James Welch drove Lemuel Gulliver ashore, for if Houyhnhnmland
is an attempt to bypass the Fair, it is so only in imagination. It shows
us Swift as drop-out, but, unlike Temple or the hermits of the Thebaid
or the hippies today, Swift took his holiday from history in an
imaginary sojourn among the impossible, rational horses, but never
fooled himself that such a solution was 'on'; Gulliver is forced to
leave Houyhnhnmland because Swift knows it is impossible to stay.
This is why Gulliver is an absurd, partly discredited figure at the
end of the book: not because he sees men as Yahoos and Europe as
diseased, for that is what the book demonstrates; not because he

admires the Houyhnhnms, for Swift too admires them; not his
diagnosis, for in this he agrees with the Giant King, the Houyhnhnm
Master and Swift himself, but his proposed cure for the disease is
what distances him from Swift and makes him ridiculous; for, in
flouting Burke's injunction to prefer nature to speculation, he believes
that history can be overcome and Utopia realised.

FIVE

THE DEAF ADDER

Inured to people who would not listen, Swift might have anticipated the critics' determination to follow the Irish in declining to heed what he says. Self-division was for him the salient characteristic of human nature – 'how inconsistent is man with himself'[1] – and he remarked the bundle of contradictions that would appear if a man should register all his opinions upon love, politics, religion, learning and the like.[2] The confirmatory evidence was within as well as around him and here above all he was unlikely to commit the blunder which he imputed to Sheridan of thinking himself an exception to all mankind. Yet the bane of Swift criticism, common to detractors and apologists alike, is a resolve to invest him with this never-possessed, explicitly repudiated consistency. Most misconceptions spring from the dogma of a unified Swift, an integrated thinker with one immutable set of beliefs shaping his work. To this end contradictions are doggedly juggled into agreement, a procedure that, with Swift, has at least the merit of keeping one busy. For Thackeray the last book of the *Travels* is so perverted that a sane man, let alone a Christian, could not have written it.[3] Yet the author was an Anglican priest who also wrote sermons and prayers. Thackeray concluded that the minister must be a fake, the religion a sham. Swift is either a careerist hunting a bishopric or a Machiavellian who prizes religion as social bulwark; off the record, he might have justified his vocation by echoing Buffon and Voltaire – *il faut un religion au peuple*, for religion is necessary even if untrue and the God who does not exist has to be invented.

The real Swift is, for Thackeray, an irreligious madman and the imposter is betrayed as the cloven hoof peeps under the hypocritical cassock in the satires, when, for example, the dogma of the resurrection is derided; 'the learned among them confess the absurdity of this doctrine; but the practice still continues, in compliance to the vulgar'.[4] He is ostensibly ridiculing the Lilliputian custom of burying the dead feet uppermost, so that, when the earth revolves at the last day, they will be ready for instant ascension, but the perspicacious reader knows that the real target is the Christian hope of rising again and easily detects the nonchalant ventriloquism – Gulliver's lips move but Swift is talking. So Thackeray denounces the 'Thoughts on Religion' as a set of excuses for concealing disbelief and combs Swift's life for confirmations of irreligion, ignoring whatever tells against this. The prayers for Stella are disregarded, the advice to the deplorably unsuitable Gay to take holy orders is cited as proof of the donor's own infidelity, that he had 'bent his pride so far down as to put his apostasy out to hire' and 'bound himself to a life-long hypocrisy'.[5] It is easy to make fun of such melodramatic extravagance, more pertinent to note that it follows naturally from a resolve to conflate Anglican divine and author of 'A Voyage to the Houyhnhnms' into one nicely manageable, easily classified, totally consistent figure.

Swift's defenders, in their anxiety to refute charges of hypocrisy and misanthropy, employ the same method to reach an opposite conclusion. If Swift was a sincere Christian, as the sermons and prayers unarguably demonstrate, then the satire cannot exhibit the sacrilegious despair detected by the Victorians. They had mistaken for Schopenhauerian pessimism what was really the robust apologetic of a bellicose Anglican and had naturally gone astray, as all must who read the satires and neglect the sermons.[6] Since Swift wrote sermons defending Christianity, he must have written satires to the same end; a Christian who is a satirist must be a Christian satirist, all the more so when he is a dean.[7] Failure to see this results in interpretations of the satire that contradict views expressed by Swift elsewhere and, therefore, it is implied, wrong, since Swift, whether in satire, sermon, tract or letter, has only one voice and only one message.[8] Not till we unite dean and satirist, so disastrously sundered by Thackeray, and read the satires as Anglican sermons, differing only in genius and form, will we truly understand them. For there is only one Swift and he is, literary gift apart, an orthodox parish priest.

Inclusion of the sermons as essential propaedeutica is a give-away once we reflect what odd sermons they would be *not* to uphold Christianity. To insist on them as indispensable guide, to search there for the satire's meaning, is really to deny the need for a guide at all, to have already predetermined the meaning, for certain *a priori* assumptions are being made as to the kind of work the satire must be. A Christian interpretation is smuggled through the back door and then triumphantly discovered, with the author's vocation certifying the critic's exegesis, while over the front door hangs the intimidating sign warning no non-Christian reading to apply. Criticism surrenders to biography and biography is a drill-sergeant hectoring the text, like a new recruit, into unquestioning obedience. The old fallacy of a necessarily integrated Swift is now used to defend him. Where Thackeray interprets the life by the vicious work, the modern apologists baptise the work on the strength of the exemplary life, but each exhibits the same insistence that life and work, all contradictions bulldozed aside, must form a single, consistent whole. One partial estimate replaces another, repeating its predecessor's blunder in claiming to be the whole truth.

It is gratifying to see the Thackeray school hoist with their own petard, but showing Swift as sincere Christian in itself neither guarantees understanding of the satire nor exhausts discussion of its provenance. The assumption that the vocation explains the work is as critically inadmissable as the assumption that the work disproves the vocation. There is no necessary identification between them and we must resist scanning the *Travels* with Christian spectacles for the evidence we are sure to find. *Compelle intrare*, the words so often used to justify the forcible conversion of heathen and heretic, are disconcertingly applicable to attempts at impressing Swift as Christian propagandist, complimentary neither to the satires, which will survive without a *nihil obstat*, nor to the Church, which will survive without the *Travels*. Look at the frantically ingenious attempts to frog-march the Struldbruggs into the Christian camp, the contortions undergone to set the episode safely within a sure doctrinal framework, the anxious juggling of an attack upon the folly of believing life is good into a respectably orthodox rebuke to blasphemers seeking earthly immortality – almost as if such critics secretly agree with Thackeray that anything more radical would discredit Swift's priesthood and expose him as time-server. And so they scrutinize the satires with an ecclesiastical blue pencil, protecting Swift from himself, censoring everything to suit his official status, taming every passage to the requirements of an Anglican pulpit, exhibiting, in flat defiance of his own warning, a resolve to fabricate a Swift forever congruous with himself, his beliefs and attitudes all of a piece.

The search for unity is ironical in one who categorized man as the self-contradictory animal and provided in his own person an outstanding example of the genus. Liberty-loving authoritarian, rationalist despairing of reason, despiser and champion of the Irish, a Christian provoked to arraign belief in God's love as a delusion of pride, a moralist who combined acceptance of psychological egoism with reverence for disinterested virtue, violent critic of party politics and ablest Tory propagandist of his day, upholding majority rights one moment ('we are the majority and we are in possession') and deriding them the next ('that happy majority, which I am confident is always in the right') – was ever writer less amenable to this attempt at unification? How reconcile his straight defence of hypocrisy in the *Project* with his aversion to it in his own life, an aversion so intense that he preferred to be calumniated as a ribald priest than risk identification with Tartuffe?

Doublethink glares through his attitude to censorship, his demands that Tindal be silenced and anti-Tory pamphleteers punished, coupled with outraged protests when Walpole cracked down on the liberty of the press. What is consistent in denouncing as seditious malcontents those who oppose one government's Treaty of Utrecht while inciting resistance to another government's Wood's Halfpence? Bolgolam's argument justifying Gulliver's execution without the formal proofs required by law is clearly held up for condemnation. He accuses Gulliver of being a secret Big-Endian and, as treason begins in the heart, a traitor who should be eliminated before he can do harm, in flat defiance of the Giant King who believes thoughts are no subjects, declines to make windows into men's souls and only acts when poisons are distributed in public. Yet when Tindal complains at too much emphasis laid upon 'merely speculative points . . . and other indifferent things', Swift retorts that men's practice proceeds from their speculations; and when Burnet denounces the execution of men who merely talked of assassinating Charles II, Swift curtly reminds him, Bolgolam-fashion, that all plots begin with talk. His case against dissenters is that they are potential if not actual rebels, committed in logic to the Church's overthrow, and that they must mean domination even when they deceive themselves that their plea is merely for equality. Similarly, freethinkers are dangerous because correct belief is crucial; those who stop believing in hell will surely drink, whore and defy the parson without fear of reprisal, for to think wrongly is to act wrongly – isn't this why free-thinking is so attractive in the first place? No atheist can be trusted; Swift knows this on *a priori* grounds, with no need for empirical evidence or individual investigation.

No single formula will accommodate all these contradictions, yet Swift was no hypocrite – he did not see the inconsistencies, for his judgements were provisional and piecemeal, not the logical formulations of a systematic philosophy. He is an artist, not a philosopher, and there is no single philosophic command that will marshal his various insights into parade-ground order. Nobody, for example, will dispute the Swift who prescribes prudential acquiescence to tradition and upholds the *status quo* against prying innovators. He detested those who spurn inherited wisdom to seek new truths in morals and religion – they are literally, what Mill ironically calls them, dissentients afflicted with the malady of thought, and society cannot survive when every man is encouraged to be his own carver. Swift's enemy is the challenger of consensus. Martin sensibly trusts to common forms, wrapped up in winter, open-necked in summer, unlike crazy Jack, manic for novelty and resolved, at whatever cost, to be original.[9] That Swift endorsed the Martin attitude is incontestable, yet it would be unsafe to adopt this as an infallible clue through the mazes of the 'Digression on Madness'. If Martin is our guide here, as he certainly is at other moments, then Swift must be cautioning us not to despise the evidence of the senses, nor pride ourselves on peering into the depths, but to settle instead for commonsense and prudential limitation. Swift was a reasonable man with a healthy contempt for unproductive metaphysics and hubristic enquiry beyond our station; the sensible man, leaving all this to moonstruck, neurotic Laputans, asked questions that he could reasonably hope to answer, the counterpart in epistemology of the practical agronomist who makes two blades of grass grow where only one used to be. So we should take things as they are, leave well alone, commendably preferring attractive exteriors to revolting interiors; Epicurus truly *is* the wise man when he creams off nature and leaves meddling philosophers to lap up the disgusting dregs.

But if prudential acquiescence is the permanent leader of Swift's values, how are we to read 'A Voyage to the Houyhnhnms' or the Strephon poems? Would it have been better had Gulliver remained the immoral jingoist elated at his country's killing-capacity or kept the traditional views of lawyers and colonizers inculcated by his education and shared by all of his sensible compatriots? He would doubtless have been happier – a prudent man would soon have switched off Radio Houyhnhnm – just as Strephon would have been happier had he gone on believing that every silk petticoat contains an angel;[10] for, distressing truth apart, where is the bonus in poking around untended bedrooms? But is 'A Voyage to the Houyhnhnms' a lament for the loss of English brainwashing, is Swift seriously prescribing prudence, a dose of jingoistic or romantic laudanum to kill the edge of the painful truth, and is his satire really a defence of the *status quo*, a literary expression of the *quieta non movere* policy of his despised enemy? Swift as radical questioner seems, at least as satirist, preferable to a Swift modelled on Walpole's inertia. If he feared the depths and recommended acceptance, he feared just as much the sublime and refined point of felicity, called the possession of being well-deceived – prudential or not, he had no wish to be taken in.

There is no gainsaying self-division in Swift or blinking the contradictions he warns us to expect. As preacher he exhorts us to respect superiors, as satirist shatters the authority sanctified elsewhere. The adversary of nonconformity is the satirist who celebrates social deviance: Lord Munodi is statistically a madman, the Giant King a nonpareil among rulers, each created in the image of Milton's Abdiel – 'among the faithless, faithful only he'. Sometimes Swift denounces the nonconformist as social menace, sometimes hails him as the one righteous person without whom no city can stand; sometimes traditional acquiescence means preserving the father's coat, sometimes it is shameful participation in communal neurosis; sometimes he wants people to obey authority, sometimes he doesn't. There is no magic shortcut, no infallible rule or ubiquitous master-interpretation that guarantees Swift's meaning in advance and makes inquiry redundant; because Swift often defends Christianity or authority or prudence, doesn't mean he always does so.

This is the more plausible in the light of his own statement that as clergyman he was constrained by certain obligations and therefore, to that extent, wrote in fetters, even if self-imposed. He was aware that reason might undermine faith but insisted that doubts arising from reason were not culpable, provided they were concealed and not allowed to influence conduct. On judgement day God will punish the wise for their want of morals and the ignorant for their want of faith, since both lapses are inexcusable, but will go easy on vice in the ignorant and scruples in the wise, since these are partly unavoidable.[11] But disbelief must always be hidden; the sceptic is a moral leper who spares his healthy compatriots by silence, by posing as a sound man. Swift flays the deliberate carriers of contagion, 'not content to possess their own infidelity in silence, without communicating it to the disturbance of mankind'[12] – a similar distinction to that which his hero, Thomas More, had made between the heretic and the contumelious heretic, and to that which the Giant King makes between those who keep poisons locked up and those who distribute them in public.

A doubting Swift would never have sought recruits, especially since providence had appointed him clergyman to defend a post and convert as many enemies as possible.[13] Nowhere, however, does he authorize us to believe that providence had also appointed him satirist for an identical duty. 'Positiveness is a good quality for preachers and orators'[14] – for how will they convince others without first convincing themselves? – but we don't know if the same positiveness is present in satire and sermon. On *a priori* grounds plus his own testimony, it is just as credible that the satires afforded relief from the admitted strain of his priesthood, providing a moral holiday from the obligatory positiveness of the preacher, despite the doubts that beset him with the rest of the wise. Perhaps he wrote as satirist simply to lash pride and self-love, with a gratifying freedom to express occasionally what the dean might have been constrained to censor.

Certainly clergyman and satirist approach the topic of habit from different directions. Swift's fascination with the power of habit and the difficulties of re-entry is plain to every reader of the *Travels*. Gulliver's comic miscalculations on his return from Brobdingnag exhibit the great force of habit and prejudice: live long enough with giants and you unconsciously adopt their standards. The Scythian Longheads owe their existence to the midwives' custom of so binding their infants' heads that they shoot upwards rather than outwards. Gradually, long heads become an inherited characteristic, without outside assistance, and 'thus did custom, from being a second nature, proceed to be a first'.[15] The joke has its serious implications, indicating an aspect of human nature exploitable by legislators and preachers: 'there is many an operation which in its original was purely an artifice, but through a long succession of ages has grown to be natural'.

Swift as preacher and would-be legislator (his most prominent appearance in this role is in the *Project* aimed at reforming morals and religion) attempted seriously to apply the lessons of habituation that find comic expression in the satires. The *Project* leans partly on the hope that mere external practice of Christianity will in time produce genuine devotion, clockwork imperceptibly becoming piety, Pascal's atheist who consents to holy water ending up a believer. Where Milton shrinks from religious *mneme*, practice by repetition leading to fading of consciousness, so that a learned act becomes automatic and living faith nods into ritual – for Milton unthinking orthodoxy is heresy – Pascal and the Swift of the *Project* anticipate instead that a mechanical, even bogus, routine will suddenly be raised to a higher cleave of being, automatism become consciousness. Swift as satirist is, by contrast, much closer to Milton in his attempt to demoralise habit, intimidate routine and break the hold of unreflective acquiescence, his unremitting campaign against the various modes of brainwashing whereby society conditions us to accept as norms or even ideals what the satirist exposes as foolish or wicked. Habit is no longer an ally but the prime target. These two facets of Swift are best highlighted by contrasting the conflicting attitudes to human nature in his work, from the optimistic attempt to ground a social ethic on Hobbesian psychology to the final despair in face of man's invincible irrationalism.

The *Project* is the most Hobbesian of Swift's writings, but affinities with the *Leviathan* view of man are manifest throughout his work. There was much in the Hobbesian analysis that might easily be adapted to the demands of Augustinian Christianity. *Leviathan* secularises the myth of Fall and Redemption, even to duplicating the *felix culpa*; because man knows himself, he fears the same greedy aggression in others, and fear produces foresight, the impulse to take precautions, and reason, which is a strategy for survival. The emergency is both caused and resolved by selfishness and it is the enlightened brand of selfishness that leads man to establish Leviathan and so save himself from the disastrous consequences of blind self-gratification. Leviathan is the political counterpart of Christ, the redeemer hauling man out of the pit he himself dug, although Hobbes's saviour dispenses with a change of heart in the beneficiary; even a nation of devils can create a just society provided they have sense and are intelligently selfish. Helvetius, taking the baton from Hobbes in the eighteenth century, sees no difficulty in legislating men into paradise: 'It is of little consequence that men be vicious; it is enough that they be intelligent . . . Laws will do all'.[16] Saints and supermen are unnecessary if only we construct a society where it pays to be honest, for only idiots pursue unremunerative evil. Selfishness is the basic reality and 'no man obeys them who they think have no power to help or hurt them'. Reward what you would encourage, punish what you would eradicate, and the thing is as good as done.

Hobbes's realistic rejection of highflown altruism or love of virtue for its own sake, when calculating man's chances of survival, chimes admirably with Swift's own outlook – Swift, who claimed that a man acquainted with his own heart already knew more evil of himself than any outsider could, was unlikely to be shocked by anything in *Leviathan*.[17] His defence of La Rochefoucauld as a teller of unpleasant truths might just as easily have been extended to Hobbes.[18] His poem anticipating his death springs from a fusion of La Rochefoucauld and Hobbes, from the former's observation that *'nous avons tous assez de force pour supporter les maux d'autrui'*, especially when these are our closest friends, from the latter's assertion that for so morally solipsistic a creature as man, Aristotle's *philanthropia* is impossible, that pity for another is really self-pity, fear of a similar calamity befalling oneself – only those as old as the invalid or with similar symptoms can sympathise.[19]

Swift's jokes about egoism are a ritual for exorcizing the Hobbesian demon he believed in and feared. He pretends puzzlement when a man for whom he can do no favours treats him with civility; if his friends have not sensibly forsaken him in Dublin, it must be because they enjoy free wine.[20] Friendship is a fiction, every man is for sale, and all men, Dissenters included, are insatiably selfish, hence the folly of concessions to avid power-seekers. It is silly to blame Dissenters but sillier still not to see what they want. Gulliver spares Lilliputian hooligans so that the Emperor will spare him, but when he is released, it is only because he is needed to destroy an enemy invasion. He intercedes for the delinquent Brobdingnagian boy because he doesn't want an unforgiving enemy, especially since the farmer is unlikely to exile his son as the Queen does the malicious dwarf. Every decision is made with an eye to the main chance. The King of Laputa pretends that the gentle descent of the island upon recalcitrant subjects is an act of mercy when he is really terrified of damaging its bottom. Swift, who delights in exposing shams and who derides, through the Giant King, the fantasy that men seek public office from sheer altruism and love of the public, must have experienced in reading Hobbes that sense of *terra firma* enjoyed by Gulliver after landing in Balnibarbi.

Human selfishness is the bedrock fact upon which any viable political or religious system must build. What the *Project* reveals is less a readiness to use *any* means than a conviction that this is the *only* means to improve public morals. 'Pure' virtue is either a chimera or else the monopoly of a tiny group of moral supermen, the heroes of Glubdubbdrib, a sextumvirate to which all ages have failed to add a seventh, but in any case totally irrelevant to ordinary humanity. It is the enlightened selfishness of Christianity that constitutes its superiority as a moral system to the great pagan philosophies. All men pursue self-interest but for some this means pleasing themselves, while some enjoy pleasing others: 'This makes the great distinction between virtue and vice. Religion is the best motive of all actions; yet religion is allowed to be the highest instance of self-love'.[21] Archbishop Marsh is as mad for study as a usurer for gold or a lecher for women, except that *his* passion is morally innocent and socially useful.[22] Highwaymen and surgeons alike seek their personal advantage, but the first harm, while the second help, society in the process, and Swift invites us to make a similar distinction between the equally selfish Whigs and Tories.[23]

So he strives to break the morbid obsession with motive, refusing, like the Giant King, to burrow into men's souls so long as their behaviour is decent. What does it matter if men are good simply because they hope for heaven? Isn't the sole motive for running a race to win a prize and wasn't the crippling defect of pre-Christian philosophy precisely this failure to guarantee an infallible reward for virtue and infallible retribution for vice? 'Human nature is so constituted that we can never pursue anything heartily but upon hopes of a reward.'[24] Bunyan's rejection of a prudential morality – 'it was my duty to stand to his Word, whether he would ever look upon me or no, or save at the last', his resolve 'never to deny my profession, though I have nothing at all for my pains'[25] – would have seemed moonshine to Swift as a programme for ordinary men, however nobly applicable to the sextumvirate (Thomas More apart, all pagans whose virtue owed nothing to calculations of eternal rewards). Swift, as would-be saviour of ordinary men, locates a feasible salvation in the analysis of human nature found in *Leviathan*.

He does his best to fit Hobbesian man into the Christian system, insisting that the early Christians, despite their apparently incredible heroism, were the same as ourselves.[26] If they loved one another so much, there was a perfectly natural reason: a tiny, threatened minority must, for survival purposes, develop such devotion, as men in a burning house unite to fight the flames. Common sense and self-

interest explain everything. Christ, commanding us to love our
neighbour as ourselves, does not expect a psychological miracle, for
he knows that charity begins at home, that another man is simply a
copy of oneself and that the original will naturally and rightly be
preferred to the copy.[27] Weber may mock Bunyan's hero for remembering wife and family only after saving himself, but the laws of
both nature and God, as interpreted by Swift, legitimize self-
preservation as the prime obligation. In other moods, Swift could
revere disinterested virtue, but he no more expected to find such a
phoenix as Thomas More than ten thousand pounds in his garden[28] –
and any system for the mass of men must be governed by reasonable
expectations. It is this modest realism that controls the ground-plan
of the *Project* for reforming morals and religion.

But how far is the *Project* a straightforward, logical scheme, based
on a foundation of sceptical common sense and genuinely concerned
that 'if abuses be not remedied, they will certainly increase', how far
a work of irony, with Swift posing as yet another of the tribe of
despised projectors, making his own absurd contribution to the
vagaries of 'this projecting age'?[29] The very use of the word, coupled
with the assurance that national regeneration is child's play, sound
ominous from one who normally scourges brash optimism. The Earl
of Berkeley, the dedicatee's husband, certainly took it as straight
pleading – he wanted a copy sent to the Queen, which he would
hardly have urged had he thought it a hoax[30] – but we today need not
feel bound by his possible incapacity for satire.

Is it satire? When Swift denies that it is a 'wild, speculative project'
and boosts it as the sole, effectual, easily implemented remedy, is he
being ironically subversive, telling us in his own playful way that
God and mammon are irreconcilable, that 'to make piety and virtue
. . . the fashion of the age' is to degrade the father's coat to the fri-
volities of *haute-couture*?[31] If we swallow the bizarre prospect of the
pious beau, do we simply join the list of Swift's satiric victims? Yet
there is surely much in the *Project* that Swift genuinely endorsed and
he opens, in typical style, with a dire diagnosis of the patient's condition as prelude to proposing not just a cure but the only cure.

This is not just clergyman's cliché; the times *are* wicked, a dying
religion lingers tenuously among the rural vulgar, and vicious people,
once secretive, now possess that heedless equanimity found in Lord
Wharton, 'beyond all sense of shame or fear of reproach'. Imperturbable iniquity enraged Swift and he campaigns to restore shame and

fear to their traditional place in the nation's moral economy. The sickness is endemic; blasphemy, promiscuity, venereal disease, alcoholism, gambling and fraud, the open sale of public offices, are rampant, with every social class cherishing its own favourite vices. National catastrophe is imminent, since 'the ruin of a state is generally preceded by an universal degeneracy of manners and contempt of religion' – *Diis te minorem, quod geris, imperas.*[32]

Proud of his realism, despising futile idealists who spin airy remedies from their imaginations, *tamquam in republica Platonis, et non in faece Romuli,*[33] Swift leaves useless recrimination to seek an effective solution. His answer is a moral takeover, Christianity acquiring a controlling interest in Vanity Fair by means of the royal patronage: if the Queen, like God, promotes the pious and sends the wicked away empty, morality and religion will become fashionable court virtues overnight. From court to London and thence to the whole nation, goodness will rage downwards like a contagion. Nor will standards fall when rascals are dismissed, since the average man is well able to run affairs and the real threat is not incapacity but dishonesty, as both prelapsarian Lilliputians and Giant King fully appreciate: 'I know no employment, for which piety disqualifies any man'.[34] Failure to implement Swift's *Project* leads straight to the shameful discovery of Gulliver's last voyage, that Yahoo institutions can only be administered by Yahoo men.

Swift does not mean to sacrifice efficiency to virtue or sack unregenerate experts for holy fools, since promotion at present is not by merit in any case. Why object to a system of controls in aid of morality while ignoring the operative system that encourages vice? What is so wrong in bribing men to be good when they are already being effectively bribed to be wicked? Society and the stage need reforming because each mirrors the other. Not till Charles II's reign did 'a criminal amour' succeed upon the stage; now modern comedies exalt vice and deride goodness, the libertine is hero and the theatre has fallen from an innocent and useful diversion to the scandal and reproach of the nation.[35] In theatre and court, art and life, the same corruption is rewarded, and the unacknowledged project already being pursued is the destruction of religion and morality. Adulterers, sodomites, prostitutes of both sexes, are, as Gulliver discovers in Glubbdubbdrib, the beneficiaries of the present system, of a public life based upon the values of Restoration comedy rather than those of the Last Judgement – Swift wants to reverse the trend and give goodness its turn. So he demands censors for stage and life alike; the Romans had them and they understood liberty at least as well as us. New laws are needed for vices like atheism, avarice and drunkenness, at present safe from legal chastisement, and inspectors should be sent on yearly circuits to keep watch on things; it all sounds surprisingly closer to Oliver's Commonwealth than one might expect in the scourge of the Puritans.

But, legislation aside, the royal patronage can work the oracle, for 'can it be imagined, that any man would openly offend against it, who had the least regard for his reputation or his fortune?' Virtue is easily yoked to worldly success, since 'there is no quality so contrary to any nature, which men cannot affect, and put on upon occasion, in order to serve an interest, or gratify a prevailing passion'.[36] Even if not abolished, vices will at least be disguised and driven under-ground, their proper habitat if they must exist at all. Swift has no objection, feasibility apart, to a nation of saints, but in a society that now honours profligacy, he will settle for external decorum, the out-ward profession of respectability. He knew, however much he might occasionally deplore, the importance of surfaces: 'a scoundrel in a gown, reeling home at midnight' is only one worthless renegade, but he discredits the whole clergy and reassures all drunkards.[37] Ap-pearances *are* important, as every sensible man knows, and so he readily admits the one objection to his scheme, its encouragement of hypocrisy.

What if it does? One genuine convert to nineteen hypocrites would be a welcome ratio and, at worst, hypocrisy is preferable to open vice; people who commence hypocrites may end up saints, dissembling themselves into piety as others do into love, the strain of pretence collapsing into authenticity. 'Our duty, by becoming our interest, will take root in our natures, and mix with the very genius of our people.'[38] Ideally, Swift favours a total offensive against immorality, including legislation to muzzle the freethinkers, but his practical sense defends him from 'airy imaginations of introducing new laws for the amendment of mankind', and he contents himself with the demand that existing laws and powers of patronage be mobilized to support Christian morals.

'Everybody will agree that the disease is manifest, as well as dangerous; that some remedy is necessary, and that none yet applied hath been effectual';[39] this is not the raving of a demented enthusiast but the temperate, measured appeal of a reasonable man initiating meaningful debate on a subject of acknowledged national concern. The tone anticipates the *Modest Proposal*, and the *Project* is similarly modest in expectation – seeking not the change of heart that Marx ridicules in utopians like Owen, but rather a change of system, not the miraculous conversion of rogues into saints, but the environmental discouragement of vice, outbidding the devil by ensuring that his valuation of man's soul is always below the market quotation for outward decency. Let God look to men's hearts, Swift will stick to their actions. Vice, like the poor, is always with us, but sensible societies and sensible men will limit immorality to its unavoidable minimum, while madmen and mad societies cosset the evils that destroy them. Like the Modest Proposer, Swift confirms his own solution by denying any real alternative: 'all other projects to this great end have proved hitherto ineffectual'.[40] Something *must* be done, what *can* be done?

Yet, despite or perhaps because of these superficial similarities, no one can miss the gulf between *Project* and *Modest Proposal*. The first is straight advocacy of a thoroughly feasible policy, its author an unashamed projector with all the confidence of his tribe – men can make these reforms if only they will. The second is savagely ironical and its chief target is not, bad as these are, landlordism, misgovernment or native fecklessness, but the projecting mentality itself, the idiot assumption of all reformers that men can hear and respond, even when the case is their own salvation. The *Modest Proposal* and the *Letter to Sympson* show Swift stalking himself, with more than the animus of Shylock hunting Antonio – giving out money gratis is sober calculation compared to the folly of setting up as saviour and attempting something that makes the academicians of Lagado seem cautiously realistic. The *Project*'s optimism, by contrast, flows from faith in man, especially Hobbesian man, the creature civilized by rewards and punishments. Hobbes's longing for security led him, in his turbulent times, to transform politics into a science and tame man's irrationalism to rules of reason. He applied his passion for geometry to this task, claiming to be the Euclid of politics, referring to the 'true science of equity and justice . . . built upon sure and clear principles'.[41] From axioms of human nature he deduced the kind of society men must maintain if they desire, as they must, peace and security. Pico della Mirandola might enthuse over man's astonishing unpredictability – 'a great miracle is man' – and celebrate his undetermined nature, his unique privilege to fashion himself, totally untrammelled, as he wills, descending to the beasts or rivalling the angels; but security, which Hobbes prizes above all, requires predictability. Pico extols freedom as the golden prerogative – 'to him it was granted to have what he chooses, to be what he wills' – while beasts and angels are immutably fixed; man has no assigned place or function in the hierarchy of creation, man *is* freedom.[42]

But what thrills Pico appalls Hobbes and his science of human behaviour is designed to redeem man from terrifying freedom and restore him to programmed security, a creature responding with reassuring invariability to a set number of limited stimuli. Not anarchic freedom but placid management is Hobbes's dream and he is, unlike Pico, confidently rational, knowing man as he knows Euclid's figures, for politics is human geometry and *Leviathan* a textbook that subdues life to a set of theorems. Mechanism explains all life in terms of motion, of appetites and aversions, and there is no life or motion that eludes scientific explanation.

Pico and Hobbes advance opposed interpretations of human nature – the one stressing wonder, novelty, unpredictability, freedom, a legacy that descends through the Romantics and Dostoevsky to modern existentialism; the other emphasizing rule, regularity, management, science, in a tradition that flows through Bentham and the utilitarians to modern behaviourism. Pico is an embarrassment to those who draw blueprints of social regeneration, Hobbes conveniently to hand for those who resent disorder and aim to manage things better. In its assumption that men infallibly respond to certain stimuli – rewards, incentives, reinforcements – and invariably pursue personal advantage, the *Project* is a Hobbesian tract. Swift does not go to Condorcet's extreme of affirming that laws will do all; his is the more modest position that laws will do enough, but underlying and legitimizing his *Project* is the same reliance on calculated management that inspired Condorcet. *Calculemus*: do this properly and the empire of irreligion will wither throughout the nation, at least visibly, and that is enough for Swift. To those who object that his plan will not turn men into angels, he replies that he only wants to persuade them to stop being brutes.

Never again is he so confidently Hobbesian, so hopeful of 'scientific' laws applied to the resolution of human problems. Hobbes tries to exorcize the spectre of social chaos by turning its cause into its means of salvation – egoism is both threat and remedy, civilizing the jungle it creates. Man is shrewdly selfish enough to see that survival entails certain sacrifices and structures and so plucks the flower safety from the nettle danger. Swift adapts Hobbes to the task of taming the jungle within. *The Project*, *The Conduct of the Allies*, *The Drapier's Letters*, the works of triumph in which he either achieves or anticipates success, are all fuelled by the conviction that enlightened egoism exists, that man is neither irretrievably vicious or cretinous, and that, if not a paragon, he is at least a learning animal who can be taught to distinguish and pursue his own best interest. These works vindicate the Hobbesian view of man as a calculable creature, responsive to a regimen of rods and carrots administered from above. The failure of this view is what induced the despair of the great satires.

Ireland is crucial as the crucible where Hobbesian hopes were tested and found wanting, where the *Leviathan* analysis of man, however legislatively attractive, proved hopelessly inaccurate. Mechanism ground to a halt in an Irish bog and Swift reached depths of prophetic despondency, identifying with the retributive deity of the comminatory psalms as he watched helplessly the unteachable wickedness of a besotted people: 'Wisdom crieth in the streets . . . But ye have set at nought all my counsel, and would none of my reproof. I also will laugh at your calamity, and mock when your fear cometh'.[43] *A Modest Proposal* fulfils this promise in expressing the savage elation of a spurned redeemer at the tribulations of those who refused the saving word. The echoes of psalms and prophets throughout his Irish writings testify to the anguish of one who described himself as 'a stranger in a strange land' and spoke of fighting with beasts not at Ephesus but at Dublin.[44] Ireland *was* a strange land, far more baffling than any visited by Lemuel Gulliver – what was a flying island to a country whose natives seemed kin to the Gadarene swine, and are the Struldbruggs, who don't know how to die, any more remarkable than the Irish, who don't know how to live? Swift skirted speculative despair as he wondered if the creatures he saw walking Irish streets were entitled to the human shapes they paraded, so outrageously deviant was their behaviour to the category of human found elsewhere.[45] Yet Ireland also gave him in his role of Drapier that supreme moment in his life when, like David, he savoured the exaltation of victory won against all the odds.

Strategically, the Drapier was forced to minimize his own achievement. With no confidence in the Irish – 'one can promise nothing from such wretches as the Irish people'[46] – and aware of their defeatist reluctance to resist Wood for fear of displeasing the King, the Drapier presents the dispute as one between a united nation and a 'little, impudent hard-ware man', 'one single, diminutive, insignificant mechanick' against a whole kingdom.[47] Wood versus Ireland is how the affair developed, but only as a consequence of the Drapier's intrepid campaign; in order to stiffen resistance, he has to belittle his own efforts, presenting as the situation's datum what was really the fruit of his own courageous stand. He is forced to deride publicly as incredible what he fears privately as imminent. Is it likely that the new Lord-Lieutenant has crossed to Ireland merely to put one hundred thousand pounds into a sharper's pocket? And, suppose the worst, what, in any case, *can* Carteret do to change Irish opinion, since all the plum jobs have already fallen to Englishmen and he has nothing left to bribe with?[48] He decries the alarmist nonsense that to reject Wood is to challenge the King; the King won't, because he can't, command people to accept the halfpence, is prohibited by law from doing so. If destruction comes, it 'must be intirely owing to ourselves', so he exhorts the Irish to forget appeals to English fairplay or Walpole's alleged sympathy, since 'the remedy is wholly in your own hands'.[49]

Yet Swift knows that but for the Drapier, Wood would have had a walkover, that the Drapier is the Horatius who alone held the bridge against an otherwise irresistible enemy. How else could so insignificant a man justify intervening in high politics? A true lover of his country cannot be 'a quiet stander-by and an indolent looker-on' while ruin approaches, for 'the care of the public is, in some degree, every such man's concern'. If Ireland's leaders did their duty, which coincides with their interest, Drapiers and Deans would not be needed.[50] In words that recall Bunyan's heroic retort to the rebuke that pedlars should be silent when degrees in divinity have spoken, the Drapier upholds the rights and responsibilities of the humblest citizen. The first letter typically links accountability and destruction: 'I cannot but warn you once more of the manifest destruction before your eyes, if you do not behave yourselves as you ought'.[51]

It is, of course, a confession of identity; 'once more', clearly indicating a repeat performance, adverts to previous publications by Swift, including his pamphlet instructing the Irish to wear their own manufactures and boycott imports. No one had listened, but here finally, as Drapier, Swift is about to achieve the miracle of Irish unity to defend Irish interests: 'the people here . . . unite as one man'.[52] Even Catholic scaremongering, the old papist bogey used so often to frustrate Irish resistance to English exploitation, had failed, when the Drapier exposed Wood's lying attempt to present the anti-coinage union as a Catholic conspiracy. Every Irishman is, gratifyingly, a good patriot, for each has the sense to see that all will be losers, those lately arrived in Ireland as much as those unlucky enough to be born there, if a debased coinage enters. The fear of bad money has effected the miracle of unity where every sensible proposal has hitherto failed and Swift for once can justifiably mock those who think 'we have neither common sense nor common senses'.[53] Reason and power are for once miraculously on the same side, and, in a startling reversal of traditional roles, it is Swift's adversaries who are impotently angry as he successfully marshals a kingdom, 'firmly united against that detestable fraud'.

The Drapier's Letters are not satire but tractarian rhetoric, in which the power of the word becomes, thrillingly, a power to determine human action and shape history; unlike the *Travels* and the *Tale*, they aim at a limited, specific target and succeeded so well that Swift could jubilantly order a ceasefire: 'the work is done and there is no more need of the Drapier'.[54] It was his Palm Sunday as Irish saviour and his elation was great: 'so the people rescued Jonathan, that he died not';[55] but if they did not betray him, it was because he had so splendidly taught them beforehand not to betray themselves. He was Drapier forever but was never again triumphant, as the miracle of enlightened self-interest faded and the Irish reverted to their usual role as 'a nation of idiots'.

Even in the *Letters* there are hints of Irish perversity and the folly of would-be saviours; Irish weavers had astoundingly condemned the pamphlet encouraging domestic manufacture of cloth as a seditious libel. Why risk oneself to help such people? The Drapier might argue that 'the universal clamour of a people must be heard', and rhetorically demand 'does not the nation best know its own wants?'[56] but at bottom Swift doesn't trust the Irish and the very existence of the *Letters* suggests public imbecility: 'if every man were wise enough to understand his own interest, which is every man's principal study, there would be no need of pamphlets upon this occasion':[57] A sensible people wouldn't need a Drapier. He protests in exasperation that he has shown them the precipice once – must he really go on doing it every morning? Nature has instructed even a brood of goslings to stick close when the kite is overhead – do the Irish lack a basic faculty possessed by the meanest animals? He chastises the printer for running out of copies of the first letter – 'let it not be your fault or mine, if our countrymen will not take warning'.[58] He expects disappointment and advocates reforms so that those who refuse to listen will not have the plea of ignorance; yet the painful probability that he will be disregarded, that they prefer precipice or kite to safety, torments him and he sees the Irish as the psalmist saw doomed Israel: 'he selleth his people for nought, and taketh no money for them'. Are our people's hearts waxed gross? Are their ears dull of hearing, and have they closed their eyes? His triumph as Drapier was a brief respite from such temptations to despair and, even while exhorting, he realized the waste of breath: 'Be not like the deaf adder, who refuses to hear the voice of the charmer, charm he never so wisely'.[59] Swift was no charmer but in their adamantine heedlessness the Irish became the unbiddable creatures he cautioned against.

Ireland wrung from Swift certain responses which were followed by chagrin and self-contempt, like a man recalling his behaviour under torture. He declared the best and most useful kind of satire to be that which laughs rather than lashes men out of their follies, and accordingly awarded the prize to Horace above Juvenal, but Ireland ruined his attempt at Horatian urbanity, compelling him to become the Juvenalian satirist he preferred to subdue.[60] The surrender to rage bred self-recrimination. He confessed to Bolingbroke the addict's despair experienced whenever he gave in to the ignoble compulsion, especially when, as in Ireland, he raged ridiculously at the irremediable.[61] Ireland frustrated the twin aims of satire, as defined by Swift. The nobler, to mend the world, posits a world capable of being mended, and Ireland failed to qualify; the less commendable aim, the satirist's satisfaction in hurting the incorrigible enemy, also misfired, for it is, on the contrary, the satirist's own unbearable pain that we sense, inadequately concealed, in the *Modest Proposal*. When he asks, 'is there virtue enough in this deluded people to save them from the brink of ruin?',[62] it is not mere rhetorical affectation but genuine anguish, and he is even driven to defend the shameful surrender to anger by pleading that only fools can remain placid under such provocation. Yet he is always aware that the greatest fool is the would-be reformer and he bitterly resents the Irish because he has made himself such a fool for their ungrateful sakes. He told Sheridan to sit down and expect no more from man than such an animal is capable of, and Gulliver pronounces the fearful verdict that man is incapable of goodness;[63] what does the advice to Sheridan mean, what *are* the limits of reasonable expectation as Swift sees them?

Swift admirably exhibits the combination of qualities that Gramsci recommends: pessimism of the intelligence and optimism of the will; he is forever sceptical about securing the improvements he always wants. His cherished realism led him to despise utopian physicians who easily cured the patients of their imaginations but did nothing for sufferers in the real world: 'There is hardly a scheme proposed for improving the trade of this kingdom, which doth not manifestly show the stupidity and ignorance of the proposer'.[64] He ridiculed such men as 'empirics', quacks who talked by rote, advising men with gout to walk ten miles every morning because exercise is good for health. Wearily, he repeats that measures suitable to every other region on earth are irrelevant in Ireland, and that, insofar as this reminder is ignored, the Irish are 'in the condition of patients, who have their physic sent them by doctors at a distance, strangers to their constitutions, and the nature of their disease.'[65]

He brushes away a proposal to buy foreign wheat against possible famine – the author means well but is ignorant, possesses, certainly, a commendably optimistic will, but, unfortunately, in addition, a fatally optimistic intelligence, and the scheme is 'visionary', for amassing the necessary funds is about as plausible as Rabelais' plan for squeezing out wind from the posteriors of a dead ass.[66] Swift, knowing the author to be a native of Dublin, pretends that he must be a stranger, since only an ignoramus from overseas could be so fatuously optimistic. He, by contrast, relentlessly faces reality, affirming the two things the Irish must consider: 'first their present evil condition; and secondly what can be done in some degree to remedy it'.[67] This is the tone of both *Project* and *Modest Proposal*, the realistic appraisal of wrongs and remedies that the visionary never achieves. *Visionary* and *utopian* are prominent terms in Swift's lexicon of abuse and he dreaded the description, well-meaning but foolish, as the greatest of insults; it is, therefore, cruelly ironical that when the insult finally came, it was self-administered.

In humiliated chagrin he was forced to see himself as yet another contemptible quack, contributing his own foolish nostrum to the heap of futilities cumbering Ireland. 'Whoever talketh without being regarded is sure to be despised': his warning to prospective preachers against empty rhetoric now returned to plague him when he found himself in Ireland as one more windy preacher talking in other people's sleep.[68] He told Pope that he disliked his own pamphlets and left them unfinished or threw them in the fire, 'chiefly because I know they will signify nothing'.[69] He freely owned it a wild imagination that any words would cure the sottishness of men or the vanity of women, and even the satisfaction of watching unheeded warnings come home to roost was minimal, since 'every human creature of common sense could foretell with as little sagacity as myself'.[70] What predominates is a sense of sheer weariness, of a mind driven beyond the limits of tolerable exasperation by 'so many abortive projects . . . so many crude proposals', by 'dreams and projects' and 'speculative people' and 'a nation so shamefully besotted' that even divine mercy is nonplussed.[71] Sisyphus, exhausted, is about to abandon his Irish boulder and retire from telling the unteachable when they go wrong, 'as I have told the public often enough but with as little effect as what I shall say at present is likely to produce'.[72] His own sensible suggestions are relegated to the same vain babbling he scorned in others, as he sees in his glass the foolish face of the full-blown projector. Short of a miracle, that celestial intervention which, following Polybius, he had barred as the last resort in interpreting human affairs, the Irish seemed wilfully, irretrievably doomed.

Hobbes had failed him in Ireland. He had banked on *Leviathan*'s unflattering portrait of man, confident that he was secure against charges of highfalutin impracticability. Instead of a company of sharp-witted calculators, all selfishly enlightened, he found himself in a madhouse whose crazily unpredictable inmates were as likely to injure themselves as attack the custodians. Ireland revealed to him, what Edgar discovers, that the worst is always on the hither side of conception. Mother Courage thanks God that men are corrupt because then they can be bribed to do what's right – we need only outbid the devil. Swift seldom asks people to sacrifice themselves, always ensures that virtue is the better offer, only, inexplicably, to have it refused. He insists that individual decency, like the art of government, is a simple business, not the monopoly of heroes and saints, but well within the grasp of ordinary men. The mystery of unprofitable depravity is thus immeasurably more perplexing. If goodness is so easy, why is it so rare? Are men idiots or possessed? In his little story of 'The Injured Lady', illustrating Anglo-Irish relations, English wickedness and Irish folly are equally bewildering. England as deluded man, casting himself away on an 'infamous creature' (Scotland) must be 'possessed' or 'bewitched', enslaved by some powder from his hideous paramour, for how else can such behaviour be explained?[73] Ireland's crass neglect of her own good is likewise so insensate as to seem another type of possession. The rational reformer is unnerved by such intractable perversion, and whether they will not or cannot save themselves is a question that may interest pedants but is equally unconsoling, whatever conclusion is reached. If only Hobbes were right, how simple the reformer's task would be. The tragic truth is that man is not rationally selfish but irrationally self-willed.

Swift's Irish discovery anticipates that of *Notes from Underground*, though his reaction is very different from Dostoevsky's. Man wants not his advantage but freedom, whatever it costs, wherever it leads, and he will do what is stupid or wicked simply to prove he is his own arbiter and to spite the architects of the crystal palace, who would make him, for his own good, a standardised unit in a compulsory millenium. Dostoevsky's book is unreason's declaration of independence, a rejection of Condorcet's *calculemus* and every other external authority in affirming the absolute primacy of the will. He mocks those baby philosophers who argue that man is programmed to pursue his best advantage; man, in Dostoevsky's tautology, wants what he wants, cherishing his freedom, including – it is, after all, the acid test – his freedom to destroy himself. A romantic existentialist like Dostoevsky can celebrate this as the triumph of human autonomy and authenticity over the crystal palace, man's perversity saving him from imprisonment in any system, however rationally compelling. As with Pico, free will is the splendidly unique characteristic.

Swift, as Hobbesian reformer, far from inciting escape from the prison-house of logic, is aghast at the havoc done by unpredictable man upon blueprints of salvation. Hobbes knows that man likes his own way but believes that he likes staying alive and being secure even more, and will normally prefer these to suicidal freedom; on what other assumption can a legislator proceed? Swift, adopting this assumption, ends up as bankrupt as a visionary who had planned for angels or Houyhnhnms rather than men. His attempt to register all men in the club of virtue by reducing the subscription to the smallest possible fee failed; expecting men to conform to *Leviathan's* specifications, he might just as well have asked them all to be Thomas More in the first place.

The creative anger both explodes and implodes, with the traitor within more detestable than the enemy without. Who are the greatest fools in the Academy of Lagado? Not those seeking to extract sunshine from cucumbers or to breed naked sheep – these are hardheaded enterprises compared to the delusions of 'those unhappy people . . . wholly out of their senses', who are trying to reform society and to make men wiser and better.[74] The real visionaries (Swift used to be one) are those who imagine such fantasies are possible. Here, as in the *Modest Proposal*, Swift becomes both satirist and target, as he derides his own exorbitant expectations.

True, Swift also enjoys, through Gulliver and the Proposer, the role of cheated redeemer, playfully and vicariously exploiting it with all the irony of one who confessed himself something of a desponder. Six months after publication, Gulliver is indignantly surprised at his book's total lack of impact, and he blames his cousin Sympson ('the trust I reposed in you') and himself ('my own great want of judgement') for the folly of trying to reform Yahoos. Swift is clearly mocking this rational redeemer, with his time-table of salvation and his scheduled paradise. Gulliver complains that he 'had reason to expect' a full stop to corruption, 'at least in this little island', within six months, and refers to the thousand, confidently-anticipated reformations as 'plainly deducible from the precepts delivered in my book'; the speaker is clearly a Euclidean moralist who expects sin and regeneration to wheel to the commands of logic and range themselves accommodatingly in theorems and syllogisms – man is to be reasoned out of wickedness, taught virtue as though it were geometry. Logic tutors life and loses its temper when the pupil proves recalcitrant.

Yet Swift's mockery of the once-confident, now crestfallen projector is also a form of self-chastisement: 'I have finished my *Travels* and am now transcribing them: they are admirable things, and will wonderfully mend the world'.[75] Swift, not Gulliver, is the speaker and there is no irony; artistic elation fuses with reformist buoyancy to produce the Everest of jubilant expectation in all his writings. Yet an uneasy sense of vulnerability is never far away: 'I never will have peace of mind till all honest men are of my opinion'.[76] For Swift, peace of mind was not to be won by artistic success alone, satire as pure art is insufficient, yet he is agonizingly aware that seldom if ever does satire achieve any mode of power beyond the linguistic: 'Satire is a sort of glass, wherein beholders do generally discover every body's face but their own'.[77] Why, then, devote oneself to so futile and unrewarding a vocation as that of satirist-reformer?

Even if, anticipating Camus's exhortation, Swift loved his rock, cherished satire for its own sake, it is difficult to imagine him content with Wilde's celebration of art as useless. There is always a jeering awareness of his own inutility, his failure to get things done – the masterly words are, finally, so far as reformation goes, far inferior to Aeolist belchings, for these have helped to kill the King and ruin the Church. Enthusiast ravings change the world while Swift's rational wisdom alters nothing. Is it surprising that we sense a hint of perplexed envy, even of reluctant admiration, as he contemplates the great madmen of the 'Digression' and ponders the mystery of their success? The split in Swift is reflected in Gulliver's quarrel with Cousin Sympson: the culpable optimism denounced by Gulliver is that expressed by Swift when he elatedly forecasts his book's reformative power, while Gulliver's pessimistic disavowal of all future striving for reform is echoed in his creator's refusal to go on prescribing a dose for the dead. The *Travels* are a masterly demonstration of buck-passing, a transfer of responsibility, as, in a chain of accusation, Swift first shifts his own reformist folly on to Gulliver and then permits Gulliver to do the same to Cousin Sympson.

Self-division is equally evident in the pretence of indifference drawn over the fury that blazes within. Gulliver prefaces his inventory of human wickedness with the claim that it does not in the least provoke him, since, as he coolly remarks, 'this is all according to the due course of things'. Giving way to anger is a descent into a rat-pit of reprehensible emotions, a betrayal of philosophic calm, and a failure to follow the exemplary Houyhnhnm attitude to Yahoo evil; the wise horses are never shocked into nerve-jangling indignation by Yahoo misdemeanours, though even their stoic control is shaken by revelations of human perversion. Just as he prefers the urbane Horace to the savage Juvenal, so Swift also ranks Demosthenes, who appealed to reason, above Cicero, master of impassioned rhetoric and exploiter of emotions, yet, ironically, at certain key moments in his writing, he seems closer to those rejected than to those preferred. He never succeeded in achieving the envied Horatian calm or in taming the anger that caused him shame. Vainly, he invokes Horace as guardian of his Juvenalian self:

> Like the ever laughing Sage,
> In a Jest I spend my Rage.[78]

but outrage erupts and, though he knows that passion may make one ridiculous, he cannot avoid 'rage and resentment' at 'the mortifying sight of slavery, folly and baseness about me'.[79]

The promise to burn the *Travels* if only the world possesses a dozen Arbuthnots is a daring bid for parity with Jehovah, who will spare Sodom if a sufficient number of good men can be found there.[80] Burning the book is reprieve, burning the city retribution, but satire and thunderbolt are assimilated to each other. The element of chastisement in Swift's satire is joined, with comic incongruity, to a second element. The Jehovah-satirist launches his bolts and they fall with the fury of thistledown. The cities of the plain are hugely diverted at the messages from heaven, the scourge of the Yahoos becomes their entertainer, a comic anarchist throwing toy bombs at a royal command performance. Complexity is compounded by the injection of a third element, as the satirist, foreseeing his comic fate, prepares for it. Cassandra studies irony and makes laughter a defence. Determined at all costs not to be ridiculed as a joke Jehovah, rantingly impotent, Swift creates a scapegoat to bear the backlash of the satirist's unheeded jeremiads. Refusing to be caught in possession of a ridiculously redundant passion, an anger that neither reforms its target nor dignifies its owner, Swift astutely palms it on to Gulliver as foolish enthusiast. Swift has the relief of flaying humanity, Gulliver attracts whatever derision the unprofitable exercise provokes.

Underlying all other divisions in Swift is that between the realist who accepts unprotestingly the world as it is and the moralist who chokes on the world's iniquity. The first advocates a 'scientific' approach to the study of man, curbing emotion, renouncing the foolish idealism that faults life for not matching our dreams, scorning romantic anguish in favour of cool analysis. One must be calm and indifferent – as well arraign the laws of chemistry as jib at human nature. The second abandons the pose of neutral observer for that of prophet, leaves the laboratory to convict men of sin. The creative conflict between these separate selves gives a unique intensity to the great satires. There is a disconcerting merging as the cheated idealist, ashamed of both futile aspiration and futile anger, reappears as disillusioned realist, expecting no more from man than he gets – this alone explains the otherwise baffling metamorphosis of Gulliver's Swift, not in the least provoked by wickedness, or the Giant King's Swift, coolly appraising from his eminence the nasty habits of odious vermin, into Yeat's Swift, 'beating on his breast in sibyline frenzy blind/ Because the heart in his blood-sodden breast had dragged him down into mankind'.[81] It is the moralist–preacher who shows how absurd moralist–preachers are: no one contradicts them and no one obeys them, they are experts who are never disproved, never consulted, never heeded. Swift's chief torment was being always right and always ignored; and, after advising young preachers only to speak when they command attention, he dismayingly found himself, an old preacher of superb skill, unaccountably suffering the same humiliation as inept apprentices. A century later Alexander Herzen confronts the same contradiction: 'on the one side, the logical consistency of thought, its successes; on the other, its complete impotence before a world deaf, mute, powerless to grasp the idea of salvation'.[82]

The world's intransigence makes Gulliver abandon all hope of reforming the Yahoo, for, with the case so clearly proved, why does the world not respond? Why does the world resist the truth, deny its redeemers, elude salvation with an escapologist's ingenuity? Why, in Swift's formulation, do men strain to enter hell when they might so easily possess heaven? Socrates has an answer which comes as providentially as the Fifth Cavalry: man pursues evil because he mistakes it for good. The problem and its solution are purely rational, a matter of mere enlightenment. Horace and St Paul are less sanguine: *video meliora proboque, deteriora sequor*; for I do not the good that I wish, but the evil that I do not wish, that I perform. The welcome simplicity of Socrates founders on the mystery of the perverse will, evil as addiction rather than mistaken choice. Swift and Herzen find no comfort in Socrates, since their torment stems from a conviction that the case is proved beyond dispute, that a genuine mistake is by now impossible, and that man either cannot or will not change, is, if in error, contumeliously so. As much as Milton's great poems, Swift's great satires interrogate a mystery, and the defeat of the godly revolution is no more stunning than the debacle of reason, God's apparent failure in England no more painful than Hobbes's in Ireland. Milton could at least hope for miracle, God returning to Puritan man as to Samson, whereas Swift, through his own self-denying ordinance as to divine intervention, is left only with the mess and the perverse creatures who make it.

Swift's deepening pessimism can be charted, as instances of individual perversion suddenly become representative of a whole people and then of humanity itself; the Earl of Wharton and Ebenezer Elliston are bad enough as aberrations, intolerable as the human average. Wharton, as presented by Swift, is a problem that he can handle only by pretending to be uninvolvedly amused when he is really upset and baffled. Swift is anxious to declare his own lack of bias, to pose as a naturalist describing a rather repulsive animal in a strictly scientific way. Wharton is strange, if not unique, in that he is truly indifferent to both condemnation and applause, 'without the sense of shame or glory, as some men are without the sense of smelling; and, therefore, a good name to him is no more than a precious ointment would be to these'.[83] Swift dissects him with a cheerful lack of compunction, assured that his subject is invulnerable, living yet stonily insensible, having achieved a 'pitch of happiness and security . . . which no philosopher before him could reach'.[84] He is an Achilles without the heel, incapable of being offended; however vitriolic the assault, he will meet his attacker right afterwards, say he is damnably mauled and then, with the easiest transition in the world, ask about the weather or the time of day.

The character-sketch is a curious blend of surprise, disapproval and, however inverted, tribute. Despite vicious living and age, Wharton shows no sign of incipient Struldbruggery, although, unlike Wilde's hero, he has no portrait in the attic assuming the burden of guilt. In his late sixties, he is still like a young man of twenty-five, the triumph of style over morality. Aschenbach's nausea in *Death in Venice* at his own image as ancient roué is a more traditional reaction to age disgracing itself than Swift's attitude of derisive amusement – he tells us how Wharton so splendidly 'acquitteth himself', then undermines the encomium by specifying the disreputable activities in which he does so. He isn't, apparently, a good liar or dissembler, but what sounds like praise is quickly cancelled, for the reference is merely to his technical shortcomings – he lies indefatigably, almost from second nature, but practice leaves him inept as ever. He has the vice, and, like Chaucer's January, is the more reprehensibly absurd because performance is so poor. He is no Tartuffe, which sounds creditable, till we learn that he goes to prayers still talking smut at the church door. He knows nothing of dignity or decorum despite his high social position, but in him nobody expects it. He projects his own insensitivity on to his victims – caring nothing himself for insult or injury, he cannot conceive that anyone could, so he will sack you one day and fall on your neck the next as though nothing had happened. He is a skilled intriguer, successfully grafting onto politics the strategies of his amours, but errs through overrefinement, like gallants who risk limbs climbing through windows when they might easily walk through doors; the direct Temple and the Giant King expose such sophistication. He has three dominant yet contradictory passions – money, power, pleasure – which he somehow contrives to combine: 'they ride him sometimes by turns, and sometimes all together'.[85]

Despite the jocular tone, Swift is troubled by Wharton's secession from traditional patterns of behaviour, his declaration of independence from humanity. Racked by his father's iniquity, Dmitry Karamazov explodes into anguished inquiry: 'Why does such a man live? Tell me, can he be allowed to defile the earth by his existence?' Swift shuns such exhibitionist despair, but the same baffled incomprehension underlines the pose of amused naturalist. How does one legislate for a man like Wharton, where is the technology of behaviour, the mode of operant conditioning or behavioural control, that will subdue him to the requirements of everyday life? All of Hobbes's optimistic premises as to calculability, his dream of a psychology purged of mystery, are threatened by Wharton. He defies existing models of behaviour as much as Gulliver violates the norms established by Lilliput and Brobdingnag. Hobbes seeks knowledge of man for purposes of control and manipulation – social engineering is the goal. Similarly, Swift assumes throughout the *Project* that consciousness is a social product, that the character-determining environment is open to human control, so that we can, if we choose, manufacture hypocrites and even some truly good men instead of shameless rogues. Swift in Ireland, struggling to believe in reform, argues, in Hobbesian style, that 'supposing the size of a native's understanding just equal to that of a dog or horse, I have often seen these two animals to be civilized by rewards, at least as much as by punishments'.[86] Wharton resists all scientific classification, will not fit into the *Project* or any other simple rods-and-carrots system. He is irrational man, who explodes, in addition to everything else, the ancient pretensions of satire.

Swift insisted that corrigible people must be chid and incorrigible people harried; even death is no sanctuary from Alecto's whip and Marlborough and Whitshed are pursued into the grave to be punished – the satirist lashes the dead, content to imagine how they would have skipped had they been alive.[87] Wharton, however, confounds the satirist, for, alive, he is insensible; not only will he not reform under the lash, he doesn't even feel it. The satirist and the sadist have at least this in common, that for each the victim's anguish must be evident if full satisfaction is to be achieved – otherwise de Sade might just as well perform upon a rubber doll. Conceive de Sade's chagrin on discovering that the living flesh upon which he has lavished his finest strokes is a wooden figure, and you have some inkling of Swift's frustration in facing Wharton – but exasperation is deeper in that Swift knows Wharton is a sentient being, who can only be exempt from pain because the satirist has botched the job. Swift, the incomparable satirist, is made to feel a bungler as he desperately seeks and fails to find the words that will wound Wharton. The easily-penetrable pose of uncaring observer is a last despairing attempt to pierce the pachyderm, a forlorn hope that contemptuous relegation of the enemy to the brute may work where nothing else will. It helps, too, to conceal the embarrassingly futile anger; Swift, having lost the battle, refuses to lose his temper too over an offender who either smiles at the lash or doesn't even notice it. Dread of appearing a bad loser is a major control of the animus in Swift's greatest work. Wharton is the supreme challenge, not as a target for reform – that is a project for the Academy of Lagado, with the naked sheep and the sunshine from cucumbers – but as a man to be hurt. Swift, forgetting reform or deterrence, seeks simply to inflict pain, to extort a human response from Wharton and elevate him to the status of Hobbesian man.

The pretence of being placidly indifferent is wafer-thin in one who, following Machiavelli's advice, longs above all to be feared, to take his place in that roster of dreaded magician-satirists whose maledictions were more terrifying than weapons. The fascination with Wharton springs from a chill realization that he is totally unafraid, affably contemptuous of the satirist's fearful power. Pope turns accusation into justifiable boast when he agrees that he *is* proud –

> proud to see
> Men not afraid of God, afraid of me:
> Safe from the Bar, the Pulpit and the Throne,
> Yet touch'd and sham'd by ridicule alone.[88]

There is no more exalted tribute to the satirist's vocation and efficacy in all literature, but, apart from one or two moments in private letters, Swift never entertains such high expectations of his chosen art – on the contrary, a major element of his art is the inutility of satire and the futility of its practitioners. He is proportionately elated when, occasionally, he catches a whiff of success. Hearing Wood's squeals of protest at the Drapier's accusations, Swift, smelling blood, tells himself and his readers that they are listening to 'the last howls of a dog dissected alive'.[89] It is a revealing image and its latent relish is

inseparable from Swift's self-conceived role towards the contumeliously unrepentant sinner: a dissector without anaesthetics.

This craving for power does not, of course, exclude a capacity for
relenting towards the contrite sinner, suing for mercy, as reflected in
Swift's treatment of John Browne, one of the Irish witnesses denounced by the Drapier for allegedly supporting Wood. Browne appealed to
have his name deleted from the list of accused, lamenting that he would
be branded villain for as long as the *Letters* should be read, 'even unto
the end of time'.[90] At this tribute to his Jove-like power, Swift
generously removed Browne's name from later editions of his text.
Wood's howls and Browne's pleas are each, in their own way, gratifying testimony to the satirist's menace, and make Wharton's insouciant
indifference the harder to swallow, for Wharton turns the tables,
makes the godlike satirist feel deflatedly foolish. In his insensitivity,
he is the opposite of Wood and Browne, indeed of Swift himself,
swift as he was to take offence at the merest hint of slight or under-
valuation.

Swift clearly regards the heedless Wharton much as Meursault's
judges in Camus's *L'Etranger* regard him – as a monster, lacking certain
qualities and characteristics vital to full human status. Unlike Pope's
atheists who tremble at the satirist, Wharton cares for neither God nor
man, and there is no judgement, here or in the world to come, that can
control or deter him. He is the satirist's nightmare. Swift futilely
taps new depths of invective, brings ever more fearful instruments
to the dissecting table, only for Wharton to grin and wink at his
baffled butcher. He is atheist in religion, Presbyterian in politics, but
chooses at present to whore with a Papist; he is 'a public robber, an
adulterer, a defiler of altars, an enemy of religion and of all that is
sacred'; he escapes perjury only because he doesn't believe in the
God he invokes to credit his lies; could he even be at heart a secret
benefactor of religion, for didn't he give one thousand pounds to the
Church in the form of a fine imposed for a nocturnal defecation upon
the altar of Gloucester Cathedral, and what other motive than love
of the Church could have possessed him to do such a thing?[91] Swift
cannot leave Wharton alone, cannot cut his losses and move on: he
will indict Verres, despoiler of Sicily (Wharton had been a sticky-
fingered Lord-Lieutenant of Ireland) because 'it shall not be objected,
the criminal was not produced, or that there wanted an orator to
accuse him'[92] – but to what purpose? The cheerfully impenitent
villain listens amused and impudently greets his accuser across the

court. As well try to reform the plague or chastise the stone that injures one's foot. Wharton is, regrettably, improbable gallows material, his peculations being guaranteed against reprisal and his other vices being of the kind lamented in the *Project* as beyond the law's scope. But every reader of Swift is indebted to Wharton, for it would be difficult to exaggerate his importance as a contributory factor in the making of the great satires, and it is the adversary's invincibility, modelled on Wharton, that inspired Swift to new heights of satiric genius in the creation of his masterpieces, *Gulliver* and *A Modest Proposal*.

Ebenezer Elliston, by contrast, was born for the gallows, but, this distinction apart, he joins Wharton in a revolt against the Hobbesian parade-ground equally awkward for those who would find there the all-sufficient discipline for restraining tumultuous man. His dying speech (he is a highwayman about to be executed) as written by Swift, reveals a man trapped in what today would be called a cycle of deprivation, doomed to wickedness from the cradle for sociological rather than Augustinian reasons, 'generally so corrupted from our childhood, as to have no sense of goodness'.[93] Far from Pico's ecstatic freedom, Elliston and his fellow criminals move towards the gallows with the monotony of an assembly line. Neither Swift nor Elliston, however, questions the justice of the system – Elliston is a villain but not, in Swift's sense, a freethinker, that is, a man using his reason to justify his wickedness. He sees hanging as the just punishment prescribed by the laws of God and man, his only criticism being, paradoxically, that he hasn't been hanged sooner. His testimony, the more valuable in that he is better educated than the mass of villains, is a refutation of Hobbes; all the carrots in creation will not keep Elliston from the rope. About to be executed, he is sorry not for his sins but for his capture. Were he pardoned even now, he would instantly resume the old trade, for he is untrained for and, more important, unwilling to take up other employment. He is as incorrigibly recidivist as the rest of his colleagues, as stunningly impenitent as those who spend their last night drunk with whores. Where Johnson believes that the thought of hanging wonderfully concentrates the mind and Pascal hopes that awareness of condemnation will jolt man into faith, Swift despondently accepts that irrationalism prevails even under the gallows-tree. Sir Henry Vane spends his last minutes impregnating his wife, Elliston's mates are hanged straight after ejaculation, and Swift is plainly perplexed by both.[94] Elliston cites two comrades who were hanged, recovered, returned to crime and became worse rogues than ever, until caught and hanged again, this time properly, 'for good and all'. The anecdote justifies attack on the foolishly dangerous mercy that only transports the offender, since this simply encourages crime and he comes back an expert.

This expertise in wickedness is, ironically, bedfellow to an overall imbecility in conduct. The key message of Elliston's address is the unhappy, sordid, sottish, doomed life of the thief, running the most appalling risks for the most minimal returns – 'risks' is in fact laughably inexact, since eventual execution is guaranteed. It is a life more miserable than the poorest labourer's, bafflingly combining the evil and the unprofitable, inevitably provoking the Houyhnhnm Master's question to Gulliver concerning the ways of European Yahoos: where is the sense, use or advantage of such an existence? Yet, as Elliston assures us, 'custom is so strong' that if he escaped, he would at once return to it. Hence he and his tribe 'ought to be looked upon as the common enemies of mankind; whose interest it is to root us out like wolves, and other mischievous vermin, against which no fair play is required'.[95] The vermin deserving only extermination reappear in the last book of the *Travels* and the Houyhnhnms, in their handling of the Yahoos, reach the same conclusions as the Irish robber. Breaking Elliston's neck is the sole remedy – it is he himself who says so and who should know better? Swift, who supports hanging now and hellfire later as the only real deterrents to evil, is in full agreement with horse and highwayman.

To a certain modern sensibility, Elliston is as much a victim as his victims, but because he cannot help himself doesn't make Swift or, astonishingly, Elliston any more tolerant and neither pleads extenuating circumstances. Blame itself is irrelevant: the Houyhnhnms no more blame the Yahoos than the stones that cut their hooves, but they still kick the stones aside; Swift no more reproaches Walpole for his depredations than the farmer does the kite that steals chickens, but if the farmer has his shotgun, he blasts the thief; and Swift tells us how ready he always is to squash a louse even if he gets no credit from it. The tolerant interpretation of crime as an illness for which the patient is not accountable is foreign to Swift, Houyhnhnm, farmer and even the doomed criminal himself – they don't dispute the compulsion but decline to make it a reason for pardon.

Elliston's significance lies in the puzzle he sets the simple mechanist, for breaking necks is a drastic sort of reform, and the fact that Swift sees no alternative reveals the gulf between the suicidal addict and the intelligent egoist premissed by Leviathan. Fortunately, Elliston is the minority case, the perverse oddity, violating the laws, legal and psychological, that the mass of sensible men obey. He is a pest but unrepresentative – this alone makes the fact of his existence tolerable. The monstrosity would be a whole nation of Whartons and Ellistons, millions shockingly neglectful of their own basic interests, void of shame and incapable of reform. This nightmare hypothesis forced itself upon Swift in Ireland, when St Paul's experience of struggling with beasts became his own. In *The Faerie Queene* Gryll is the pathological exception, triumph of willed bestiality, from whom one can only turn away – 'Let Gryll be Gryll, and have his hoggish minde'. One must want to be saved. In Ireland, however, beasts and madmen have triumphed, Gryll and the Gadarene swine are national archetypes, and the proselytysers of lunacy of the 'Digression on Madness' have carried the country in a landslide conversion. Out of this bedlam came *A Modest Proposal*.

All of the warring elements noted in Swift assemble to create the unique intensity of the *Proposal*. Horace and Juvenal, Demosthenes and Cicero, urbanity and ferocity, reason and outrage, acceptance and revulsion, the raisonneur's detachment and the prophet's fury, combine in a sustained piece of clinical savagery that engages the whole man to a degree unapproached in his previous writings. These elements are, of course, also present in the *Travels* but not in so concisely dramatic or fiercely concentrated a form. Disgust cohabits with a calm appraisal of the project as a fair, cheap, above all easy method of managing the hundred and twenty thousand Papist beggars born annually in Ireland, transforming useless, abandoned people into valuable citizens and giving them a chance to achieve a status in life otherwise irretrievably beyond them. The most precocious disciple of Elliston will scarcely attain self-sufficiency as a thief till he's at least six and meanwhile how will they survive the period of apprenticeship before the craft is mastered? The proposer is, like Swift, keen on home-based industries and the great advantage of turning these pauper children into a saleable commodity is that 'the goods' are entirely of 'our own growth and manufacture'. The proposal proceeds with the logical precision of a feasibility study: keep twenty thousand aside for breeding in the ratio of three females to one male – since marriage is a custom not much regarded by our savages, no susceptibilities will be offended – and sell the rest as food to 'persons of quality and fortune'. The benefits will be many, though economic benefits understandably prevail: the gain to the gross national product if fewer pigs and more children are eaten, the anticipation of a time when mothers will compete to see who can bring 'the fattest child to market', the splendid fillip to the catering trade, and so on. Market forces clearly rule when the slogan is procreate for profit and marriage aims at replenishing the restaurants rather than the earth.

The same good economic sense shows in the praiseworthy refusal to let resentment, however justified, defeat calculation; the plump young girls of Dublin, who will not forgo foreign luxuries, deserve to be eaten, but it would be foolish to do it just when they are about to become breeders, like eating next year's seed-corn. Nevertheless, the proposer's values are not limited to economics and he proudly lists the benefits, social and moral, that will accrue. Maternal love will flourish, infanticide and abortion become unknown, marriages increase, husbands care for their pregnant wives at least as well as for their cattle – even the most sottish Irish husband does not kick the sow when she is about to litter and if wives can be raised to the level of pigs, what a breakthrough that would be! – and the nation will be wonderfully united: instead of quarrelling with each other, like the Jews as the Romans stormed Jerusalem, the Irish will close ranks against English exploitation. Anticipating Joyce's Citizen–Cyclops, the Proposer modestly offers himself as the Irish Moses, with a programme of painless, affluent liberation, an easy exit from Egypt. There will also be a welcome decrease in the number of Papists, the principal breeders and 'our most dangerous enemies', thus placating Protestant fears of threatened Catholic resurgence.[96] No other passage in the *Proposal* so decisively separates Swift from the persona, for Swift despised such fears, regarding them as either malicious propaganda by power-hungry dissenters or alarmist hysteria, papists-under-the-bed dementia, 'the real terror only of fools'.[97] There is no need to eat Catholic babies to guarantee an already assured Protestant supremacy and from so tainted a source the argument exposes the hypocrisy of those who would subvert the established church under the cover of a united Protestant front against Popery. Eating Catholic babies may, however, be the sole answer to Ireland's economic ills, unless an effective alternative is speedily found.

The measure admittedly leaves untouched the problem of the destitute old, but the Proposer chides those 'desponders' who magnify this, for the old are rotting away on schedule, dying off as fast as can reasonably be expected. The scheme will restore Ireland to the comity of civilized nations, all of which encourage marriage and procreation; it may be somewhat unusual, but it is, after all, for Ireland alone and for nowhere else on earth, past, present or future. Other countries will adopt more orthodox solutions but these are precisely what will not work in Ireland. For a disease so desperate, the remedy must be unique. Sinn Fein, ourselves alone, is the slogan trumpeted by this patriot too, though in a sense very different from the men of 1916. The inescapable question remains: how are over one hundred thousand useless mouths to be fed? Weary of vain, idle, visionary thoughts – Swift's self-recrimination at his own futile efforts envenoms the Proposer's pen – he now offers his own proposal, solid, practical, unobjectionable: 'Therefore, let no man talk to me of other expedients'. There has been too much talk, too much sequestering into Atlantic and Utopian polities, too many well-meaning 'empirics' with impossible cures, and the Proposer demands an embargo on all schemes without at least a fighting chance of implementation. In this spirit he makes his offer; those who gag at cannibalism, that trifling step from metaphorical to literal ingestion, when the landlords go the whole hog and do in fact to the children what they have as good as done to the parents, are challenged to solve the problem in another, equally effective way.

A Modest Proposal despairs of politics – politics, as an art for rational man, cannot be pursued in a madhouse and Ireland must seem to the sensible the bedlam that Europe seems to the Houyhnhnm. The parodic element reveals self-division as the Proposer ridicules the Swift who really did try to be 'a preserver of the nation'. The brutally-dismissed other expedients include the sensible policies urged so unavailingly by Swift as straight reformer and the disillusioned saviour retaliates with a scheme custom-built for Ireland that only a moral cretin could seriously endorse. Both sides of Swift war upon each other with marvellously creative consequences and produce a satire of stunning complexity in which meaning contends with meaning and catharsis is denied the reader. There is no solution within the text, instead deliberate impasse, unlike the *Project* where Swift unironically accepts the inevitable hypocrisy as a charge upon the accompanying benefits. Thackeray errs badly when he refers to Swift entering the nursery with the tread of an ogre, for the advocacy of cannibalism is ironically provocative, a challenge to procure the same advantages in any other way. In a number of serious pamphlets Swift had told the Irish what to do and had been insultingly ignored; when, finally, he recommends cannibalism as the only remedy, he expects, not indignant protest, but a viable alternative.

'Such creatures are not to be reformed':[98] Swift's verdict on Whitshed, the Drapier's enemy, is equally applicable to Elliston and Wharton and then, by dismaying extension, to Ireland itself. The Irish proved a nation of 'such creatures', as incrimination spread in a widening arc of contagion, from isolated individuals to a whole people to mankind itself. In the last book of the *Travels* all men have applied for Irish citizenship, humanity is an Irishman, incapable of amendment by precept or example. The satirist–charmer retreats in baffled disgust as the adders remain defiantly deaf.

SIX

CURIOSITY AND CONTAMINATION
FORBIDDEN KNOWLEDGE IN *GULLIVER'S TRAVELS*

That Swift approved of curiosity cannot be doubted. His satiric aim, says Leavis, is the intimidation of habit, his persistent message, for Quintana, is 'Look again! It is not as it seems'.[1] Without the saving power of curiosity we go through life torpidly accepting surfaces and the danger of becoming slovenly habituated to prevailing custom and ancient assumption is a major theme throughout Swift's work, and especially so in the *Travels*, inculpating not just the characters but also the readers of the book. We are uneasily aware of being person- ally prime targets of the writer's mockery – expecting to be diverted, we speedily sense our own vulnerability, rather like being out in the open with a crack marksman training upon you. Being the tracker of Swift's meaning rather than the prey can be just as unnerving. We know that meaning is there but just as we are about to corner it, it slips away, taunting us to chase after in some totally different direc- tion. The book is Janus-faced, forever offering an alternative reading, another way of construing the evidence that confounds the hard-won conclusions just achieved.

Is Gulliver an image of despair or hope? We note how easily he is brainwashed without even realizing it – that being a *sine qua non* of the process – and when we see Lilliputians, Brobdingnagians, Laputans, even Houyhnhnms, all exhibiting the limitations of a conditioned outlook, we suspect that perhaps the English too are involved in this universal predicament and that there are, ourselves included, no privileged observers. Pavlov rules, O.K., is the dismaying graffito a modern reader finds scrawled over the *Travels*. Gulliver avoids blinding and death in Lilliput only because he still hasn't been educated to accept royal vindictiveness as the normal routine – it is 'the precipitancy of youth' that makes him run away. The older, more experienced Gulliver knows retrospectively that the punishment was reasonably light and, similarly circumstanced, would stay and take his medicine. Knowledge and experience are euphemisms for a brain-washing process that teaches us to tolerate the humdrum atrocity and the mature Gulliver mirrors our own hopelessly imprisoned state. But perhaps the ease of brainwashing in the *Travels* is meant to alert us to our own peril, a summons to vigilance rather than a wail of despair, with Gulliver as cautionary example, behaving like a fool in Lilliput so that we can stop being fools in England. Gide claimed he wrote *The Immoralist* to stop being him; perhaps the *Travels* is the supreme instance of literature as therapy, Gulliver so marvellously rendered in art to help us defeat the Gulliver in our lives. For, if after seeing his follies so fully exhibited, how absurdly he mistakes con-ditioning for truth, if, after all this, we persist in promoting the relative and contingent in our own lives as absolutes, we have only ourselves to blame. After such knowledge, what forgiveness?

Gulliver is the most tractable of conformists, with a chameleon facility for blending unprotestingly with new landscapes. He easily becomes a Lilliputian patriot and partisan, referring in a very short time to 'our Emperor' and 'our wine' in opposition to Blefuscan rivals. The smooth assumption of Lilliputian norms is shown as he unironic-ally affirms the Emperor's superiority in being at least a nail's breadth taller than the rest of his court. So impressive a distinction under-standably strikes awe into fellow-Lilliputians and Gulliver's admira-tion indicates how far he has gone in taking out citizenship papers. He is soon thoroughly indoctrinated in the new values, a splendidly receptive subject for transplantation, destitute of the antibodies that cause rejection. The elation of the Man Mountain at pygmy favours, his thrill at becoming the Emperor's 'useful servant' or kissing the Empress's fingertips, exhibit in full the vanity he claims to disavow. When he conveys 'his most humble respects' to the monarch 'whose virtues had so justly filled the whole world with admiration', we are not to interpret this as the stock encomium found in the baggage of the career politician everywhere;[2] it is rather a sign of his talent for forgetfulness, for Lilliput *has* become the whole world and his vision has shrunk to pygmy dimensions – unlike Uriah Heep, he really is humble. His fury at the charge of adultery is fanned when he reflects that his accuser, as all the world knows, is only a *Glumglum*, whereas he himself has scaled the dizzy heights of *Nardac*.

This total immersion in the new norms shows the extent to which he has become mentally a little man, unoffendedly accepting the Lilliputians as his peers and basing his defence against adultery on hierarchical distinctions rather than the physiological absurdity of the accusation. This counter-attack upon the treasurer as his inferior in rank follows immediately upon what he clearly regards as an act of almost foolhardy daring – his naming of the two spies who have slandered him; we are to gauge the depths of his indignation from the recklessness of so open a denunciation: 'I will name them, and let 'em make their best of it'.[3] Vittoria Corombona, back to the wall and hedged round by enemies, does not display a braver spirit. Gulliver's mind has become totally Lilliputian, the larger world he comes from forgotten, no mental citadel still intact from which he can survey with amused detachment the absurd antics of these foolish little men.

His informant on court politics, briefing him on the High-Heel–Low-Heel split, remarks that the Low Heels are now on top – a political truth that Gulliver must have observed, having been blazed forth to all by the royal heels being a fourteenth part of an inch lower than the rest of the court. Gulliver's descent into Lilliputian standards is revealed in the insultingly casual nature of his adviser's parenthesis – 'as you cannot but observe'[4] – but Gulliver has forfeited the right to feel insulted, has barred himself from retorting that such trifles as a *drurr* are far beneath his attention, has in fact no inclination to do so; what his eye cannot even see looms large in his mind. The Giant King's ridicule of English party politics as unworthy the attention of a serious man is vetoed to Gulliver, up to his neck in the petty follies of Lilliput; where the Giant King reflects the Olympian derision of Jove in 'The Day of Judgement', the Man Mountain shares the values of his tiny companions, mentally as much a Lilliputian as his hosts. It's a small world: cliché is transformed into moral truth for the habituated Gulliver.

Brainwashing, the power of habit, the displacement of one set of established ideas by another, hinted at from the book's beginning, appears explicitly as a major theme towards the end of the first voyage. But before that we have the comedy of the Lilliputian scholars' blank incomprehension at Gulliver's account of the great world.[5] Gulliver cannot be human in their sense of the word since a hundred such creatures would quickly devour all the food in the world; he must therefore have fallen out of the sky, come from the moon or a star. The logic is impeccable, given the closed system of Lilliputian conditioning – Lilliputian knowledge forbids the possibility of a society of Gullivers and what they know is not on the agenda for debate or revision. Swift's favourite comic strategy of highlighting the discrepancy between word and deed provides a launching-pad for the habituation theme. When the Emperor talks of lenity, everyone braces himself for atrocity, just as when Big Brother promises plenty, all tighten their belts. Hearing the mild decision – blinding followed by slow starvation – the naive Gulliver confesses to being 'so ill a judge of things that I could not discover the lenity and favour of this sentence'.[6] His bad judgement saves his life when he decamps rather than accept so mild a chastisement, but he is a bad judge only in assuming a perfect congruence between word and deed, sentence and act, instead of exposing their fearful discordance.

Gulliver's flight opens the door for Swift's critique of 'knowledge' as conditioning, habituation to what is contingent and relative as though it were immutable and absolute. The innocence of ignorance is Gulliver's salvation, just as an uncritical submission to experience would have destroyed him. It follows that a certain kind of knowledge is as damaging as radiation exposure, killing the instinctive response in replacing the human with the habitual. We shall return to this theme later, when, in a dramatic reversal, those exemplary figures, the Giant King and the Houyhnhnm Master, already praised for their inquisitive zest, are suddenly held up for our admiration as saintly obscurantists who will have no truck with wickedness, even to the extent of knowing it.

'A Voyage to Brobdingnag' develops the two major themes initiated in Part One: the status of knowledge in its relation to opinion and experience and the value of knowledge in its relation to progress and morality. The Brobdingnagian scholars, like their colleagues in Lilliput, are too frozen epistemologically, too locked into perceptual habits, even to begin to understand Gulliver – they lack the essential humility that leaves the true scholar open to new insight. They, too, function within a closed system where everything is already categorised, so that Gulliver's arrival is, like ice in Siam, a contradiction of all existing experience. Their various attempts to explain him failing, they fall back upon sport of nature in a sonorous Brobdingnagian equivalent of *lusus naturae*, which sounds impressively scientific but is merely a new label for old ignorance, finally no more useful than Aristotle's occult causes. It is the Giant King, not his scholars, who achieves the remarkable breakthrough of actually listening to Gulliver's own account of himself and deciding that it 'might possibly be true'.[7] The invincible dogmatism of the scholars, treating Gulliver as a problem to be solved on strict *a priori* grounds in accordance with the unchallengeable requirements of a sacrosanct system, is transcended; he becomes instead a problem belonging to the order of experience, to be solved by an appeal to empirical evidence, which must, of course, include what he himself says. The King learns when he listens, opening his mind to the possibility of a truth ruinous to his present creed. It was an identical epistemological humility that Cromwell solicited when he begged his parliamentary brethren to consider that they just might be mistaken and there is no doubt that Swift, in exhibiting this intellectual adaptability to the new, intends the King as an exemplary figure.

Gulliver in Brobdingnag is, however, swamped by the new to a point where identity itself becomes problematic. The comedy of the first two voyages comes from seeing a man forget himself in adapting far too freely to new external reality. In Lilliput a giant declines mentally into a little man, in Brobdingnag a midget develops megalomaniac pretensions. Before long Gulliver is referring affectionately to the forty-foot-tall Glumdalclitch as 'my little nurse', acidly to the thirty-foot-tall dwarf as 'a malicious little cub'. The average Brobdingnagian would quite legitimately speak thus and Gulliver, who throughout his stay in Brobdingnag dodges mirrors to avoid being reminded of his insignificance there, now exists in his mind's eye as a full-grown giant. Soon after arriving at court, he cultivates a giant attitude towards English vanities as the minute follies of tiny, worthless creatures – he would, he assures us, laugh just as heartily at English aristocrats mimicking human grandeur as his captors laugh at him. His blasé dismissal of the Brobdingnagian temple as not up to the standard of Salisbury Cathedral – it is only three thousand feet high and he feels entitled, on relativistic grounds, to chide its want of height[8] – conveys with comic exactitude how wonder and awe are inexorably tamed by habit. The servitude of perceptual habit, its torpedo effect upon the imagination, are to be seen in the giants as well as in Gulliver. The Queen lacks her husband's empathic power, the mental generosity that, if only occasionally, allowed him to see things from a Gulliverian perspective. Brobdingnagian blinkers prevent her from appreciating Gulliver's courage in repulsing the giant wasps, for what is a menace to him is only a nuisance to her – hence her blunder in ridiculing as timidity what she should praise as daring.[9]

The moment of re-entry is, as the astronauts tell us, the most dangerous of all, the point of maximum peril when the voyager, grown used
to space, suddenly becomes subject again to atmospheric demands
with potentially destructive consequences. Analogously, Gulliver's
returns to normal life also reveal the shock of re-entry. Even away
from Brobdingnag, in his swimming house in the ocean, he is dominated by giant assumptions. He knows that his rescuers are Englishmen
but has forgotten that Englishmen are not giants and his mental
picture of a man is of someone around seventy feet tall. This explains
his irritation at the delay in getting him on board – why doesn't one of
the sailors simply lift the box out of the sea with his fingers as even
little Glumdalclitch or the dwarf could have done? Such ravings
make his rescuers think they have a madman to deal with, and, if to
carry the attitudes and assumptions of one society into another, vastly
different society, is to be a madman, then Gulliver fits the bill.

But the trouble is disorientation, not lunacy, jet-lag in its most
outrageously conceivable form rather than anything certifiable.
Looking at his fellow Englishmen with eyes schooled to Brobdingnagian dimensions, he is stunned at their pygmy size and sums them
up, in a purely physical notation free from moral animus, as 'the most
contemptible little creatures'. The rescuing captain can't understand
why the castaway shouts when he talks, but for more than two years
Gulliver has had to shout to be heard and he goes on doing so when
there is no longer any need. Once when Sheridan was denouncing
human frailties, Swift silenced him with the caustic enquiry, 'How
came you to claim an exception from all mankind?'[10] We can, if we
wish, direct the same question at Gulliver, but it is not really applicable
to someone who is victim rather than Pharisee, the prisoner of habit
rather than a monster of pride. He battles to readjust to unfamiliar
England against 'the great power of habit and prejudice' and the
tyranny of environment; 'my ideas were wholly taken up with what
I saw on every side of me', he says of his life in Brobdingnag, explaining how total immersion in the milieu had equipped him to wink
at his own littleness as people do at their own faults.[11] England seems
another Lilliput where he shouts at those he meets in the street
to get out of his way before he tramples them underfoot. The voyage
ends in the comic reunion with his family, he thinking his wife and
daughter unaccountably dwindled, they thinking him demented. We
begin to be uneasily aware of the great power of habit and prejudice
in our own lives, suspecting that it is not just in physical matters that
we are so conditioned.

The conviction that perceptual imprisonment is ubiquitous, that what we arrogantly take for cognition is merely custom, habits successfully pretending to be truths, is reinforced when we find even the wise horses included in the circle of dogmatic error. In Lilliput and Brobdingnag Gulliver is an inconvenient fact disrupting ancient systems of knowledge. Rather than amend their systems, the scholars dismiss him as a liar or explain him away as the kind of freak that even the best systems have to tolerate from time to time. The Houyhnhnm Master has the laudable curiosity to ask questions but shares with the rest of us the reluctance to entertain answers which overturn cherished truths. When, in response to the invitation to state how he got there, Gulliver tells how he sailed from his own country in a great wooden vessel with a number of his fellows, the horse concludes that his wonderful Yahoo is either mistaken or lying. The horse knows it is impossible for a country to exist beyond the sea, just as he knows that the Houyhnhnms are not shipbuilders nor the Yahoos navigators. How then can Gulliver be telling the truth? The question is settled on *a priori* grounds in terms of the unquestioned assumptions of Houyhnhnm thought.

The folly of arguing on such grounds without considering empirical evidence is emphasized in the Houyhnhnm inventory of Gulliver's defects relative to his brother brutes in Houyhnhnmland, culminating in the charge that he cannot walk with security, since, if either of his hinder feet slip, he must inevitably fall.[12] It is deliberately ironical that the Houyhnhnm should select as the supreme instance of Gulliver's perverse folly in opposing nature, thus handicapping himself in the struggle to survive, the one decision that enabled man to dominate the world in a way never achieved by any other animal – the crucial decision to stand upright, to become *homo erectus*, upright man. Even a rational horse cannot imagine the advantages of going on two legs rather than four; all its equine prejudices, inherited from countless generations of ancestors, prevent an understanding of this aberrant, suicidal Yahoo who has altered nature so much for the worse in a whole catalogue of deleterious mutations: face too flat, nose too prominent, eyes badly situated, and so on.

But the fault-finding is itself faulty, based on a radical misconception, a horse's fatuous attempt to legislate for men. The Houyhnhnms know what nature has programmed them to know and such knowledge is ideal for them, but because it comes straight from the horse's mouth doesn't mean that it's good for us, and in their intolerant attribution of their own norms to Gulliver, they repeat the blunder of the scholars of Lilliput and Brobdingnag. On the eve of his expulsion, Gulliver, looking from a hilltop with his pocket-glass to spy the nearest land, sees about five leagues away a small island which the sorrel nag, lacking all conception of any country but his own, mistakes for a blue cloud. [13] *Quantum sumus, scimus*: we know what we have been programmed to know and the sorrel nag knows there is no land but Houyhnhnmland. But Gulliver knows better and islands are not clouds, however much one venerates those who say they are.

If perceptual prisons are to be broken and limited vision corrected, a narrow parochialism not mistaken for truth, then intellectual curiosity and a readiness for new ideas, a 'scepticism' towards custom facilitating its abandonment when necessary, are the tools of liberation. Swift's admiration for such agility is manifest in the Giant King and the Houyhnhnm Master who creditably hear Gulliver out, bravely renouncing the dogmas that label him liar the instant he contradicts the conventional wisdom of Brobdingnag and Houyhnhnmland. Yet it is these same exemplary figures, praised for their openness to experience and their patient attention to Gulliver, who suddenly halt, indignantly declining to cross thresholds of cognition over which Gulliver invites them.

One of the difficulties of the *Travels* is that it deals with a cluster of associated subjects – habit, curiosity, enquiry, knowledge – in two totally opposed ways that furnish two totally opposed sets of instructions for its readers. Gulliver can be seen as the book's hero in certain full interpretations of that word. A modern reader, fresh from Dostoevsky's Grand Inquisitor and *Brave New World*, might reasonably regard Gulliver in Brobdingnag as the hero as lover of freedom, refusing to trade it for comfort or security. All through his captivity and not simply during his initial period of maltreatment and exploitation, he chafes against the indignity done to human nature in his person, regarding himself as universal human representative. Even when he is treated kindly by Glumdalclitch and the King, he goes on longing for freedom and return to England – 'I wanted to be among people with whom I could converse upon even terms'[14] – he doesn't want to be anybody's pet and is mortified when he learns of the plan to find a female upon whom he can breed. To father a posterity little better than canaries is a secure but intolerable future and he prefers the risks of freedom to the shameful ease of servitude.

Perhaps this is an anachronistic way of regarding him, distorting

Swift's intentions through twentieth-century spectacles; perhaps
Swift was not so impelled as we are to applaud the heroism of this
particular decision, since the perplexing priorities of freedom and
security did not press upon him with quite the insistent urgency that
they do today – although the student of Hobbes was clearly aware of
them. But there can be no question of Gulliver's relevance to Swift
in what a modern reader might consider his other role as hero – not
ethical hero, preferring hazardous liberty to the degrading comfort of
Brobdingnag, not the champion of human dignity against the behaviourist psychologists and genetic engineers who will programme
him for happiness, but hero of truth, scientific hero, always looking,
always seeking, intrepidly intent on finding out, whatever the cost.
That Swift had this in mind in creating Gulliver is indisputable; the
only doubt is in determining the degree to which he underwrote this
notion of the hero as truth-seeker, upheld it as unreservedly exemplary.

The *Travels* testify to Swift's affection for truth-seekers. The
Giant King and the Houyhnhnm Master are eager to learn about
European affairs, especially our history, that central humanist concern
to which Swift himself was so committed. The one moment when little
Grildrig is treated with total respect is when he gravely rebukes the
King for his irresponsible levity towards Europe, arguing that a prince
of such excellent understanding should be ashamed of the novice
blunder of identifying size with reason, thereby dismissing Europe
with contempt just because it is little.[15] If men can learn even from
insects, why not Brobdingnagians from Europeans? It is one of the
rare moments in the whole book when Gulliver speaks without any
intervening irony on his creator's behalf as Swift discards his satiric
mask to appear as straight man. This direct appeal to the civilized
virtues – politeness, wholesome curiosity, the respect owed to others
until it is forfeited by misconduct – evokes the civilized response:
'The King heard me with attention, and began to conceive a much
better opinion of me than he had ever before. He desired I would give
him as exact an account of the government of England as I possibly
could . . . he should be glad to hear of anything that might deserve
imitation'.[16]

The respite from satire is now over, for although the King, chastened
and attentive, sits, metaphorically speaking, at Gulliver's feet, eager
to learn, what he hears is valuable only in the sense of negative
imitation – studying Europe, he learns how Brobdingnag must *not*

behave. The climactic irony is that the dignified appeal ushers in the shameful revelations, Gulliver's most impressive moment in Brobdingnag leads on to his most ignominious; treated at last as a rational being, given all the time he needs to persuade his host how admirable we Europeans are, he leaves him instead convinced that we are 'the most pernicious race of little odious vermin that Nature ever suffered to crawl upon the surface of the earth'.[17] Nor can we dismiss this as the careless verdict of a half-hearted student, unwillingly conscripted for tuition and paying only fitful attention. Gulliver has five audiences, each several hours long, to state his case, before the King, in a final session, using extensive lecture notes, gets his chance to question the teacher. Any one of us would be delighted to have so assiduously intelligent a student so urgently devoted to his subject.

The Houyhnhnm Master takes even greater pains to learn all he can about Europe, for while Gulliver could already speak the language when he met the King, the Houyhnhnm has to spend three months teaching Gulliver, giving 'many hours of his leisure' to a crash course in the Houyhnhnm tongue, before getting back 'some tolerable answers' – sufficient testimony to the horse's eagerness to learn. Gulliver's conversations with the Houyhnhnm are an extended, detailed account of what has already been presented in précis in his sessions with the Giant King. One chapter in Brobdingnag suffices for Gulliver's five lectures and the final tutorial, whereas in Part Four three chapters are needed to describe European civilization, followed by a fourth in which the horse sums up what he has learned. But there is the same basic pattern in both voyages: the tribute to Gulliver as someone worth listening to, the laudable curiosity of the host in his zest for instruction, the same slashing summation of man as pest – 'little odious vermin', 'that instead of Reason, we were only possessed of some quality fitted to increase our natural vices'.[18] In each case, the verdict is based upon an application to the problem that testifies to the lively curiosity of the interlocutor's mind; Swift clearly approved of people who liked finding out and who exerted themselves to do so.

We need only look for further confirmation at the people he dislikes in the *Travels* and the reason for it. The generalised evil of the Yahoo apart, the two great cautionary subgroups within the book, representing finally one specific variety of shortcoming, are the Laputans and the Struldbruggs. Each, in their respective ways, exhibits a blinkered egoism which finds nothing in the world worthy of contemplation outside the narrow preoccupations of the self. The trouble with the Laputans, for Swift, is not just that they have enrolled in the wrong faculty and are reading the wrong syllabus of subjects; it is rather that they shamefully snub the rest of the university and especially those revered subjects without which, Swift insists, there is no true, humane education. The list of subjects in the Giant King's 'defective' education, as lambasted by the corrupt Gulliver, still smarting from his gunpowder fiasco – morality, history, poetry and mathematics (but only applied mathematics, with immediate utility for improving everyday life) – alerts us to those fields of study that Swift unreservedly admires.

Conversely, there is a clue to his curt dismissal of metaphysics, music and pure mathematics in his explanation as to why *Paradise Lost* is a greater poem than Thomson's *Seasons*. Whereas Thomson's is a purely descriptive poem dealing only with nature, a landscape without figures, Milton provides not just description but, much more important, a crucially significant human action.[19] We appreciate this tribute to Milton as a kind of historian all the more when we recall Swift's own lifelong devotion to the study of history as the central humane discipline. Like the Giant King and the Houyhnhnm Master, Swift is deeply interested in the doings of men, in human nature and its manifold ways of organizing itself in different societies, and Gulliver inherits this interest from his creator. He sets out on his third voyage with 'the thirst I had of seeing the world, notwithstanding my past misfortunes, continuing as violent as ever'.[20]

Ironically, this rage for experience, this craving for other men and other lands, send him to a people so stonily incurious to anything outside their circle of interest that their wives yawningly commit adultery under their noses without being noticed. The Laputans live steeped in metaphysical speculation, 'always so wrapped up in cogitation that [they are] in manifest danger of falling down every precipice'.[21] Swift offers a new variation on the old joke about the absent-minded professor which goes back at least as far as Thales. Thales, we are told, was so busy speculating about solar eclipses that he fell down a well that yawned before him, Archimedes so engrossed in a geometrical problem that he didn't hear his killers approaching. The everyday business of ordinary life – and even the indispensable business of preserving life – flow unheeded past such men as they concentrate exclusively upon cornering some elusive abstraction. Are they great heroes or great fools? If the Laputan philosophers are a reliable guide, Swift is clearly in no doubt as to where to place them.

Such men do not know how to live, have sacrificed life to thought, and are so besotted with futile abstractions that they have no room for the wider curiosity that alone makes civilized life possible. They are fanatics of learning, as equally ridiculous and unpleasant as their counterparts in religion. When Gulliver first climbs aboard the flying island it is, significantly, the vulgar who show interest in the remarkable stranger, their philosopher masters being 'altogether unmoved by the sight of my foreign habit and countenance' – just as we later hear how the common people and the women lead the timely rebellion, totally supported by Swift, against the intellectuals' preposterous plan to abolish language altogether and replace words with things in conversation.[22] One sees why Orwell, despite other major differences, had a great affection for the good, old-fashioned, no-nonsense Swift, scourge of snootily pretentious airy fairy élitists.

First introduced to the king's presence, Gulliver has to wait over an hour before being even noticed, as the king 'was then deep in a problem'. Learning *per se* was not something that bowled Swift over, especially when it was divorced from the decencies of civilized life. He looked upon the great scholar Bentley as a Yahoo with a doctorate, a man whose vast expertise, far from helping him to be courteous and humane, merely enabled him to be rude with impunity, providing a secure academic base for his disgraceful manners. The moonstruck meanderings of Laputan world-makers were even less impressive than Bentley's pedantic boorishness. When Gulliver tells the Laputans that he doesn't need a flapper to summon him back to everyday concerns or civilized discourse, he immediately falls from grace in a society where being rapt is a sacramental sign and all the best people have flappers. They have two obsessive interests – music and pure mathematics; in every other area of human activity they are either deliberately ignorant or unbelievably inept. They worship theory, which means that they cannot make a decent suit of clothes or build a proper house, since their dexterity on paper is allied to contempt for the practical application of any skill. All their discoveries are, appropriately, in the stars and they easily outstrip European astronomers. Swift stays unimpressed – who, starstruck lunatics apart, cares about the theory of comets and what practical good can accrue to man from such learned lumber? Thales fell down a hole, harming only himself, but it's no joke when the country is falling apart and its so-called rulers are either at the bottom of wells or wandering beyond the moon.

Comic nemesis has, however, fittingly caught up with them as obsession deepens into pure mania. They have become catastrophists and doomwatchers, neurotically poised for the end of the world through collision with a comet, the death of the sun or some other heavenly disaster. So rooted is this terror that they cannot even rest or enjoy 'the common pleasures or amusements of life'. Swift as defender of the common pleasures of life is such an unusual role that we are sent back to scrutinize even more closely the culprit philosophy that interferes so regrettably with everyday amusements. Thales, we perceive, is neither admirable nor even funny; the lovably amusing absent-minded professor shades into the inhuman scholar–scientist, 'so abstracted and involved in speculation that I never met with such disagreeable companions'.[23] Gulliver's completely justified resentment comes to a head when, after learning the language and able to answer the king's questions, he finds that the king wants to hear only about European mathematics and has not the slightest interest in the laws, government, history, religion or manners of the various countries known to Gulliver – the university has dwindled to a chair in pure mathematics, with every other discipline discarded as worthless. No wonder Gulliver is disgusted. The king's preference in instruction is in itself enough to condemn him in Swift's eyes. What a waste of Gulliver's experience, what a deplorable sense of priorities, and what a depressing dearth of curiosity – the contrast with the eager inquisitiveness of the Giant King is deliberately glaring.

The other great negative example are the Struldbruggs. Gulliver, longing for England, has just turned down a good offer from the King of Luggnagg to stay on at his court, when he suddenly hears of the Struldbruggs and is seized with an altruistic joy that someone, somewhere, has cheated the otherwise universal doom of death. All thoughts of family and homeland vanish as he decides to spend the rest of his life among the happy beneficiaries of man's most ancient, pervasive, ubiquitous dream – the gift of immortality. Camus's Outsider in the death cell dreams deliciously that just once the condemned man escapes as the inexorable march of events miraculously falters; the Struldbruggs are apparently the realization of that dream: 'Happy nation where every child hath at least a chance for being immortal!'[24] It is one of the very few occasions when Swift employs the exclamation mark in the *Travels* and its use is to deepen the ironic contrast when deluded rapture is routed by harsh reality.

The dream of eternal life becomes the nightmare of never dying, the horror of being a Struldbrugg, for it is he, not the man in the death cell, who is truly condemned. Their futile, zombie existence is made plain in the appallingly incurious faces they turn towards life. When Gulliver is presented to them as a great traveller who has seen all the world, they have not a single question to ask him apart from begging money – the whole of man's life has shrivelled to a *slumskudask* and immortality is used for cadging handouts.[25] Orwell borrows the Struldbruggs in order to expose his hero to a similarly disillusioning experience. Winston Smith, his head ringing with the mystical assurance that salvation is in the proles, overhears in a prole pub an old man demanding from an uncomprehending barman the long dis- carded measure of a pint. Hoping that he has finally found a repository of ancient wisdom who can tell him about life before Big Brother, he invites him to discuss the great changes since he was a young man. The old man has lived through the whole frenzied career of western man in the twentieth century but can only remember that the beer used to be better and that he once wore a top-hat at a funeral. Helpless- ness floods over Winston as he realizes that there is no living mind here but simply a rubbish heap of worthless detail.[26] There is no more hope in the old prole than Gulliver finds in the Struldbruggs and in both cases the really sickening discovery is that they neither know nor want to know, that their ignorance is a fate which is, nevertheless, in some sense also a choice.

If the incurious Laputans and know-nothing Struldbruggs are the book's villains, it would seem reasonable to regard the restlessly inquiring Gulliver as its hero. He first goes travelling because his business fails and he can't make it ashore, but thereafter he is an addict, victim of what Pascal diagnoses as our prime ailment, an inability to sit quietly at home. Money, no longer the motivation, is useful only for persuading his wife to let him go, the inconvenient absence more than balanced by the financial gain to the family. What he craves is new experience, the thirst for the world he refers to as he sets out on his third voyage – he can no more turn down a ship than an alcoholic can a drink. 'I continued at home with my wife and children about five months in a very happy condition, if I could have learned the lesson of knowing when I was well': so begins the final voyage but the reader has long realized that Gulliver prefers the risks of travel to the wellbeing of a stay-at-home, sedentary existence.

Gulliver travels and he travels to acquire new knowledge, new experience, new sensation – he is man not as Pascal would have him be but as he regrettably is. Gulliver's predatory pursuit of knowledge is most strikingly demonstrated in the voyage to Brobdingnag and it is no coincidence that Swift here develops his most searching critique of how man should comport himself with regard to new discoveries, welcoming them indiscriminately or cultivating a wary suspicion that will help sift what is valuable from what is pernicious. 'Having been condemned by Nature and Fortune to an active and restless life . . .' – thus Gulliver, only two months home from Lilliput, explains his decision to set out once more.[28] It is the same restless, investigative mind that causes him to be stranded in Brobdingnag, for he begs to go ashore with the longboat seeking fresh water to see the country and 'make what discoveries I could', and it is while he is busily researching that the fate of Archimedes seems to have fallen on him.[29] His companions, pursued by the monster, abandon him, and the itch for knowledge exposes him to destruction.

Gulliver as hero–victim of the scientific impulse, comic brother to Thales and Archimedes, those fellow sufferers for truth's sake – it is not too wildly absurd a supposition, though what Swift might say is another matter. But that Swift admires those who strive after knowledge, despises the lazily incurious, is beyond question. And who else in fact or fiction has been so avid for books that he has used ladders and scaffolding to get at them, so keen on self-instruction that he has combined it with gymnastics, as Gulliver does in Brobdingnag? How many of us would consort with the spirits of the dead to improve our knowledge of history? Gulliver is a hero of learning, lining up with the Giant King and the Houyhnhnm Master rather than with the Laputans and Struldbruggs. If we look at the content of what, generally speaking, he seeks to know – the manners, history, government, politics, and so on of the various peoples he encounters – we find a syllabus of study already heartily approved by his creator. Why is it, then, that Gulliver is not the book's unqualified hero? Why, paradoxically, is the declension from heroism clearest of all at certain key moments when his determination to pursue truth at all costs earns him Swift's condemnation, not praise?

The clue given at the opening of the book's final chapter will carry us through these difficulties. Gulliver is simultaneously defending the plainness of his book in style and content and denouncing the Münchhausens who aim at sensation; he too could have astonished us with a host of tall tales had he not preferred instruction to amusement and sacrificed ornament to truth.[30] Every traveller should try to make men 'wiser and better', writing always for their amendment rather than their approbation. This is, of course, pure comedy, Swift smiling to himself as his stolid narrator sells ludicrously short the astonishing inventive genius that went to the creation of the *Travels* – for what more could a tribe of Münchhausens have given us in the way of fantastic adventure? But there is another sense in which it is straight-forwardly serious, for Swift did write to make men wiser and better – it is the justification and overriding criterion to which he repeatedly adverts; it is also of crucial importance in determining his attitude towards intellectual curiosity and a guide through what we might otherwise misinterpret as inconsistency and contradiction.

Swift commends but does not idolize intellectual curiosity. The pursuit of knowledge *à l'outrance* is, he believes, in certain circum-stances, no more legitimate than the unbridled pursuit of power. Nietzsche argues that power must express itself unconfinedly to be power at all, that a quantum of withheld power is a logical contra-diction, that failure to act proves incapacity to do so. A man without power submits, a man with it retaliates; the idea of a power choosing submission rather than action, disciplining itself to passivity, is for Nietzsche nonsensical, is at the root of his quarrel with Christianity, his hostility to Christ as rival and competitor. Gulliver, with the power to crush Blefuscu, refuses to do so on the ground that the act is immoral, where a would-be Nietzschean like Raskolnikov is drawn to commit the act precisely because it is immoral, for how else can one be a superman without committing sin? Yet most of us think that even sordid old pawnbrokers have a right to live and applaud Gulliver's decision as the welcome triumph of right over might – we endorse Isabella's words as to the excellence of having a giant's strength and agree that, at least occasionally, it is tyrannous to use it like a giant.

We are, in other words, not Nietzscheans when it is a question of physical power. We do, however, adopt a Nietzschean stance towards the matter of intellectual power – any voluntary restriction here, any limit freely agreed, seem to us like the perverse self-immolation that Nietzsche saw in Pascal. But if we are less sympathetic to the demand that intellectual, no less than physical, power should discipline itself in setting bounds to its aspirations, this is because we regard intellec-tual power as a totally unqualified good – we are the Nietzscheans of intellect, believing that nothing must stay its uninhibited progress. Swift does not agree. He avoids our inconsistency by urging that the pursuit of knowledge, as of power, should be circumscribed by moral considerations and he does this all the more insistently because, like his compatriot Burke, he is warily suspicious of intelligence. Against the exponents of the *arcana imperii* tradition, he repeatedly asserted that the art of government was a simple, straightforward business, well within the capacity of the average man, distrusting the experts who claimed alone to possess the secret.[31] The Lilliputans, with Swift's approval, prefer honest men of everyday talent to the clever rogues who line their pockets – what, finally, is more frightening than an evil genius? The Houyhnhnms expel Gulliver for fear the wonderful Yahoo will someday defect to his brutal brethren, taking his superior expertise with him. The unfettered intellect, uninstructed by morality, is the major bogey darkening Swift's pages. So the moralist in Swift feared curiosity when it made men neither wiser nor better but carried them to contamination instead of enlightenment. In Brobdingnag we see how the search after knowledge becomes a mode of depravation.

Brobdingnag, giant in its horrors as in all else, magnifying twelve-fold what we might otherwise evade or take casually in our stride, thrusts every ailment and mutilation, every nasty item in the lives of man and beast, before our horrified gaze; wens and tumours, blotches and smells, food smeared with flies' excrement, lice crawling pig-size through clothes, all is inescapably present, the daily routine of Gulliver's life. Short of plucking out his eyes, he cannot avoid all this – but what shocks us, perhaps, is that he doesn't really want to, is indeed enjoying in some queer way the fascination of disgust. Far from averting his eyes and hurrying away, Gulliver looks – and, despite a heaving stomach, he looks entranced, resolutely repressing nausea for the sake of the information and experience acquired. His one regret after almost throwing up at the loathsome lice is that he hasn't his dissecting instruments with him – a remarkable tribute to the scientific spirit, that lust to know, so characteristic of western man, for he surely realizes, as does the anatomist of the *Tale* with the beau's carcass, that the deeper he cuts, the more hideous will be the mess.

In a letter of Byron's is an arresting passage presenting in almost canonical form this modern attitude towards experience, the idea that unwavering openness is the greatest commandment, unflinching audacity towards new sensation the greatest virtue.[32] Describing a double guillotining which he bravely attended despite temptation to stay away, he tells how, in his state of excited apprehension, 'my hand shook so that I could hardly hold the opera glass', then supplies the rationale for forcing oneself to so distressing an experience: we must look closely at everything, once. Kant, rejecting happiness, tells us we are given life in order to do our duty; Byron tells us what this duty is. We must resist the tempter who would have us desert our post, our observation post, for not to look, shirking the experience, stigmatizes the coward and weakling. We meet here the essential initiation rite of western man, the test which alone certifies the transition from adolescence to maturity, analogous to those rituals where primitive peoples wound themselves to prove their courage. In each case, the rationale is identical: we emerge from the ordeal fortified and stronger.

George Steiner argues that the axiomatic assumption of western civilization is the belief that man and the truth are companions, that mental inquiry must move forward, such motion being both natural and meritorious in itself, since man's proper relation to the truth is one of pursuer.[33] Western man *must* go on seeking truth; other civilizations unmoved by this compulsion are not demonstrating some miraculous free choice or feat of innocence, rather the stigma of adverse ecological and genetic circumstance – they *lack* the exhilarating, hazardous curiosity that makes western man the hero of truth. 'We cannot turn back. We cannot choose the dreams of unknowing.' The Nietzschean compulsion towards power is reinterpreted in intellectual terms. However fearful the knowledge, we must embrace it like a Christian with the Cross, assured that agony is the only way to salvation.

Today, we are told, for the first time the axioms of scientific beneficence and uninterrupted advance are being questioned, but this exaggerates, for the axioms, however seductive, were never unanimously approved. What has happened is that certain developments in the modern world have made us more willing to listen to the great dissenters, isolated voices from the past cautioning against the unfettered intellect, warning of the need to keep the scientific spirit on a moral rein. When Steiner quotes Tito Perlini on the fetishism of fact – 'raised to the status of an autonomous idol, the *fact* is an absolute tyrant before whom thought can do nothing but bow down in silent worship' – we recall Pascal's injunction not to make an idol of truth.[34] And how, after reading the final chorus of *Doctor Faustus*, can we doubt that the fatality of knowledge was suspected long before Freud or Jacques Monod? Most relevant of all to *Gulliver's Travels*, we find Milton in *Paradise Lost* ascribing the invention of gunpowder to Satan and denouncing this hellish discovery as a desecration of heaven's beauty. There is no need to wait until today for a rebellion against the tyrannical obscurantism of rational, scientific truth, since this is precisely what the Giant King, that lover of new discoveries, does when he ostracizes the fact of gunpowder, declines even to know it far less use it. Is is a triumph all the more remarkable in that this refusal, contrary to Steiner's thesis, issues from strength not deficiency, from breathtaking moral integrity rather than adverse circumstance.

Gulliver in Brobdingnag is the paradigmatic western man, ready to pay any price for new experience. He hurries along to the Brobdingnagian execution, because, although he 'abhorred such kind of spectacles . . . my curiosity tempted me to see something that I thought must be extraordinary'. His investigative courage is suitably rewarded, for the spouting blood is like the great *jet d'eau* at Versailles and the bounce of the decapitated head can be heard a mile away – what a shame had some squeamish misgivings robbed him of such novelty.[35] Today he would take his camera and tape-recorder to capture the moment for ever. A camera is what comes to mind as he describes the horrors of European warfare to the Houyhnhnm Master – a steady, unexcited recording of what happens, totally free of moral prejudice or human emotion. Decapitations and massacres are as real as sunsets, and the camera, repudiating preferences, reproduces with detached accuracy whatever encounters its lens. We do not look to a piece of scientific equipment for moral discriminations since it deals only with what is and knows nothing of ought, and it is possible for a man to become himself a scientific machine in this sense, investigating reality regardless of moral consequences.

The Giant King and the Houyhnhnm Master are not scientific in this sense but are instead representative of those other civilizations deficient in that boundless curiosity that admits no limit to its rovings. Despite an exemplary enthusiasm for new knowledge, there are times when they prefer ignorance. Gulliver begins his account of the gunpowder incident with an air of embarrassed regret, yet laudably determined to tell the whole sorry tale to its pitiful end. He would have preferred to conceal or gloss over it – but truth is imperative. His embarrassment is of that vicarious kind which the sensitive feel when someone else behaves badly. Anticipating a shower of royal gratitude, he has offered the King that fruit of civilization, greatest gift of western man, the secret of gunpowder. The King is, unaccountably, horrified and attributes the invention to 'some evil genius, enemy to mankind', for who else could have been 'the first contriver' of a device so wicked?[36] One could almost believe he has been reading Milton, for Satan is the first manufacturer of high explosives and Raphael tells Adam that when the armaments industry starts up again it will be a son of Satan who will do it. His love of new discoveries notwithstanding, the King would rather abdicate than utilize such hideous power and he warns Gulliver that he won't be just spectating at executions if he ever mentions the matter again.

Gulliver can only explain so bewildering a reaction as a deficiency in the scandalized party. The King is 'secluded from the rest of the world', victim of 'the miserable effects of a confined education', and we Europeans, unhampered by nice, unnecessary scruples in our voracious hunt after new discoveries, must charitably discount this when judging – for how can we expect a backwoods barbarian to be arbiter for civilized Europe or permit such provincial narrowness to dictate to our sophistication? This, Gulliver concludes sorrowfully, is what happens when people miss the advantages of a European education – 'a strange effect of narrow principles and short views!' – and the major benefit of all is our liberation from superstitiously foolish misgivings in tolerantly welcoming every new scientific breakthrough.

As Gulliver shakes his head over the deplorable prejudices of his giant host, he anticipates the knowing pedagogue of the final voyage smiling at the naive ineptitude of his Houyhnhnm pupil before the facts of European warfare. Gulliver's chief problem as instructor is that there is no common ground of shared experience nor even a reciprocal vocabulary that he can exploit. How describe a Europe radically discontinuous with Houyhnhnm society, how can the innocent comprehend the depraved, Parson Adams nod sagely as the Marquis de Sade unfolds his sinister tale? The Yahoo alone as sole link makes possible an interchange between Gulliver and the horses, otherwise there could only be silence or Houyhnhnm monologue. By using the Yahoo as a templet for European corruption, a grid for identifying civilized depravity, Gulliver is able to speak so that the horses are not completely baffled; but the templet is only approximate, the grid neither precise nor detailed enough to cover the full range of civilized behaviour.

The Yahoo is only a subset, however large, of universal evil and the Houyhnhnm remains blessedly ignorant of the unnatural vices of Europe because there is no natural domestic model against which he can even begin to understand. Even with the illumination of Yahoo example, he is dumbfounded by the catalogue of European crime – Gulliver labours, desperately reaching for circumlocutions, to be understood, and, even when he makes the breakthrough, the horse's 'understanding' is simply prelude to an even more horrified amazement. Knowing *how*, as Winston Smith discovers, is triflingly inconsequential when set against the infinitely more baffling problem of knowing *why*. The Houyhnhnm 'was wholly at a loss to know what could be the use or necessity of practising those vices'.[37] He is, in fact, painfully realizing that use and necessity, the criteria of the rational intelligence, are wholly inapplicable in solving the *mysterium iniquitatis*, suffering the same bewildered anguish as Othello trying to make sense of Iago's malice. When Gulliver pities the simpleton who doesn't know about high explosives, we recall another simpleton whose rapturous praise of the Struldbruggs causes his knowing listeners to smile. But where *his* ignorance came from not knowing better, the horse's comes from not knowing worse.

Yet the Houyhnhnm is also intentionally ignorant and, from a certain standpoint, culpably so; he too, like the Giant King, commands silence on the ground that curiosity can go too far, that there are doors best left unopened, depravities best unheard. 'He thought his ears being used to such abominable words, might by degrees admit them with less detestation.'[38] Byron's injunction to see everything once is rejected since defilement must have a beginning and the addict was once merely curious. Experiment may end in disaster. The horse educates Gulliver in the Houyhnhnm tongue to be in turn educated in European affairs – but it isn't so much education, a leading out, as computer-programming, a feeding in; the Houyhnhnm, no computer, finally rebels when the material being fed becomes so foul as to reach danger level. Pollution accumulates until he suffers 'a disturbance in his mind', and, far from being ashamed of this as a sign of evasive immaturity, he cherishes it as a kind of moral alarum essential to self-preservation. There can be moral as well as physical contagion and the rage for experience can be as deadly as any corporeal fever. Exemplary in their readiness to admit new knowledge, the Giant King and the Houyhnhnm Master are equally so in the wise prophylaxis that shuts out moral infection.

Swift, conforming to the Pascalian prescription for true greatness, moves between two extremes in his enquiry into the triad of habit, curiosity and knowledge.[39] On the one hand, he attacks slothful conditioning as the foe of knowledge, and, following Cromwell, urges the intellectual sluggards to think that they might be mistaken. On the other hand, he endorses established moral convictions and recommends an entrenched dogmatism against the novel perversions of trendy innovators. The pressure of the real as embodied in the brutal facts of commonplace corruption provokes in Swift's heroes the attitude of the French at Verdun: *ils ne passeront pas*. Yet there is no real contradiction, despite the apparent confusion that the heroes are praised for the same reason as the villains are condemned: they will not learn. The only absolute recognized by Swift is the moral good of man and, in obedience to this, all knowledge is segregated into three categories – what we must know, however unpalatable, because without it we are lost; what we may know, so long as it is not given a false priority; and what we must not know because it is the knowledge forbidden by heaven. This division explains how Swift can both praise and condemn curiosity, uphold and expose habit, welcome and shun knowledge. It explains how certain forms of ignorance can be regarded as good and certain feats of wilful ignorance as blessed; and we are no longer puzzled when strenuous strivers after knowledge are transformed into saintly dunces with an even greater demand upon our admiration. At the end of *Paradise Lost* Adam, in a kind of graduation ceremony, takes leave of his final tutor Michael, 'greatly instructed' and with his 'fill of knowledge'. When we inspect the ensuing curriculum we find that it is essentially a moral education, a course in right living. The delighted archangel confers on his student the degree *summa cum laude*: 'This having learned, thou hast attained the sum / Of wisdom; hope no higher . . .'[40] Swift will be content if those undergoing his course of instruction pass out with similar qualifications.

SEVEN

THE DISPLACED PERSON

Gulliver travels to find himself. As much as *Oedipus* or *Der zerbrochene Krug* the action is a search for identity, its ultimate question as shocking as that posed by the twentieth-century death-camps: not 'where is God?' but, much more appallingly, 'where is man?' In pursuit of this mystery, Swift employs throughout certain recurring images and themes – giants and girls, sexuality and vermin – as aids to identification.

The opening voyage, addressing a personal dilemma as well as universal concerns, is the most autobiographical; in the figure of the baffled giant, Swift investigates his own captivity in Lilliput. One of the most bitter sensations known to man is the consciousness of failure affixed to a conviction of ability. When the man is not merely talented but a genius, the agony of bewilderment, of unjustified self-reproach, is commensurately greater, and the mystery of defeat, forever soliciting explanation, can become a mode of diabolic torment. That Swift saw himself as both genius and failure we need not doubt, for his own word is the evidence. 'What a genius I had when I wrote that book!'[1] The note of elated discovery and gratified pride in his own belated tribute to the *Tale* only enhances and authenticates the sense of accomplishment he experienced in the rereading; and the reception of the *Travels* as recorded by Johnson – 'It was received with such avidity that the price of the first edition was raised before the second could be made; it was read by the high and the low, the learned and illiterate. Criticism was for a while lost in wonder'[2] – must surely have ratified in him the conviction of his old power. He had, in addition, other spectacular triumphs. The purpose of *The Conduct of the Allies*, says Johnson, was to persuade the nation to a peace, and never had pamphlet more success.³ In *The Drapier's Letters* he had, single-handed, defeated a government attempt to exploit Ireland – and, for Swift, saving the Irish was a labour that might have confounded Hercules himself.

The ordinary man shakes his head in perplexity on hearing such a life described as failure; what, he wonders, would Swift have accepted as success? Yet genius remains inconsolable; if there is one indisputable fact about Swift, it is his bitter, invincible conviction of defeat. We might pardonably exaggerate by describing him as a man programmed for defeat, and the great fish which he just missed catching as a boy was indeed, as he told Pope, to haunt his whole life as prophetic admonition, symbol of all those near things that darkened his career.⁴ The man whose pantheon of heroes was an assembly of spectacular failures – Brutus, Junius, Socrates, Epaminondas, Cato, More – was acutely sensitive to the obstacles cumbering the path of heroic virtue in a spiteful, petty, levelling world. He caustically supplies the one infallible test of a true genius: all the dunces are inveterately leagued against him. He provides the recipe to those seeking advancement through the power of the word:

> Write worse then if you can – be wise –
> Believe me 'tis the way to rise.⁵

The pain of personal failure, the sense of wasted endeavour, of words marshalled to no creative purpose – doses prescribed for the dead, appeals to animals incapable of amendment, the charmer's skill squandered on deaf adders – all this hangs heavy over Swift's work, is indeed, paradoxically, the source of its greatness. No other writer of genius has so much made the foolish futility of words the master-theme of his achievement, and it is this that partially justifies Leavis's pronouncement about great powers exhibited consistently in negation and rejection.⁶

Failure is less tantalising when the great man falls through some excess or shortcoming, the tragedy of *hamartia* as defined by Hamlet, 'the stamp of one defect' that pulls ruin upon a whole array of virtues. This helps to assuage whatever dismay we feel at Antony bested by Octavius or Coriolanus broken by the tribunes. Great men undoubtedly, but the reconciling pity is that greatness should be so lamentably vitiated. The reconciling element disappears, however, when heroism perishes with no *hamartia* to dull the edge of pain. The defeat of goodness is for Swift as nerve-jangling as Aristotle predicted, and we need only read Swift on More's fate at the hands of 'Henry the Beast' to appreciate how unappeasably angry he could become at the spectacle of unmerited suffering – the greatest Englishman of all time murdered by the worst.[7]

Swift re-echoes the perplexed anguish of the Psalmist: how long, O God? Why does God forget his servant, hide in the seasons of distress? Why do the good fail, the wicked flourish? Why is the genius doomed to die like a poisoned rat in a Dublin hole while mediocrities monopolize power? Nor is it simply his own personal debacle that torments him. His friend Bolingbroke provides yet another confirmatory instance of the same perverse law that condemns great ability to impotence. In his poem 'On the Death of Dr Swift' there is a footnote telling us that Bolingbroke 'is reckoned the most universal genius in Europe', but that Walpole, dreading his gifts, has conspired with George I to keep him in the political doldrums.[8] The mystery remains: how has an intellectual giant like Bolingbroke been outmanoeuvred and outsmarted by a commonplace rascal like Walpole? What is this strange moral equivalent of Gresham's Law which continually awards victory to Lilliputians, while the colossus, superior gifts notwithstanding, is lucky to escape with eyesight and life?

There is plausible internal evidence that Swift uses Lilliput to explore certain crises in his own life or in the lives of his friends; the giant's 'eminent service' in extinguishing the blaze in the royal apartments which so offends the Empress that she declines ever again to enter the polluted palace, is an allegory of Queen Anne's outraged resolve never to advance the author of the *Tale* – or, alternatively, of the royal ingratitude towards Bolingbroke who had put the nation in his debt by concluding the Peace of Utrecht. Both book and treaty are giant achievements, maligned by pygmy malice. Gulliver, lodged in the profaned temple, desecrated some years before by an unnatural murder, recalls Swift's revulsion at the execution of Charles I, always for him, as his sermon on the royal martyr shows, the nadir of revolutionary evil.[9] But, detailed interpretation apart, there is clearly something in the image of the bemused giant, curiously impotent despite enormous power, that holds intense personal interest for Swift. Not that Gulliver *is* Swift; on the contrary, he is in his role as wide-eyed *ingenu* laughably different from his sharp, knowing creator. The ropedancing and the crawling under sticks which so fascinate him as ceremonies unknown to the rest of the world are sickeningly familiar to Swift as the contemptible cantrips of power-seekers everywhere.

But, however unlike in other ways, Gulliver as giant among pygmies is an apposite metaphor of Swift in his society, just as Gulliver's unavailing efforts to live decently and usefully, placing his great powers at the public service but forever frustrated by the envy of little men, is a thinly disguised rendition of his creator's unhappy fate.

Gulliver visits fantastic countries without ever leaving the real world. The veracity he is so touchy about is never really in doubt and his appeal to his long sojourn among the honest horses as verification of his story, is superfluous. Escapist is thoroughly inapplicable to a book which entraps us while pretending to visit exotic regions. Johnson's outrageous dismissal of the *Travels* – a mere matter of thinking of big men and little men with everything else at once falling into place[10] – is unpardonable; what about flying islands and crazy academies, hideous immortals and sorcerers' realms, rational horses and Yahoos? Yet this perverse judgement is relevant to the first two voyages and can help us identify their salient characteristics: the only thing fantastic in Lilliput or Brobdingnag is Gulliver himself, so that it *is* finally nothing more remarkable than a question of relationships between big and little men.

These worlds are perfectly credible, totally recognizable – naturally enough, since they are both our own, diminished and magnified in powers of twelve. Gulliver impatiently waves away the printer's plea for changing the original text; how can he be prosecuted for what has happened so long ago and far away? – thus betraying these travels into remote nations as investigations of contemporary England.[11] Kinship is established when Gulliver spots his first Lilliputian, a human creature not six inches high, with a bow and arrow in his hands and a quiver at his back, while he himself lies pinioned, sword at his side, pistols in his pocket. Unsurprisingly, Lilliput has the same dismal record of war and massacre as England – six feet or six inches, it is the same bellicose, destructive animal. Far from 'remote', Lilliput's problems in warfare, political careerism, religious intolerance, are those of Europe. Not the country nor its customs and concerns, but Gulliver's status within it – this creates the elements of fantasy and fairy-tale, establishes it as the children's classic. Giants are a norm in fairy-tale and 'A Voyage to Lilliput' presents a metamorphosis as startling as any in Ovid or Kafka.

Gulliver changes. Shipwrecked an ordinary man on a Pacific beach, he loses consciousness and is reborn nine hours later a giant. Lest we miss the gestation symbolism, he tells us afterwards his stay in the new universe was just over nine months. How seems the world to someone who awakes to a twelvefold increase in stature? Swift supplies a comic analogue to Marlowe's Faustus, an examination of the benefits and perils of being suddenly raised far above ordinary mortals. Its picquancy is a function of Swift's own Olympian self-awareness linked to his sense of restriction and confinement, a fettered giant in his irksome Dublin exile. The dream of power is as old as the dream of immortality and the latest import from American comic books via television in the awesome figure of the Incredible Hulk, who uses his prodigious strength to right wrongs and foil villains, is testimony to the dream's staying-power, in however debased a form. The ordinary man fancies that, given giant power or eternal life, all things are possible, but just as in Part Three Swift destroys the dream of immortality by depicting it as a Struldbrugg nightmare, so in Part One he explodes equally naive expectations by showing that the giant Gulliver fares no better in Lilliput than his intellectual counterparts, Jonathan Swift and Henry St John, do in eighteenth-century England. 'A Voyage to Lilliput' scrutinises the fate of the giant in society by presenting him in certain representative guises: as Polyphemus, Hercules, Samson, and also as intellectual titan, bringer of new truth to ordinary men.

Irony is present from the start in the simultaneous recreation of Gulliver as giant and prisoner. His first impulse to resist as a match for their greatest army is followed by a prudential decision to submit, the linguistic problem circumvented by calling upon the sun as witness of the promise.[12] The Lilliputians evince a similar capacity for prudential morality. They don't try to kill him while he sleeps, sensibly, since the aroused giant would have burst his bonds and caused a blood-bath. The initial relationship between giant and little people is a perfect *exemplum* of Swift's lifelong thesis that decency and commonsense, morality and reason, are ideal bedfellows, that men go to heaven with half the pains of the hellward journey.

The irony of Gulliver's dual status – giant and captive – is, however, soon matched in the ambivalent Lilliputian response. He is, clearly, a notable acquisition; when he eats and drinks, they exhibit an ecstatic proprietary pride in the doer of these wonders. When, freed from the ropes but securely chained, he at last stands erect, they gasp with delighted astonishment. Their attitude to him is rather like Magwitch's to Pip: my gentleman, our giant. But pride competes with other considerations. Like a modern nuclear reactor, Gulliver is both promise and threat, at once source of power and fear, and, however gentle and obedient, he poses serious problems for his hosts' technology. What if he breaks loose, runs amok, causes famine or plague? Even if they manage to kill him, will not the stench of the monstrous carcass produce disastrous environmental pollution? Can they afford so costly a luxury with the consequent strain upon their tiny resources? – he needs six hundred domestics and armies of craftsmen of all kinds from joiners to tailors, he consumes daily enough food to keep 1728 Lilliputians alive, the removal of his excreta requires a squad of labourers with wheelbarrows working a full shift.[13]

His everyday acts are potential catastrophes: a man who extinguishes conflagrations simply by urinating might be welcome in London in 1666 or Chicago in 1871, but always there is the fear that he might just as easily drown the government as save the city. His mere presence is a peril in town or country. He must stick to the highways and stay out of the fields where a stroll would mean total devastation. Visiting the metropolis, he has to wear a short coat for fear of destroying buildings and there is a two hours' curfew to avoid a massacre of citizens. What if he sleepwalks? or sneezes? It's like living with a petro-chemical complex on the doorstep. Every time he relieves himself, the health authorities face a major crisis in pollution disposal, the modern equivalent of a giant oil tanker wrecked daily on your coast. When he eats and drinks the spectacle is magnificent, but pride in his prowess and aesthetic delight are tempered by a frightened glance at the ravaged foodstore or the ledgers of a desperate exchequer. And yet the Lilliputians clearly find it a comfort to have a giant on their side and the high risks of his maintenance nag less when he puts on a fearsome display of the latest European weaponry; waving his scimitar or firing his pistols, he appeals to the same emotions, brings the same comforting reassurance, as do the newest NATO missiles or the massive Warsaw Pact armaments rolling through Red Square.

From the start he decides to be a 'good' giant, earn his parole by contradicting the stereotype of the wicked ogre. His first conscious impersonation is of a mock Polyphemus.[14] When the hooligans who stone him are delivered to him by the military for punishment, he puts them in his pocket and takes one out, like the Cyclops with the companions of Ulysses, as though he were about to eat him. The officers' dismay gives way to rejoicing when instead he uses his

terrible knife to cut the culprits' bonds before gently setting them free
– the ogre is really a genial giant, forever obliging and anxious not to
disturb. He passes with full marks this clemency test and in a remarkable demonstration of power and magnanimity completely fulfills
Isabella's injunction to the great ones of the world:

> O, 'tis excellent
> To have a giant's strength, but it is tyrannous
> To use it like a giant.[15]

The policy of being a model prisoner seems to pay off when the
Emperor, hearing of the incident, decides to give Gulliver a chance to
prove himself 'a useful servant'. He becomes a kind of court entertainer or circus strong-man, a Samson desperately eager to placate his
captors by feats of strength and entertainments, using his handker-
chief as exercise ground for the royal cavalry, straddling his legs to
provide an imposing triumphal arch for the full military parade.
Mildness reaches a charming apogee as the natives dance in his hand
and the children play hide-and-seek in his hair – there could be no
more striking proof that the passage from Polyphemus to lovable
giant has been fully accomplished.[16]

After such exemplary behaviour, it comes as no surprise when he at
last obtains his freedom. With freedom, however, we have the first
hint of something rotten in Lilliput. Gulliver is freed not as reward for
good conduct but to frustrate an enemy invasion, and but for this
emergency might have lain in chains for ever. Swift's own experience
in securing the remission of first fruits for the Church of Ireland
taught him how sweet people seeking favours could be, how un-
gratefully curt after you had delivered. Gulliver, like Swift, delivers;
he guarantees Lilliput against aggression by walking off with the
enemy fleet, his spectacles a shield against arrows. Without the stir
of one Lilliputian scientist, the nation acquires a new, stunningly
invincible weapon that blows skyhigh the armaments parity with
Blefuscu. But when the Lilliputian Emperor, insatiable for world
empire, avid to become literally as well as panegyrically lord of the
universe, spurns an advantageous peace, like the Whig hawks, and
demands unconditional surrender, the reduction of Blefuscu to a
colony, and universal dragooning into the Little Endian Church, the
tool rebels, the weapon declines to be used: Gulliver, refusing to be an
instrument for reducing a free people to servitude, withdraws his
giant labour. The invasion threat over and Blefuscu, like Louis XIV

at Utrecht, ready to treat, Gulliver declines to pulverise them into unconditional surrender. In response, forgetting all his debts to Gulliver, the Emperor begins plotting his death and the way is clear for Gulliver's two further impersonations of harassed, tormented titanism, Hercules and Samson.

Before this, however, we have the spectacle of Gulliver as intellectual giant, bringer of new, startling truth to little men and meeting the customary fate attending such giants ever since Plato's philosopher returned to the cave to enlighten its inhabitants about the world outside. The giant's flagrant capitulation to the petty follies of Lilliputian politics has already been noted. Certainly, Gulliver, in consequence of his ludicrous complaisancy, has only himself to blame if the little people treat him as a born Lilliputian with the full set of petty prejudices; but, at the same time, there is something absurdly egotistic in the easy assumption that whatever concerns a Lilliputian must also be of obsessive interest to a giant – a *drurr* may be crucial in Lilliput but Gulliver has to take it on trust. The very uncomplaisant god of 'The Day of Judgement' surveys scornfully the petty wranglings of the odious vermin who dare to make him a party to their disputes before squashing them all underfoot.

It is, therefore, comically appropriate that smack in the middle of this display of egotism, Swift should insert a devastating critique of the Lilliputian reaction to Gulliver's news of the giant world. The little people credit only one world, that divided between their two great empires.[17] They reject Gulliver's account of Europe on *a priori* grounds as incompatible with established truth, applying in the process pygmy reasoning and Lilliputian standards to the whole universe. Gulliver must have fallen out of the sky, from the moon or a star, since clearly a hundred such creatures would speedily eat the world to death – 'world' is obviously a synonym for Lilliput. The logic is impeccable given the closed system of Lilliputian conditioning – and against the walls of this system Gulliver beats in vain in his attempt to persuade his hosts to a radical reappraisal of reality. There is no evidence in the text that he is exasperated by their resolve not to be enlightened, but this simply emphasizes the temperamental gulf between Swift and Gulliver, for, similarly circumstanced, the greatest single torment of Swift's life was his inability, despite all his art and striving, to make people see.

If Gulliver as intellectual giant can be contemptuously ignored, Gulliver as good servant turned awkward is another matter, especially when his maintenance cost is remembered. Even a docile Gulliver comes dear; when refractory, the opportunity cost of his upkeep becomes totally unacceptable. Lilliputian vindictiveness gathers against the recalcitrant giant all the more readily when the budget is on the agenda. Gulliver's myopia is nowhere more humorously demonstrated than when, thinking he is honouring the royal host, he overeats scandalously, while the Treasurer Flimnap sourly looks on, thinking not only of his 'faithless' wife but of the depleted exchequer.[18] The Lilliputians by now want rid of him – what good is an intractable giant? But the dilemma is painful; exiled, he might cross to Blefuscu and take both fleets with him. The overriding priority is how safely to jettison this disobliging encumbrance, and, in the context of the parallels already established between Lilliputian and European history, it is appropriate that the methods of elimination proposed should resemble closely the tragic ends of the two mightiest heroes in western mythology, Hercules and Samson.

It is fitting that the jealous treasurer should conceive a plan of strewing a poisonous juice on Gulliver's shirts to make him tear his flesh and die in torture: the shirt of Flimnap, Lilliputian replica of the shirt of Nessus, the device whereby Hercules, that other victim of love and jealousy, is untimely destroyed. The second, more merciful plan, proposed by Gulliver's friend, the Secretary Reldresal, looks back to Samson's treatment by the Philistines. Blinding the giant is in every sense the ideal solution: it will confirm 'all the world' in its appreciation of imperial mercy, it will suitably acknowledge the giant's former services before he turned nasty, and it will make him totally dependent on his captors for the rest of his life. Strong as ever, he will be able to 'see' only through his master's eyes; he will be braver than ever, for dangers unseen cannot deter, and he need fear no longer for his eyes, the one concern that almost frustrated the removal of the enemy fleet.[19] The Emperor's decision is a compromise between death and blinding; Gulliver is to be blinded, then gradually starved to death – boring operations can begin in distant parts of the kingdom to find areas suitable for disposing of the noxious carcass to prevent atmospheric pollution.

Gulliver, to whom this plan is leaked through the loyalty of a high placed friend (Philby in Lilliput), can now only react. He is being forced to his dismay into the role of Samson, and the always unstable relationship of guest and host has now clearly declined into that of captive and captor, victim and executioner. Propaganda about royal mercy notwithstanding, he recoils from the role of docile, tractable giant, eyeless in Lilliput at the mill with slaves, but equally he rejects with horror the part of heroic, defiant Samson, pelting the tiny metropolis to pieces with stones, pulling the whole guilty empire crashing down upon his puny enemies. Far from hero, Gulliver is comic as he desperately cudgels his brain trying to see the lenity of the imperial sentence or shrinks from harming the Lilliputians in grateful remembrance of that exalted title of *Nardac* so graciously bestowed upon him in happier days.

Salvation comes to him, ironically, by way of inexperience, his character as *ingénu*, young, rash, foolishly precipitate, as Swift supplies a delightfully comic instance of the advantages that sometimes accrue from being a fool among knaves. He simply decides to leave Lilliput and let the little people live as they did before he arrived. With greater maturity, deeper knowledge, a fuller acquaintance with the ways of princes, he would have seen the Emperor's unbelievable mercy, have embraced joyfully so mild a chastisement as mere blinding. He avoids it because, young and blessedly ignorant, he is still headstrong enough to disregard expert advice. The radical critique of habituation posing as knowledge, the merely provisional, relative and contingent claiming to be absolute and immutable, first seen in the offhand dismissal of Gulliver's European 'fantasies' by the little people, is now redirected towards Gulliver himself as target as he confesses shamefacedly, on the basis of subsequent experience, what a fool he was in saving his eyes. Such 'knowledge' as he has since then acquired is, Swift implies, as damaging as exposure to the stench of a dead giant, as fatal as radiation sickness, in the manner in which it weakens and finally deadens the instinctive human response, the intuitive moral reaction, to straight evil; adaptation to certain modes of experience is the disease that destroys humanity.

The international crisis sparked off by the flight to Blefuscu, which attains comic heights with the Emperor of Lilliput demanding in egotistic abandon the instant return of the defector in chains, is only defused when Gulliver finds a boat from the giant world. What better solution to the impasse than Gulliver's unimpeded departure? The Emperor of Blefuscu observes the conventions by politely asking him to stay on as *his* servant, but is mightily relieved when the Man-Mountain just as politely declines. Both empires are at last free 'from so insupportable an encumbrance' and can cheerfully return to the mutual massacre that Gulliver's intervention threatens to end;

Golding's officer sails away from the island, in Swift's version, and leaves the boys to Beelzebub. The little world has no place for giants who will not abet its corruption; it will always prefer Barabbas to Christ, Flimnap to Gulliver,Walpole to St John.

Gulliver's leaving the world of the little people is the last ironical juxtaposition of Swift's giant with his own situation. Gulliver sails easily away from Lilliput, captivity ended, an innocent in the evil political world yet miraculously endowed with the power to leave it behind. Swift, shipped off to his Dublin exile, is still the captive giant, cruelly aware of the stink of political life, yet powerless, despite all his great powers, to master, amend or even escape it. Gulliver is liberated from Lilliput, Swift remains as agonizingly imprisoned among *his* little people as ever.

Gulliver leaves Lilliput to seek himself, for he is not at home with the little people. Swift's restless search, using travel as a metaphor, contrasts sharply with Pascal's recommended quietism. Pascal knows what ails us: an inability to sit quiet in one little room.[20] Only on reaching that littlest room of all, the grave, is the frenzied hunt after distraction ended, the last unalterable identity assumed – eternal prisoner or heir to paradise. Swift avoids such otherworldly speculation, his preferred categories being reason and animalism rather than heaven and hell. He always resists committing himself unequivocally to what man cannot know; 'if the way to Heaven be through piety, truth, justice, and charity, she is there'.[21] The search for comfort concerning his dead mother includes, characteristically, a scintilla of scepticism, a hint of doubt, if only in its mode of formulation; a conclusion is implied rather than affirmed and he and we together are left to hope that it is unchallengeable. Swift will assert only the empirically indisputable and his kingdom is very much of this world, what happens to men here and now his concern. Discussing heaven, he chooses predictably the negative mode; we know, not what goes on there, but what doesn't – neither marriage nor giving in marriage.[22] It is what men do on earth – rope-dancing in Lilliput, amassing shining stones in Yahooland, marrying and giving in marriage in England – that obsesses Swift. Where Pascal is interested only in the identity disclosed in the grave, the *Travels* pursues identity in this life and does so by forbidding in advance any pretended distinction between an alleged human nature (*animal rationale*, God's image, etc.) and the deeds of men. 'Th'art the deed's creature': our deeds possess and define us, we think them ours but we are theirs, and we discover ou‒

selves in the mirror of everyday life rather than in some final judgement after death. And so, against Pascal's advice, Gulliver is sent on
his travels to gather the data enabling a final assessment of human
nature to be made. The present aim is to show the part played by
Gulliver's girls in reaching this verdict, the importance of sexual
evidence in the *Travels* in defining human nature, how indeed at
certain points in the text the sexual test assumes crucial significance
not only thematically but as a structural principle in the book's
organisation.

Gulliver travels because Swift needs evidence; only with the dossier
complete and the prosecution case invincible, is he allowed to give up
the sea and write his memoirs. To ask therefore why Gulliver returns
from Lilliput is like asking why Hamlet doesn't kill Claudius in the
prayer-scene – the short answer is that there are three voyages and
two acts to go. But this, undeniable if trite, refers to the needs of the
artist rather than the demands of the art. To leave matters as shockingly obvious as this is to convict the writer of ineptitude or literary bad
manners. Genius is the synchronization of external requirement with
internal necessity so that what has been willed seems also inevitable:
what Shakespeare and Swift want is what Hamlet and Gulliver
decide. Thy will be done on earth as it is in heaven; *en la sua voluntade
e nostra pace*: the words would be as appropriate in the mouths of
Hamlet and Gulliver as in that of God's submissive subject. The
Creator's world is a masterpiece ruined by characters who insist on
doing their own thing.

Swift's literary strategy is of course very different from Shakespeare's; his gift is enlisted under satire and he never refines himself
out of existence – behind the persona we suspect always a real presence and the guarded scepticism that made him, in the matter of Irish
coinage, distrust the apparently honest Maculla as much as the rascally
Wood, is equally evident in his relations with his own literary
creations.[23] From the narrator of the *Tale* to Gulliver, the Drapier and
and Modest Proposer, his characters are always delegates, never
representatives; they say and do only what he wants. If we accept
Keats's definition of the poet as having no character or identity, a
chameleon forever 'filling some other body', delighting as much in an
Iago as an Imogen, then we must deny the title to Swift. Hack, Gulliver,
Drapier, Proposer, do not relate to Swift as Timon, Lear, Antony to
Shakespeare. Swift never set characters free in this sense because he
never trusted anyone to speak for him – any persona who had tried

anticipating Burke's line with the electors of Bristol would soon have got short shrift. Nevertheless, Swift is as aware as Shakespeare of art's exigencies; Gulliver's return from Lilliput, as much as Hamlet's delay, is motivated internally and not just because Swift is hankering for Brobdingnag. No more than Hamlet does Gulliver know that he's a fiction, at his creator's beck and call; the relationship is rather that identified by Augustine when discussing man's free will and divine foreknowledge: God knows *and* man is free. The artist, like the Creator, foresees what the character will choose.[24]

Gulliver *is* needed for Brobdingnag but the internal justification is that giants cannot live with ordinary people without becoming their conquerors, tools or victims. Gulliver is no conqueror – never once in Lilliput does he use his giant strength to hurt anyone or even retaliate when attacked. He is willing to be a tool, but not to the degree required by pygmy megalomania, so the only part left him is that of victim. Even his complaisancy, however, does not extend to suicide or passive martyrdom. He cannot remain permanently in Lilliput; sooner or later, he will be killed or forced to kill in a pre-emptive strike against his enemies. He is a displaced person, nowhere more strikingly revealed than in his sexual position. Reproduction is one of the chief characteristics by which we identify living organisms and the life of the ordinary man includes among its essential elements sex as well as sleep and food. Saints and the Dean of St Patrick's may have different needs and priorities, but high on the average human agenda is the instinct to mate and procreate – and Gulliver is indisputably the ordinary, everyday representative of eighteenth-century English humanity. Swift's book is founded upon the fact that so unimaginatively banal a man could never have invented such fantastic places, and he is so manifestly not Scheherezade that the surest testimony of their existence is his telling us so – he is as incapable of such marvellous lies as the Houyhnhnms themselves.

His ordinariness is evident in the circumstances of his marriage, when, taking advice, he decides to alter his condition. He marries because everybody does; it is normal, almost routine, and he is the last man to challenge the prevailing orthodoxy, preferring, in sexual as in other matters, the human average.[25] But in Lilliput he is barred from sexuality, fated to everlasting celibacy. The superb sexual equipment which excites the admiration of the soldiers marching between the bestrid legs of the colossus is, paradoxically, useless; big may be beautiful, but in Lilliput only at the sacrifice of utility value, at least as an organ of reproduction. As a fire extinguisher, he is priceless, as an object of aesthetic admiration, unique, but this very uniqueness certifies him unfit for Lilliput. The eunuchs who, in Yeats's graphic description, crowd round Don Juan as he enters hell, enviously contemplating his mighty thigh, are presumably right to be envious, hell being what it is, or are very foolish eunuchs indeed, but sexual envy is certainly the last thing to direct towards Gulliver in Lilliput.

The Man-Mountain, taker of fleets, invincible in war, is simultane-ously not really a man at all, being forbidden full human participation. That Swift intends this is plain from the superb comedy of Gulliver hotly protesting his innocence of adultery in Lilliput, indignantly spurning the slanderous allegations of liaison with a court lady. So proud at having been made a *Nardac*, he is commensurately furious at being labelled adulterer, completely failing to see that in his position the honour is just as absurdly misplaced as the libel.[26] A major irony of the *Travels* is Gulliver's susceptibility to brainwashing, his smooth accommodation to new environments. Swift's Olympian view sets him above such relativistic follies; Gulliver may think he's a Lilliputian but Swift knows better, and nowhere is the delusion more hilariously exposed than in these solemn protestations of sexual innocence. Gulliver returns from Lilliput not just because another voyage impends but because he has no future with the little people. They are, as he points out at the end of the *Travels*, not even worth conquering, and their final irrelevance to man as an abiding home is dramatised most vividly in terms of total sexual disparity. If you can't sleep with them, you can't live with them: it is, after all, the truism from which biology begins.

In Brobdingnag the total reversal of situation leaves the underlying constant unaffected – voluntary permanent residence is still un-acceptable and for the same reason. The giants, unlike the Lilliputians, can of course keep him prisoner. The little people are relieved to see him go, for the miniature balance of power is disastrously upset – Gulliver is both misfit and menace in Lilliput because he is greater than man. In Brobdingnag he is misfit because his insignificance makes him the prey of rats, dogs and monkeys. Trifles, literal and culinary, threaten his existence: drowning in the soup, stifling in the cream, falling from the table, being pecked to death by birds or stung to death by bees; even reading a book is both strenuous and hazardous, like the regimen of an Olympic athlete. Glumdalclitch frets over little Grildrig as though he were an incubator baby, forever at risk. The forfeiture of manhood is again, though in a very different way, dramatised by exhibiting the stranger as complete sexual misfit. The contemptuous impudicity of the maids of honour torpedoes any claim to manhood he might make. His greatest uneasiness is that they use him with a total lack of ceremony, like a creature of complete inconsequence, stripping naked in his presence, uninhibitedly and insultingly, with no attempt at concealment.

It is a peeping Tom's dream and in Marlowe's *Faustus* Robin lasciviously loiters on thoughts of a life blessed with such magical powers as Gulliver possesses, but Gulliver, in his position of 'privilege', far from being turned on, is disgusted and humiliated. The Brobdingnagian beauties, all blotches, moles and hairs, repel rather than tempt, are styptics to the erotic imagination as they urinate copiously and with blatant abandon in his prescence – what a Brobdingnagian Strephon can only discover in foolhardy exploration is obligingly displayed to Gulliver's nauseated gaze. It is this casual, open indifference that he finds so humiliating, and his sense of shame is merely intensified when indifference modulates into deliberate stripteasing. It is, significantly, the handsomest of the girls, a lively sixteen-year-old, who takes the greatest liberties with the manikin, frolicsomely seating him, helpless and fuming, astride her nipple, 'with many other tricks, wherein the reader will excuse me for not being over particular'.[27] But, as Swift well knows, the reader is not so easily fobbed off – his imagination has been triggered and he cannot help but be intrigued as to the kind of games they get up to in Brobdingnagian bedrooms.

The young lady is not some teenage erotomaniac; her conduct would doubtless be very different were a real man present and her first trick is in any case impossible with a male of her own species. Gulliver is, for her, simply not a man at all, just a little instrument for making fun or provoking sexual jokes (the more uproarious when set against his outraged expression), possessing finally no more dignity than a dildo. No wonder he persuades his nurse to contrive some excuse for not seeing that young lady any more, for nowhere else in Brobdingnag (and only once more in the whole of the *Travels*) is his sense of shame and degradation so forcibly impressed on him. Bad enough to be stroked condescendingly by the Giant King and called little Grildrig, so insulting to his humanity, but the obscene jests of the playful teenager strike at the very root of his manhood, emasculate him entirely. Helpless in the hands of the giantesses, writhing vainly against loathsome submission to the monstrously magnified flesh, Gulliver could serve as emblem to Spinoza's section of the *Ethics* dealing with the passions and entitled, significantly, 'Of Human Bondage'.

Gulliver naturally dreams of liberty amid such degradation. The Giant King, bent on keeping him, commands as overriding priority the acquisition of a female of Gulliver's race upon whom he can breed. Far from feeling grateful at this projected catering for his sexual needs, he sees this as the greatest insult of all and prefers death to 'the disgrace of leaving a posterity to be kept in cages like canary birds, and perhaps in time sold about the kingdom to persons of quality for curiosities'.[28] He is now what the cattle of Lilliput were to him: a species of animal worth cultivating for its curiosity value but little else, and that the curiosity value may have a commercial spin-off leaves the intrinsic triviality unchanged. The envisaged sale of his descendants is the ultimate mortification; Gulliver shares the view, so superbly dramatized in the *Modest Proposal*, that the reduction of men to items of merchandise is the clinching denial of their humanity. The twin assumptions of the *Modest Proposal* – to be bought and sold is the sign of an object, to be kept for stud purposes the sign of an animal – are foreshadowed as Gulliver, anticipating the fate of the Irish poor, confronts both degradations in Brobdingnag, and the great bird that carries him out of the land of giants restores him to a society where his status as man will be renewed.

This claim to a unique human status is the central problem of the *Travels*. Swift was acutely aware of environment and custom in providing the standards by which we compare and judge: a great horse to a Welshman is a little one to a Fleming.[29] The search for a basic human identity, some irrefutable constant infallibly certifying recognition, is pursued through all the voyages and it is intentionally mortifying that the only constants discovered are shameful. The relaxation of tension in the third voyage is attributable to Gulliver's ceasing to be an actor and becoming instead a detached observer. He surveys cynically the curious antics of Laputan ladies deceiving their starstruck husbands, a feat so easy that adultery becomes a yawn. He discovers that female perversity is the same the world over, a constant distinguishing all the daughters of Eve; he admits that the story of the great lady who deserts a loving, generous husband for an old deformed footman who beats her daily smacks more of Europe than Lagado –

but 'the caprices of womankind are not limited by any climate or nation, and . . . are much more uniform than can easily be imagined'.[30] Gulliver would doubtless have cited Emma Bovary, Anna Karenina and Connie Chatterley as further conformations of this judgement. But in Part Three sex is other people's problem, not Gulliver's.

In Lagado sexual vanity is exploited by a shrewd chancellor into an inland revenue dream; men pay taxes as sexual *conquistadores*, their own returns accepted as gospel truth. Women are assessed on their own declared beauty and skill in fashion, but 'constancy, chastity, good sense and good nature were not rated, because they would not bear collecting'.[31] Glubdubbdribb reveals the filth behind history, the great European houses riddled with bastardy and syphilis. The standard route to high title and fortune is sodomy, incest or the selling of a wife or daughter.[32] Gulliver's role as observer of sexual problems is nowhere more evident than in his introduction to the Struldbruggs. The Luggnagians are not so sadistic as to condemn married Struldbruggs to everlasting misery; the union of two immortals is unchallengeable ground for divorce, the spots on the foreheads clear proof of irreparable breakdown. Gulliver's delusions of bliss eternal vanish when he sees the immortals – 'the most mortifying sight I ever beheld, and the women more horrible than the men'.[33] Swift resumes the attack, begun in Brobdingnag, against the false, fleeting attractiveness of the female; the face that launched a thousand ships will seem shockingly different through a microscope or when Helen is a mass of wrinkles, and those romantics who talk glibly of loving for ever should wait till they see a Struldbrugg woman. Cumulatively, these unflattering observations throughout Part Three may signal the beginnings of a shift away from the affectionate husband of the first two parts, grieving over his lost wife and children, towards the alienated misogynist of the last voyage, returning from Houyhnhnmland with much the same view of woman as Young Goodman Brown brings back from the forest; but it seems more sensible to ascribe these general reflections to Gulliver's function within Part Three as observer rather than participant.

Certainly the satiric impact of Part Four derives from an opening in which Gulliver appears as loving husband and father. His home life, all those acid comments on women notwithstanding, is still normal – 'I left my poor wife big with child'.[34] Conjugal rights and wedded love are clearly on a good footing and the narrator laments the decision to go seafaring again, leaving wife and children after five months of happiness, failing to learn the lesson of 'knowing when I was well'. What happens to transform him from loving husband to raging misogynist? As much as *Oedipus*, 'A Voyage to the Houyhnhnms' charts a passage from unreflecting innocence to shocking awareness of pollution. Gulliver is initially as convinced as Oedipus that he is in no way related to the surrounding corruption. Disgust is his sole reaction, as, stifled by the excremental onslaught, he faces his Yahoo brethren. A more imaginative man might have afterwards recalled the problems his own animal nature had set the Lilliputians, but he experiences no hint of recollection or identity, no tremor of affinity, simply intense antipathy for the most revolting of all the creatures he has encountered. The Yahoo is for him completely other. It is the horses who first spot the resemblance; to his 'everlasting mortification' they refer to him as Yahoo and later, when comparisons are made, he has to admit in his heart that the abominable creature beside him is 'a perfect human figure'.[35] Only his clothes prevent the horses from making a total identification. Like a criminal overlooked in a line-up by a confused witness, he gains a temporary reprieve, but knowledge grows within and the rest of the book is an exercise in species identification, during which the evidence accumulates and drives him reluctantly towards admission of kinship. The long search for man's essence is almost over and the last, irrefutable proof of his Yahoo nature is the sexual test as irresistible criterion of species definition.

The evidence adduced is both negative and positive: the contrasting life-styles of Houyhnhnm and Yahoo, rational creature and brute; the methodology is that of the field scientist, anthropologist or ethologist – provisional, empirical, pragmatic. That a creature is truly rational should be as demonstrable from its sexual behaviour as from every other aspect of its life. The formal structure of the Voyage is as logical as 'To his Coy Mistress'. The hypothesis of rationality is tested against Houyhnhnm practices and sustained. Their attitude to sex and marriage is clearly intended as exemplary, an intelligent combination of eugenics and population control, the rational power employed to tame the domain of libido. Procreation is the sole aim; once achieved, intercourse stops. They produce one offspring of each sex and only if a casualty occurs do 'they meet again'.[36] They avoid the elaborate courtship and financial haggling inseparable from fashionable European marriage: 'The young people meet and are joined, merely because it is the determination of their parents and friends; it is what they see done every day, and they look upon it as one of the necessary actions in a reasonable being'.[37]

There can be little doubt as to which side Swift would have favoured in the present debate within Britain's Indian community as to whether the traditional system of arranged marriage should prevail or give way to the western practice of individual choice determined by love. And the same justification urged by Indian conservatives in support of the ancient way is advanced by Swift in his eulogy of Houyhnhnm wedlock – marital violation is unknown among the horses, since the perfervid emotional atmosphere that spawns Medeas and Clytemnestras, Isoldes and Cleopatras, is simply not present. 'The married pair pass their lives with the same friendship and mutual benevolence that they bear the others of the same species who come in their way; without jealousy, fondness, quarrelling, or discontent.'[38] It is the ban on fondness, the odd man out in a group of otherwise unopposedly bad qualities, that arrests attention as signifying a loss of control that disqualifies one as *animal rationale*. Female Houyhnhnms are properly educated – given, that is, the same education as males, so that they are not simply, as in Europe, viviparous animals. Taking all these as the characteristics of a rational species with regard to sexual activity, Swift challenges us to measure man against this proffered standard. The conclusion is negative: in every way man differs from the rational horses.

By contrast, Yahoo sexuality confirms the already frightening physical resemblance to man. With the aid of his Houyhnhnm tutor, Gulliver discovers the elementary biological truth that all members of a species look and behave alike in all important respects, that, even if similarities are not always immediately obvious, they soon become apparent once group characteristics are ascertained. He quickly perceives the blatant irrationalism of Yahoo sexuality. They are, he learns, uniquely disgusting in that the female will admit the male even after conception, an infamous brutality of which no other sensitive creature is guilty. They swing between 'fondness' and 'quarrelling', rampant copulation and a bitter intersexual strife found nowhere else in nature. Desire is unbridled and unregulated; the female will periodically lure the young male into the bushes while simultaneously counterfeiting fear, exuding at such times a 'most offensive smell'.[39] Listening to the catalogue of their transgressions, Gulliver tremblingly awaits the revelation of the unnatural appetites of Europe, for surely here, as in all else, there is kinship too? But the horses know nothing of these perversions; men have, apparently, the edge in sophisticated depravity, 'and these politer pleasures are entirely the production of art and reason on our side of the globe'.

Throughout Swift's writing, from *The Mechanical Operation* onwards, there is a preoccupation, if not indeed fascination, with the dark irrationalism of sex. In Captain Creichton's memoirs there is the anecdote of the covenanting preacher who, on the run, hiding in a maid-servant's bed while the soldiers seeking his life searched the house, nevertheless managed to get the girl pregnant; and Swift, clearly intrigued, recounts elsewhere a similar story of a nobleman, in the death-cell to which treason had brought him, impregnating his wife shortly before his own execution.[40] One easily imagines Swift shaking his head as he pondered these incongruities, divided between baffled amusement and scornful indignation. His sense of the rational is so patently offended by the discordance of a creature, for whom the grave yawns, pursuing sexual appetite, manifesting in so bizarre a fashion the irrational drives that rule him. Such incidents must have seemed to him too disturbingly akin to the situation of insects whose last living act is fertilising the female that devours them. Meditating on this, Swift foreshadows his compatriot Beckett: 'They give birth astride of a grave, the light gleams an instant, then it's night once more.'[41]

The sexual identity of man and Yahoo is undeniable. Against all the evidence there is only man's verbal denial, supporting it his everyday conduct. The insistence on praxis, so crucial to Swift's life and work – as he wrote to Bolingbroke, 'I renounce your whole Philosophy, because it is not your Practise'[42] – is nowhere better exemplified than in the final voyage. Gulliver clings to the myth of his differentiation, but the Yahoos know better; when they see his naked arms and breast, they claim him as their own. The exposed beauties of Brobdingnag were no more exposed than he now. For the first time we see him as family man, holding an infant in his arms, the reality of Yahoo fatherhood emphasized when all his attempted tender ministrations end in the child soiling him, an occupational hazard of every father since Adam nursed Cain. Gulliver as Yahoo father textually precedes Gulliver as Yahoo lover, but the illogicality is artistically appropriate, for the latter role is the book's climactic terminus.

When, bathing stark naked in the river, Gulliver so inflames the young female Yahoo that she leaps hungrily upon him, we have the last piece of the jigsaw, the ultimate, undeniable proof of kinship. Only the sorrel nag's timely intervention saves him, forcing her to withdraw: 'she quitted her grasp with the utmost reluctancy' and 'stood gazing and howling all the time I was putting on my clothes'.[43] The comedy incapsulates the grief of unrequited love, with the young Yahoo as desolate as Troilus looking towards the Greek camp where the lost Criseyde now lies. For the Houyhnhnms it's a great joke, but for Gulliver it's the end of the line, finis to self-deception; he must be a real Yahoo 'since the females had a natural propensity to me as one of their own species'. *Quod erat demonstrandum*. Reproduction will out.

It is so easy, in sharp contrast to Lilliput and Brobdingnag, for a family man from England to go on being so in Yahooland. Gulliver, who as a young man had been an avid reader of travellers' tales, must have read stories about sexual intercourse between African women and male apes – read and rejected them as contrary to nature, since breeding across species was regarded as incredible. He knows (it is what so unnerves him in the bathing incident) that the necessary characteristic of a species is a readiness to breed together. Here is identity at last, self-recognition with no possibility of error. When the Yahoo girl leaps upon him, she is really saying, with an irony Nathan never intended, thou art the man. *Ecce homo*.

With grim comedy Swift reveals Gulliver struggling from the hold of his would-be lover, aware, to his intense mortification, that in the deepest sense he can never escape her again, for he is hers by right and by nature. Who can argue with the sex glands? It is the shame of Brobdingnag carried to its furthest pitch; there he was helpless only because of a secondary, relative attribute, his size, now the humiliation is both primary and essential. After the blind alleys of Lilliput and Brobdingnag, he has found his proper niche, is at last sexually in the right place, a sexual equal, a possible mate, a Yahoo; like Antony, though in horror rather than delight, he can finally say, 'Here is my space'. It follows that the horrified rejection of the female Yahoo adumbrates the future repulse of her sister, Mary Gulliver; the crushing disappointment of the amorous Yahoo is given its appropriately refined form in Mary's complaint of neglect in the epistle Pope wrote for her:

> Welcome, thrice welcome to thy native Place!
> – What, touch me not? what, shun a Wife's Embrace?
> Have I for this thy tedious Absence born,
> And wak'd and wish'd whole Nights for thy Return?

In her chagrin at the unaccountable retreat to the stables, Mary even descends to sexual innuendo: 'What mean those visits to the Sorrel Mare?'[44] But, however understandable in a discarded wife, there is no call for the reader to find more in the text than Swift has made clear: *not* hippomania, a new set of perversions, but an admission by man of Yahoo guilt. Gulliver's 'native Place' looks decidedly unattractive in a context of Yahoo parallelism and the erstwhile lover of mankind has at last truly seen himself, in a lake in Houyhnhnmland.

And what, after all, *is* his 'native Place', where has Gulliver's sixteen-year search for man taken him? To *animal rationale*, glory of creation? – or to a species of animal incapable of amendment, a vicious *lusus naturae*? Corresponding to these warring definitions are two opposed versions of man's origins. The *Travels*, predictably, displaces the ancient myth of Genesis, of the child of God, made in his image but driven for sin from the Garden, with a new, naturalistic account of human beginnings from which any hint of a special relationship with a Creator is rigorously excluded. Houyhnhnm tradition has it that the Yahoos are not indigenous, but that many ages ago two of these brutes appeared together upon a mountain, whether produced by the heat of the sun upon corrupted mud and slime, or from the ooze and froth of the sea, was never known; so prolific were they in breeding that within a short time they had overrun and infested the whole nation.[45] The divine injunction to increase and multiply, with its accompanying promise of the earth as fief, is set aside for a view of human increase as the noisome proliferation of vermin. This degraded report of our first parents looks forward to Wilberforce's interpretation of Darwin or man's advent as described in Golding's *The Inheritors*, rather than backwards to Milton's noble pair, descending in tragic dignity after their ejection from Eden to the challenge of the world below. True, it is the unchristian Houyhnhnm who speaks, but where in the *Travels* is the proof that he is mistaken, that man is not brute but *imago Dei*? Can we seriously doubt on the evidence of his sexual behaviour to which category he belongs?

The origin of Yahoo man as stated in this Houyhnhnm anti-Genesis is the climactic scandal of a scandalous book. From its day of publication, amid the chorus of delighted acclamation, sounded an adversary voice that spoke for outraged humanism. The artistry, on such a view, only made the offence the more unpardonable. It was a 'bad' book and Bolingbroke, reacting to his friend's masterpiece as Lord Longford to an inspired pornographer, tells us why: it was 'a bad design to

depreciate human nature', and if the design had been executed with
the highest genius, so much the worse for its perverted motivation.[46]
The root of the offence is easy to find. More than a century before the
traumatic scandal of Darwin, the *Travels* declines to distinguish man
from the rest of the animal universe but instead decisively relegates
him to the brutes. 'If the book be true . . . religion is a lie . . . and men
and women are only better beasts.'[47] This was a typical nineteenth-
century reaction to Robert Chambers' *The Vestiges of Creation*, a
rudimentary dry-run for Darwin's epochal work. When *The Origin of
Species* appeared, its deliberately mild and unprovocative tone did
not save it from the fury of those who found there an appalling interpretation of the world. The superintending providence of God over
nature and with it the uniquely privileged position of the human race
as centre and *raison d'être* of creation seemed totally discredited. Even
the docile Darwin could not refrain, if only in a private letter, from
mocking his indignant critics: 'Here is a pleasant genealogy for
mankind'.[48]

The 'better beasts' and 'pleasant genealogy' have already surfaced,
however unscientifically, in the *Travels*, with the man–Yahoo
identification and the Houyhnhnm version of human evolution. The
dismissal of Genesis and special creation, of the revered distinction
between human and animal, anticipates the central Darwinian idea of
an underlying unity in the development of life and it is no consolation
to mortified man to find himself deposed as perfection of nature by a
creature so patently unreal as a rational horse. Either man is *animal
rationale* or there is no such thing. The scandal of the *Travels* is its
apparent espousal of the latter alternative. Man, priding himself as
star of the show, is demoted to a contemptible extra. No wonder that
vous autres, the star's idolators – a party to which Gulliver as lover of
mankind also belonged before his last voyage – were offended; they
were meant to be. Even those, like Bolingbroke, who had broken with
orthodox religion, still upheld, perhaps the more fiercely, a secularised
version of man as *imago Dei*, creation's masterpiece. The eighteenth-
century backlash of deists and rationalists against the black legend of
human nature promulgated by Augustinian Christianity and its
naturalistic fellow-traveller, Hobbesian psychology, helped boost the
benevolent view of man. The standard homiletic denunciations of
man as sink of iniquity, routine in seventeenth-century Calvinism,
were becoming increasingly repugnant to rational philosophers of the
Bolingbroke kind. Swift, with his mission to vex, surely welcomed the

anger that his book would incite in such quarters.

Not just the Lilliputians but we too watch with puzzled consternation as, from the opening pages, Gulliver's animal attributes, gargantuanly enlarged, are thrust provocatively upon our attention. Swift was no Darwin; he set out to antagonize in a deliberate display of exhibitionist coat-trailing designed to enrage the champions of human dignity. When Gulliver, lying bound on the beach, urinates, it is for the little people the equivalent of Niagara, a fearful torrent whose noise and violence stun them – one of the few occasions, significantly, when we look *with* the Lilliputians rather than *at* them. Later, Gulliver's home, the morally polluted temple, becomes literally so when, caught in the Swiftian dilemma between urgency and shame, the chained giant creeps inside to excrete.

Why does Swift drag such detail before us, domiciling us to a landscape of torrential urine and giant excrement, an effluent society where the body's prodigious waste can threaten plague or douse conflagrations? It is almost as though Gulliver, after his nine-hour sleep on the beach of Lilliput, has reverted to monstrous infancy, his bowel and bladder movements a matter of public concern and discussion – we must wait for Leopold Bloom before the hero's excretory functions are again assumed to be of significant interest to the reader. Gulliver justifies the exhibitionism in his self-exculpatory insistence that only once was he guilty of such uncleanliness, for afterwards he always defecated *al fresco* to make the removal of the offensive matter quick and relatively easy. He adduces this as proof of his personal hygiene, in indignant rebuttal of what detractors have nastily insinuated since his book was published. But if self-vindication is a plausible explanation of Gulliver's indiscreet disclosures, if he is driven by a commendable anxiety to be distinguished from lunatics like Jack in the *Tale* with his disgusting slogan, 'he which is filthy, let him be filthy still', this nevertheless leaves undecided why Swift determinedly trumpets such goings-on.[49]

It only becomes intelligible (as other than a personal hang-up) on the assumption that Swift attacks human pride by rubbing our faces in the mess we make and pretend not to notice. He solicits outrage with these baited revelations, banking on being accused, like Gulliver in his letter to Sympson, 'of degrading human nature', for how else will he be able to launch that stinging parenthesis – 'for so they have still the confidence to style it'?[50] Bolingbroke, blundering into the trap, is answered even before he protests. The inventory of identification between man and beast is, accordingly, as exhaustive as possible, the mass of evidence exposing man's animalism piled high in a last bid to provoke the urgency of the rational response. Man, distressingly, blatantly animal, must prove his rational component, and when he arrogantly assumes the high, unearned title of *animal rationale*, Swift scornfully uncovers his sordid secrets, exhibiting them, like Gulliver's excreta, to full public view. Jack's antinomian plunge into brutality, his ardent capitulation to the inescapable filth, recurs as Gulliver unprotestingly endorses the sickening catalogue of human depravity – rape, mugging, perversion, murder – as 'all according to the due course of things', beyond complaint and correction. Gulliver's modest proposal is that man continue, without recrimination, the incurable Yahoo he is, if only he desert the one astounding offence for which he can be faulted: pride. Let him cherish his natural defects but renounce his unnatural one – a renunciation the more feasible for Gulliver in his bafflement at how such an animal acquired such a vice. The privilege of filth claimed by Jack is insultingly tossed by Gulliver to Yahoo man.

It is, of course, dangerous to assume that Swift underwrites this easy relegation of man to Yahoo, no more accountable for his misdeeds than for the movement of his bowels or the pressure on his bladder. But neither can we complacently assume that Swift is ridiculing a glaring category-confusion in Gulliver's failure to distinguish between reprehensible because corrigible immorality and the ineluctable facts of being human. The relationship between guilt and responsibility is as central to Swift as to Kafka – and as puzzling to determine; our answer should emerge from a grappling with the text, not a prior assumption as to what he *must* have meant. From the guilt of being human under an extreme Calvinist dispensation to the guilt of being Jewish in Hitler's Europe, men have often been schooled to feel the iniquity of an imposed fate, condemned for what they cannot control.

Swift certainly claimed to have consistently observed in his satire the distinction between what is and what is not corrigible – only conceited ugliness and strutting folly are legitimate targets:

> His Satire points at no Defect
> But what all Mortals may correct.[51]

To justify this claim, the troublesome prominence of man's animalism in the *Travels* must be seen as serving a reformative purpose; the brute facts, so long kept locked away, are turned loose to roam the streets so that man will have to take refuge in the house of reason. The mystery of Judas is explained by De Quincey as a desperate bid to force Jesus's hand, the betrayed messiah compelled to manifest his power. In a similar mood of moral *jusqu'au boutisme*, of vexation at the long un-fulfilled pledge, Swift delivers man to his animal drives so that his very survival depends upon an analogous manifestation of reason. In each case, the ostensible hostility, the act of betrayal (Bolingbroke's 'bad design') – prove you are the Son of God, prove you are *animal rationale* – mask a desperate longing for the 'adversary's' triumph. The partner-ship of *animal* and *rationale* has, for Swift, hitherto been distressingly uneven, with the substantive having all its own way; it is long overdue for the adjective to stop being a sleeping partner and assert instead its rights as the major shareholder.

Hence the strategic emphasis on animalism, the menace made so frightening that reason, with back to the wall, must conquer or perish. Swift's 'realism' is very different from Machiavelli's. *The Prince* presents political man as he is and must be, with no hint of shaming him into going and sinning no more. Swift, by contrast, is an under-cover man, a double agent whose real allegiance is to morality. The *Travels* presents animal man, noisomely offensive, all according to the due course of things, but with a challenge to change what is alleged to be incorrigible. We are meant to protest the portrait's partiality, to demand, in addition to the undeniable animal, the rational being, the complementary and redeeming truth of human nature. Swift, that prince of trappers, entices us to make this crucial protest and then invites us to make good our claim. It will not be allowed on the near-miraculous exploits of a sprinkling of moral supermen like the Glub-dubbdrib sextumvirate – no more than Milton will Swift let men be saved by a deputy or scramble into heaven on the coat-tails of heroes and saints; free-loading is strictly forbidden. Nobody pretends that Shakespeare and Newton are representative of man's ability in poetry and mathematics; why do we cheat by claiming that More and Brutus represent us morally? The everyday deeds of ordinary men are the only admissible evidence for judgement. Swift, meanwhile, strenu-ously devil's-advocating, will continue to present man as 'perfect Yahoo' (despite his impertinent snobbery towards his brother-brutes), dismissing *animal rationale* as merely a parvenu's pretext for cutting embarrassing relatives.

Man's vaunted uniqueness totters as Swift invades certain pri-vileged areas – love, marriage, parenthood – where human beings have long thought themselves securely separate from the animal world, with a demand for the impostor's extradition. The myth of superiority is challenged. That Lilliputian ideas of the parent–child relationship differ so radically from our own is a consequence of their honest resolve to rank man with his animal brethren. They reject the attempt to refine sex into romantic love, seeing behind the sublimation only biological categories. For them the conjunction of male and female is founded upon the great law of nature which ensures the propagation and continuation of the species – men and women, like other animals, are joined together by motives of concupiscence.[52]

In tiny detail as in sustained assault Swift challenges highfalutin romanticism, unceasingly reminding man and his mate of their animal lineage. Glancing at the Laputans' crazy obsession with music and mathematics, Gulliver casually remarks that when they want to praise the beauty of a woman 'or any other animal', they do so in terms taken from these subjects.[53] The derogatory linking is the more insulting in its unemphatic, throwaway context; Gulliver's innocent aside masks his creator's provocative malice, the relish which places 'other' and 'animal' in venomous conjunction. In Brobdingnag the magnified flesh so meticulously exhibited gives the manikin a sense of claustrophobic nausea; the monstrous breast of the wetnurse, its hideous nipple so minutely observed, achieves an effect antipodal to the pornographer's art. The Brobdingnagian beauties turn Gulliver's stomach, not his head. Swift's campaign to maim the erotic impulse – what led Aldous Huxley to protest that a poem like 'A Beautiful Young Nymph Going to Bed' is worse than pornography[54] – springs from his belief that man is much more animal than he admits. Hence the harshness of his onslaught on romantic delusion. Romanticism – interpreted by Swift as a fatuous attempt to elevate unavoidable biological drives to a status higher than the rational, the flesh impudently presuming beyond its limits – is a major target in his work from youth onwards.

His first, false excursion along the road of eulogistic, exalted poetry (made, perhaps, with Temple's dislike of satire in mind) ends with a denunciation of the Duessa from whom he has broken free. The high poetic afflatus is brutally discarded as he turns to his true mate, verse satire, at once far more sensible and far less starstruck:

> There thy enchantment broke, and from this hour
> I here renounce thy visionary pow'r;
> And since thy essence on my breath depends,
> Thus with a puff the whole delusion ends.[55]

Swift's decent muse, like a country virgin accosted by gallants or a young Houyhnhnm strayed among Yahoos, recoils disgusted from the 'cattle she has got among' and departs as fast as she can.[56] The delusion incorporates the fraud of romantic love as well as the phoney inspiration of romantic poetry. As trenchantly as Flaubert, Swift documents the disastrous consequences of romantic delusion, from the maidservant who causes the palace fire in Lilliput through dozing over a romance to the sordid heroine of 'The Progress of Love', projecting herself as love's victim, as helpless as Racine's Phèdre: '*C'est Vénus toute entière à sa proie attachée*'. Phyllis justifies her shameful elopement with the butler on the eve of her wedding to another man, her family's choice, with the blasphemously threadbare appeal to love as heavenly dispensation:

> It was her Fate, must be forgiven,
> For Marriages are made in Heaven.[57]

Swift prefers the Lilliputian view that marriages are of the earth, earthly, and comes, so contemptuous is he of Phyllis and her tribe, close to Iago's cynical reductionism – in her case, love *is* simply a lust of the blood and a permission of the will.

Swift's scornful intensity reflects his fear that so shameless an affront to self-restraint marks the fall into Yahoo bestiality, the point where the human definitively regresses into the zoological. Phyllis, rushing back to the zoo, is merely the sophisticated counterpart of the amorous she-Yahoo leaping upon the naked Gulliver, with the towering additional impudence that she dresses up her lust as the will of heaven. How much more decorous than this sordid imposture is the Houyhnhnm system of arranged marriage, how much superior eugenically in providing simultaneously for individual sex drives and the healthy perpetuation of the species, with no surrender to romantic folly. It would be misleading to say that in Houyhnhnmland eugenics prevails over love, for there is simply no contest. European women, by contrast, lamentably educated, woefully irrational, are 'useless animals', good only for breeding – and for breeding badly. Love is, in Swift's lexicon, a capitulation to sexual abandon that guarantees the deterioration of the species in a flagrant disregard of elementary eugenics. Far from translating man, as its devotees claim, to a higher plane, it simply takes him down to the 'Old Blue Boar' at Staines, to a cat-and-dog existence interspersed with prostitution, pimping and gonorrhea – such is Swift's ironical vision of the 'progress' of love.

The progress of love is the regress of man.

Parental love suffers a corresponding dislodgement. Human beings cannot point to tenderness for their young as signalling a superiority, since the impulse, in both human and animal, proceeds from the same strictly natural principle. Swift anticipates Kant's insistence that a love dictated by nature can neither claim nor accept moral credit. Why should a child, any more than a kitten or a piglet, feel grateful to its parents for the alleged gift of life? How can a pair of animals humped in concupiscence, with no thought of benefiting a third party, in a 'love-encounter' of sheer self-gratification, be a suitable target for gratitude? The sad discrepancy between Houyhnhnm reason and human irrationalism is highlighted in the vocabulary of their differing sexual codes. The Houyhnhnms 'meet together' in a programme of planned procreation aimed at one offspring of each sex; wherever the desired balance is not achieved, they obligingly swap around until every family has its correct quota, after which intercourse ceases – they only 'meet again' where casualties have occurred and the depletion has to be made good.

The whole business of sex and procreation among the virtuous horses is a disciplined, rational synchronization of needs and resources, like the x-efficiency dream of modern economic theorists.[58] The contrast with Lilliputian (and human) messiness is glaringly exposed in the expression 'love-encounters', hinting at the haphazard and casual, at something unpremeditated and adventitious in the sexual act; children come as by-product, the credit of an impersonal nature, with procreation apparently as outwith human control as the laws of science.[59] Where a Houyhnhnm might therefore legitimately feel grateful to his parents for deliberately deciding to conceive him, similar emotion would be absurdly misplaced in a Lilliputian or European. The sole obligation stipulated in Lilliput is that of fathers towards children, the duty to support one's offspring, however inadvertently conceived. When Gulliver leaves on his second voyage, he shows how well he has absorbed this lesson by scrupulously providing for his family. The money he makes from exhibiting and then selling the tiny cattle guarantees the Gullivers from cadging public charity – if irresponsible as progenitor, he is commendably responsible as provider.

As well as challenging man's unique status in these hitherto privileged areas of love and parenthood, violating sanctuaries where humanity has long thought itself safe from pursuit, Swift also mercilessly erodes other traditional distinctions that have reassuringly fenced off man from beast: to be an object of merchandise or financial exploitation, to be part of the food chain, to be kept for breeding purposes. Gulliver's tiny cattle persuade his rescuers that he is not a madman but it is not just his moral credit they save – back home he displays them for cash and then sells them for a high profit. An identical fate awaits Gulliver in Brobdingnag where he switches from exploiter to exploited, worked almost to death in daylong exhibitions by the greedy farmer before being knocked down to the Queen.

Gulliver has difficulty in deciding which he resents more: this cruel exploitation, 'the ignominy of being carried about for a monster' and shown for cash – an indignity which the King of Great Britain, similarly circumstanced, would have likewise had to thole; or Glumdalclitch's tearful resentment at her father for deceiving her yet again, as he had with the pet lamb, promised to her but sold to the butcher as soon as it was fat.[6] Better, of course, to be the girl's pet than her father's freak attraction, but the insult to human dignity is equally mortifying. Gulliver's cold farewell to the exploiting farmer reveals his resentment, though he himself felt no qualms over the Lilliputian cattle – naturally enough, assuming the axiomatic gulf between man and beast fixed in Eden when God made Adam lord of creation, with dominion over all creatures, to use as he thinks fit. Man's cherished distinction, by contrast, is that he is not, on pain of forfeiting his unique dignity, exploitable; he is an end in himself, not to be used, otherwise his special status is denied and he becomes just another beast with a market value.

Even in Lilliput, though without knowing it till later, Gulliver is a valuable commodity, a hot property. Brought to the metropolis, he is as big a box-office draw as King Kong and the secretaries of state make a killing in ticket sales.

But in Brobdingnag the humiliation comes from seeing, but being powerless to stop, his own exploitation. The amused delight he provokes there stems from his amazing simulation to a human being, a rational creature – he is for the giants a charming forgery, a marvellously ingenious imitation, which the mind knows as such even while the eye is pleasingly deluded. Any claim to human status is straightaway denied when his giant captor sets the newly-found creature on all fours as its natural mode of locomotion. Stand up though he may, all his efforts to be accepted as *homo erectus* misfire. The Houyhnhnm master is similarly perplexed at the gentle Yahoo's strange folly in going around on his rear legs – cannot he see the advantages that accrue from his brother brutes' sensible decision to stay foursquare on the earth? Why go perversely against nature and one's animal lineage for the sake of so futile an affectation? But whatever the direction of the attack, whether from giants who see him as an ingenious clockwork device or *lusus naturae*, or from horses puzzling over this curious Yahoo, it is always Gulliver's human status that is in question; big or small, commodity or freak, target of marvel or derision, Gulliver is throughout his travels stripped of dignity, reduced to the level of a Lilliputian sheep or a dancing bear or a Bedlamite in his cell with the day-trippers bent on diversion enjoying his antics.

The animal's vulnerability is most obvious in the ease with which it becomes some other creature's dinner, whether bred to that end by man himself or falling victim to a superior predator. Returning from Lilliput, Gulliver loses a sheep to the ship's rats and later finds its bones picked clean. The incongruity of a live sheep carried off and eaten by rats becomes nightmare in Brobdingnag when European man fights for his life against the giant rats and narrowly escapes, thanks to his sword, the fate of his tiny sheep. No more vivid illustration of man as animal – as extremely vulnerable animal – is conceivable than Gulliver desperately parrying the rat attack, the lord of creation a whisker away from being a rodent's lunch.

The terror of being eaten alive modulates into the shame of being kept as a stud animal. The gravest affront to Gulliver as human being, paralleling the more specific onslaught on his male dignity at the hands of the Brobdingnagian women, comes with the Giant King's direction that a female be found upon whom the manikin can breed and so perpetuate his species. Gulliver, on such a view, is significantly no different from the Lilliputian cattle he tries to encourage in England. On the assumption of his unique status as man, he takes this as the greatest of insults, but just as validly, his giant captors, on *their* assumptions, would reject this claim with derision. The giant rats see him as a meal, the giant people as a pet, to be treated kindly but never as an equal. Gulliver in Brobdingnag is handled with the same easy disdain as he himself has already shown towards inferior creatures – what he has done unto others is now done unto him until separate identity becomes blurred as man merges with beast.

There are two key moments in Brobdingnag which anticipate the final damning identification with the Yahoo. The first is when the monkey kidnaps Gulliver in the conviction that he is a young one of the species and tries to feed him, cramming its partly-digested filth into his mouth, and, with true paternal solicitude, 'patting me when I would not eat'.[61] The monkey claiming Gulliver as child, the female Yahoo seeking her mate, are each offering, in these crucial areas of rearing and breeding, clues to the real identity beneath the pose. The second is when the Giant King delivers judgement on European man as little odious vermin crawling on the earth's surface (Epicurus's chosen home), and, recalling the giant lice rooting through the beggars' rags, we realize, appalled, that these are what he has in mind.[62] Louse and Yahoo represent the nadir of Swift's meditations on man's bestiality, the lowest stages in the regression from human to zoological existence charted throughout the *Travels*. Man slides dismayingly down the life-chain, from human to animal to noisome pest, starting off as rational, ending as fit only for extermination.

The difference between animal and pest is the difference between *A Modest Proposal* and 'A Voyage to the Houyhnhnms'. Gulliver as animal anticipates the shock of the children of the Irish poor suddenly becoming items on a butcher's price list or courses on a menu. 'A child just dropt from its dam' is indistinguishable from a newly-littered piglet, save that in Ireland the piglet is better cared for – one of the proposal's merits is that its implementation may persuade Irish husbands to treat their pregnant wives at least as well as their livestock. What an advance it would be, what a breakthrough in solving the Irish question, if the Irish were somehow *raised* to animal level and managed to pass themselves off as two-footed cattle, beasts in all else save this strange habit of walking erect. That this is the destiny against which Gulliver in Brobdingnag rebels as the worst of degradations – to be tended and bred like an animal – simply proves that the Irish poor are far worse off than little Grildrig among the giants; and it is a measure of Ireland's plight that the only solution is a grateful surrender of human dignity.

A Modest Proposal presents the Irish as animals but not vermin, a useful addition to the food supply, comparable to the cows of Lilliput rather than the lice of Brobdingnag. Fit for human consumption: it is a kind of compliment and the extreme remedy of converting infants into meat to solve a population problem is no more inhumane and far more rational than reliance on starvation and infanticide. It is, after all, only this doomed surplus who end up in the kitchens; are cleavers any worse than the deaths to which we at present equably condemn them? A problem basically economic evokes a solution unchallengeably rational, given that the creatures in question do not differ significantly from other cattle. There are simply too many Irish for the needs of a healthy economy, so why not manage the Irish poor as we already manage Irish pigs – so many for stock, for breeding, for the slaughterhouse, as the market requires? The market rules and if we dislike the idea of people bred to its demands, we had better find a feasible alternative, for the surplus dies daily in any case. The frisson comes from hearing people discussed in terms of cattle control, units in a process that ignores all values but economic.

The Yahoo, by contrast, like the Jew under Hitler, is a problem in pest control, sanitary rather than economic, the cleansing of the world, not the regulation of the market. The Modest Proposer seeks the optimum number of Irish, not their extermination; but even *one* Jew or Yahoo left alive is an affront, a breeding pair a menace, to the sanitationists of Houyhnhnmland and the Reich – the aim *is* genocide. How to eliminate the Yahoo is the one debate in Houyhnhnmland and, ironically, the sole lesson his masters think worth learning from their gentle Yahoo is the castration technique that will extirpate his species forever without recourse to wholesale massacre. Did not the Emperor of Lilliput favour blinding and castration to summary execution as a gentler method of destroying the awkward giant? Imagine the unexceptionable zest with which the Nazi extermination apparatus would have been welcomed by the horses in solving *their* sanitation problem. The Irish are fit for food, the Yahoos only for extermination.

Swift's exasperation in Ireland is real enough. Every section of society is condemned for its lavish contribution to the nation's ruin: a drunken, improvident poor; a middle class sottishly selfish; a leadership venal and afraid. The note of bitter elation sounding through *A Modest Proposal* is sustained by a conviction that a guilty nation is getting its deserts. Ireland was made for Swift, catalyst for his pedagogic despair, confirming in him a wider application of the verdict he once passed on the people of Leicester: 'a parcel of wretched fools'.[63] Even the basic sagacity and will to self-preservation of the animal seemed lacking among the Irish; the national totem was the Gadarene swine and Dublin was Swift's Ephesus, where, like St Paul, he was conscious of fighting with beasts.[64]

Nevertheless, we detect a contrary impulse in Swift that made him champion as well as chastiser of this people. Ireland's unforgivable failure to help herself notwithstanding – and Swift's own twelve-year campaign to promote reform from within shows how much could have been done – the system imposed upon her from abroad was unjust and vindictive. Foolish accomplices in their own ruin, the Irish are also victims, as hampered and misgoverned as the wretched citizens of Balnibarbi. London rule is at least partly responsible for Irish distress, whereas we have no ground for believing that the Houyhnhnm have made the Yahoos any worse than nature created them; on the contrary, but for the efficient policing of the horses, the Yahoos would run ungovernably wild, destroying themselves and everything else. Certainly, a major target of the proposal is the Irish themselves – Swift is furious at fools who connive at their own destruction; but equally undeniable, in however oblique and qualified a form, it is also a defence of an exploited people against rapacious predators. There is no such competing or balancing element in Swift's attitude to the Yahoo, no rage at the exploiter to temper contempt for the victim nor pity for the oppressed to mitigate anger at the fool. In contrast to the double face of the Irish – villain and victim – the Yahoo appears as singly, irredeemably vermin; there can be nothing but relief and satisfaction at his suppression or even extermination, however achieved.

The events attending the expulsion from Houyhnhnmland make this vividly clear. Gulliver's leave-takings of the different countries he visits are dramatically appropriate, matching his role during residence. At the opening of the final chapter of Part One he finds 'a real boat' and the Lilliputian adventure is over. Resuming real manhood, he ends the petty predicaments of Lilliput by simply leaving them – the Man-Mountain deciding to go, where is the power to stop him? He is, contrastingly, carried out of Brobdingnag by the giant bird, as helplessly subject to superior force as throughout a sojourn in which things are forever being done *to* him, whether by monkeys or maids-of-honour. He is taken leisurely to Japan, like the tourist he is throughout the third voyage, in a ship assigned him by the King of Luggnagg, but his vital involvement in the action of Part Four is reflected in the climactic expulsion that ironically echoes the leaving of Lilliput – ironically, because the surface similarity of single-handedly preparing his own departures from Lilliput and Houyhnhnmland masks crucial differences.

Outward preparation is similar but inward disposition is transformed. That he leaves Lilliput with relief, Houyhnhnmland with dread, dramatises the transition from lover of mankind to misanthrope, and the metamorphosis is visible in his preparations for

departure. In Lilliput he greases the boat, which so opportunely
floats his way, with the tallow of three hundred tiny cows. We accept
this unblinkingly as being, among other things, what cows are for – to
be used by men as men see fit, in accordance with God's promise in the
Garden. But the attitude of the Houyhnhnm and their disciple
Gulliver towards the Yahoo intentionally causes the reader discomfort.
The easy brutality, the untroubled assumption that no treatment is
too bad for them, that vermin have no rights and scruples are absurd,
are all part of the book's provocation.

Before the catastrophe, Gulliver unexcitedly relates how he did his
shoe repairs with the skins of Yahoos dried in the sun and collected
birds' feathers with springes made of Yahoo hair; sentenced to
expulsion, he casually describes how he built his canoe, covered with
Yahoo skins, its chinks sealed with their tallow to keep out the sea.
One last twist is given with the information that, the older animals
being unsuitable, he made the sail from the skins of the youngest
Yahoos.[65] Old scores are settled, old insults wiped out, as Gulliver,
with vengeful relish, perhaps reflects that the boy who soiled, the
girl who attacked him, have ended up in his sail. The casual callous-
ness is underscored by the tearful farewell to the revered Houyhnhnm
and the last solicitous exhortations of the sorrel nag. It is the same
strange amalgam of tears and extermination, emotion and brutality,
sentiment and atrocity, as appears in many of those who manned the
death camps and the key in both cases is identical – pity is absurd when
exterminating vermin.

But, as Swift well knows, this is no longer a matter of Lilliputian
cows and he manipulates a significant shift in our response, a vague
unease, a half-stifled disapproval trembling towards articulation. Old,
reassuring distinctions between man and beast are now so darkened
that the ground gives beneath us and we are left stateless in a realm
where brute and human promiscuously merge – Orwell is never more
Swift's pupil than at the end of *Animal Farm*. Discomfort is intensified
by Houyhnhnm attitudes: that the Yahoos cannot help what they are
does not make the horses more tolerant and their one recurring debate
is merely procedural – a massacre of the pests in one genocidal swoop
or the milder policy of male castration and gradual extinction. The
reader's unease (deepened by a recollection of the Emperor of Lilliput's
similar interpretation of mildness) testifies to the deadly accuracy of
Swift's aim in Part Four; driven throughout towards unwilling alliance with the Yahoos, we are now much too close for comfort. While

the cows of Lilliput left us totally untroubled, the Yahoos of Houyhn-hnmland, lacking only our clothes and the jabber we call language, are our kinsmen, however unwelcome, and we are meant to feel a twinge of fearful resentment at their treatment – blood *is* thicker than water, more precious than tallow. Their fate and Houyhnhnm callous-ness alike disturb us and there is no need for Redriff to see how thoroughly Gulliver detests his own kind – the material sealing his canoe is proof enough. The question of sadism does not arise; rather, Gulliver's attitude anticipates and intensifies that of the Modest Pro-poser towards the Irish: an untroubled assumption that the creatures in question are either animal or vermin. Even in *A Modest Proposal* the door is not closed on *Endlösung*; it needs only one more step from man as animal to man as pest in 'A Voyage to the Houyhnhnms'.

EIGHT

THE RADICAL SCEPTIC

Assaying his scepticism is the most hazardous task in all Swift. Its presence is undeniable, its kind a matter of intense dispute. Some today still find the key in the malicious jibe that he was a divine who was hardly suspected of being a Christian, that he had at best only a surface to defend; yet Thackeray's easy assumption that only an infidel could have conceived the Yahoo wears increasingly thin as the sincerity of Swift's Christianity is vindicated. The opposite, equally unwarranted assumption is to take the satire as Christian equivalent of the queen's shilling and the satirist as recruiting-sergeant for the Church. Even if true, these propositions should emerge from, rather than, as they sometimes do, precede, a reading of the text. Scepticism, not faith, is surely the immediate imprint of the work upon the reader who comes to it without preconceptions as to what it should or must mean; but if we train the page to parrot certain opinions, it will naturally provide them on request.

Yet so portmanteau a term as scepticism is scarcely definitive – there is a species hospitable to religion, another acridly dissolvent of all belief. We may, nevertheless, legitimately limit enquiry. Swift is not a sceptic in any technical philosophical sense. Such men cultivated *ataraxia*, the state of serene indifference and imperturbability, and, despite various attempts at impersonation, the role was incompatible with his partisan temper, his need for commitment: 'It is a miserable thing to live in suspense; it is the life of a spider.'[1] Unable, on his own admission, to stop fretting over the misdeeds of the ungodly, he was plainly incapable of *ataraxia*; a detachedly imperturbable Swift is even less credible than Thackeray's melodramatic distortion.

But other strains of scepticism tax credibility less when associated

with Swift. The religious wars, ending in stalemate, had unintention-
ally fostered the growth of unbelief. Fanatics had butchered each
other so that doubters could deride both; free-thinking rationalists
were the intellectual beneficiaries of the Westphalia compromise, and
Christians were inevitably affected. Pascal is acutely aware of the
sheer aleatory nature of belief, the haphazard determinants of dogma,
how a change of climate or three degrees of latitude can reverse the
whole of jurisprudence, how the entry of Saturn into Leo marks the
origin of a certain crime, how justice is bounded by a stream and truth
on one side of the Pyrenees is error on the other.[2] The strength of
scepticism is doubly certified in such a source and one perceives how
devastating such relativism could be when trained against established
dogma. Gone is the pugnacious confidence of *The Song of Roland* –
Christians are right, pagans are wrong. Which Christians? The wars
of religion undermined faith. Milton called them the wars of truth but
their aftermath was doubt, and it is Pascal's scepticism that heralds
the future, Milton's assurance that looks to the past.

Even in Milton's time a growing number of thinkers reacted with
astonished consternation to the spectacle of men slaughtering each
other over breathtakingly unverifiable assertions about God, his
Church and the way he wanted men to live and society to function.
Swift himself, good Anglican though he was, is driven to denounce
such presumption:

> You who in different Sects have shamm'd,
> And come to see each other damn'd;
> (So some Folks told you, but they knew
> No more of Jove's Designs than you)[3]

No sceptic could better this rebuke to those impertinently claiming to
be heaven's plenipotentiaries, for since God himself speaks, who can
contradict him?

By Swift's day the great doctrinal issues that had riven Europe for
two centuries were coming to seem to many what the wrangling of
Byzantine ecclesiastics seemed to Gibbon – a clutter of contemptible
squabbles, not worth losing one's temper over, far less one's life.
Even a belligerent Anglican can adopt such a perspective confronting
the wars of Lilliput. Six rebellions, one monarch executed, another
exiled, thousands of martyrs, a long, savage war between the world's
two chief nations, all because people cannot agree on how to shell an
egg. Each side accuses the other of heresy against fundamental

doctrine enshrined in the Holy Blundecral, which sounds ominously to be all blunder. Since Lilliput is Europe, it devises the same sceptical solution of *cuius regio eius religio*: to stop the carnage caused by the clash of unverifiable 'truths', the magistrate must decide how men are to act, let belief be what it will.[4]

For the martyrs and all those who prefer death to surrender, there is not a scintilla of admiration or even respect; Swift has come to bury, not praise, sectarian man, and he heaps the ridicule high. Where another writer might have seen heroism, however misguided, as well as absurdity – there is a parallel situation when the Lilliputian Emperor, like Satan or Prometheus defying omnipotence, draws his tiny sword to deter the Man-Mountain[5] – Swift sees and ensures we see only the folly of the business; god-defiers and fanatics alike evoke his contempt, not admiration. All the participants, martyrs and persecutors, killers and killed, are plunged in idiocy, with their savage zeal in inverse ratio to the dispute's triviality. Gulliver tells the wise horse that the bloodiest European wars are those caused by differences in opinion, especially over trifles. Among the trifles listed, in what really amounts to a sceptic's view of Reformation polemic, are whether flesh be bread or bread flesh, whether the juice of a certain berry be blood or wine.[6] The interpretation of Christ's words at the Last Supper was probably the single most contentious Reformation controversy, dividing Catholic from Protestant and Protestant from Protestant. Precisely what does Swift mean by having Gulliver dismiss it as a trifle, and how, if at all, are we to distinguish Lilliputian follies over eggs from the section entitled 'Christianity' in Voltaire's *Philosophical Dictionary*, where the man to whom, in de Maistre's phrase, hell had given all its powers, derides the bloodily absurd schisms of the early Christians?

Scepticism was, of course, a tempting weapon for the orthodox to use against enthusiasts and Swift is the most eminent of those who surrendered. The risks were great. The bantering spirit was supposed to lay the persecuting one, but what was to stop it, once having tasted blood, from hunting a new quarry in religion itself, as the *Tale of a Tub* so superbly demonstrates for many readers? What if the neighbour who has obligingly helped to eject a troublesome intruder, suddenly declines to leave and starts taking over the house? What is undeniable is that an awkwardly large number of readers sense some such takeover in the *Tale*, that few leave the book convinced, as Swift claims he intended, that Anglicanism is to be clutched as the pearl of great price, the admirably sensible course between lunatic extremes. Rather than recommend any form of Christianity, the book mows down every religious sentiment incautiously straying within range of its satiric guns. Christians who adopted the techniques of scepticism to ridicule their separated brethren – Swift with dissenters, Pascal with Jesuits – had made a simple but profound miscalculation: thinking it fine to have the laughers on their side, they found themselves on the side of the laughers.

Swift's scepticism presents special difficulties because there are two distinguishable strains in his work, two antithetical ways of regarding the darkness, one welcoming, the other condemnatory. At times he exhibits a scepticism akin to Pascal's, serving religion, employed, like the Baptist, in straightening the way of the Lord; to this end he recommends a darkness that humbles and chastens, preparing man for submission. But the satires resist this kind of labelling. Their scepticism is not, without begging questions, Pascalian, but neither is it Voltairean, levelled against orthodoxy in the interest of a new faith; Swift would have despised the aims of the Encyclopedists. It is neither instrument nor propadeutic but radical scepticism for its own sake, with no compensatory faith, religious or humanist, to offset the brutalities of existence, no payoff beyond the aesthetic reward. It aims neither at making us Christians nor useful members of the *philosophes'* remodelled heavenly city, merely at truthful presentation; jarring occasionally with religion, it is even more implacable towards Enlightenment optimism.

Pascal and Voltaire are enemies because they are competitors, selling the same product for different firms, disagreeing as to the location, not the possibility, of happiness. For Pascal man is corrupt, life a vale of tears, terrestrial felicity a myth seducing man from God; Voltaire, by contrast, attacks religion for denigrating man, and *his* heaven is a rational society on earth, to be achieved when the infamous thing is finally crushed. Christians are at once too sceptical and too credulous, disbelieving in man and swallowing dogma. For Pascal, holding that 'the only good thing in this life is our hope of another', happiness as a social programme is mere folly: 'unbelievers are the most credulous. They believe in Vespasian's miracles in order not to believe in those of Moses'.[7] His commitment to original sin severs Swift from the *philosophes*; despising the earthly paradise, tight-lipped about the heavenly one, he exposes in the satires happiness as a fraud, the hedonist as enemy. Such satire is a no-go area to any kind of consolation, including the Christian; if we do find it there, it is because we have unwittingly entered the import business.

Undeniably present is an epistemological pessimism which, though often supporting religious belief, occasionally threatens it; suspicion of human reason sometimes deepens to a level inhospitable to any creed. Generally, however, his scepticism was comfortably housed in Christianity and it was only occasionally that the lodger turned refractory. Scepticism did not, for him, lead to toleration since fallible men must not dogmatize, but to reliance on traditional wisdom when all is uncertain. His target is the epistemological optimist, whether Milton, Descartes or Bacon. An intellectual euphoria inspires both the conviction that truth always overcomes error in an open encounter and the theory of the *veracitas dei*, the insistence that what is clearly seen must be true, or else God, who created our intellect, is a cheat. Bacon's version is the *veracitas naturae*; faithfully read, the book of nature cannot mislead. Epistemological pessimism, by contrast, rejects reason's mastery of truth and is invariably partnered by a dark view of human nature. A variant is epistemological traditionalism, belief that, lacking immediately discernible truth, we must settle for authority or slide into chaos. Against this, rationalism demands the right to criticize or repudiate any authority as based on mere prejudice or accident.[8]

From Pyrrho onward the sceptic has often been traditionalist and conservative, with the *via dubitantis* a recognized highway to faith.[9] Hume might mock, but for many the journey from philosophical sceptic to believing Christian has been perfectly serious. Swift and Pascal are Christian Pyrrhonists, evincing the same dark view of human nature, the same distrust of systematic philosophy, formal logic and subtle argument. Contempt for philosophers is a major theme in Part Three of the *Travels*; in Glubdubbdribb Aristotle's shade routs his wordy commentators, dismisses Scotus and Ramus as sophisticated fools, and confesses his own and his successors' errors, calling all philosophies mere fashions that flourish briefly before dying.[10] Newton's defence of Wood reinforced Swift's hostility towards scientists arrogantly blundering out of their specialism and in the *Battle* his references to Descartes, Gassendi and Hobbes are uniformly scathing.[11] His anti-scientific philippics are better seen as a campaign against intellectual pride than as the touchiness of an arts graduate.

His allegiance to the Church rests on a conviction that it is the chief buttress of culture against nature and it is as likely that he came to Christianity via pessimism as vice versa. His contrasting attitudes to the mysteries of original sin and the Trinity, each equally obligatory for the orthodoxy of his day, are revealing.[12] He is embarrassed by the Athanasian Creed, grudgingly accepting the incomprehensible doctrine as a necessary admission fee to Christianity, whereas the axiom of human depravity is empirically undeniable in a world so manifestly implicated in some terrible aboriginal calamity. Where the other mysteries require the Church's *imprimatur*, that of original sin verifies the institution that teaches it – Christianity is sooner discredited than the corruption of man as 'all according to the due course of things'.

Hence his refusal to defend religion by theologico-philosophical argument, his rage at those who stupidly abetted freethinkers by doing so. We need religion as we need our dinner, wickedness makes Christianity indispensable, and there's an end of it. Thackeray interprets this as cynicism, yet Pascal, surely no cynic, similarly argues for religion in a way closer to Voltaire than Aquinas. This new apologetic reflects a shift from metaphysics to psychology, from ontological proofs to the believer's requirements, with the god of the philosophers making way for the god of the psychologists. Bayle protests against the view that religion alone can tame the human animal, insisting that religion and morality are independent, that there are virtuous atheists and wicked Christians. Swift consigns virtuous atheists to the same bestiary as contains griffins and unicorns, and assumes with Dr Johnson that insurance premiums on the silver will automatically increase when the guests are infidels.

So singlemindedly does Swift battle for religion as a deterrent that it is no surprise if many conclude that the institution was all he upheld, the surface all he defended. The prayers for Stella alone contradict this, but his secretive, almost trappist attitude to the sacramental–spiritual side makes the error intelligible. Thackeray was both puzzled and irritated by the pains Swift took to keep his personal devotions concealed; why all this tiptoeing about the house as though Diocletian sat in Dublin Castle, this extravagant return to the catacombs in a land so safely and thoroughly Christian? But, as the *Argument Against Abolishing Christianity* shows, Swift does not share Thackeray's certitude concerning Christian civilization, and he might also have directed his critic to a famous passage forbidding us, at risk of being Pharisees, from letting our right hand know what our left is doing. Nevertheless, all this leaves Swift vulnerable as ever to the charge that he argues for religion simply as the sanction of ethics, with God as the great policeman, impossible to elude or hoodwink.

Pessimism towards man makes the church's institutional value the greater. The 'Thoughts on Religion', misconstrued as a set of excuses for not professing disbelief, reveal rather epistemological despondency, his conviction that the mass of men are as well qualified for flying as thinking.[13] His sceptical case for Anglicanism is applicable to any established religion, bishops or bonzes, and, while this is tactical since Anglicanism *is* established, his belief in the unavoidability of error is quite sincere: 'Laws penned with the utmost care and exactness, and in the vulgar language, are often perverted to wrong meanings; then why should we wonder that the Bible is so?'[14] It is a dangerous argument for a reformed churchman, inviting the Catholic retort that the appeal to scripture is really a disguised appeal to individual readers of scripture, with all the attendant anarchy involved. The only remedy, an infallible custodian of scripture, was urged by Catholic propagandists, willing to exploit scriptural obscurity in driving Protestants towards total scepticism or submission to Rome. Caught in the dilemma of every reformed conservative who wants no more revolution, Swift falls back upon the Pyrrhonistic tautology that Anglicanism must be accepted because it is accepted.

He similarly employs epistemological pragmatism to denounce Jack and praise Martin, the one for preferring ruinous 'purity' to sensible adaptation, the other for making survival his priority. The Socinian attack on Christ's divinity is irresponsible because the doctrine is entrenched, historically certified, and the attempted demolition will simply produce riots: 'to remove opinions fundamental in religion is impossible, and the attempt wicked, whether those opinions be true or false; unless your avowed design be to abolish that religion altogether'.[15] A conservative infidel might have said as much. Swift is even prepared to allow missionaries to play down or suppress altogether the doctrine of the Incarnation as too strong for potential converts, 'but, in a country already Christian, to bring so fundamental a point of faith into debate, can have no consequences that are not pernicious to morals and public peace'.[16] Truth is the last ground he will argue upon as long as history, tradition, consensus and individual fallibility can be summoned against the innovating enemy. He shares with Hobbes and Pascal a craving for order as he contemplates fearfully the anarchy generated by the claims of the individual conscience and concludes that truth is elusive, to be haggled over till doomsday with no other consequence than mutual exacerbation. Plato dreams of the sage chosen as king; Pascal will settle for the present ruler's eldest son as a claimant far easier to identify and far less likely to provoke dissension.

A similar scepticism underlies Swift's advice on right and wrong ways of defending the Christian mysteries. Distaste for doctrinal dispute shows in his unease towards Athanasius, like a sensible gentleman obliged to acknowledge an uncouth relation. He explains apologetically the creed's origin as anti-Arian polemic, grudgingly concedes that it might edify those who decipher it, but disavows even this by saying that it contains 'some nice and philosophical points which few people can understand'.[17] Christians should stick to scripture–doctrine and ignore these misconceived attempts to meet the Arians on their own subtle ground – Swift, clearly, would have dealt with Arius in a very different way. The sermon's peroration reveals relief at having done with the subject forced upon him 'by the occasion of this season' – the awkward relation gratefully packed off to the country for another year.

The theological refinement that amuses Gibbon upsets Swift; he scourges preachers who lard their sermons with the tags of church councils and medieval scholastics, a vandalism as bad as that inflicted by the fashion-crazy brothers upon the sweet simplicity of the father's coats. Mysteries, by definition inexplicable, must be left unprobed; debating them simply multiplies unbelievers, for many an apostate would be still devoutly Christian if foolish clerics had remembered that religion is not geometry. Swift detested Anthony Collins but agreed with him that nobody doubted God's existence until Dr Clarke tried to prove it. His own strategy for defending the faith is very different. What right have men baffled by nature, by the growth of plant or animal, to cross-examine providence? If God in his wisdom chooses to darken commands as a means of testing faith and increasing dependence, who are we to cavil?[18] The propadeutic qualities of scepticism, so mockingly canvassed by Hume, are seriously advanced by Swift as he follows Sir Thomas Browne in teaching the haggard and unreclaimed reason to stoop to the lure of faith.

Rather than defend religion rationally, Swift prefers to impugn the attacker's motive. Here, too, his division of mankind into fools and knaves holds true, for, if only fools use reason to defend mysteries, only knaves use it to subvert them. Since 'reasoning will never make a

man correct an ill opinion, which by reasoning he never acquired',
Swift refuses to honour Yahoo pretexts with reasoned refutation.[19]
Eagerly he takes the short step from asserting that 'men of wicked
lives would be very glad there were no truth in Christianity at all', to
concluding that 'men always grow vicious before they become unbelievers'.[20] Arianism is revived, not out of zeal for truth, 'but to
give a loose to wickedness, by throwing off all religion'.[21] Predictably,
he flays Christian rationalists who answer fools in their folly, when
the one thing needful is to unmask evil men.

So standard is this tactic in Swift that it startles to find him treating an
opponent differently, as when, condemning the Jacobite Charles
Leslie, he makes the completely uncharacteristic qualification, 'but I
verily believe he acts from a mistaken conscience, and therefore I
distinguish between the principles and the person'.[22] Leslie had, for
Swift, the merit of supporting a lost cause, and so, however wrong,
gets credit for selfless dedication. It is selfishness masquerading as
principle that angers Swift and his lenity towards Leslie is seldom
extended to other enemies – instead, he flatly refuses to distinguish
between principle and person, argument and motive. If Burnet is
bitterly anti-Tory, it is because he has 'no visible expectation of
removing to Farnham or Lambeth'. If Milton writes in favour of
divorce, what else is to be anticipated from a man so unhappily
married? If Tindal is a foe to the Church, his rascality is sufficient
explanation.[23] Swift ignores the possibility that conclusions may be
sound even if motives are questionable and behaves as if exposing
men were the same as refuting arguments. Ironically, his own work
is often misconstrued as the rancour of a political has-been and failed
careerist.

Rational argument is, on such a view, mere window-dressing while
the real business goes on elsewhere: Henry's genitals, Louis's rectum,
the Duchess of Kendal's bedroom. Reason serves the passions, confers
respectability on the irrational desires that incite action. 'The thoughts
are to the desires, as scouts and spies, to range abroad, and find a way
to the thing desired.'[24] Pope versifies this Hobbesian insight:

> On life's vast ocean diversely we sail,
> Reason the card, but passion is the gale.[25]

Believing this, Swift is free to accuse atheists of willed disbelief:
'The preaching of divines helps to preserve well-inclined men in the
course of virtue; but seldom or never reclaims the vicious.' How can

a doctor save a patient determined to die? Unamuno distinguishes between him who cannot and him who will not believe, and interprets the psalm accordingly: the wicked man has said *in his heart* there is no God. The good man, tragically compelled to say it in his head, never consents in his heart, is never a voluntary atheist nor wills God's annihilation.[26] This Romantic theme of believing heart versus unbelieving head – 'I should go with him in the gloom, / Hoping it might be so' – is precisely what Swift denies in condemning freethinkers; all atheism is voluntary, every freethinker an intending libertine. 'Mr Hobbes's saying upon reason may be much more properly applied to religion; that, if religion will be against a man, a man will be against religion';[27] *nihil cognitum quin praevolitum.* Atheism is not an intellectual stance, nor even, what Pascal calls it, an intellectual deficiency, but the moral equivalent of the leper's scales, irrefutable sign of corruption within. 'For, of what use is freedom of thought, if it will not produce freedom of action; which is the sole end, how remote soever in appearance, of all objections against Christianity?'[28] This is clearly intended to end rather than initiate argument – so inclusive an indictment removes the need to examine any individual difficulty.

Swift defends the mysteries, not rationally like Tillotson or Paley, but by arguing that the clergy have nothing to gain from them, hence no motive to deceive.[29] Those who are not on the take at least deserve to be heard, an argument recurring in Swift's writings, straight and satiric. Denouncing those who conceal Ireland's miseries for selfish reasons, he vindicates his own altruistic indignation with the reminder that he owns not one spot of ground in the whole island.[30] The modest proposer disclaims any personal profit from his scheme as his youngest child is nine and his wife past child-bearing.[31] Papal impositions, lacking scriptural authority and patently inspired by avarice, belong with Milton's pamphlet and Burnet's history, but, by the same token, why distrust Anglican mysteries? Whatever its merits, the argument is not to be found in Aquinas or Hooker. Swift ignores the obvious rejoinder that Anglicans may be mistaken, though not tricksters, not because he hasn't thought of it but because he detests controversy of that kind. He deserts metaphysics for psychology because he is happier scrutinising motives than squabbling over ontological futilities. This new apologetic reflects a growing unease that reason, once handmaid of revelation, had turned fickle and was dallying with the irreligious enemy. So flighty a helpmeet was unlikely to be courted by Swift.

Reason's defection was indicated by the loss of the initial capital or the straight substitution of 'reasoning'. Hobbes freely admits that Leviathan's reasoning is fallible – it doesn't matter since a law is authoritative simply as the sovereign's will; *Leviathan* is the climax of the late-scholastic displacement of reason by will. Swift likewise demotes reason from its former eminence, presenting it as an arithmetical faculty, open to error: 'according to Hobbes's comparison of reasoning with casting up accounts; whoever finds a mistake in the sum total, must allow himself out; although, after repeated tryals, he may not see in which article he hath misreckoned'.[32] He reaches the sceptical conclusion that 'Reason itself is true and just, but the reason in every particular man is weak and wavering, perpetually swayed and turned by his interests, his passions and his vices'.[33] It is the proud, star-fixed rationalist who ends in the ditch where his lower parts seduce him, emblematic proof of reason's descent in the world.

Swift is not decrying reason in any sense that would link him with Blake's energy or Lawrence's vitalism – he would never have admitted that the Yahoos have all the life or that their life is worth having, but he would have agreed that the Houyhnhnms have all the reason, for that is what he intends. They have it so incontestably to convince man how thoroughly unjust is his own misappropriation of the title of *animal rationale*. Swift is no enemy of reason but of man's claim to possess it, when all experience indicates how distressingly meagre is his portion. Far from advocating irrationalism, he insists that every man must, to his limit, obey the reason God gives – 'he cannot do otherwise, if he will be sincere, or act like a man'. This respect can even induce him to talk like a Cartesian: 'if I should be commanded by an angel from heaven to believe it is midnight at noon-day; yet I could not believe him'.[34] All that we perceive clearly is true, for God is not a juggler. But what, for Swift, *do* we see clearly and what, in Houyhnhnm terms, does reason mean? The rational horses employ, paradoxically, neither ratiocination nor deduction; theirs is an angelic illumination, an intuitive perception, of moral truth, without need of argument or deliberation. Man, neither angel nor Houyhnhnm, forced to act upon opinion and speculation, is, by contrast, forever prone to error. In addition, his physical nature perverts his reason, and Swift never permits men to forget the bodies that thwart high rational aspiration. He playfully compares man to a broomstick, emblem of an inverted tree; man too is a topsy-turvy creature, head where heels should be, in the dust – but behind the fun is tragedy, for if reason cannot deliver us from the body of this death, what remains?[35]

Obviously, religion. Lacking Houyhnhnm certitude, man must seek salvation in faith and embrace the chastening darkness, the scepticism that preserves him from becoming that most outrageous of creatures, a freethinker. Since to boast of one's brightness is Luciferian, man must welcome the dark religion that stresses his weakness and fallibility. Swift recommends submission to the 'good' darkness, with its humbling but redemptive self-effacement. It is no easy surrender. Swift is no placid fideist; he tells us that not only are men plagued by doubts, but that, tormentingly, these doubts are bred by their God-given reason. Faith is the heroic vocation, freethinking contemptibly easy. The problem, as in Houyhnhnmland, is one of pest-control. Doubts will breed despite us, but we must contain and discourage them, with the human will as department of sanitation.[36] The wicked man fosters mental vermin, the diabolic man maliciously strives to pollute others, the good man keeps his home as clean as possible and never dreams of infecting his neighbour's.

This 'good' darkness prepares us for humility, the recognition that we must not be our own carvers, but the darkness denounced in the satire is that encouraging pride and self-assertion. Swift taps new deeps of epistemological pessimism in showing that man avoids rather than misses truth, ingeniously connives at his own deception. Ignorance, like atheism, is voluntary, for man has the same vested interest in delusion as in infidelity. Swift's scepticism is far more shocking than the *que sais-je* attitude of Montaigne. He detests those who, undermining religion in the name of their own delusion, think men will be happy once freed from 'superstition' and 'prejudice'. These irresponsible meddlers are the Strephons of epistemology, preferring dreams to reality: the 'metaphysical' reality that truth and happiness are rivals, the 'practical' reality that religion is our one stay against chaos.

Yet, in Swift too, these usually coexisting truths may occasionally conflict, when, in 'The Day of Judgement' or *The Mechanical Operation*, the joy of assured salvation is derided as the supreme delusion. Venturing beyond the Christian barrier, the satires show a nightmare world of triumphant nihilism, raking all human institutions with a devastating scepticism, exposing life as a vast deception, pronouncing sentence of death on human nature, for man is on trial, and not God but humanity is challenged to prove its existence. Pascal's diagnosis of human wretchedness without knowledge of God is intended to force a straight choice between despair and faith, an Augustinian solution for Augustinian man. If there is no solution in Swift's satire, it is because he so splendidly succeeds in not providing one, neither in the absurd hero who flays humanity nor in those who self-defensively reject him as a fool. An art supplying its own internal solution, serving as pretext for postponing the mandatory reformation, would have provoked Swift's scorn as the last evasion of sophisticated Yahoos, enlisting aesthetics to thwart amendment. Swift's art, by contrast, anticipates the Marxist ambition of abandoning interpretation for change, and his satire dislocates the world from habitual perspectives to enforce the case for reform. The reader must move beyond feeling to decision if the world is to be wonderfully mended. For Stephen Dedalus such art is pornography or didacticism, impure and improper, deplorably kinetic, rather than the aesthetic stasis which is, for him, ideal. But aesthetic stasis is for Swift an unforgivable indulgence as he sees London and Dublin fall to the Yahoos. His is a literature of emergency; sufficiently an artist to appreciate that the easiest form of existence is in art, he is enough of a reformer to experience a puritan distrust of this very easiness, of how insidiously it can entice artist and audience from the prime duty of amendment.

Wretchedness in the *Pensées* is merely a provisional conclusion within a dialectic, not truth but a rung on a ladder towards it, and in the dialectic's final stage, self-knowledge and happiness coincide. There is, deliberately, no equivalent stage in Swift's satire. If, as has been argued, tragedy is possible only for agnostics and Manicheans, since a hint of heaven spoils the effect, this perhaps explains why Swift's satire seems curiously close to tragedy, its hero denied any compensation for the anguish of insight.[37] Gulliver settles blissfully in his Houyhnhnm paradise – superior to Adam's in harbouring no Eve – so that grief will be the greater when it is irretrievably lost, for, unlike Adam, there can be no return. Paradise is the forfeit of knowledge, whether it be the loved one's boudoir, the Epicurean surface, the naif's dream of immortality, the river bank after the great fish has just escaped. Only truth-dodgers, immune to reality, can cling to paradise; knowledge divorces happiness and Swift supplies no hint of a future reconciliation.

Even in his religious writings, he handles heaven with embarrassed reticence, and for one so hard on pre-Christian philosophers for failing to provide a commensurate reward for virtue, his own exploitation of Christianity's great advantage is strangely meagre. His sole comment on the beatific vision is the Hobbesian advice to avoid such meaningless jargon;[38] all he knows or tells of heaven is that marriages are not made there and he would not speak at all if the depraved Phyllis did not make heaven a shield for filth. A similar reluctance underlies his intriguing remark concerning Adam that 'the text mentioneth nothing of his Maker's intending him for, except to rule over the beasts of the field and birds of the air'.[39] Pascal's image of man as exiled king, pretender to heaven, is surely closer to the traditional Christian view of man's destiny than Swift's strict interpretation of Genesis, but so fierce is his antipathy to pride that he suspects even the expectation of heaven. When he creates his own Eden, Swift corrects not just the logic books but God too in making the horse the presiding creature; man puffed up by Genesis will be deflated by *Gulliver*.

The sneer that the churchman was not a Christian becomes intelligible, however mistaken, when one recalls how astonishingly little is known about his faith. He would have considered such curiosity impertinent, but, deliberate reticence or not, he is equally successful concealing his faith in the satires as in screening the family devotions in Dublin – indeed, only an act of faith on our part will discover it. We know the *Pensees* were written to make infidels Christians but we have no such assurance concerning the *Travels*. Using Swift's official status to dictate meaning to the work is like brandishing the crucifix to scare away other readings as though they were vampires, for the text itself justifies us no further than seeing the world as a place of filth and folly, where you pay for truth by forfeiting happiness.

The force of the 'Digression on Madness' comes from a masterly deployment of these major themes. There is, first, the concern with origins to discredit enemies; the Aeolists reflect their founder's lunacy, and, like all such innovators, military, religious, philosophical, should be in Bedlam, natural home of all independent carvers. Yet only unsuccessful madmen end there; the fashionably mad are feted instead of chained, lionized in drawing-rooms rather than locked in dungeons, sustained by the plaudits of countless brother-madmen. Triumphant lunatics demand satiric attention as representative men who reveal society as a wider bedlam that gets the leaders it deserves. Socrates answered the sneer about incompetent philosophers by arguing that his very virtues disqualify the philosopher from governing an evil society; how can a good man run a death-camp? Swift shows that even evil men squander the camp's resources, that our madhouses are a cruel waste of manpower. Instead of commissioning the psychopath to lead Yahoos hired to kill, we throw him into a cell where he injures only himself, when he might just as easily and much more usefully be annexing new dominions for the crown; the megalomaniac is lost to the episcopate for mere lack of a mitre; the lunatic, dabbling in excrement, has all the qualities required for the Royal Society.[40] How can such a waste of madness be justified? In Houyhnhnmland Gulliver likewise discovers that our most trumpeted institutions, Army, Law, Church, Medicine, Science, have their Yahoo equivalents, cruder but substantially similar; new European is but old Yahoo writ large.

Madness supplies not only a meritocracy but also a basis for happiness, since, in a delusion-free world, 'there would be a mighty level in the felicity and enjoyments of mortal men'.[41] The *Tale*, with its chilling revelation that in the inside things are good for nothing, its warning that, since nature insists on putting her best furniture forward, it is temerarious to dig deeper, is as nihilistically powerful today as when it shocked contemporaries. A good nose and keen eyesight ruin romantic love. Brobdingnagian beauties are so only for those who know no better. Strephon must devote himself to Celia's fair exterior and stay clear of her bedroom, if he wants happiness and not truth. Curiosity being midwife to disenchantment, Swift accordingly supplies a new definition of wisdom to suit psychological hedonism: 'He that can, with Epicurus, content his ideas with the films and images that fly off upon his senses from the superficies of things; such a man, truly wise, creams off nature, leaving the sour and the dregs for philosophy and reason to lap up'.[42]

The target is mindless happiness, the enemy the carefree hedonist. Swift parts irretrievably from those apostles of happiness, the *philosophes*, in being too sceptical for that company of self-styled sceptics. The *Tale* is a seventeenth-century product and, compared to the seventeenth-century *libertins*, the *philosophes* are optimists, dismantling the City of God only to rebuild it with more modern materials, rejecting paradise for progress and identifying truth with happiness.[43] But for Swift truth is an ordeal requiring a special fortitude and the Swiftian hero opposes the Epicurean sage in declining a happiness that is a perpetual possession of being well-deceived.[44] Whatever ministers to happiness is suspect, even religion itself when it forgets its chastising role and pervertedly placates a sense of human importance. Donne's claim that the sinner too is God's creature and contributes to his glory even in damnation is for Swift the old detestable egoism in Sunday clothes. The dogma of divine solicitude may mask human vanity; arrogantly posing as God's image, man is really his antithesis, just as he is antipodal to the Houyhnhnm, the truly rational creature he presumes to be. So anxious is Swift to destroy such pride that he risks a God-forsaken world where the mere claim to divine attention is proof of corruption:

> Who can believe with common-sense
> A bacon-slice gives God offense?
> Or, how a herring hath a charm
> Almighty anger to disarm?
> Wrapt up in majesty divine,
> Does he regard on what we dine?[45]

Or on what we do? In his zeal to deny a Puritan hot line to heaven, he comes dangerously close to denying any line whatever. The wars of Lilliput, the irreverence about Eucharist and resurrection, can be so interpreted as to save appearances for the Anglican apologist. But difficulties crowd in as he blitzkriegs pride: 'It is a sketch of human vanity for every individual to imagine the whole universe is interested in his meanest concern' – an arrogance reaching its apogee in the dissenting preacher communing with God: 'Who that sees a little paltry mortal droning and dreaming and drivelling to a multitude, can think it agreeable to common good sense that either heaven or hell should be put to the trouble of influence or inspection upon what he is about?'[46] Certainly the target is home-brewed inspiration, but who, where inspiration is the theme, can claim not to be a little paltry mortal? The passage works as Anglican propaganda only for those assured that all the drivellers are on the other side and it is difficult to control such scepticism like a tap, dousing the Puritan enemy while keeping the church safely dry. Is pride confined to the left, belief in divine concern a delusion of sectaries? Swift's imprudent mode of attack nudges him towards a dubious company for a dean: Spinoza who says that thinking triangles would conceive a triangular god; Voltaire's dervish who points out that when the sultan sends a ship to Egypt, he gives no thought to the mice in the hold; Arnold's Mycerinus, bleakly discovering that, even if they exist, the gods are 'careless of our doom'; Nietzsche, denouncing the doctrine of God's love and the arrogance that poses as modesty – 'they have a way of raising their eyes to heaven which I cannot endure' – and concluding that such impudence cannot be branded with sufficient contempt.[47]

In this fantasy of divine concern, man resembles the Lilliputian politician who assumes that a *drurr* is as crucial to Gulliver as to him, when what looms large in Lilliput is beneath the man-mountain's perception. The discrepancy between God and man is infinitely greater than that between Gulliver and Lilliputian, yet man forever diminishes God to his own trivial dimensions. The Giant King and Swift's Jove are un-Christian gods surveying our doings with contempt rather than love. So incensed is Swift by the attempt to bridge the infinite qualitative gulf between God and man that he retaliates with a jeering deity who enjoys himself hugely in damning all men as idiots. This sadistic joker is irreconcilable with any religion; he sports with men as the President of the Immortals with Tess, though, significantly, Swift, unlike Hardy, sides with the tormentor. Even those who insist that satirist and clergyman are indivisible will wish to avoid such a god when judgement day comes.

Scepticism is here too intense, pessimism too bitter, to accommodate Christianity, and if Thackeray's charge of infidelity is still mistaken, it is not so outrageously baseless as some suppose. The Christian, be he Origen or Holy Willie, generously extending salvation even to the devil or restricting it to a privileged remnant, must believe at least in the possibility of redemption. Swift's satire arraigns the belief itself as the child of pride. Even the prayer-book is blamed for catering to man's self-esteem: 'Miserable creatures! How can we contribute to the honour and glory of God?' – and Swift openly declares that in his revision this pretentious prayer would disappear. If complacency is bad, religious complacency is monstrous.[48] In a mad world where ignorance is bliss, Swift's hero, preferring to be sadly wise, chooses sanity and the opprobrium of all resentful madmen. Even half a hero, as Gulliver's example shows, is enough to provoke the defensive derision of those with a phobia for truth.

We are assured that Gulliver's 'truth' is not his creator's, that, far from endorsing the man–Yahoo identification, Swift ridicules the blunder in his supremely comic portrait of a clown who loses everything on the horses.[49] Gulliver is a tribute to the efficiency of Houyhnhnm propaganda, his defection from humanity a triumph for the equine Ministry of Truth, and, in a highly comic analogue of Orwell, the 'hero' ends just as deludely loving his indoctrinators. This is the true parallel to Gulliver's conversion – not the Damascus road or the Platonic cave but the brainwashed victims of modern totalitarianism.

Adulation is irrational enough to survive expulsion and the thoroughness of indoctrination is attested in the fanatical intransigence towards his fellow-men. Since Swift makes it plain that men are not Yahoos, we are to treat all this like any other party-line distortion; Gulliver's Houyhnhnmland dossier is about as reliable as the encomia brought back from the Soviet Union by Stalinist hacks, deceiving themselves and others into believing that they had seen the future and that it worked – Gulliver's distinction is to think it neighed. Only the brainwashed could miss the dissimilarities between man and Yahoo so emphasized by Swift; Gulliver as victim is to be pitied, ridiculed, condemned, but on no account trusted.

Yet Gulliver never claims complete physical identity; the real gravamen, more disturbing and difficult to dispute, is the moral affinity rather than the surface resemblance. Churchill, the Duchess of Kendal and Walpole are not hairy and unkempt, lack web feet and claws, but Churchill's rapacity is the Yahoo lust for shining stones, the grand lady is sexually a she-Yahoo, and the crawling lickspittle of Yahoo politics is indistinguishable from the prime minister. Are we to dismiss *Animal Farm* because Bolsheviks have no tails? What does it matter to the satiric attack that the Yahoos are amphibious and men are not, if bestial habits are shared? For, if so, to plead wrongful arrest by exhibiting our feet and fingers is a waste of time.

Equally futile, when the challenge is to identify the essential constituents of human nature, is reliance upon clothes and language. Swift's undergraduate logic textbook serenely affirmed man as *animal rationale*, with the horse as convenient converse.[50] Gulliver's experience confounds these definitions, so that he wonders why people, so readily crediting Lilliput and Brobdingnag, will not believe in Yahoos, especially when our cities teem with them, with the minor difference that they wear clothes and speak a kind of jabber. Is outrage at relegation to the brutes justified? In his debate with Stillingfleet, Locke insisted that one must possess reason to be a man. Clothes are merely accidental, shape and appearance equally inconclusive, since baboons and idiots have both but lack reason. Swift invents an additional, equally irrational category, calls it Yahoo, and shows that humanity, a few master spirits apart, belongs here, with no more right to be called rational than baboons. A creature behaving like a Yahoo is a Yahoo, clothes, language and high claims notwithstanding. The otherwise intractable problems of the Irish yield once these ingenious human simulations are treated as the animals they are. Men in the

Travels differ from Yahoos only in refined perversion, with European man, self-elected quintessence of humanity, especially obnoxious. If Gulliver is a fool for believing this, so too is Swift; we are still free to laugh but not to assume that Swift shares our amusement.

If we must convict Gulliver of folly, his offence is just at our elbow: he rashly tells hedonistic narcissists the truth and the furious response is predictable. Swift insists that *le moi est haissable* because man's prime transgression is self-love, surpassing vice itself, allowing men to boast of behaviour that should make them cringe: 'I never wonder to see men wicked, but I often wonder to see them not ashamed'.[51] So implacably does Swift pursue self-love that for some readers the hunt becomes obsessive, satire modulating into sadism, the correction of faults to a perverted probing of wounds – the irony forsakes its moral purpose and, rather than mending the world, explores its unmendability. Unable to forgive man for being a vertebrate mammal, Swift breaks his own rule of exposing only what is corrigible. For what kind of correction is implied in Gulliver's final verdict that, pride excepted, all vice is according to the due course of things? Like his creator, Gulliver is puzzled by pride rather than sin, as he calls for self-recognition rather than an impossible virtue. Satire self-destructs: we simultaneously see ourselves and how unteachable we are.[52]

How far is Swift implicated in this despair? Is it genuine or simply strategic, a fury assumed to evoke reform? Bolingbroke pioneered the dogma of factitious despair when he told Swift that if he despised the world as much as he pretended, he would not be so angry with it.[53] It is an attractive argument, for why write satires at all if men cannot profit from them? Yet, minimal though this is, can we uneasily detect even here a whiff of the complacency Swift abhorred?

The question is the more pertinent when set against Swift's major satiric theme of man's genius for self-exculpation, his gift against all evidence for seeing himself as harmlessly virtuous, innocent victim of corrupting institutions or adverse circumstance, which he is laudably trying to reconstruct or overcome. The talent for alibi angers Swift – the *bovarysme*, the insuperable power to conceive things as other than they are, the *mauvaise foi* of which Sartre's Garcin in *Huit Clos* is master. An ability to dream a life divorced from action and impervious to evidence is the badge of Swiftian man. Garcin insists that his behaviour somehow belies his essence, and, in a clash between shameful existence and gratifying fiction, the dream triumphs. Swift shares Johnson's fear of the imagination that preys on life and Garcin would have seemed to him one more victim of a representative disease, a ubiquitous schizophrenia.

The sickness is not confined to individuals: the English claim to be a Christian people is, as the *Argument* shows, as preposterous as Garcin's to heroism; the Irish call themselves men but behave like beasts; men everywhere commit atrocities, never doubting their claim to be rational beings. This ingenious duplicity drove Swift towards a fury objectified in the greatest piece of 'existentialist' literature ever written. Gulliver is a comedy of *Angst* and crisis which anticipates a major existentialist lesson: that there is no human nature apart from the deeds of men, that we are what we do, with no hidden self to appeal to against the testimony of daily life, that there is no essence apart from existence. Long before Kierkegaard, part of Hobbes's nominalistic case consisted in contrasting the abstract virtue of human nature with the actual deeds of individual men and Middleton gives classic conciseness to this cardinal existentialist tenet: 'Y'are the deed's creature'. The brutal blocking by De Flores of Beatrice Joanna's flight from responsibility is reenacted as Swift, in an analogous act of justified defloration, shatters the dream of innocence which is man's refuge from truth.

Swift's satire demands an end to duplicity, with word and deed reconciled, man confessing himself the Yahoo he is or proving himself the rational being he claims to be. Action is crucial since without it words are mere wind, a futile repetition of Master while the Father's will is flouted. This emphasis upon action links Swift with men to whom he is otherwise implacably opposed. His differences from Milton, for example, are the more striking when their similarity of experience is remarked. Each suffered personal and political disappointment following upon splendid success, but out of Milton's anguished interrogation of God came the great poems with their insistence that 'nothing is here for tears', out of Swift's quarrel with history came the great satires, the despairing rejection of 'all visionary hopes', the vile prospect of dying in Dublin like a poisoned rat in a hole.

Similarly, the same creed in different men may issue in vastly different consequences. Belief in predestination sanctions for some a fatalistic resignation, for if the future is already determined, why not sit back and let it happen? Most Puritans, however, utilised the doctrine to rouse men from passivity, exhorting them to cooperate with God in creating the inevitable future. A deceptively trivial passage in *Silas Marner* supplies an insight into this attitude of mind.

Doctor Kimble, complimenting Miss Lammeter on her excellent pork pies, fears that the batch may be ended. Priscilla reassures him; she can easily make some more and 'my pork pies don't turn out well by chance'.[54] 'Chance' is the dirtiest word in George Eliot's lexicon; her strongest disapproval is for those who pray over instead of mastering their ovens, relying on heaven's help to avoid self-help, waiting wind-falls from providence. Priscilla Lammeter is the spiritual daughter of Oliver Cromwell and her attitude towards pork pies would have won fervent commendation from the warriors of the New Model, for she is reasserting, in a humble domestic context, the central thesis of seventeenth-century Puritanism: that God's future is accomplished through human instruments, that his Kingdom, like good pork pies, is not to be had by sitting and waiting. Most Calvinists were, perhaps paradoxically, men of intense activity; the crucial question attending man at the Last Judgement, said Bunyan, would not be 'Did you believe?' but 'Were you doers, or talkers only?' – only the doers would be saved. Cromwell thundered the same truth: 'God doth not always deliver His people by miracles, it behoveth us to reform our-selves'.[55] The words summon to action like a lambeg drum, con-demning the dropout who trusts pork pies to turn out well, whether he prays over his oven or lets it rust to scrap.

Its contingent nature, its element of conditionality, is what dis-tinguishes Christian promise from pagan fate. The story of Oedipus is a tautology, simply unpacking the contents of the name: the deeds are a necessary predicate, for Oedipus is a parricide as a bachelor is an unmarried man – only ignorance prevents our seeing what the gods already know. At the end of the action, the spectator raised to godlike omniscience, he recognizes the analytic nature of the statement: Oedipus can only do what the gods have determined his name to mean. With Macbeth it is otherwise. His name bears no predetermined meaning and whatever meaning it acquires as the play proceeds is self-injected. Even at the end his status is problematic – 'this dead butcher' is merely one view with which we need not agree. When the witches hail him as future king, the statement is synthetic – they indicate a destiny that depends completely upon his cooperation. Above all, they do not point the way towards kingship over Duncan's body; that discovery and decision are his, and his 'fate' will occur only if he consents to it. The Judaeo-Christian promise is conditional: the promised land is for those who observe the covenant, victory comes only when Moses holds his arms high, the reward not just of faith but effort.

Puritanism was an anti-fatalistic creed, a cure for passivity, a doctrine for the energetic: 'our rest we expect elsewhere', said Cromwell, while Milton insists that only a faith which acts is counted living.[56] Bunyan assigns to talkers the same fate as met the brisk lad, Ignorance. The supreme exponent of the philosophy of action as opposed to contemplation was Gerrard Winstanley, for whom it is 'action whereby the creation shines in glory', while, in contrast, 'words and writings were all nothing and must die, for action is the life of all, and if thou dost not act thou dost nothing'.[57] Cromwell, Milton, Bunyan, Winstanley: it is not the sort of company in which one expects to find Swift. Great though the differences within the foursome, they present a united front against the arch-apologist of Anglican supremacy. Nevertheless, opposed as they are, Swift shares a similar devotion to the *vita activa* as the one proof of 'faith' and borrows elements of their activist strategy on behalf of his own Augustan defence of reason. Just as Levellers and Quakers alike insisted that faith issue in works, so Swift devises his new definition, *rationis capax*, not as acquittal but challenge, not as the summation of an argument but as a hypothesis awaiting verification; he throws the definition as one throws a gauntlet, not a lifebelt. Men are not meant to shelter behind it from the charge of being Yahoo, but to grasp this last opportunity of refuting the accusation in the only valid way: by demonstrating their putative capacity for reason in action. Otherwise, faith in human reason is as dead as the dead faith despised by Milton and all the words 'proving' man's reason are 'nothing and must die'.

Where action ceases, thought's impertinent':[58] Swift shares Rochester's contempt for words totally out of kilter with things. That he loved words is clear to the newest newcomer to his pages and it is the lover of language who carries to a delightful *reductio ad absurdum* the Royal Society's campaign for linguistic clarity; in the language department of the Academy of Lagado words have been abolished and only things remain, as men converse mutely by pointing to the articles which their servants unpack from their shoulders.[59] But the *Argument Against Abolishing Christianity* reveals how thoroughly he despised words sundered from reality, language used to promote delusion rather than truth. No other great writer is so concerned to distinguish between language and reality, to pursue words as liars, showing how easily they are used to say the thing which is not. And so he ridicules the notion, dear to Orwell, that a change in language means a change in the structure of reality. Pass acts of Parliament out-

lawing every concept denoting man's moral and physical defects,
extirpate them from the language – he awakes next morning the same
filthy animal, the essential reality untouched.[60] Abolish the names of
the factions into which men divide for purposes of aggression – they
will still go on killing each other, inventing new names to justify the
slaughter, for it is the slaughter, not the names, they love. Dignify man
with the title of *animal rationale* – what difference if his behaviour
remains incorrigibly Yahoo? Preach Christianity from every pulpit in
the land, let every politician, every editorial, proclaim us a Christian
people – mere jabber if our real religion, as evidenced by our actions,
is the bank rate and the balance of payments. Swift mercilessly compels
words to unmask, language is driven into the open where it can be
hunted and trapped. Among the many things he shares with Burke is
an insistence on conduct as 'the only language that rarely lies'.

This explains why he savages in the *Argument* not the enemies of
Christianity, odious though they are, but its 'friends', who defend it
with arguments so shoddy as to be more damaging than direct attack.
Swift upholds real Christianity against this gimcrack imitation, but,
since each version goes by the same name, only the test of action can
distinguish the true from the spurious. Every major work of Swift's
aims at action and bitterness often comes from the dispiriting awareness that words are being asked to do too much, falling like futile seed
on stony ground. There is anger in the *Argument* against those who
smugly accept words for deeds, assuming a congruence between
language and reality, names and things; but the deeper rage is the
satirist's for himself at the inefficacy of *his* words, for, whatever he
says and however powerfully he says it, he knows that real, primitive
Christianity has gone for ever. Hence the 'negativism' sensed by some
readers of Swift's satire. He compensates for his pessimism as to the
practical outcome – restoration of real Christianity, Irish reform, an
end to Yahoo man – by a commensurate delight in retaliation, a gusto
in lashing those too lost to listen; life being what it is, one can only seek
revenge. But beneath the elated chastisement is the self-recrimination
of the satirist, bitter that his words bounce harmlessly off pachy-
dermatous reality. Like the Emperor of Lilliput making his long speech
to the newly-captured, totally uncomprehending Gulliver, the satirist
is simply indulging himself. No other writer has written so magnifi-
cently about the futility of words or exposed so scathingly the inadequacy of language.

When the words did succeed, he was correspondingly exhilarated.

The Drapier's Letters is a great activist manifesto, a summons to action, and his role as Drapier was so intensely satisfying because he proved himself therein not just a master of words but a shaper of action, stopping unjust authority dead in its tracks, uniting, for a brief, ecstatic moment, an exploited people against the oppressor. Swift as Drapier gratifyingly felt himself to be a doer rather than a talker, and success was the sweeter in being achieved against the full coercive power of established authority. Words, for once, had deliciously proved their effectiveness against brute reality, taking it by the scruff of the neck and kicking it out of Ireland. Swift's word had conquered the world. His other great practical triumph, *The Conduct of the Allies*, where, like a Cromwell of literature, he had also marshalled words towards effective action in upholding the peace proposals of the Tory government, had not been so supremely satisfying. It is his most effective manifesto on the side of authority, but, triumph though it was, it reveals a Swift who is simply spokesman, however inspired, for an established power group, a propagandist for what others had decided, even if he agreed with the decision. The Drapier's elation, however, comes from a sense of having achieved, single-handed, total victory over authority, welding together, through sheer literary power, what had been hitherto a feckless, defeated people, of having created, not simply directed, a great act of successful resistance. The *Letters* are a monument to the power of the unsupported word, victory against all the odds, the word as deed, and it marks Swift's triumphant initiation to the ancient tradition of Irish satirist-magicians.

The paradox of Swift, with his belief that words without action are worthless, is that his most memorable writings are those inspired to controlled fury by consciousness of failure, by a heartrending sense of the inadequacy of words to achieve results, and hence by a determination to make words their own reward, since no other return – aims accomplished, policies implemented – is forthcoming. The despair of repeated defeat motivates the greatness of such work, his art is supreme when his back is to the wall. *The Conduct of the Allies*, *The Drapier's Letters* and *The Partridge Papers* are, by the measure of mission accomplished, the most effective writings, but those bitter with failure achieve greatness because they miss practical success. The sense that primitive Christianity is hopelessly unattainable hones the bladelike scorn of the *Argument*; the regulated rage of the *Modest Proposal* follows upon the discarding of his own eminently sensible advice to the Irish as impracticable dreaming; and the final contemptuous assumption of the *Travels*, that man is a programmed Yahoo, is Swift's interim verdict pending the outcome of his challenge to be proved wrong.

The peculiar intensity of the satire at such moments is the product of two opposing impulses contending for supremacy within it: an insistence, Puritan in its stringency, that words should produce action, poised against the harsh realization that no significant action is possible, beyond the words themselves. Swift's consummate art is, for its creator, in a real sense inadequate, inferior substitute for the denied reformation. One of our greatest shapers of language makes his theme, astonishingly, the shortcomings of language, the inutility of words. The whole thing would be inexplicable without the Puritan thread through the labyrinth – the futility of faith without works, words without action. Take Winstanley to a logical conclusion and literature becomes irresponsibly dilettante, a sad diversion from the *vita activa* of politics, for words and writings are nothing and must die, and if thou dost not act thou dost nothing – a recipe for the rejection of art, the abandonment of literature. Accept with Flaubert the primacy of the word, cherishing it as superior to the deed, and the life of action becomes vulgar and limited, disdained by the noble spirit – art becomes the one meaningful pursuit. Swift's dilemma comes from his fuller humanity, from lacking the limitations that blessed Winstanley and Flaubert: too great a writer to forsake words as ultimately irrelevant, yet too involved in public affairs to rest easy in some palace of art, too much an artist to side with Winstanley, too much a citizen to approve Flaubert. Hence the predicament, especially in those works created out of a sense of irremediable defeat; for there, as much as for Flaubert, words are the only significant action, yet they are also what Winstanley condemned – nothing, mere reminders of failure.

Swift is just as committed as his Puritan adversaries to the need for action, but lacks the optimistic assurance with which they fronted the future. History was for them the track record of divine achievement. Cromwell, convinced that the God of Battles had enlisted with the New Model, could easily discover 'some glorious and high meaning in all this' – 'all this' being the process which had carried a Cambridge squire to the pacification of the British Isles – but he also knew how much he himself had contributed to the miracle. 'The Lord was with Joseph and he was a lucky fellow.'[61] Cromwell's 'luck' was inseparable from the diligent courage he brought to the shaping of God's future. Confidence in divine purpose reflects a massive self-confidence, a jubilant confrontation of challenges sure to be over-come. Hence the easy dismissal of apparently trivial, or even sordid, means, whereby the future had been hewn from possibility, for no-thing else counted provided the self triumphed and providence was fulfilled. Cromwell cautions against an over-scrupulous investigation of means instead of exclusive concentration upon ends: 'It's easy to object to the glorious actings of God, if we look too much upon instruments'.[62] This is a winner's philosophy, the view of one inter-ested only in results. Swift, by contrast, is forever looking upon instruments, relentlessly subjecting them to a lynx-like scrutiny in order to discredit the alleged providential character of events by exposing their depraved provenance; a close look at the disgusting instruments will silence all the impious nonsense about the glorious actings of God – if the means are so disgraceful, how can the end be good?

Herodotus' account of how Darius became King of Persia exactly conveys Swift's view of historical causation, of the disreputable skulduggery in which great transformations originate. The story of Darius, in its fusion of religion, sex and political ambition, is char-acteristically Swiftian; we recall how one of the Emperor of Lilliput's cushions, i.e. mistresses, saved Flimnap–Walpole after a nasty fall from the political highwire – the Duchess of Kendal, like Herodotus' mare, is mistress of history as well as of George I. Glubdubbdribb teaches how senates and courts are governed by pimps and whores, how many great men owe their success to sodomy, incest and the eager prostitution of wives and daughters. Clearly, the coming of the Christian dispensation meant, for Swift, no essential change in the way history is made and careers advanced – behind every political success is a clever groom with a mare or a slush-fund.

Cromwell might ascribe his rise from squire to Lord Protector to the irrefutable workings of God; Swift follows Pascal in emphasizing the stink, the brute idiocy of the historical process: 'Cromwell was about to ravage the whole of Christendom; the royal family had been brought down, and his own would have been established forever but for a small grain of sand that formed in his bladder. Rome itself would have trembled beneath him, but once that little gravel was there, he died, his family fell from power, peace reigned, and the king was restored'.[63] A horse in rut, Cleopatra's nose, a grain in a bladder: such is the stuff of history. Swift employs the same insight to brilliant satiric purpose in the 'Digression on Madness'. Who would be so foolish as to trace God's glory working through lust and fistulas, to imagine God Almighty using erections and cancer of the rectum to accomplish his purposes? Gulliver, alerted to the filth beneath the façade of history, declines a providence that employs such instruments as John Churchill and the Duchess of Kendal, and the whole doctrine provokes in Swift a nauseated contempt at the blasphemous reduction of God to a labourer in the world's sewer.

Underlying his dispute with the Puritans are radically opposed interpretations of God and his meaning for humanity. For Swift, God signifies stability, obedience to tradition, stoic fidelity to ancestral faith, whereas for Cromwell God is the authority legitimizing change, a revolutionary, not a stabilising principle. The God conceived by Cromwell as present in history is Jehovah, Lord of hosts, manifesting himself at Naseby and Dunbar; Swift's pessimism proposes a very different model, God present as at Gethsemane or Golgotha, not Jehovah but the crucified. But a crucified God, a victim, exemplary in patient submission to suffering and death, was of no practical use to militants determined to conquer the earth and destroy their enemies. Milton's Christ is not the man of sorrows but the young commander of the campaign in heaven, at mere sight of whom Lucifer's forces, like royalists facing Oliver, quail and break; or he is the patient strategist of the wilderness, frustrating Satan's wily manoeuvres to outflank and entrap him. He is not the Redeemer, dying for men, but the second Adam, a model of aggressive resistance to evil, teaching us not to renounce the world but to master it. Such mastery entails not resigned acquiescence to history as juggernaut, but man in the driving seat, supremely confident of his ability to handle the controls; for man does not suffer history, he makes it.

The praxis so basic to Puritanism reveals itself in Calvin's impatient dismissal, as useless to humanity, of a mystifying God, *Deus absconditus*, who rebuffs man's co-operation by keeping his purposes obscure: 'What avails it, in short, to know a God with whom we have nothing to do?'[64] The secret of Calvinist dynamism lies in the alliance of knowledge and action, otherwise knowledge is meaningless. Faith is always applied, a preparation for works; as well no God as a dumb God, for confidence in a communicating deity alone injects purpose into human action. God is seventeenth-century shorthand for man's faith in his own power to plan, direct and change the future. To the enemies of Puritanism this certitude is arrogance, a minority's device for dictating the future to all mankind, and when power merged with prophecy, as in Cromwell, the doctrine of providence seemed indistinguishable from justification by success.

Not only Puritan warriors, of course, predict as inevitable what they strive to achieve or consecrate their drive to dominate as the will of God. An immense endowment of will, energy and determination, wherever found, is invariably harnessed to a sense of mission, a conviction that its possessor is the instrument of God or history. Lunacharsky attributed Lenin's love of power to two things, a sense of infallibility plus an incapacity, priceless in the aspiring dictator, to put himself in the position of an opponent. Both are revealed in Lenin's assertion that 'the dictatorship of revolutionary classes has often been expressed, supported and carried out by the dictatorship of individual persons' – which, translated, simply states Lenin's right to command the party which commands the revolution.[65] Lenin's consistency resides less in any organisational theory than in a conviction that his views must always prevail, because he sees himself, not as an individual prone to error, but as the class-consciousness of the proletariat in visible form. Solzhenitsyn exposes this astounding egotism as he imagines Lenin pondering his role in the coming revolution: 'He did not want power for its own sake, but how could he help taking the helm when all the rest steered so incompetently? He could not let his incomparable qualities of leadership atrophy and go to waste?'[66] There is a striking resemblance to the Cromwell of the 'Horatian Ode', for Marvell, too, sees the Lord Protector not as an individual but as a historical force, personification of the English Revolution, destiny on horseback, power seeking him rather than vice versa – save that Marvell's ambivalence towards his hero is very distant from Solzhenitsyn's biting exposure of Lenin's presumption.

Did Lenin perhaps have Cromwell in mind when he referred to the justified dictatorship of individual men? The parallel is certainly undeniable in the shared assumption of infallibility, the intolerance of criticism, the ability to change course, adopting what they have just come from condemning without once doubting their essential, immutable rightness: for how can God be mistaken or history lose its way? That one justifies his claim to rule by the will of God, the other by historical necessity, is relatively trivial, a mere difference of terminology. Each commands the future, with Cromwell as ready as Lenin to tame a recalcitrant majority, willing, in his phrase, to give one man a sword wherewith to cow the nine dissentients who blindly resist. Cromwell's constant appeal to God should not disguise the essential kinship with the Russian atheist – a kinship claimed by Stalin when he insisted to H. G. Wells that the Bolsheviks were simply doing in Russia what the Lord Protector had long since done in Britain, and that those who admired Cromwell had no right to condemn his political legatees.[67]

The recourse to God to justify his political somersaults does not, of course, convict him of hypocrisy; God and providence are the established language, the accepted categories, of the period, and Cromwell no more means to deceive than Arnold when he appointed himself secretary to the *Zeitgeist*, or we, supporting our theses with the help of historical laws and socio-economic trends. Nevertheless, a reference to providence by Cromwell was invariably prelude to a change of policy, God's name invoked to ease the shock of the new departure. As today, it was the radical, revolutionary elements in society who monopolized prediction – the conservative cherishes the past, futurity is the revolutionary's homeland. But what is strange to us is that in the seventeenth century materialism was the ideology of the politically conservative, buttress of the *status quo*, while God was the principle of change, providence a strategy for overthrowing established hierarchies: 'Behold, I make all things new'. God and providence are the seventeenth-century equivalent of historical necessity, legitimizing the violence required by the new future: Cromwell knows that God wants Charles I beheaded just as Lenin knows that history has consigned the Romanovs to the dustbin. What obscures this for us is that as messianic Puritanism waned, religion became a stabilising element, supporting the established order. Today, with the emergence in the Third World of 'liberation' theologies, we are in a privileged position, denied for three centuries, to appreciate at first hand the dynamic impulse of seventeenth-century Puritanism and the fear it inspired in supporters of established authority. We are witnesses to a potentially explosive fusion of Jesus and Marx, of the Magnificat and the Manifesto, as certain Christians insist that God's will requires social justice, including the overthrow, by violence if necessary, of repressive regimes.

It is impossible to exaggerate the 'activist' element in Puritanism; Marvell wrote of making destiny a choice,[68] but dynamic Puritanism converted choice into destiny, ambitions into decrees of fate. Belief in providence was simply a stage on the road towards man's assumption of total responsibility, God and providence were terms under cover of which man stalked his own sense of mastery. Hence Swift's angry contempt for Puritan claims to intimacy with providence as covertly legitimizing an earthly takeover, his unremitting campaign against the doctrine as the rationalization of aggression. From *The Mechanical Operation* to *The Partridge Papers*, from Captain Creichton's memoirs to a poem like 'The Day of Judgement', he exposes the doctrine as a species of forgery, uttering personal ambitions as the will of heaven. 'When the minds of men are once erroneously persuaded that it is the will of God to have those things done which they fancy, their opinions are as thorns in their sides, never suffering them to take rest till they have brought their speculations into practice.'[69] Hooker's shrewd observation is reformulated by Swift with the free-wheeling gusto that characterises the *Tale* as he defines this practice as a form of madness: 'what a man's fancy gets astride on his reason, when imagination is at cuffs with the senses, and common understanding as well as common sense is kicked out of doors; the first proselyte he makes is himself, and when that is once compassed, the difficulty is not so great in bringing over others; a strong delusion always operating from without, as vigorously as from within'.[70] Swift ridicules the claim to a special relationship with deity in an attempt to sap the sense of certitude that fuels Puritan aggression. What use, demands Calvin, is a God who does not communicate? The god of Swift's poem breaks silence only to tell men what damned idiots they are in presuming to know his mind.

Even in a piece so playful as *The Partridge Papers*, Swift wages the old struggle against the old adversary. His exuberance and sense of fun are aspects of his work and character which completely eluded the gloomy, embittered portrait by Thackeray and others in the nineteenth century. One of the major services of twentieth-century criticism was to rescue Swift from the straightjacket of the misanthropic madman, and to this end Swift's own injunction, '*Vive la bagatelle!*', has been effectively pressed into service. But the playfulness often encompasses a core of seriousness and what looks pure game sometimes yields on investigation a latent significance. Swift clearly relished his annihilation of Partridge and the reader admires the satiric mastery which left the hopelessly outmatched astrologer spluttering ineffectually that he was still alive. But was it no more than inspired fooling that motivated the greatest satirist of the age to turn his full gifts upon so wretchedly inferior an opponent? Swift versus the egregious almanac-maker is the most grotesque of mismatches, and we wonder at his gleeful dissection of a vulgar charlatan at a time when he was pressed hard with the defence of Church and State. Doubtless there was an element of holiday in his excursion into the prediction business, relief from the strain of guiding Queen Anne's heedless ministers; but he was also striking hard at something he despised, using the hoax to ventilate disgust. The *Tale* makes clear his detestation of quack preachers and bogus prophets, always mad, often dangerous. To men of sense, Partridge was simply ludicrous; to a man of Swift's hypersensitive discernment, so apprehensively aware of the contagion of madness, Partridge was a potential menace, to be regarded much as port health authorities regard a ship from a cholera coast. His virulent anti-Catholicism could be manipulated not just by the enemies of Rome but by those set on subverting the Church of England – Swift's selectively partisan memory recalled how Laud's 'Romanism' had served as one major pretext for the great rebellion, and there were still many in England who responded to the epithet 'Romanist' in the spirit with which 'republican' is widely received in Ulster today.

We must remember, too, the contemporary close interlinking of science and magic – only retrospectively can we separate what is 'rational' in seventeenth-century science from what is not. A decade before the Royal Society there was a Society of Astrologers in London. It was a serious subject, the Civil War contributing greatly to its growth and prestige. The revolutionary period, with its significant millenarian component, had produced a new profession, that of the prophet, and the prophets were to a man ideological warriors for Parliament against King, propagandists greatly influencing morale.[71] Hobbes in his history of the war identified prophecy as 'many times the principal cause of the event foretold', and one of the leading prophets, William Lilly, hit the jackpot by publishing his forecast of royal disaster on the same day as the Battle of Naseby. Cromwell himself consulted an astrologer to ascertain his chance of re-election in a new parliament.

Our historical imagination must be liberated if we are to understand how astrology was regarded by many intelligent men in the seventeenth century. For us it is like that archaic superstition which marks Michael Henchard as a man of the past, using wise men and magic to predict the harvest, while his young, successful rival studies agronomy, economics and the market, a man of the future employing the newest scientific knowledge. But in the seventeenth century, many, especially on the Puritan side, looked upon astrology as a nascent science, a means of predicting the future, in much the same way that sociology is regarded today. Partridge in 1708 is, of course, a far cry from the prophets of the New Model, but Swift discerned in him a lineal descendant of the men who had helped to turn the world upside down, identifying the same deluded fanaticism, now blessedly bereft of the power to behead archbishops and kings. Where we see only a fool, Swift saw a once malignant enemy whom the whirligig of time had made delectably vulnerable. Remembering the trials of William Joyce and Ezra Pound for wartime propaganda on behalf of the Axis, we can better appreciate Swift's attitude towards Partridge. The annihilation of the miserable almanac-maker is no more an attack on one isolated lunatic than 'A Beautiful Young Nymph Going to Bed' is the dismemberment of one wretched streetwalker. Partridge and Corinna are, for Swift, emblems of pernicious social evils whose eradication is necessary for sound national health.

The sheer fun of the writing, the splendidly comic way in which Swift uses the prophets' strategy against themselves – the inspired retaliation of assuming the irrefutability of prediction (the device noted by Hobbes as playing so significant a part in the victory over Charles I) – should not obscure the latent seriousness of intention. Protest as he will, Partridge is a dead man from the moment Bickerstaff says so, and even at this late date it must have afforded Swift immense satisfaction to deal thus with the degenerate descendants of those whose words had helped propel Charles to the scaffold. That Swift is a great comic genius is undeniable, and *'Vive la bagatelle!'* is a happy slogan for advancing *this* Swift against the gloomy monster paraded by Thackeray, but, as always, there is danger in the pendulum's swing. We purchase the comedy too steeply if it means overlooking other significant element in the work. Seriousness may not always be in the fun, but we should certainly always be alert to the possibility in a writer whose distinguishing characteristic is a unique power to fuse the comic with the grave, levity with crisis, like a vaudeville Cassandra or Pascal plus pratfalls.

Swift's three great triumphs of impersonation are the roles of Gulliver, Bickerstaff and the Drapier. But the last words spoken by Gulliver, the letter of reproach to cousin Sympson, express chagrin at having wasted his breath, in foolish compliance with his cousin's request, in trying to reform the Yahoos – an absurd project, a visionary scheme, which he has done with for ever. Words are useless; the sensible man is driven towards silence. But the words of Bickerstaff and M. B., Drapier achieve a signal triumph over reality – foiling Wood and Walpole, making a corpse of a living man. Killing is the quintessential historical deed, initiating the whole historical process: Cain and Abel, Romulus and Remus; the headless king is final proof of Cromwell's power. The literary doing to death of Partridge is the most startlingly dramatic instance of the word as deed. Bickerstaff's hoax prediction actually caused the Company of Stationers to strike Partridge's name from their rolls, with the result that his almanac was automatically suspended – a corpse cannot prophesy. It is impossible to conceive a more striking demonstration of the power of the word; the most activist of Puritans, even Winstanley himself, would have been totally satisfied at so matchless a congruence between word and deed.

Yet Swift's habitual greatness is a gift for discovering incongruence, for exploring the ironic gap between word and deed, and concluding, mortifyingly, that, while words may condemn, they cannot save. The work pivots on the existentialist proverb that actions speak louder than words, that a man's true belief is best ascertained from his conduct, not his creed. Profession and practice war with each other in Ireland to produce a nation of Beatrice Joannas. Angry repudiation of Yahoo kinship provokes in Swift the same response as in De Flores – only fools get angry with mirrors. Whether in truants, fallen women or condemned criminals, Swift despises evasion, and in the conveniently culpable devil he detects and derides the scapegoat syndrome. Satan is innocent, misdemeanours are no more made in hell than foolish amours in heaven: we are all the deeds' creatures. Swift scorns excuses as Bunyan short cuts, and a wise reader will no more seeks them in his work than a defendant look for comfort to his prosecutor.

Yet the tendency to invent lifelines for self-esteem to cling to is revealed in the scramble to find reassurance in the *rationis capax* hypothesis. If the Houyhnhnm is *animal rationale*, then man is not, but Swift's more modest suggestion is clutched with relief by those anxious to secure him as defence counsel. Gulliver, seduced by the more ambitious definition, naturally turns pessimist when utopian perfectionism jolts against reality and then swings full circle towards despair, but Swift's moral realism spared him the folly of expecting too much. The *vous autres* letter to Pope reveals not pessimism but a realistic apprasal of man's potential, and this sense of the possible, so lacking in Gulliver, kept Swift from misanthropy.[72] The *rationis capax* definition proves that Gulliver's despair is culpably self-induced, since for Swift man is not Yahoo.

Yet the 'existentialist' framework of the final voyage makes any real distinction between the two definitions irrelevant. *Rationis capax* is a hypothesis, not a conclusion, a challenge, not a reassurance, not an acquittal but a signal for the case to begin and the evidence to be assembled. No amount of *a priori* theorizing about human nature will suffice – verbal assurances, arguments and syllogisms are inadmissible in a court where there is no such thing as reason, only evidences of reason. Empiricism is mandatory; the man who claims he can rise early must stop lying in bed till noon. *Rationis capax* is tested and rejected within the *Travels*. Reason merely makes man more dangerous than the Yahoo, and human behaviour leaves Gulliver, Houyhnhnm and Swift all equally perplexed. It is pointless to extort consolation from the more moderate definition, when the satire shatters both. The parallel of man and Yahoo so powerfully established, it is hard to believe we can escape with a mere promise to deliver, an undertaking of future good. Our misreading of the *Travels* is largely attributable to the inertia of an inappropriate model. We imagine ourselves in an English court where one is innocent till proved guilty, but in Swift's court guilt is assumed and innocence has to be demonstrated. Swiftian man, like Eugene O'Neill's derelicts, is so morally overdrawn – aspirations located in a future which, with every second of postponement, hurtles away – that Swift insists on hard cash; within the *Travels rationis capax* is just another worthless cheque from a hopeless bankrupt.

Gulliver's penultimate folly of expecting reformation within seven months is balanced by man's apparent inability to reform ever – there is no escape from the world of fools and knaves. Such comedy is a Greek gift, its concealed cost biting exorbitantly into our self-esteem as we laugh, to our own condemnation, at the fool who would reform Yahoos, When Gulliver, abandoning Lagado, disgustedly renounces all such visionary schemes, is it so misconceived to catch echoes of Swift mocking his own fatuity in prescribing a dose for the dead? *This* is judgement day, reform now or never. The challenge shirked, Swift not unreasonably concludes that he confronts a braggart whose achievements are all on paper: those who can, do; those who can't, claim to be *rationis capax*. Gulliver's temporal expectations are finally no more absurd than the injunction to go and sin no more, which might just as easily provide amusement for moral realists; and if amendment in seven months is ludicrous, how are we to describe the impracticability of the demand 'this night I require thy soul of thee'? Yet even the fool was not so foolish as to ridicule so derisively brief a grace-period or offer to instruct the speaker in the realities of depravity.

The strongest charge against Gulliver is his outrageously neurotic behaviour towards his wife, his family and his saviour, Don Pedro. Yet absence of neurotic symptoms doesn't guarantee mental health and there may be neurotic societies as well as neurotic individuals. Abolishing symptoms is futile, unless mental hygiene is the prevention of symptoms. Neurosis may even be a kind of early-warning system, alerting us to deepseated, undetected social evils, the truly hopeless victims of which are not the extravagant protesters but the well-adjusted conformists, docilely inured to the intolerable. This calm adjustment is the measure of their abandonment. Lord Munodi and Gulliver are statistically both madmen, neurotically at odds with communal values; but, feeling no loyalty to Balnibarbi, we easily discover in Munodi the one sane man in a mad society, *Athanasius contra mundum*. Gulliver, by contrast, threatens us, and, in sensible self-defence, we dismiss him as absolutely mad, citing his preference for stables over houses as clinching proof of derangement. Gulliver is indeed neurotic and we are well-adjusted, but, in a book about brainwashing, it might be prudent to ponder the victim's identity. He blunders about foolishly where we are poised and sure-footed, but perhaps our very agility should cause us concern. In Orwell's dystopia Winston Smith is a lunatic, in the country of the blind the hero needs only a minor operation to become normal, and Socrates, Christ and Thomas More are all bad company men – assume the organisation's impeccability and the deviationist must be a criminal. Reasonable men accept the world, which is why progress depends upon the unreasonable. Gulliver unhappy may be preferable to untroubled Epicurus, and his veneration for the horses is not necessarily proof of lunacy, the debate ended, but perhaps a challenge to each reader to show that he, for one, is superior company to the residents of stables; the horse-lover is to be proved wrong, not assumed so.

This means taking man's demotion seriously and if this is offensive, then Swift has succeeded, for his vocation is to offend. He strives to hurt and is furious at failure; Wharton as unassailable enemy was a standing reproach to Swift. Ironically, the ingenious evasion of insult recurs in certain modern interpretations of the satire which reduce scathing denunciation to affable comedy. Thackeray accused Swift of entering the nursery with the tread of an ogre; today the nursery is again secure, the ogre transformed to a genial giant straight from Disneyland. Insult is outlawed in these Whartonian refusals to take Swift seriously and the result is the emasculation of work whose greatness is inseparable from its genius for outrage. We are assured that Swift presents, in the beau and the Yahoo, not man as he is, but a nightmare vision of what he might be, that the Europe revealed to Giant King and Houyhnhnm master would be appalling if real, but is, luckily, only the product of Gulliver's disordered imagination, which, however distressing for him, need cause us no concern.[73] Wharton himself could not have produced a more reassuring exegesis of a work which convicts man as worse than Yahoo and European history as a nightmare from which we cannot awake.

Does this make Swift a complete pessimist? To answer one must distinguish between the constructive effort of the man and the destructive vision of the artist. The example of Beckett today, resistance hero and celebrant of futility, shows how a writer may, as man, utilize in the world of actuality the instruments of action, and simultaneously, as artist, shatter their brittle significance. Swift is Beckett's ancestor, his satire an expression of despair, his life a refusal to surrender. At moments in his writing peculiarly Swiftian, radical scepticism intensifies to a revulsion from life and the seemingly incurable follies of men. Some readers shy away from this as too discreditable for pardon, demanding that literature in general and Swift in particular should console; our prejudice that all literature is on the side of the angels is doubly strong when the writer is in holy orders. Yet the preface to *Pendennis* gives the needful reply: 'If truth is not always pleasant, at any rate truth is best'. It is Swift's 'truth' that concerns us, not the doctoring of his work for the sake of our self-assurance. This dark misanthropy is merely the most extreme instance of something intermittently sensed in Shakespeare, Tolstoy, Lawrence, and other great writers, and we must scrutinize our motives for recoil – a desire to think well of ourselves, pride in our social adjustment, a refusal in the presence of evil to emulate Prospero before Caliban: 'This thing of darkness I acknowledge mine'. But, regret it or not, we must face Swift's pessimism, knowing at least that it never sapped his courage or weakened his sword-arm. The greatest of desponders is also the bravest of fighters, always grumbling, never surrendering. The genius of the work defies imitation, the heroism of the life is exemplary.

NOTES

CHAPTER ONE

[1] *Works*, X, 4.

[2] 'Liberty and Terror: Illusions of Violence, Delusions of Liberation', *Encounter*, October 1977, 34–41.

[3] *Works*, IX, 222.

[4] Quoted by Christopher Hill, *God's Englishman: Cromwell and the English Revolution*, 1970, 109.

[5] 'Politics vs Literature: An Examination of *Gulliver's Travels*', *The Collected Essays, Journalism and Letters of George Orwell*, ed. Sonia Orwell and Ian Angus, London, 1968, IV, 210.

[6] *Ulysses*, London, 1964, 49.

[7] *Fact and Fiction*, London, 1961, 32.

[8] Alexander Solzhenitsyn, 'The Smatterers', *From Under the Rubble*, London, 1976, 261.

[9] *Works*, XI, 159.

[10] George Steiner, *In Bluebeard's Castle: Some Notes Towards the Redefinition of Culture*, 1974, 103–4.

[11] *Works*, 11, 113.

[12] *The Poems of John Dryden*, ed. James Kinsley, Oxford, 1958, 1, 33.

[13] *Works*, I, 241.

[14] *Works*, IX, 151; IV, 49–50.

[15] Abram Tertz (Andrey Sinyavsky), *A Voice from the Chorus*, London, 1977, 24.

[16] Denis Donoghue, 'The Brainwashing of Gulliver', *The Listener*, 4 November 1976, 578–9.

[17] R. L. Colie, 'Gulliver, the Locke–Stillingfleet Controversy, and the Nature of Man', *History of Ideas Newsletter*, New York, 11, 1956, 58–62.

Irvin Ehrenpreis, 'The Meaning of Gulliver's Last Voyage', *REL* July 1962, 18–38.

[18]*Works*, XI, 280.
[19]*Works*, XI, xxxvi.

CHAPTER TWO

[1]Quoted by George Woodcock, *Anarchism: A History of Libertarian Ideas and Movements*, Harmondsworth, 1963, 7.

[2]Quoted by James Joll, *The Anarchists*, London, 1964, 137.

[3]Ricardo Quintana, *Swift: An Introduction*, 1955, 30.

Louis A. Landa, Introduction to the Sermons, *Works*, IX, 123.

[4]*Works*, 11, 16; V, 224.

[5]*Works*, 11, 2.

[6]John D. Seelye, 'Hobbes's Leviathan and the Giantism Complex in the First Book of *Gulliver's Travels*', *JEGP*, 60, 1961, 237.

[7]*Two Treatises on Government*, ed. with an introduction by Peter Laslett, 1960, 377–8.

[8]*Leviathan*, ed. with an introduction by Michael Oakeshott, 1955, 197, 218.

[9]*Works*, XI, 57.

[10]*Works*, XI, 43; *Leviathan*, op. cit., 5, 209.

[11]*Works*, IX, 244.

[12]*Works*, IX, 152.

[13]Friedrich Nietzsche, *The Birth of Tragedy* and *The Genealogy of Morals*, trans. Francis Golffing, New York, 1956, 178.

[14]*The Republic*, trans. H. D. P. Lee, Harmondsworth, 1955, 91.

[15]*Works*, IX, 32.

[16]*Works*, IX, 32.

[17]Orwell, *Politics vs Literature*, op. cit., IV, 213.

[18]Irvin Enrenpreis, 'Swift and Liberty', *JHI*, XIII, 1952, 131–46.

[19]*Works*, V, 379, 251, 445; X, 39.

[20]*Works*, III, 124; II, 245; X, 124–5.

[21]*Works*, II, 258, 268; V, 35.

[22]*Works*, III, 124.

[23]*Works*, VII, 380.

[24]*Lives of the Poets*, ed. G. Birkbeck Hill, Oxford, 1905, 11, 361.

[25]*Works*, II, 124, 26; XII, 162.

[26]*Works*, IX, 240.

[27]Quoted by Robert Conquest, *Lenin*, London, 1972, 123.

[28]*Leviathan*, op. cit., 6.

[29]*Ibid.*, 218.

[30]*Works*, II, 94.

[31]*Two Treatises on Government*, op. cit., 424.

[32]*Essays on the Law of Nature*, ed. Wolfgang von Leyden, 1954, 212–13.

[33]*Two Treatises on Government, op. cit.*, 298.

[34]*Ibid.*, 295.

[35]*Leviathan, op. cit.*, 103.

[36]*Two Treatises on Government, op. cit.*, 319.

[37]*Ibid.*, 346.

[38]*Works*, II, 15.

[39]*Works*, I, 141.

[40]*Works*, I, 142.

[41]*Works*, IV, 247.

[42]*Works*, IV, 115.

[43]*Works*, II, 88.

[44]*Works*, I, 279; VI, 195.

[45]Louis Teeter, 'The Dramatic Use of Hobbes's Political Ideas', *ELH*, 3, 1936, 145.

[46]*Works*, II, 74.

[47]*Leviathan, op. cit.*, 116.

[48]*Grace Abounding to the Chief of Sinners*, ed. Roger Sharrock, Oxford, 1962, 120–1.

[49]*Works*, IV, 49. *Pensées*, trans. with an introduction by Martin Turnell, London, 1962, 221.

[50]*Works*, XI, 55.

[51]*Works*, II, 6.

[52]*Works*, IV, 39.

[53]*Lives of the Poets, op. cit.*, I, 220.

[54]*Works*, IX, 161.

[55]Louis I. Bredvold, *The Brave New World of the Enlightment*, University of Michigan, 1961, 7–27.

[56]*King Lear*, ed. Kenneth Muir, New Arden Shakespeare, 1964, V, 111, 209.

[57]*The Works of Beaumont and Fletcher*, Variorum edition, 1912, IV, 255.

[58]*Leviathan, op. cit.*, 234.

[59]*Ibid.*, 139.

[60]*The Social Contract*, trans. Maurice Cranston, Harmondsworth, 1968, 52–3.

[61]Quoted by Barbara Ward, *Faith and Freedom: A Study of Western Society*, London, 1954, 41.

[62]Robert W. Babcock, 'Swift's Conversion to the Tory Party', *Essays and Studies in English and Comparative Literature*, University of Michigan, 1932.

[63]*Religion and the Rise of Capitalism: A Historical Study*, London, 1926, 5.

[64]*Works*, II, 74.

[65]*Leviathan, op. cit.*, 227.

[66]*Works*, II, 89.

[67]*The Second Treatise of Civil Government* and *A Letter Concerning Toleration*, ed. J. W. Gough, Oxford, 1946, 148–9.

[68] *Works*, II, 89.

[69] *Works*, IX, 151; IV, 49–50.

[70] *Works*, IV, 50.

[71] *Works*, IV, 43–4.

[72] *Leviathan, op. cit.*, 355.

[73] *Hobbes*, 1904, 150.

[74] *Leviathan, op. cit.*, 306, 360.

[75] *Works*, II, 5–6.

[76] *A Letter Concerning Toleration, op. cit.*, 124–5.

[77] *Works*, II, 11.

[78] *Poems*, II, 579.

[79] *Works*, II,100, 94.

[80] *Works*, II, 122.

[81] *Works*, II, 3.

[82] *Corr.*, III, 118.

[83] *Oeuvres Complètes*, Bibliothèque de la Pléiade, Paris, 1957, 439.

[84] *Works*, II, 35.

[85] *An Enemy of the People*, trans. Michael Meyer, London, 1963, 14.

[86] *Works*, II, 6.

[87] *Grace Abounding, op. cit.*, 120.

[88] *Works*, II, 6; IX, 157.

[89] *Works*, II, 94.

[90] *A Letter Concerning Toleration, op. cit.*, 133.

[91] *Works*, II, 6.

[92] *Works*, II, 74.

[93] *Leviathan, op. cit.*, 355.

[94] *Aquinas: Selected Political Writings*, ed. A. P. d'Entreves, Oxford, 1948, 153.

[95] *Works*, XII, 244–5.

[96] *Works*, II, 11–12.

[97] *Works*, II, 11.

[98] *Leviathan, op. cit.*, 35.

[99] *Pensées, op. cit.*, 151.

[100] *Works*, XII, 244.

[101] *Works*, XII, 89.

[102] *Corr.*, II, 465; *A Letter Concerning Toleration, op. cit.*, 160.

[103] *Works*, XI, 33–4.

[104] *Works*, IX, 261.

[105] *Works*, IX, 261.

[106] *Works*, IX, 263.

[107] *Boswell's Life of Johnson*, ed. G. Birkbeck Hill, Oxford, 1954, II, 249.

[108] *Leviathan, op. cit.*, 327, 307–8.

[109] *Works*, IX, 150–1.

[110]*Leviathan, op. cit.,* 41.

[111]*Ibid.,* 188.

[112]*Works,* IX, 150.

[113]*Life of Johnson, op. cit.,* II, 126.

[114]*Leviathan, op. cit.,* 327, 395.

[115]*Pensées, op. cit.,* 164.

[116]Owen Chadwick, *The Secularization of the European Mind in the Nineteenth Century,* Cambridge, 1975, 23–8.

CHAPTER THREE

[1]*Leviathan, op. cit.,* 84.

[2]Isaiah Berlin, *Four Essays on Liberty,* Oxford, 1969, 118–72.

[3]*Works,* XI, 86.

[4]*Works,* XI, 206.

[5]*Works,* XI, 272–3.

[6]*Leviathan, op. cit.,* 86.

[7]*Works,* I, 129.

[8]*The World Turned Upside Down: Radical Ideas during the English Revolution,* 1972, 15.

[9]*Works,* II, 114–15.

[10]*Works,* I, 126.

[11]*The World Turned Upside Down, op. cit.,* 223.

[12]*Corr.,* V, 118.

[13]*Works,* I, 177.

[14]*Works,* I, 176.

[15]*The World Turned Upside Down, op. cit.,* 198–9.

[16]*Ibid.,* 159–62.

[17]Herbert Marcuse, *An Essay on Liberation,* Harmondsworth, 1972, 37.

[18]Thomas Mann, *Doctor Faustus,* trans. H. T. Lowe-Porter, Harmondsworth, 1971, 103.

[19]*Poems,* II, 497.

[20]*Works,* I, 103–8; Herodotus, *The Histories,* trans. Aubrey de Selincourt, Harmondsworth, 1969, 213.

[21]Quoted by Ferdinand Mount, 'Revolutionaries: Their Mind, Body and Soul', *Encounter,* December 1977, 61.

[22]*Works,* I, 122. See *Gulliver's Travels and Other Writings,* ed. Louis A. Landa, Oxford, 1976, footnote 343.

[23]*The World Turned Upside Down, op. cit.,* 254.

[24]*Ibid.,* 257.

[25]*Works,* I, 244; *Journal to Stella,* ed. Harold Williams, Oxford, 1948, 11, 658.

[26] *Works*, VI, 9.

[27] *Works*, IX, 10–11.

[28] *Poems*, I, 222–5.

[29] *Works*, IX, 263.

[30] *Works*, IX, 253.

[31] Quoted by Hill, *The World Turned Upside Down*, op. cit., 150.

[32] *Ibid.*, 271, 276, 298.

[33] *Works*, I, 184.

[34] *Works*, I, 188.

[35] Quoted by Hill, *The World Turned Upside Down*, op. cit., 247.

[36] *Works*, I, 108.

[37] *Works*, I, 187–8.

[38] *Works*, I, 189.

[39] *Works*, I, 174.

[40] *Works*, XI, 132.

[41] *Works*, I, 189.

[42] *Works*, I, 190.

[43] *Works*, IX, 85–94.

[44] *Works*, IX, 89.

[45] *Works*, IX, 89.

CHAPTER FOUR

[1] *Life of Johnson*, op. cit., II, 238.

[2] *Corr.*, III, 179.

[3] *Works*, IX, 63–81. See IX, 65, 66, 67, 68, 77.

[4] Patrick Delany, *Observations upon Lord Orrery's Remarks on the Life and Writings of Dr Jonathan Swift*, London, 1754, 266.

[5] *Works*, I, 244.

[6] *Works*, I, 150.

[7] *Works*, XI, 198.

[8] *Works*, I, 73.

[9] *Works*, XI, 159.

[10] *Works*, XI, 161.

[11] *How Conservatives Think*, ed. with an introduction by Philip W. Buck, Harmondsworth, 1975, 33, 30.

[12] *Ibid.*, 47, 49–50, 51.

[13] *Works*, XI, 160–1.

[14] *Works*, IX, 261.

[15] R. W. Hepburn, 'George Hakewill: the Virility of Nature', *JHI*, XVI, 2, 1955, 135–50.

[16] A. E. Case, *Four Essays on 'Gulliver's Travels'*, Princeton, N.J., 1945, 124.

[17]*The Works of Lord Macaulay*, ed. Lady Trevelyan, 1875, VI, 317.

[18]Ernest Tuveson, 'Swift and the World-Makers', *JHI*, XI, 1950, 72.

R. F. Jones, *Ancients and Moderns: A Study of the Rise of the Scientific Movement in Seventeenth-Century England*, Washington University Studies, St Louis, 1961, 146; R. F. Jones, 'The Background of *The Battle of the Books*', *The Seventeenth Century: Studies in the History of English Thought and Literature from Bacon to Pope*, Stanford, Calif., 1951; J. B. Bury, *The Idea of Progress: An Enquiry into its Origin and Growth*, 1920; Frank E. Manuel, *Shapes of Philosophical History*, Stanford, Calif., 1965.

[19]Christopher Hill, *The Century of Revolution*, 1961, 180.

[20]*Works*, XI, 43; IX, 156–7.

[21]*Works*, I, 242.

[22]Kathleen Williams, 'Restoration Themes in the Major Satires of Swift', *RES*, New Series, XVI, August 1965, 266.

[23]*Fact and Fiction*, 1961, 32.

[24]Sir William Temple, *Five Miscellaneous Essays*, ed. S. H. Monk, Ann Arbor, Mich., 1963, 39–40.

[25]*Works*, IV, 246; XI, 119.

[26]*The Poems of John Dryden, op. cit.*, I, 32.

[27]*Temple, op. cit.*, 95.

[28]*Works*, XI, 235–6.

[29]*Works*, I, 87.

[30]*Works*, I, 79–80.

[31]*Works*, IX, 73.

[32]*Works*, IX, 245.

[33]*Works*, I, 179.

[34]*Works*, IX, 233, 73, 241–50.

[35]R. S. Crane, 'Anglican Apologetics and the Idea of Progress, 1699–1745', *MP*, XXXI, 1934, 273–306, 349–82.

[36]*Pensées, op. cit.*, 111.

[37]*Works*, IV, 30.

[38]*Works*, IV, 45.

[39]*Works*, IV, 42.

[40]*Works*, IV, 246.

[41]Quoted by Jones, *Ancients and Moderns, op. cit.*, 193, 183.

[42]*Works*, XI, 116, 181–2.

[43]*Works*, I, 147.

[44]*Works*, I, 81.

[45]*Works*, IX, 264.

[46]*Works*, II, 47, 60–1.

[47]Quoted by Manuel, *op. cit.*, 70.

[48]*Works*, XI, 44, 116, 180, 185–6, 198

[49]*Works*, XI, 256.

254

[50] *Works*, XI, 121–2.

[51] *Works*, XI, 240–1.

[52] *Works*, IX, 263.

[53] *Poems*, II, 579; *Works*, I, 167.

[54] *Works*, I, 114.

[55] *Works*, IV, 243, 246.

[56] J. Leeds Barrell, 'Swift and the Struldbruggs', *PMLA*, LXXXIII, 1958, 43–50; Ernest Tuveson, 'The Dean as Satirist', *UTQ*, XXII, 1953, 368–75; George Falle, 'Swift's Writings', *UTQ*, 34, 1964–65, 294–312.

[57] *Works*, IX, 263.

[58] *The Myth of Sisyphus*, trans. Justin O'Brien, Harmondsworth, 1975, 11.

[59] *Works*, XI, 44.

[60] Samuel Beckett, *Endgame*, London, 1958, 35.

[61] William Godwin, *Enquiry Concerning Political Justice and its Influence on Morals and Happiness*, ed. F. E. L. Priestley, Toronto, 1946, II, 209. See also James Preu, 'Swift's Influence on Godwin's Doctrine of Anarchism', *JHI*, XV, 1954, 371–83.

[62] Orwell, *Politics vs Literature, op. cit.*, IV, 215–16; J. S. Mill, On Liberty, *Essays on Politics and Society, The Collected Works of John Stuart Mill*, XVIII, ed. J. M. Robson, University of Toronto, 1977, 219–20.

[63] *Works*, XI, 183.

[64] *Works*, XI, 260–1.

[65] *Works*, I, 217.

[66] Quoted by E. H. Carr, *What is History?*, Harmondsworth, 1964, 74.

[67] *Works*, I, 180.

[68] *Works*, V, 144, 154.

[69] *Works*, IX, 144; *Corr.*, II, 356.

[70] Erasmus Lewis on Harley; quoted by Falle, *Swift's Writings, op. cit.*, 297–8.

[71] *Corr.*, III, 329.

[72] *Corr.*, III, 274; Pope to Swift.

[73] *Works*, I, 242.

[74] *Works*, V, 27–34; XI, 180; I, 222.

[75] *Poems*, II, 361; see also *Poems*, II, 567.

[76] *Works*, I, 226, 229.

[77] *Works*, I, 233–4.

[78] *On Liberty, op. cit.*, 238.

[79] *Works*, II, 103–4.

[80] *Works*, II, 94.

[81] *Works*, IV, 14.

[82] *Works*, IX, 5.

[83] *Works*, II, 63, 5.

[84] Z. S. Fink, 'Political Theory in *Gulliver's Travels*', *ELH*, XIV, 1947,

151–61. See also Preu, *op. cit.*, 371; Basil Willey, *The Eighteenth Century Background*, 1957, 103.

85Manuel, *op. cit.*, 6.

86*Works*, XI, 252; I, 109–10.

87*Works*, XI, 236–7.

88*Religion and the Rise of Capitalism*, *op. cit.*, 35, 105, 163.

89*Works*, XI, 243.

90*Works*, XI, 257.

91Manuel, *op. cit.*, 3.

92*Plays*, trans. Elisaveta Fen, Harmondsworth, 1960, 281–2.

93*The Wild Palms*, London, 1954, 109.

94Orwell, *Politics vs Literature*, *op. cit.*, 219.

95*Oblomov*, trans. David Magarshack, Harmondsworth, 1967, 123–4.

96*Complete Works of Oscar Wilde*, London, 1977, 1081, 1082.

97*Oblomov*, *op. cit.*, 104.

98'Looking Back on the Spanish War', *The Collected Essays, Journalism and Letters*, *op. cit.*, II, 260–1. *Nineteen Eighty Four*, Harmondsworth, 1958, 59–60, 71–2.

99*The Pilgrim's Progress*, ed. J. B. Wharey, second edition revised Roger Sharrock, Oxford, 1960, 89.

100*Areopagitica, The Works of John Milton*, New York, 1931, IV, 318.

101C. J. Rawson, *Gulliver and the Gentle Reader: Studies in Swift and our Time*, 1973, 31–2.

102*Corr.*, III, 383.

103*Corr.*, III, 501; IV, 505; III, 340; II, 30; II, 449; III, 375.

104*Corr.*, II, 330.

105*Corr.*, III, 9.

106*Corr.*, IV, 383.

107*Corr.*, III, 488.

CHAPTER FIVE

1*Works*, IV, 245.

2*Works*, I, 244.

3*Works of William Makepeace Thackeray*, London, 1869, XIX, 162–3.

4*Works*, XI, 42.

5Thackeray, *op. cit.*, 154.

6Louis I. Bredvold, 'The Gloom of the Tory Satirists', *Pope and His Contemporaries: Essays Presented to George Sherburn*, ed. J. L. Clifford and L. A. Landa, 1949, 2–3.

7Tuveson, *The Dean as Satirist*, *op. cit.*, 368.

8Kathleen Williams, *Jonathan Swift and the Age of Compromise*, 1959, preface.

256

[9]*Works*, I, 125.

[10]*Corr.*, I, 4.

[11]*Works*, I, 243.

[12]*Works*, IX, 159.

[13]*Works*, IX, 262.

[14]*Works*, I, 241.

[15]*Works*, I, 175.

[16]*A Treatise on Man*, trans. W. Hooper, London, 1777, II, 299, 301.

[17]*Works*, IX, 360.

[18]*Corr.*, III, 118.

[19]*Poems*, II, 554. *Oeuvres Completes, op. cit.*, 409.

[20]*Corr.*, V, 31. See also *The Correspondence of Jonathan Swift*, ed. F.Elrington Ball, London, 1914, VI, 5.

[21]*Works*, V, 243.

[22]*Works*, V, 211.

[23]*Works*, VI, 133–4.

[24]*Works*, IX, 244.

[25]*Grace Abounding, op. cit.*, 101.

[26]*Works*, IX, 171.

[27]*Works*, IX, 232.

[28]*Works*, XIII, 80–1.

[29]*Works*, II, 63, 44.

[30]*Works*, II, Introduction, xx.

[31]*Works*, II, 47.

[32]*Works*, II, 57.

[33]*Works*, XII, 299.

[34]*Works*, II, 49.

[35]*Works*, II, 56.

[36]*Works*, II, 50.

[37]*Works*, II, 54.

[38]*Works*, II, 59.

[39]*Works*, II, 61, 62.

[40]*Works*, II, 57.

[41]Quoted by C. B. Macpherson in Introduction to *Leviathan*, Harmondsworth, 1968, 10.

[42]'The Dignity of Man', in *The Portable Renaissance Reader*, ed. James Bruce Ross and Mary Martin McLaughlin, Harmondsworth, 1978, 476, 478.

[43]*Works*, XII, 23.

[44]*Corr.*, III, 341; IV, 79.

[45]*Works*, XII, 65.

[46]*Corr.*, III, 9–10.

[47]*Works*, X, 18–19.

[48]*Works*, X, 57–8.

[49] *Works*, X, 21, 63.

[50] *Works*, X, III, 108.

[51] *Works*, X; 4.

[52] *Works*, X, 57.

[53] *Works*, X, 55.

[54] *Corr.*, III, 93.

[55] Quoted by Davis, Works, X, Introduction, xx.

[56] *Works*, X, 30, 43.

[57] *Works*, X, 111.

[58] *Works*, X, 22, 134, 24.

[59] *Works*, X, 43, 22.

[60] *Works*, XII, 33.

[61] *Corr.*, III, 382.

[62] *Works*, IX, 16–17.

[63] *Corr.*, III, 95; *Works*, XI, xxxiv.

[64] *Works*, XII, 79.

[65] *Works*, XII, 8.

[66] *Works*, XII, 22.

[67] *Works*, XII, 66.

[68] *Works*, IX, 214.

[69] *Corr.*, III, 434.

[70] *Works*, XII, 68, 71.

[71] *Works*, XII, 66, 67, 81.

[72] *Works*, XII, 66; *Corr.*, III, 355.

[73] *Works*, IX, 8.

[74] *Works*, XI, 171.

[75] *Corr.*, III, 87.

[76] *Corr.*, III, 103.

[77] *Works*, I, 140.

[78] *Poems*, II, 635.

[79] *Corr.*, III, 289.

[80] *Corr.*, III, 104.

[81] *Collected Poems of W. B. Yeats*, London, 1979, 268.

[82] Alexander Herzen, *From the Other Shore and The Russian People and Socialism*, trans. Moura Budberg and Richard Wollheim, with an introduction by Isaiah Berlin, London, 1979, 31.

[83] *Works*, III, 178.

[84] *Works*, III, 178.

[85] *Works*, III, 181.

[86] *Works*, XII, 88.

[87] *Corr.*, IV, 74; *Poems*, I, 296–7.

[88] *The Poems of Alexander Pope*, ed. John Butt, 1939, IV, 324–5.

[89] *Works*, X, 54.

[90]Quoted by Davis, *Works*, X, Introduction, xv.
[91]*Works*, III, 179, 28, 68–9.
[92]*Works*, III, 27.
[93]*Works*, IX, 40.
[94]*Woeks*, V, 270; IX, 38.
[95]*Works*, IX, 41.
[96]*Works*, XII, 114.
[97]*Works*, XII, 258.
[98]*Works*, XII, 25.

CHAPTER SIX

[1]F. R. Leavis, 'The Irony of Swift', *The Common Pursuit*, 1972, 75. Ricardo Quintana, *The Mind and Art of Jonathan Swift*, 1953, 65.
[2]*Works*, XI, 38.
[3]*Works*, XI, 49.
[4]*Works*, XI, 32.
[5]*Works*, XI, 33.
[6]*Works*, XI, 56.
[7]*Works*, XI, 88.
[8]*Works*, XI, 98.
[9]*Works*, XI, 93–4.
[10]*Corr.*, III, 94.
[11]*Works*, XI, 132.
[12]*Works*, XI, 226.
[13]*Works*, XI, 265.
[14]*Works*, XI, 123.
[15]*Works*, XI, 111.
[16]*Works*, XI, 111.
[17]*Works*, XI, 116.
[18]*Works*, XI, 111, 232.
[19]*Corr.*, IV, 53.
[20]*Works*, XI, 137–8.
[21]*Works*, XI, 144.
[22]*Works*, XI, 144, 169.
[23]*Works*, XI, 157.
[24]*Works*, XI, 192.
[25]*Works*, XI, 197.
[26]*Nineteen Eighty Four*, op. cit., 77.
[27]*Works*, XI, 205.
[28]*Works*, XI, 67.
[29]*Works*, XI, 69.

[30] *Works*, XI, 275.

[31] Edwin B. Benjamin, 'The King of Brobdingnag and *Secrets of State*', *JHI*, XVIII, 1957, 572–9.

[32] *The Works of Lord Byron*, ed. Rowland E. Prothero, London and New York, 1900, IV, 126.

[33] *In Bluebeard's Castle*, op. cit., 106, 104. See also 'Has Truth a Future?', *The Listener*, 12 January 1978, 42–6.

[34] *Pensées*, op. cit., 334.

[35] *Works*, XI, 103–4.

[36] *Works*, XI, 119.

[37] *Works*, XI, 228.

[38] *Works*, XI, 232.

[39] *Pensées*, op. cit., 164.

[40] *Paradise Lost*, ed. Alastair Fowler, London, 1976, 637–8.

CHAPTER SEVEN

[1] *The Works of Jonathan Swift*, ed. Sir Walter Scott, 1814, I, 90.

[2] *Lives of the Poets*, op. cit., III, 38.

[3] *Ibid.*, 18.

[4] *Corr.*, III, 329.

[5] *Poems*, II, 361.

[6] Leavis, op. cit., 86.

[7] *Works*, XII, 181–2; V, 247.

[8] *Poems*, II, 560.

[9] *Works*, XI, 11; IX, 219–31.

[10] *Life of Johnson*, op. cit., II, 319.

[11] *Works*, XI, xxxiv.

[12] *Works*, XI, 7.

[13] *Works*, XI, 29, 13.

[14] *Works*, XI, 15.

[15] *Measure for Measure*, ed. J. W. Lever, New Arden Shakespeare, London, 1965, II, 11, 108–10.

[16] *Works*, XI, 22, 24, 26.

[17] *Works*, XI, 33.

[18] *Works*, XI, 48.

[19] *Works*, XI, 54.

[20] *Pensées*, op. cit., 175.

[21] *Works*, V, 196.

[22] *Works*, I, 244.

[23] *Works*, XII, 94–5.

[24] *Basic Writings of Saint Augustine*, ed. with an introduction by Whitney J. Oates, New York, 1948, II, 64–9.

[25] *Works*, XI, 4.

[26] *Works*, XI, 49–50.

[27] *Works*, XI, 103.

[28] *Works*, XI, 123.

[29] John Locke, *An Essay Concerning Human Understanding*, ed. with an introduction by John W. Yolton, Everyman's Library, London, 1964, I, xxvi, 5.

[30] *Works*, XI, 150.

[31] *Works*, XI, 173–4.

[32] *Works*, XI, 182–3.

[33] *Works*, XI, 198.

[34] *Works*, XI, 205.

[35] *Works*, XI, 213–14.

[36] *Works*, XI, 252.

[37] *Works*, XI, 253.

[38] *Works*, XI, 253.

[39] *Works*, XI, 248.

[40] *Works*, V, 130, 270.

[41] *Waiting for Godot*, 1965, 89.

[42] *Corr.*, III, 354.

[43] *Works*, XI, 251.

[44] *Minor Poems*, ed. Norman Ault and John Butt, London, 1954, 276–9.

[45] *Works*, XI, 255.

[46] *Corr.*, III, 183.

[47] *The Origin of Species*, ed. with an introduction by J. W. Burrow, Harmondsworth, 1968, 29.

[48] *Ibid.*, 16.

[49] *Works*, I, 122. See *Gulliver's Travels and Other Writings*, ed. Louis A. Landa, 1976, 343.

[50] *Works*, XI, xxxv.

[51] *Poems*, II, 571.

[52] *Works*, XI, 44.

[53] *Works*, XI, 147.

[54] *Do What You Will*, 1931, 93–4.

[55] *Poems*, I, 55.

[56] *Poems*, I, 50.

[57] *Poems*, I, 224.

[58] *Works*, XI, 252.

[59] *Works*, XI, 44.

[60] *Works*, XI, 80–1.

[61] *Works*, XI, 106.

[62] *Works*, XI, 116, 97.

[63] *Corr.*, I, 5.

64*Corr.*, IV, 79.
65*Works*, XI, 265.

CHAPTER EIGHT

1*Works*, I, 244.
2*Pensées, op. cit.*, 139.
3*Poems*, II, 579.
4*Works*, XI, 33–4.
5*Works*, XI, 14–15.
6*Works*, XI, 230.
7*Pensées, op. cit.*, 231.
8Karl Popper, *Conjectures and Refutations: the Growth of Scientific Knowledge*, London, 1963, 4–5.
9Louis I. Bredvold, *The Intellectual Milieu of John Dryden: Studies in Some Aspects of Seventeenth-Century Thought*, University of Michigan, 1934, 16–46.
Jacques Maritain, 'The Political Ideas of Pascal', in *Redeeming the Time*, 1946, 29–45.
10*Works*, XI, 181–2.
11*Works*, I, 142, 152, 156.
12*Works*, IX, 159–68.
13*Works*, IV, 38.
14*Works*, IV, 248.
15*Works*, IX, 261.
16*Works*, IX, 262.
17*Works*, IX, 160.
18*Works*, IX, 164, 165.
19*Works*, IX, 78.
20*Works*, IX, 159, 78.
21*Works*, IX, 160.
22*Works*, IV, 79–80.
23*Works*, IV, 81; II, 67, 91, 68.
24*Leviathan, op. cit.*, 46.
25*An Essay on Man*, ed. Maynard Mack, London, 1950, 67–8.
26*The Tragic Sense of Life*, trans. J. E. Crawford Flitch, London, 1962, 185–6.
27*Works*, IX, 80.
28*Works*, IV, 38.
29*Works*, IX, 77.
30*Works*, XII, 5.
31*Works*, XII, 118.
32*Works*, II, 15. See *Leviathan, op. cit.*, 26.

[33] *Works*, IX, 166.

[34] *Works*, IX, 161.

[35] *Works*, I, 240.

[36] *Works*, IX, 262.

[37] I. A. Richards, *Principles of Literary Criticism*, London, 1924, 246. See also W. B. C. Watkins, *Perilous Balance: The Tragic Genius of Swift, Johnson and Sterne*, Princeton, N.J., 1939.

[38] *Works*, IX, 66.

[39] *Works*, IX, 264.

[40] *Works*, I, 111–13.

[41] *Works*, I, 109.

[42] *Works*, I, 110.

[43] Carl Becker, *The Heavenly City of the Eighteenth Century Philosophers*, New Haven, Conn., 1959, 30–1.

[44] See Edward W. Rosenheim, Jr., *Swift and the Satirist's Art*, Chicago, Ill., 1963, 179–238.

[45] *Poems*, III, 149.

[46] *Works*, I, 167.

[47] *The Twilight of the Idols* and *The Anti-Christ*, trans. with an introduction by R. J. Hollingdale, Harmondsworth, 1968, 156, 158.

[48] *Works*, IX, 263.

[49] Martin Kallich, 'Three Ways of Looking at a Horse: Jonathan Swift's Voyage to the Houyhnhnms Again', *Criticism*, II, 1960, 122–3; Calhoun Winton, 'Conversion on the Road to Houyhnhnmland', *SR*, LXVIII, 1960, 21.

[50] R. S. Crane, 'The Houyhnhnms, the Yahoos and the History of Ideas', in *Reason and the Imagination: Studies in the History of Ideas*, 1600–1800, ed. J. A. Mazzeo, 1962.

[51] *Works*, IV, 251.

[52] See A. E. Dyson, *The Crazy Fabric: Essays in Irony*, 1965, 1–13. John Lawlor, 'Radical Satire and the Realistic Novel', *Essays and Studies*, 8, 1955.

[53] *Corr.*, III, 121.

[54] *Silas Marner*, Harmondsworth, 1967, 154. See also 126, 142.

[55] Quoted by Hill, *God's Englishman, op. cit.*, 231, 235.

[56] *Ibid.*, 227, 230.

[57] Hill, *The World Turned Upside Down, op. cit.*, 312.

[58] Quoted by Hill, *The World Turned Upside Down, op. cit.*, 334.

[59] *Works*, XI, 169–70.

[60] *Works*, II, 32.

[61] Quoted by Hill, *God's Englishman, op. cit.*, 242.

[62] *Ibid.*, 245.

[63] *Pensées, op. cit.*, 158.

[64] Quoted by Hill, *God's Englishman, op. cit.*, 219.

[65]Quoted by Robert Conquest, *Lenin, op. cit.*, 28.

[66]*Lenin in Zurich*, trans. H. T. Willetts, Harmondsworth, 1978, 48.

[67]Hill, *God's Englishman, op. cit.*, 269.

[68]*The Poems and Letters of Andrew Marvell*, ed. H. M. Margoliouth, revised edition, Oxford, 1971, 1, 85.

[69]Richard Hooker, *Of the Laws of Ecclesiastical Polity*, ed. Georges Edelen, Cambridge, Mass., 1977, 1, 49 (spelling modernised).

[70]*Works*, 1, 108.

[71]Hill, *The World Turned Upside Down, op. cit.*, 70–3.

[72]*Corr.*, 111, 118.

[73]Harold Kelling, '*Gulliver's Travels*: A Comedy of Humours', *UTQ*, XXI, 1952, 371–2. See also Edward Stone, 'Swift and the Horses: Misanthropy or Comedy?', *MLQ*, X, 1949, 367–76; John F. Ross, 'The Final Comedy of Lemuel Gulliver', in *Swift: A Collection of Critical Essays*, ed. Ernest Tuveson, Englewood Cliffs, N.J., 1964, 71–89; S. H. Monk, 'The Pride of Lemuel Gulliver', in *Eighteenth Century English Literature: Modern Essays in Criticism*, ed. James L. Clifford, New York, 1959, 112–29.

ABBREVIATIONS USED

Works   *Prose Works of Jonathan Swift*, ed. Herbert Davis, Oxford, 1939–68.

Corr.   *The Correspondence of Jonathan Swift*, ed. Harold Williams, Oxford, 1963–5.

Poems   *The Poems of Jonathan Swift*, ed. Harold Williams, Oxford, 1937.

ELH   *A Journal of English Literary History*

JEGP   *Journal of English and Germanic Philology*

JHI   *Journal of the History of Ideas*

MLQ   *Modern Language Quarterly*

MLR   *Modern Language Review*

MP   *Modern Philogy*

PMLA   *Publications of the Modern Language Association of America*

PQ   *Philological Quarterly*

REL   *Review of English Literature*

RES   *Review of English Studies*

SP   *Studies in Philology*

SR   *Sewanee Review*

UTQ   *University of Toronto Quarterly*

SELECT BIBLIOGRAPHY OF
SECONDARY SOURCES

Acworth, Bernard, *Swift*, London, 1947.

Adams, Robert M., *Strains of Discord: Studies in Literary Openness*, Ithaca, N.Y., 1958.

Allen, Don Cameron, 'The Degeneration of Man and Renaissance Pessimism', *SP*, XXXV, 1938, 202–27.

Allen, J. W., *A History of Political Thought in the Sixteenth Century*, London, 1928.

Allison, Alexander W., 'Concerning Houyhnhnm Reason', *SR*, LXXVI, 1968, 480–92.

Atkinson, Geoffroy, *The Extraordinary Voyage in French Literature before 1700*, New York, 1920.

Babcock, Robert W., 'Swift's Conversion to the Tory Party', *Essays and Studies in English and Comparative Literature*, University of Michigan, 1932, 133–49.

Baker, D. C., 'Tertullian and Swift's *A Modest Proposal*', *Classical Journal*, LII, 1957, 219–20.

Ball, Albert, 'Swift and the Animal Myth', *Transactions of the Wisconsin Academy of Sciences, Arts and Letters*, XLVIII, 1959, 239–48.

Barroll, J. Leeds III, 'Gulliver and the Struldbruggs', *PMLA*, LXXIII, 1958, 43–50.

Becker, Carl, *The Heavenly City of the Eighteenth-Century Philosophers*, New Haven, Conn., 1959.

Beckett, J. C., 'Swift and the Anglo-Irish Tradition', in *Focus: Swift*, ed. C. J. Rawson, London, 1971, 155–70.

——, 'Swift: The Priest in Politics', in *Confrontations: Studies in Irish History*, London, 1972, 111–22.

——, 'Swift as an Ecclesiastical Statesman', in H. A. Cronne, T. W. Moody, and D. B. Quinn (eds.), *Essays in British and Irish History in Honour of James Eadie Todd*, Frederick Muller Ltd., 1949; repr. in *Jonathan Swift:*

A Critical Anthology, ed. Denis Donoghue, Harmondsworth, 1971, 153–68.

Benjamin, Edwin B., 'The King of Brobdingnag and Secrets of State', *JHI*, XVIII, 1957, 572–79.

Bennett, H. R., 'Jonathan Swift, Priest', *Anglican Theological Review*, XXXIX, 1957, 131–8.

Berwick, Donald M., *The Reputation of Jonathan Swift*, 1781–1882, Philadelphia, Pa., 1941.

Brady, Frank (ed.), *Twentieth Century Interpretations of 'Gulliver's Travels'*, A Collection of Critical Essays, Englewood Cliffs, N.J., 1968.

Bredvold, Louis I., *The Intellectual Milieu of John Dryden: Studies in Some Aspects of Seventeenth-Century Thought*, University of Michigan, 1934.

——, *The Brave New World of the Enlightenment*, University of Michigan, 1961.

——, 'The Gloom of the Tory Satirists', in *Pope and His Contemporaries: essays presented to George Sherburn*, ed. James L. Clifford and Louis A. Landa, Oxford, 1949.

——, 'A Note in Defence of Satire', *ELH*, VII, 1940, 253–64.

Brown, James, 'Swift as Moralist', *PQ*, XXXIII, 1954, 368–87.

Brown, Norman O., *Life against Death: The Psychoanalytical Meaning of History*, London, 1959.

Bullitt, John M., *Jonathan Swift and the Anatomy of Satire: A Study of Satiric Technique*, Cambridge, Mass., 1953.

Bury, J. B., *The Idea of Progress: An Enquiry into its Origin and Growth*, London, 1920.

Carnochan, W. B., 'The Complexity of Swift: Gulliver's Fourth Voyage', *SP*, LX, 1963, 23–44.

——, '*Gulliver's Travels*: An Essay on the Human Understanding?', *MLQ*, XXV, 1964, 5–21.

——, *Lemuel Gulliver's Mirror for Man*, Berkeley, Calif., 1968.

——, 'Swift's *Tale*: On Satire, Negation, and the Uses of Irony', *Eighteenth-Century Studies* No. 1 (autumn 1971), 122–44.

——, 'Augustan Satire and the Gates of Dream: A Utopian Essay', *Studies in the Literary Imagination*, V, No. 2 (Oct. 1972), 1–18.

——, 'The Consolations of Satire', in *The Art of Jonathan Swift*, ed. Clive T. Probyn, Plymouth and London, 1978, 19–42.

Case, Arthur E., *Four Essays on 'Gulliver's Travels'*, Princeton, N.J., 1945.

Chadwick, Owen, *The Secularization of the European Mind in the Nineteenth Century*, Cambridge, 1975.

Clarke, John R., *Form and Frenzy in Swift's 'Tale of a Tub'*, Ithaca, N.Y., 1969.

Clayborough, Arthur, *The Grotesque in English Literature*, Oxford, 1965.

Clifford, James L., 'Swift's Mechanical Operation of the Spirit', in *Pope and His Contemporaries: essays presented to George Sherburn*, ed. James L. Clifford and Louis A. Landa, Oxford, 1949, 135–46.

——, (ed.), *Man Versus Society in Eighteenth-Century Britain: Six Points of View*, Cambridge, 1968.

——, (ed.), *Eighteenth-Century English Literature: Modern Essays in Criticism*, New York, 1959.

——, 'The Eighteenth Century', *MLQ*, XXVI, 1965, 111–34.

Clubb, Merrel D., 'The Criticism of Gulliver's Voyage to the Houyhnhnms, 1726–1914', *Stanford Studies in Language and Literature*, Stanford, Calif., 1941, 203–32.

Colie, R. L., 'Gulliver, the Locke–Stillingfleet Controversy, and the Nature of Man', *History of Ideas Newsletter*, II, New York, 1956, 58–62.

Cook, Richard I., *Jonathan Swift as a Tory Pamphleteer*, Seattle, Wash., and London, 1967.

Crane, R. S., 'Anglican Apologetics and the Idea of Progress, 1699–1745', *MP*, XXXI, 1934, 273–306, 349–82.

——, 'Suggestions towards a Genealogy of the Man of Feeling', in *Studies in the Literature of the Augustan Age*, ed. R. C. Boys, Ann Arbor, Mich., 1952, 61–87.

——, 'Review of Martin Kallich's Three Ways of Looking at a Horse: Jonathan Swift's "Voyage to the Houyhnms Again" ', *PQ*, XL, 1961, 427–30.

——, 'The Rationale of the Fourth Voyage', in *Gulliver's Travels*, ed. Robert A. Greenberg, New York, 1961, 300–7.

——, 'The Houyhnhnms, the Yahoos and the History of Ideas', in *Reason and the Imagination: Studies in the History of Ideas, 1600–1800*, ed. J. A. Mazzeo, New York, 1962, 231–53.

Cranston, Maurice and Peters, R. S. (eds.), *Hobbes and Rousseau: A Collection of Critical Essays*, New York, 1972.

Darnall, F. M., 'Swift's Religion', *JEGP*, XXX, 1931, 379–82.

——, 'Swift's Belief in Immortality', *MLN*, XLVII, 1932, 448–51.

Davie, Donald, 'Academism and Jonathan Swift', *Twentieth Century*, CLIV, 1953, 217–24.

Davies, Hugh Sykes, 'Irony and the English Tongue', in *The World of Jonathan Swift*, ed. Brian Vickers, Oxford, 1968, 129–53.

Davis, Herbert, *Stella: A Gentlewoman of the Eighteenth Century*, New York, 1942.

——, 'The Conciseness of Swift', in *Essays on the Eighteenth Century* presented to David Nichol Smith, ed. J. R. Sutherland and F. P. Wilson, Oxford, 1945.

——, 'Recent Studies of Swift: A Survey', *UTQ*, VII, 1938, 273–88.

——, *Jonathan Swift: Essays on his Satire and Other Studies*, Oxford and New York, 1964.

——, 'Swift's Use of Irony', in *The World of Jonathan Swift*, ed. Brian Vickers, Oxford, 1968, 154–70.

——, 'Swift's Use of Irony', in *Irony in Defoe and Swift: The Uses of Irony*, by Maximilian E. Novak and Herbert Davis, Los Angeles, Calif., 1966.

Dennis, Nigel, *Jonathan Swift: A Short Character*, New York, 1964.

DePorte, Michael V., *Nightmares and Hobbyhorses: Swift, Sterne and the Augustan Idea of Madness*, San Marino, Calif., 1974.

Dircks, Richard J., 'Gulliver's Tragic Rationalism', *Criticism*, II, 1960, 134–49.

Dobrée, Bonamy, 'Swift, 1715–1745', in *English Literature in the Early Eighteenth Century 1700–1740*, The Oxford History of English Literature, VII, Oxford, 1959, 432–74.

——, 'The Jocose Dean', in *Swift: Modern Judgements*, ed. A. Norman Jeffares, London, 1968, 28–46.

Donoghe, Denis, *Jonathan Swift: A Critical Introduction*, Cambridge, 1969.

——, (ed.), *Jonathan Swift: A Critical Anthology*, Harmondsworth, 1971.

——, 'The Brainwashing of Gulliver', *The Listener*, 96, November 1976, 578–9.

——, (ed.), *Swift Revisited*, Cork, 1968.

Dyson, A. E., 'Swift: The Metamorphosis of Irony', *Essays and Studies*, N.S., XI, 1958, 53–67; repr. in *The Crazy Fabric: Essays in Irony*, London, 1965, 1–13.

Ehrenpreis, Irvin, *The Personality of Jonathan Swift*, London, 1958.

——, *Swift: The Man, His Works and the Age, I: Mr Swift and his Contemporaries*, London, 1962.

——, *Swift: The Man, His Works and the Age, II: Dr Swift*, London, 1967.

——, 'Swift and Liberty', *JHI*, XIII, 1952, 131–46.

——, 'The Meaning of Gulliver's Last Voyage', *REL*, III, 1962, 18–38.

——, 'Jonathan Swift', *Proceedings of the British Academy*, LIV, 1968, 149–63.

——, 'Dr S——t and the Hibernian Patriot', in *Jonathan Swift, 1667–1967: A Dublin Tercentenary Tribute*, ed. Roger McHugh and Philip Edwards, Dublin, 1967, 24–37.

——, 'Swift and the Comedy of Evil', in *The World of Jonathan Swift*, ed. Brian Vickers, Oxford, 1968, 213–19.

——, 'Swift's Letters', in *Focus: Swift*, ed. C. J. Rawson, London, 1971, 197–215.

Elder, Lucius W., 'The Pride of the Yahoo', *MLN*, XXXV, 1920, 206–11.

Elliott, Robert C., *The Power of Satire: Magic, Ritual, Art*, Princeton, N.J., 1960.

——, *The Shape of Utopia: Studies in a Literary Genre*, Chicago, Ill., and London, 1970.

——, 'Gulliver as Literary Artist', *ELH*, XIX, 1952, 49–63.

——, 'Swift's Satire: Rules of the Game', *ELH*, XLI, no. 3, 1974, 413–28.

——, 'Swift's "I"', *Yale Review*, LXII, No. 3 (spring 1973), 372–91.

Ewald, William Bragg, Jr., *The Masks of Jonathan Swift*, Cambridge, Mass., 1954.

Falle, George, 'Swift's Writings', *UTQ*, XXXIV, 1965, 294–312.

——, 'Divinity and Wit: Swift's Attempted Reconciliation', *UTQ*, XLVI, 1976, 14–29.

Ferguson, Oliver W., *Jonathan Swift and Ireland*, Champaign, Ill., 1962.

——, 'Swift's Saeva Indignatio and *A Modest Proposal*', *PQ*, XXXVIII, 1959, 473–9.

Figgis, J. N., *Political Thought from Gerson to Grotius: 1414–1625*, New York, 1960.

Fink, Z. S., 'Political Theory in *Gulliver's Travels*', *ELH*, XIV, 1947, 151–61.

Firth, Sir Charles H., 'The Political Significance of *Gulliver's Travels*', *Proceedings of the British Academy*, IX, 1919–20, 237–59.

Fitzgerald, Robert P., 'The Structure of *Gulliver's Travels*', *SP*, LXXI, 1974, 247–63.

Foot, Michael, *The Pen and the Sword*, London, 1957.

Foster, Milton P. (ed.), *A Casebook on Gulliver among the Houyhnhnms*, New York, 1961.

Frantz, R. W., 'Swift's Yahoos and the Voyagers', *MP*, XXIX, 1932, 49–57.

French, David P., 'Swift, the Non-Jurors and Jacobitism', *MLN*, LXXII, 1957, 258–64.

——, 'Swift and Hobbes – A Neglected Parallel', *Boston University Studies in English*, III, 1957, 243–55.

Fritz, Kurt von, *The Theory of the Mixed Constitution in Antiquity: A Critical Analysis of Polybius' Political Ideas*, New York, 1954.

Frost, William, 'The Irony of Swift and Gibbon: a Reply to F. R. Leavis', *Essays in Criticism*, XVII, 1967, 41–7.

Frye, Roland Mushat, 'Swift's Yahoo and the Christian Symbols for Sin', *JHI*, XV, 1954, 201–17.

Fussell, Paul, *The Rhetorical World of Augustan Humanism: Ethics and Imagery from Swift to Burke*, Oxford, 1965.

——, 'The Frailty of Lemuel Gulliver', in *Essays in Literary History presented to J. Milton French*, ed. Rudolf Kirk and C. F. Main, New Brunswick, N.J., 1960, 113–25.

Geering, R. G., 'Swift's Struldbruggs: The Critics Considered', *Journal of the Australian Universities Language and Literature Association*, VII, 1957, 5–15.

Gill, James E., 'Man and Yahoo: Dialectic and Symbolism in Gulliver's "Voyage to the Country of the Houyhnhnms"', in *The Dress of Words: Essays on Restoration and Eighteenth Century Literature in Honor of Richmond P. Bond*, ed. Robert B. White, Jr., University of Kansas, 1978, 67–90.

Godwin, William, *Enquiry Concerning Political Justice and its Influence on Morals and Happiness*, ed. F. E. L. Priestley, Toronto, 1946.

Goldgar, Bertrand A., '*Gulliver's Travels* and the Opposition to Walpole'.

in *The Augustan Milieu: Essays presented to Louis A. Landa*, ed. H. K. Miller, E. Rothstein and G. S. Rousseau, Oxford, 1970, 77–101.

Gray, James, 'The Modernism of Jonathan Swift', *Queen's Quarterly*, LXVII, 1960, 11–17.

Greenberg, Robert A., 'Swift's *Gulliver's Travels*, Part IV, Ch. III', *Explicator*, XVI, 1957, item 2.

——, 'A Modest Proposal and the Bible', *MLR*, LV, 1960, 568–69.

Greene, Donald, 'Swift: Some Caveats', in *Studies in the Eighteenth Century, II, Papers presented at the Second David Nichol Smith Memorial Seminar Canberra 1970*, ed. R. F. Brissenden, Canberra, 1973, 341–58.

——, 'The Education of Lemuel Gulliver', in *The Varied Pattern: Studies in the Eighteenth Century*, Toronto, 1971, 3–20.

Hall, Basil, ' "An Inverted Hypocrite": Swift the Churchman', in *The World of Jonathan Swift*, ed. Brian Vickers, Oxford, 1968, 38–68.

Halewood, William H., 'Plutarch in Houyhnhnmland: A Neglected Source for Gulliver's Fourth Voyage', *PQ*, XLIV, 1965, 185–94.

——, '*Gulliver's Travels*, I, vi', *ELH*, XXXIII, 1936, 422–33.

Harrison, G. B., 'Jonathan Swift', in *Social and Political Ideas of Some English Thinkers of the Augustan Age, 1650–1750*, ed. F. J. C. Hearnshaw, London, 1928, 189–209.

Hart, Jeffrey, 'The Ideologue as Artist: Some Notes on *Gulliver's Travels*', *Criticism*, II, 1960, 125–33.

Harth, Philip, *Swift and Anglican Rationalism: the Religious Background of 'A Tale of a Tub'*, Chicago, Ill., 1961.

Harth, Philip, and Peterson, Leland D., 'Swift's *Project*: Tract or Travesty?', *PMLA*, LXXXIV, 336–43.

Hearnshaw, F. J. C. (ed.), *The Social and Political Ideas of Some Great Thinkers of the Sixteenth and Seventeenth Centuries*, London, 1926.

——, (ed.), *Social and Political Ideas of Some English Thinkers of the Augustan Age, 1650–1750*, London, 1928.

Hepburn, R. W., 'George Hakewill: The Virility of Nature', *JHI*, XVI, 1955, 135–50.

Highet, Gilbert, *The Anatomy of Satire*, Princeton, N.J., 1962.

Hill, Christopher, *The Century of Revolution*, London, 1961.

——, *God's Englishman: Cromwell and the English Revolution*, London, 1970.

——, *The World Turned Upside Down: Radical Ideas during the English Revolution*, London, 1972.

——, *Milton and the English Revolution*, London, 1977.

Hill, Geoffrey, 'Jonathan Swift: The Poetry of "Reaction" ', in *The World of Jonathan Swift*, ed. Brian Vickers, Oxford, 1968, 195–212.

Hodgart, Matthew, 'Gulliver's Travels', in *Swift Revisited*, ed. Denis Donoghue, Cork, 1968, 25–39.

——, *Satire*, London, 1969.

Holloway, John, *The Charted Mirror: Literary and Critical Essays*, London, 1960.

——, 'Dean of St. Patrick's: A View from the *Letters*', in *The World of Jonathan Swift*, ed. Brian Vickers, Oxford, 1968, 258–68.

Horrell, Joseph, 'What Gulliver Knew', *SR*, LI, 1943, 476–504. Introduction to *Collected Poems of Jonathan Swift*, London, 1958.

Huxley, Aldous, 'Swift', in *Do What You Will*, London, 1931, 93–106.

A. Norman Jeffares (ed.), *Fair Liberty Was All His Cry: A Tercentenary Tribute to Jonathan Swift, 1667–1745*, London and New York, 1967.

Johnson, J. W., 'Swift's Historical Outlook', in *Swift: Modern Judgements*, ed. A. Norman Jeffares, London, 1968, 96–120.

Johnson, Maurice, *The Sin of Wit: Jonathan Swift as Poet*, New York, 1950.

——, 'The Structural Impact of *A Modest Proposal*', *Bucknell Review*, VII, 1958, 234–40.

——, 'Swift and "the Greatest Epitaph in History"', *PMLA*, LXIII, 1953, 814–27.

Jones, Myrddin, '*Further Thoughts on Religion*: Swift's Relationship to Filmer and Locke', *RES*, N.S., IX, 1958, 284–6.

Jones, Richard Foster, *Ancients and Moderns: A Study of the Rise of the Scientific Movement in Seventeenth Century England*, St Louis, Miss., 1961.

——, 'The Background of The Battle of the Books', in *The Seventeenth Century: Studies in the History of English Thought and Literature from Bacon to Pope*, Stanford, Calif., 1951.

Jones, W. T., *Masters of Political Thought: Machiavelli to Bentham*, London, 1947.

Jourdan, G. V., 'The Religion of Dean Swift', *Church Quarterly Review*, CXXVI, 1938, 269–86.

Kallich, Martin, 'Three Ways of Looking at a Horse: Jonathan Swift's Voyage to the Houyhnhnms Again', *Criticism*, II, 1960, 107–24.

Kay, John, 'The Hypocrisy of Jonathan Swift: Swift's *Project* Reconsidered', *UTQ*, XLIV, 1974, 213–22.

Kaye, F. B., 'The Influence of Bernard Mandeville', *SP*, XIX, 1922, 83–108.

Kelling, Harold D., '*Gulliver's Travels*: A Comedy of Humours', *UTQ*, XXI, 1952, 362–75.

——, 'Reason in Madness: *A Tale of a Tub*', *PMLA*, LXIX, 1954, 198–222.

Kelsall, M. M., '*Iterum* Houyhnhnm: Swift's Sextumvirate and the Horses', *Essays in Criticism*, XIX, 1969, 35–45.

Kermode, J. F., 'Yahoos and Houyhnhnms', *Notes and Queries*, CXCV, July 1950, 317–18.

Kiernan, Colm, 'Swift and Science', *Historical Journal*, 14, 1971, 709–22.

Kinkead-Weekes, Mark, 'The Dean and the Drapier', in *Swift Revisited*, ed. Denis Donoghue, Cork, 1968, 41–55.

Kliger, Samuel, 'The Unity of *Gulliver's Travels*', *MLQ*, VI, 1945, 401–15.

Knight, G. Wilson, 'Swift and the Symbolism of Irony', in *The Burning Oracle*, London, 1939, 114–30.

Knox, Ronald, *Enthusiasm: A Chapter in the History of Religion with special references to the Seventeenth and Eighteenth Centuries*, Oxford, 1950.

Korshin, Paul J., 'Swift and Satirical Typology in *A Tale of a Tub*', in *Studies in the Eighteenth Century, II, Papers presented at the Second David Nichol Smith Memorial Seminar Canberra 1970*, ed. R. F. Brissenden, Canberra, 1973, 279–302.

Krailsheimer, A. J., *Studies in Self-Interest from Descartes to La Bruyère*, Oxford, 1962.

Landa, Louis A., *Swift and the Church of Ireland*, Oxford, 1954.

——, 'Swift's Economic Views and Mercantilism', *ELH*, X, Dec. 1943, 310–35.

——, 'Review of Potter's Swift and Natural Science', *PQ*, XXI, 1942, 219–21.

——, 'Note on Irvin Ehrenpreis's *The Personality of Jonathan Swift*', *PQ*, XXXVIII, 1959, 351–3.

——, 'Jonathan Swift: Biographical Evidence', in *Studies in the Literature of the Augustan Age*, ed. R. C. Boys, Ann Arbor, Mich., 1952, 176–97.

——, 'Swift, the Mysteries and Deism', *Studies in English*, University of Texas, 1944, 239–56.

——, (ed.), *'Gulliver's Travels' and Other Writings*, Oxford, 1976.

Lawlor, John, 'Radical Satire and the Realistic Novel', *Essays and Studies*, N.S., VIII, 1955, 58–75.

Leavis, F. R., 'The Irony of Swift', in *The Common Pursuit*, London, 1972, 73–87.

Leyburn, Ellen Douglass, *Satiric Allegory: Mirror of Man*, New Haven, Conn., 1956.

McDowell, R. B., 'Swift as a Political Thinker', in *Jonathan Swift, 1667–1967: A Dublin Tercentenary Tribute*, ed. Roger McHugh and Philip Edwards, Dublin, 1967, 176–86.

McKenzie, Gordon, 'Swift: Reason and Some of its Consequences', in *Five Studies in Literature* by B. H. Bronson *et al.*, *University of California Publications in English*, VIII, 1, Berkeley, Calif., 1940, 101–29.

Mack, Maynard, 'The Muse of Satire', in *Studies in the Literature of the Augustan Age*, ed. R. C. Boys, Ann Arbor, Mich., 1952, 218–31.

Manuel, Frank E., *Shapes of Philosophical History*, Stanford, Calif., 1965.

——, (ed.), *Utopias and Utopian Thought*, London, 1973.

Maritain, Jacques, 'The Political Ideas of Pascal', in *Redeeming the Time*, trans. H. L. Binsse, London, 1946, 29–45.

Maxwell, J. C., 'Demigods and pickpockets: the Augustan myth in Swift and Rousseau', *Scrutiny*, XI, 1942, 34–9.

Mercier, Vivian, *The Irish Comic Tradition*, Oxford, 1962.

Mesnard, Jean, *Pascal: l'homme et l'oeuvre*, Paris, 1951.

Mezciems, Jenny, 'Gulliver and Other Heroes', in *The Art of Jonathan Swift*, ed. Clive T. Probyn, Plymouth and London, 1978, 189–208.

Mintz, Samuel I., *The Hunting of Leviathan: Seventeenth-Century Reactions to the Materialism and Moral Philosophy of Thomas Hobbes*, Cambridge, 1962.

Monk, Samuel Holt, 'The Pride of Lemuel Gulliver', in *Eighteenth Century English Literature: Modern Essays in Criticism*, ed. James L. Clifford, New York, 1959, 112–29.

Moore, J. B., 'The Role of Gulliver', *MP*, XXV, 1928, 469–80.

Morris, John, 'Wishes as Horses: A Word for the Houyhnhnms', *Yale Review*, LXII, No. 3 (spring 1973), 355–71.

Mortimer, Ernest, *Pascal: the Life and Work of a Realist*, London, 1959.

Murray, Patrick, 'Swift: The Sceptical Conformist', *Studies*, LVIII, 1969, 355–67.

Murray, W. A., 'Review of Frye's Article on Swift's Yahoo and the Christian Symbols for Sin', *JHI*, XV, 1954, 599–601.

Nelson, William (ed.), *Twentieth Century Interpretations of 'Utopia': A Collection of Critical Essays*, Englewood Cliffs, N.J., 1968.

Newman, Bernard, *Jonathan Swift*, New York, 1937.

Nicolson, Marjorie, *Science and Imagination*, London, 1956.

——, 'Milton and Hobbes', *SP*, XXIII, 1926, 405–33.

Oakeshott, Michael, 'The Moral Life in the Writings of Thomas Hobbes', in *Rationalism in Politics and Other Essays*, London, 1962, 248–300.

Ong, Walter J., 'Swift on the Mind: The Myth of Asepsis', *MLQ*, XV, 1954, 208–21.

Papajewski, Helmut, 'Swift and Berkeley', *Anglia*, LXXVII, 1959, 29–53.

Paulson, Ronald (ed.), *The Fictions of Satire*, Baltimore, Md., 1967.

—— (ed.), *Satire: Modern Essays in Criticism*, Englewood Cliffs, N.J., 1971.

——, 'Swift, Stella and Permanence', *ELH*, XXVII, 1960, 298–314.

——, *Theme and Structure in Swift's 'Tale of a Tub'*, New Haven, Conn., 1960.

Peake, Charles H., 'Swift and the Passions', *MLR*, LV, 1960, 169–80.

——, 'The Coherence of *Gulliver's Travels*', in *Focus: Swift*, ed. C. J. Rawson, London, 1971, 171–96.

Pinkus, Philip, 'Swift and the Ancients–Moderns Controversy', *UTQ*, XXIX, 1959, 46–58.

——, 'Sin and Satire in Swift', *Bucknell Review*, XIII, No. 2, 1965, 11–25.

Potter, George R., 'Swift and Natural Science', *PQ*, XX, 1941, 97–118.

Preu, James, 'Jonathan Swift and the common man', *Florida State University Studies*, XI, 1953, 19–24.

——, 'Swift's Influence on Godwin's Doctrine of Anarchism', *JHI*, XV, 1954, 371–83.

Price, Martin, *Swift's Rhetorical Art: A Study in Structure and Meaning*, New Haven, Conn., 1953.

——, *To the Palace of Wisdom: Studies in Order and Energy from Dryden to*

Blake, New York, 1964.

Probyn, Clive T. (ed.), *The Art of Jonathan Swift*, Plymouth and London, 1978.

——, 'Swift and the Human Predicament', in *The Art of Jonathan Swift*, Plymouth and London, 1978, 57–80.

Quintana, Ricardo, *The Mind and Art of Jonathan Swift*, Oxford, 1936; repr. London with additional notes and bibliography, 1953.

——, *Swift: An Introduction*, London, 1955.

——, 'Situational Satire: A Commentary on the Method of Swift', *UTQ*, XVII, 1948, 130–6.

——, '*Gulliver's Travels*: The Satiric Intent and Execution', in *Jonathan Swift, 1667–1967: A Dublin Tercentenary Tribute*, ed. Roger McHugh and Philip Edwards, Dublin, 1967, 78–93.

Rawson, C. J., 'Order and Cruelty: A Reading of Swift (with some comments on Pope and Johnson)', *Essays in Criticism*, 20, 1970, 24–56.

——, *Gulliver and the Gentle Reader: Studies in Swift and our Time*, London and Boston, Mass., 1973.

——, 'The Character of Swift's Satire', in *Focus: Swift*, ed. C. J. Rawson, London, 1971, 17–75.

——, 'The Nightmares of Strephon: Nymphs of the City in the Poems of Swift, Baudelaire, Eliot', in *English Literature in the Age of Disguise*, ed. Maximilian E. Novak, Berkeley, Calif., 1977, 57–99.

Reichert, John F., 'Plato, Swift and the Houyhnhnms', *PQ*, XLVII, 1968, 179–92.

Reiss, Edmund, 'The Importance of Swift's Glubdubbdrib Episode', *JEGP*, LIX, 1960, 223–8.

Rogers, Katherine M., ' "My Female Friends": The Mysogyny of Jonathan Swift', *Texas Studies in Literature and Language*, I, 1959, 366–79.

Rogers, Pat, 'Swift and the Idea of Authority', in *The World of Jonathan Swift*, ed. Brian Vickers, Oxford, 1968, 25–37.

——, *Grub Street: Studies in a Subculture*, London, 1972.

——, *The Augustan Vision*, London, 1974.

——, 'Gulliver's Glasses', in *The Art of Jonathan Swift*, ed. Clive T. Probyn, Plymouth and London, 1978, 179–88.

Rosenheim, Edward, Jr., *Swift and the Satirist's Art*, Chicago, Ill., 1963.

——, 'The Fifth Voyage of Lemuel Gulliver: A Footnote', *MP*, LX, 1960, 103–19.

Ross, Angus, 'The Hibernian Patriot's Apprenticeship', in *The Art of Jonathan Swift*, ed. Clive T. Probyn, Plymouth and London, 1978, 83–107.

——, 'The Social Circumstances of Certain Remote Nations', in *The World of Jonathan Swift*, ed. Brian Vickers, Oxford, 1968, 220–32.

Ross, John F., *Swift and Defoe: a study in relationship*, Berkeley, Calif., 1941.

——, 'The Final Comedy of Lemuel Gulliver', in *Swift: A Collection of Critical*

Essays, ed. Ernest Tuveson, Englewood Cliffs, N.J., 1964, 71–89.

Ross, Ralph, Schneider, Herbert W., Waldman, Theodore (eds.), *Thomas Hobbes in his Time,* University of Minnesota, 1974.

Said, Edward, W., 'Swift's Tory Anarchy', *Eighteenth-Century Studies,* No. 1 (autumn 1969), 48–66.

Sams, Henry W., 'Swift's Satire of the Second Person', *ELH,* XXVI, 1959, 36–44.

Seelye, John D., 'Hobbes's Leviathan and the Giantism Complex in the First Book of *Gulliver's Travels'*, *JEGP,* LX, 1961, 228–39.

Sherburn, George, 'Methods in Books about Swift', *SP,* XXXV, 1938, 635–56.

——, 'Jonathan Swift', in *A Literary History of England,* ed. A. C. Baugh, New York, 1948, 857–69.

——, 'Errors Concerning the Houyhnhnms', *MP,* LVI, 1958, 92–97.

——, 'Rasselas Returns – To What?', *PQ,* XXXVIII, 1959, 383–4.

Speck, W. A., *'The Examiner* Examined: Swift's Tory Pamphleteering', in *Focus: Swift,* ed. C. J. Rawson, London, 1971, 138–54.

——, 'From Principles to Practice: Swift and Party Politics', in *The World of Jonathan Swift,* ed. Brian Vickers, Oxford, 1968, 69–86.

——, 'Swift's Politics', *University Review,* Dublin, IV, 1976, 53–71.

Starkman, Miriam Kosh, *Swift's Satire on Learning in 'A Tale of a Tub',* Princeton, N.J., 1950.

Steiner, George, *In Bluebeard's Castle: Some Notes Towards the Re-definition of Culture,* London, 1974.

——, 'Has Truth a Future?', *The Listener,* 99, Jan. 1978, 42–6.

Stone, Edward, 'Swift and the Horses: Misanthropy or Comedy?', *MLQ,* X, 1949, 367–76.

Stout, Gardiner D., Jr., 'Speaker and Satiric Vision in Swift's *Tale of a Tub',* *Eighteenth-Century Studies,* No. 2 (winter 1969), 175–99.

——, 'Satire and Self-Expression in Swift's *Tale of a Tub',* in *Studies in the Eighteenth Century, II, Papers presented at the Second David Nichol Smith Seminar Canberra 1970,* ed. R. F. Brissenden, Canberra, 1973, 323–39.

Strauss, Leo, *Natural Right and History,* Chicago, Ill., 1953.

Stromberg, Roland N., *Religious Liberalism in Eighteenth-Century England,* Oxford, 1954.

Suits, Conrad, 'The Role of the Horses in "A Voyage to the Houyhnhnms"', *UTQ,* XXXIV, 1965, 118–32.

Sutherland, James, 'Forms and Methods in Swift's Satire', in *Jonathan Swift, 1667–1967: A Dublin Tercentenary Tribute,* ed. Roger McHugh and Philip Edwards, Dublin, 1967, 61–77.

Sutherland, John H., 'A Reconsideration of Gulliver's Third Voyage', *SP,* LIV, 1957, 45–52.

Sutherland, W. O. S., Jr., 'Satire and the Use of History: Gulliver's Third Voyage', in *The Art of the Satirist: Essays on the Satire of Augustan England,*

Austin, Tex., 1965, 107–25.

Tallman, Warren, 'Swift's Fool: A Comment upon Satire in *Gulliver's Travels*', *Dalhousie Review*, XXXIX, 1961, 470–78.

Taylor, Aline Mackenzie, 'Sights and Monsters and Gulliver's 'Voyage to Brobdingnag', *Tulane Studies in English*, VII, 1957, 29–82.

Teeter, Louis, 'The Dramatic Use of Hobbes's Political Ideas', *ELH*, III, 1936, 140–69.

Tilton, John W., '*Gulliver's Travels* as a Work of Art', *Bucknell Review*, VIII, Dec. 1959, 246–59.

Torchiana, Donald T., 'W. B. Yeats, Jonathan Swift and Liberty', *MP*, LXI, 1963, 26–39.

Traugott, John, 'A Voyage to Nowhere with Thomas More and Jonathan Swift: *Utopia* and "The Voyage to the Houyhnhnms"', *SR*, LXIX, 1961, 534–65.

——, 'Swift's Allegory: The Yahoo and the Man of Mode', *UTQ*, XXXIII, 1963, 1–18.

——, 'The Refractory Swift', *MLQ*, XXV, 1964, 205–11.

——, 'Swift, Our Contemporary', in *Focus: Swift*, ed. C. J. Rawson, London, 1971, 239–64.

——, '*A Tale of a Tub*', in *Focus: Swift*, ed. C. J. Rawson, London, 1971, 76–120.

—— (ed.), *Discussions of Jonathan Swift*, Boston, Mass., 1962.

Tuveson, Ernest, 'The Dean as Satirist', *UTQ*, XXII, 1953, 368–75.

——, 'Swift and the World Makers', *JHI*, XI, 1950, 54–74.

——, 'Swift: The View from within the Satire', in *The Satirist's Art*, ed. H. James Jenson and Malvin R. Zirker, Jr., Bloomington, Ind., and London, 1972, 3–27.

—— (ed.), *Swift: A Collection of Critical Essays*, Englewood Cliffs, N.J., 1964.

Vickers, Brian (ed.), *The World of Jonathan Swift*, Oxford, 1968.

——, 'Swift and the Baconian Idol', in *The World of Jonathan Swift*, 87–128.

——, 'The Satiric Structure of *Gulliver's Travels* and More's *Utopia*', in *The World of Jonathan Swift*, 233–57.

Viner, Jacob, 'Satire and Economics in the Augustan Age of Satire', in *The Augustan Milieu: Essays presented to Louis A. Landa*, ed. H. K. Miller, E. Rothstein and G. S. Rousseau, Oxford, 1970, 77–101.

Voigt, Milton, *Swift and the Twentieth Century*, Detroit, 1964.

Ward, David, *Jonathan Swift: An Introductory Essay*, London, 1973.

Wasiolek, Edward, 'Relativity in *Gulliver's Travels*', *PQ*, XXXVII, 1958, 110–16.

Watkins, W. B. C., *Perilous Balance: The Tragic Genius of Swift, Johnson and Sterne*, Princeton, N.J., 1939.

Watt, Ian, 'The Ironic Tradition in Augustan Prose from Swift to Johnson', in *Focus: Swift*, ed. C. J. Rawson, London, 1971, 216–38.

Webster, C. M., 'Swift's *Tale of a Tub* compared with Earlier Satires of the Puritans', *PMLA*, XLVII, 1932, 171–8.

——, 'Swift and Some Earlier Satirists of Puritan Enthusiasm', *PMLA*, XLVIII, 1933, 1141–53.

——, 'The Satiric Background of the Attack on the Puritans in Swift's *A Tale of a Tub*', *PMLA*, L, 1935, 210–23.

——, 'Notes on the Yahoos', *MLN*, XLVII, 1932, 451–4.

Wedel, T. O., 'On the Philosophical Background of *Gulliver's Travels*', *SP*, XXIII, 1926, 434–50.

Westgate, R. I. W. and MacKendrick, P. L., 'Juvenal and Swift', *Classical Journal*, XXXVII, 1942, 468–82.

Wilding, Michael, 'The Politics of *Gulliver's Travels*', in *Studies in the Eighteenth Century, II, Papers presented at the Second David Nicol Smith Memorial Seminar Canberra 1970*, ed. R. F. Brissenden, Canberra, 1973, 303–22.

Williams, Kathleen, *Jonathan Swift and the Age of Compromise*, Lawrence, Kansas, 1958.

——, 'Gulliver's Voyage to the Houyhnhnms', *ELH*, XVIII, 1951, 275–86.

——, 'Restoration Themes in the Major Satires of Swift', *RES*, N.S., XVI, 1965, 258–71.

—— (ed.), *Swift: The Critical Heritage*, London, 1970.

Wilson, James R., 'Swift's Alazon', *Studia neophilogica*, XXX, 1958, 153–64.

——, 'Swift, the Psalmist and the Horse', *Tennessee Studies in Literature*, III, 1958, 17–23.

Winton, Calhoun, 'Conversion on the Road to Houyhnhnmland', *SR*, LXVIII, 1960, 20–33.

Wolper, Roy S., 'Swift's Enlightened Gulls', *Studies on Voltaire and the Eighteenth Century*, LVIII, 1967, 1915–37.

Yeomans, W. E., 'The Houyhnhnm as Menippean Horse', *College English*, XXVII, 1966, 449–54.

Yunck, John A., 'The Skeptical Faith of Jonathan Swift', *The Personalist*, XLII, 1961, 533–54.

Zimmerman, Everett, 'Gulliver the Preacher', *PMLA*, 89, 1974, 1024–32.

INDEX